The Listener's Musical Companion

BOOKS BY B. H. HAGGIN

A Book of the Symphony (1937)

Music on Records (1938)

Music on Records (1941)

Music for the Man Who Enjoys "Hamlet"
1944, 1960—Republished in 1983 as *Music
for One Who Enjoys "Hamlet"*

Music in The Nation (1949)

The Listener's Musical Companion (1956)

Conversations with Toscanini
1959, 1979—revised and republished in 1989
in *Arturo Toscanini: Contemporary Recollections
of the Maestro*

Music Observed
(1964—republished in 1974 as *35 Years of Music*)

The Toscanini Musicians Knew
1967, 1980—revised and republished in 1989
in *Arturo Toscanini: Contemporary Recollections
of the Maestro*

The New Listener's Companion and Record Guide (1967, 1978)

Ballet Chronicle (1970)

A Decade of Music (1973)

Discovering Balanchine (1981)

Music and Ballet 1973–1983 (1984)

Arturo Toscanini: Contemporary Recollections of the Maestro
1989—revised and edited by Hathaway.
Combines *Conversations with Toscanini*
with *The Toscanini Musicians Knew*
and new material

The Listener's Musical Companion

New Edition

B. H. HAGGIN

Compiled and Edited by

THOMAS HATHAWAY

New York   Oxford
OXFORD UNIVERSITY PRESS
1991

Oxford University Press

Oxford   New York   Toronto
Delhi   Bombay   Calcutta   Madras   Karachi
Petaling Jaya   Singapore   Hong Kong   Tokyo
Nairobi   Dar es Salaam   Cape Town
Melbourne   Auckland

and associated companies in
Berlin   Ibadan

First Published by Oxford University Press, Inc., New York, new edition, 1991

First issued as an Oxford University Press paperback, new edition, 1991

Oxford is a registered trademark of Oxford University Press

Library of Congress Cataloging-in-Publication Data
Haggin, B. H. (Bernard H.), 1900–1987
The listener's musical companion / B. H. Haggin
compiled and edited by Thomas Hathaway. —New ed.
p. cm.   includes bibliographical references and indexes.
ISBN 0–19–506374–0
ISBN 0–19–506375–9 (pbk.)
1. Music appreciation. 2. Composers.
I. Hathaway, Thomas. II. Title.
MT6.L14L6   1991   781.1'7—dc20
90–40982

1 3 5 7 9 8 6 4 2

Printed in the United States of America
on acid-free paper

IN MEMORY OF

KARL F. REULING

1931–1991

Foreword

This book is intended primarily for those who, wishing to select a few out of the hundreds of works available on records, want to know which of these works are the greatest—in range and depth of communicated experience and emotion, in mastery of the resources of the medium; which works are enjoyable though of lesser stature; which are of little consequence though by great composers; which to acquire first, which later, which not at all. As against the writing that encourages readers to find the meaning of a piece of music in its historical background and the events of the composer's life, this book encourages them to find it in the internal operation of the piece itself—by listening to it.

Part One offers a discriminating survey of some of the greatest works in our Western musical literature and points out what to listen for in them. An introductory chapter explains how the author arrived at the musical judgments found in this book, and how his insights as a professional listener can help readers to develop musical judgment of their own. A second introductory chapter describes what it is that music (and music alone) communicates.

In Part Two the author directs the reader to some of the best writing about music past and present, and provides three chapters on musical procedures and forms, in which he describes the life he perceives in certain pieces of music in order to help readers to hear it for themselves in the other music discussed in the book.

Part Three concerns musical performance. The author describes what distinguishes a good one from a bad one, and then describes the work of the outstanding musicians of the twentieth century. A list is provided of good recordings of the principal works discussed in Part One, and there are indices of musical terms, performers' names, book-titles, and general subjects.

Although this book is intended primarily for people who listen for pleasure, there is enough discriminating critical writing on various aspects of music of a kind not usually found in introductory guides that it should be valuable as supplementary reading for students in general educational courses, as well.

Contents

vii

CONTENTS

CONTENTS

About This Edition

In preparing this edition (the eighth) I have not treated Haggin's book as a relic of its time, to be preserved without change, but as a work he had intended should be useful. To that end—and to answer readers who will ask "What did Haggin think about this piece . . . or that composer?"—I have incorporated into the text some of the supplementary remarks he made in the record reviews he appended to successive editions. These record supplements provided him with an occasion to draw attention to worthwhile composers and pieces he hadn't mentioned before, and they expanded the range of the original chapters considerably. I found material of this kind in his writing outside the book, also, and I have incorporated some of that as well.

Compiling the edition this way was made possible by the consistency of Haggin's writing style over his lifetime—in vocabulary, sentence-structure, and manner of ordering his thoughts. This permitted me in most instances to juxtapose material written many years apart without altering any of it. Where syntax required, however, I have changed the word-order or supplied connecting words or phrases. Because all of the substance remains Haggin's, I have not spoiled the appearance of the page by indicating every change of this kind with brackets and ellipses. Brackets are used only where I have extended a list of compositions, books or performances beyond the ones Haggin mentioned himself, or where I have inserted remarks of my own.*

---

* While I have been scrupulous never to put into Haggin's mouth statements he didn't utter himself, I will call attention to two paragraphs—on page 120—

xi

Other alterations I have made are as follows:

I have eliminated or revised any statements that are no longer true (e.g. that Berlioz's *The Trojans* has never been performed by a major American opera company).

I have divided the now far more comprehensive chapter about twentieth-century European music into two chapters.

I have eliminated Haggin's discussion of jazz as a separate chapter and inserted most of the material at the end of the expanded "Great Performers" section instead. Haggin did not write about jazz performed after the 1940s, and consequently this chapter, unlike the others, no longer constituted a current introduction to its subject. On the other hand, the material fits well where I have put it, since Haggin is discussing the recorded performances of jazz players.

I have moved the "Criticism" chapter from the end of Part One to the beginning of Part Two, to better set it off from the chapters about composers.

I have moved part of Haggin's description of Grützmacher's fake Boccherini B-flat Cello Concerto, formerly part of his discussion of musical ethics in connection with Musorgsky's *Boris* in Chapter 15, to the new section about Boccherini in Chapter 9.

I have replaced the larger part of the "Performance" chapter (about Casals, Schnabel and Toscanini, who, as performers, are discussed in much the same terms in Chapter 28) with Haggin's more recent comments on general aspects of musicianship and current performance practice. I have moved this performance chapter from the end of Part One to the beginning of Part Three, where, as Chapter 27, it introduces Haggin's recollections of the great performers of the century in Chapter 28. And I have ex-

---

concerning the five-act Italian-language version of Verdi's *Don Carlo* that I did have to write myself using some of his words. The observations Haggin made at different times about the editions of this opera were tied up with his objections to other people's ideas about them—a director's about which version to produce, a scholar's about the worth of certain parts, a conductor's about how much to include in a recording—and for once it was impossible to extract Haggin's remarks from their original contexts and assemble them as written into a summary of his thinking about the subject. The observations, then, are his; the form in which they appear is a paraphrase.

panded the latter, originally called "Great Performances of the Past," to include his comments on performers of today.

In the chapter "Recommended Recordings," I have replaced Haggin's by now dated reviews of the recordings of his time with a select list of current good records that are likely to remain available for some years. Where practical I have listed recent records Haggin heard and recommended himself; where that was not useful, I have made recommendations of my own. But I have not included every record Haggin ever approved of even if it remains in the catalogue. Some performances he included only because they were the best at the time. Some he admired once but came to like less later on. Some that he continued to enjoy have been supplanted by newer versions of equal merit and better recorded sound. And in the case of Baroque and pre-Baroque music, the style of "period" performance has changed so radically and so often in recent years that it seemed best to mention only the most brilliant and enduring of the older records (and, needless to say, only the most brilliant and enduring of the new ones).

Concerning the chapters on musical forms, most readers of previous editions have treated them as supplementary material, to be read after the sections on composers and performance. I have decided to accept this fact, and to move them from the beginning of the book to the back, as Chapters 24 and 25. (Haggin had been prepared to be even more accommodating: in a letter to the book's first publisher he wrote that these two chapters, which "were included to make the book informative to the widest possible audience . . . could be omitted" entirely.)

To these two chapters I have added a third containing Haggin's later essay, "Three Mozart Andantes." From the essay I have removed two passages—the analogy between a Mozart concerto and a stage play at the beginning, and the description of the Andante of K.467 at the end (hence "*Two* Mozart Andantes," not three, in the new chapter's title)—both of which Haggin had copied with little change from the "Mozart" chapter in this book, where they still appear. In place of them in the essay I have inserted the discussion of ritornello concerto form originally found in the "Mozart" chapter. There this passage had had to be insinuated as a parenthetical digression, which those who had not read the chapters on musical procedures were advised they could skip; as the introduction to the new "Andantes" chapter, it becomes an integral part of a section given over to forms and procedures.

Finally, where Haggin, following the usage of his time, employed the masculine pronoun where today we would use "one," "he or she" or the third person plural, I have changed his wording. Haggin established the precedent for this himself when he altered the title of a later edition of one of his books—from *Music for the Man Who Enjoys Hamlet* to *Music for One Who Enjoys Hamlet*.

Toronto, 1990   Thomas Hathaway

Editor's Acknowledgments

I am indebted to Sheldon Meyer, Joellyn M. Ausanka, and Leona Capeless of Oxford University Press, for their interest and help in revising this book for republication. I am grateful, also, to *Commentary, Commonweal, Encounter, The Hudson Review,* I.H.T. Corporation (for *The New York Herald Tribune*), Lincoln Kirstein (for *Hound and Horn*), *The Nation, The New Republic,* and *The Yale Review,* for their kind permission to use material that first appeared in their publications.

For assistance of various kinds, I am indebted to the following: above all to Karl F. Reuling, for initially directing my attention to material by Haggin that would enhance the new edition of this book, for doing much of the research for the expanded "Great Performers" chapter and for the list of recommended recordings, and for reading the entire manuscript. To Victoria Ellis Hathaway, for editorial assistance over the entire period of the book's preparation. To a person who wishes to remain anonymous, for research and advice for the revision of the chapters about composers; to Dr. Dietrich Bartel, for reading the Bach chapter for errors; to Michael Shavelson for reading the Mahler chapter; and to Alfred P. Haft, Jr., for calling attention to an error in the Berlioz chapter. To Michael Gray, Robert K. Dodson, Karl F. Reuling, and one other, who wishes to remain anonymous, for researching the sources of some of the quotations in the book; to Steven Wassmansdorf, for, among other things, compiling composers' names and dates for the ends of chapters; and to Greta Dentay for proof-reading German titles and texts. To Jack Curtis, for providing me with his index of Haggin's record reviews from 1974 through 1986; and to Edward M. Campbell, Raoul Gersten, and John A. Santoro, for information about current recordings of music before 1800. To Harris Green, Thomas Jackson, Dr. Grant Jones, Mary Armitage Jones, Jeffrey Kraegel, Mary McGeer, Terry Teachout, and Eliot Wagner, for proof-reading. To Ben Raeburn and Rose Hass, formerly of Horizon Press, and to Christina E. Blake of Rutgers University Press, for providing material relating to previous editions of the book. And to Marshall Beil and Dr. Renate Dische, for legal and other advice.

T. H.

Author's Acknowledgments
(1956, 1971)

The initial idea of this book came from Mel Evans; and [chapters 1 and 2, and 24 and 25] embody suggestions from Mr. Evans and Barbara Heyman. In addition I am indebted to Robert E. Garis, Paul Bertram and Charles B. Farrell for their critical reading of the manuscript; and to Mr. Farrell for the information about the Boccherini Cello Concerto in B flat and other such matters, and for help with technical problems, with the proofs, and with the general index.

The Elaine Music Shop, the Doubleday Book Shop and Philip L. Miller made it possible for me to hear some of the recordings that were not made available by a few of the record companies. And Walter Toscanini, with the assistance of his secretary, Eugenia Gale, provided other recordings that I needed to hear.

The Commodore Music Shop supplied information about recordings of jazz.

I am indebted to Greg Audette, for his help in the revision of the recordings section.

PART ONE

1

Introduction
The Reader and the Critic

The first chapters of this book are what I have thought would be helpful to people who have just begun to be interested in music—interested, for one thing, in discovering whether they get from music anything like what they get from a novel, a play, a poem, a painting. And three chapters in Part Two (24, 25 and 26) supplement these opening chapters by providing a description of musical procedures and forms from which readers should not be deterred by the quotations in musical notation: all one is asked to do is to try letting the eye follow as one listens—something readers will, I think, find not only possible, but helpful in impressing what they hear on their minds. The knowledge of the procedures and forms will be helpful in the same way as the discussion of meaning in music in Part One; and an additional benefit from this material will be detailed acquaintance with several great pieces of music. But readers can, if they prefer, skip Chapters 24 through 26.

After the first two chapters the book offers a critical survey of the literature of music, addressed not only to the newly interested reader but to all—whatever their musical experience and understanding—whose interest in music gives them further interest in what critical perception may reveal in it. I have written in the expectation that readers are going to do their own listening and reach their own conclusions about what they hear; and that I will be merely pointing out things for them to listen to and evaluate.

Which is to say that I will be performing the function of the critic; and I think it would be good for me to state at the outset what I understand this function to be.

The critic is a music-lover and listener like his readers: he is the expert and professional listener, who is assumed to have greater powers of perception and judgment than the amateur, and therefore to be able to make his readers aware of things in the music which they mightn't notice by themselves. He functions as a sort of guidepost, saying in effect: "I hear this happening at this point"—after which his reader listens and may say: "Yes, I hear it too." But the reader also may say: "No, I hear *this*." That is, the critic uses his powers to animate those of his reader—but only to animate, not to dictate: what he says about a piece of music is true for the reader only if it is confirmed by the reader's own ears. And each critic writes for the group of people who have found his perceptions and evaluations sufficiently confirmed by their own experience.

Underlying what I have just said is the fact that criticism does not, as some people think it must, offer the one possible and correct opinion, arrived at by measuring the piece of music with a set of established caliper-like esthetic principles for determining the good and the beautiful. The piece of music is a special kind of communication; the critic reports the effect of that communication on a mind operating not with impersonal esthetic principles but with personal sensitiveness, perception and taste; and the communication may impress different minds differently. The critic, then, reports not what is true, but what is true for him, and what becomes true also for the reader who finds it to be so when he or she listens to the piece.

All this to prepare the reader for the discovery in this book that I too have, as a critic, done my own listening and evaluating—the discovery, that is, of opinions which occasionally differ from those of other critics and even from that awesome authority, accepted opinion. Accepted opinion finds greatness in every note set down on paper by a great composer like Bach or Mozart; I hear in some works—and must report hearing—dull products of a routine exercise of expert craftsmanship. Accepted opinion holds some symphonies and concertos of Brahms to be works of tremendous profundity, and there was a time when they impressed me that way; but today I hear in them only the pretension to profundity. And on the other hand I esteem Tchaikovsky, to whom accepted opinion condescends.

There would be no need of preparing the reader for such dissents in a book about literature. But anyone conditioned by the announcements of music on the radio, the notes on record envelopes, the program notes at concerts, the reviews of these concerts in newspapers, needs to be prepared for the shock of a questioning of the accepted valuation of a theoretic exercise by Bach, a potboiler by Mozart, an imitation of Beethoven by Brahms, a piece of slick trash by Puccini or Ravel.

The survey that follows, then, offers a reasoned exercise of judgment and taste, which—since it is reasoned—is not dogmatic, and in fact induces a similar exercise of judgment and taste by the reader. In sum: I am bound to report what I hear; and readers then are free to find what I say to be true or not true for them. That is our relation in this book.

Readers who are guided by this book will, admittedly, miss certain works that the author thinks are overrated; but they will experience other, greater works by the same composers; and they will also experience works by other composers that accepted opinion underrates. The total of what is given is more than most readers will be able to acquire on records for a long time—before the end of which they will have reached the point where they will have tastes of their own, and will know whether they want to accept my judgment or reject it.

I should perhaps mention that if I take more space for Berlioz than for Haydn it isn't because I consider Berlioz greater than Haydn: the space in each instance is what is required by what I think needs to be said about each composer. And the same for differences in treatment of the composers—e.g. the inclusion of detailed analysis of particular works, or of quotations in musical notation, in one instance and not in another.

And I should, finally, speak of the difficulties in writing about music—primarily the difficulty in using words about a means of communicating what words cannot communicate. I operate on the assumption that it is legitimate to speak of the *Benedictus* of

Beethoven's *Missa Solemnis* being about the blessedness at the heart of things, even though precisely what Beethoven "says" about this blessedness is something to be learned only from the music.

2

The Meaning of Music

I said that a piece of music is a communication. And if you are one of those to whom a Beethoven symphony is a lot of meaningless noises, you may say: "Tell me what it communicates"—meaning of course "Tell me in words." But the simple inescapable fact of the situation is that what Beethoven says in those sounds cannot be told in words.

Someone observed once that art is not superfluous—by which he meant that the artist produces it to communicate something he can't communicate in any other way. You can see this most clearly in poetry: the particular images and overtones of sense and feeling from the lines

> When to the Sessions of sweet silent thought
> I summon up remembrance of things past

are communicated only by this particular assemblage of words; and you won't get them from a statement in other words like "When in hours of meditation I recall the past."

So with painting. In one of his finest essays, *Music at Night,* Aldous Huxley writes about two paintings of the Virgin, one by Piero della Francesca, the other by Tura—about how they observe the same current symbolical conventions but differ "in the forms and their arrangement, in the disposition of the lines and planes and masses," and how as a result of this pictorial difference they "say" different things. Huxley describes what he thinks those

7

different things are; but the point of his essay is that words cannot really tell us what the two paintings "say," and that we can learn this only from the paintings—from Piero's "welding together of smooth and beautifully balanced solidities," from Tura's intricate lines and writing surfaces—themselves.

This is true also of the grave, powerful, massive emotions to which, says Roger Fry, we are compelled by a Cézanne still-life—by the way a few apples and pears, commonplace objects entirely without emotional associations, are "reduced to pure elements of space and volume" and "coordinated and organized by the artist's sensual intelligence." That is, Fry can describe those emotions as grave, powerful and massive; but we can discover what they really are only from that organization of elements of space and volume on the canvas.

So with the piece of music, an organization of sounds which don't, like words, refer to external objects, but do have internal coherences that are meaningful to an ear sensitized to them. Huxley's example in his essay is the *Benedictus* of Beethoven's *Missa Solemnis;* and he says correctly that it is a statement about the blessedness at the heart of things, but that no words can give us any knowledge of what Beethoven felt this blessedness to be—that we can learn this only from the music.

Actually, Cézanne compels us to those grave, powerful, massive emotions not just with one painting of apples and pears but with many; and the state of inner illumination and superearthly exaltation that Beethoven attained in his last years is communicated to us not just in one piano sonata or string quartet but in a number of works. And from this you may understand that our interest in a work of art is an interest not just in its meaning but in this meaning as embodied, made explicit in the organized detail of the work of art, and as newly and differently embodied and made explicit in the organized detail of each work of art. We are interested in those grave, powerful, massive emotions as they are communicated by each different painting of apples and pears by Cézanne; in that state of inner illumination and superearthly exaltation as it is communicated by each different piano sonata or string quartet of Beethoven.

If then you don't understand what Beethoven "says" it is because the sounds he uses are not a meaningful language for you; and the thing to do is to learn this language as you would any other. If you enjoy folkmusic, jazz or musicals that is because the musical language is one you do understand—the one you learned, as you did English, by hearing it from earliest childhood. Probably, if you had heard Beethoven as early, as much, and as long as the music you like now, you would understand him as well; and if you want to acquire an understanding of Beethoven's vocabulary and ideas (for actually his language is the basic one of all Western music, popular and serious) you will have to live with them and get to know them as well as those of the music you are familiar with already.

Which is to say that you will have to listen to Beethoven's music, and keep listening. That, fortunately, is all you will have to do: music is easier than French in this respect. With French you have to learn the things the words refer to, and the grammar that organizes them in statements; but the meaning of a statement by Beethoven is an internal coherence of the sounds that you will apprehend directly from them by listening to them, or not at all.

And so try the experiment of listening to the beginning of the third movement of Beethoven's Trio Op. 97 (*Archduke*)—just the two statements of the piano that are echoed by the violin and cello, no more; and just once. Listen to it once again the next night, and every night for a week or two or as long as you care to continue the experiment. The passage may say as little to you after a month as it did the first night—in which case you will have to accept the fact that Beethoven and you are not for each other. But on the other hand it may, one of those nights, suddenly come alive for you and begin to make a definite though indefinable sense; and this will be the beginning of an understanding of music, the opening up of a new world of artistic experience as rich and stimulating as that of literature or painting. One thing is certain, however: if you don't get the meaning of Beethoven's statement from the statement, you won't get it from anything else.

There are some whose disappointing experiences with music lead them to argue that a piece of music must have within itself the evidence of its having been produced by a certain human being in a certain time and place, and to conclude from this that if they were told something about the composer and his period they would be better able to understand his music. And there are books which "treat music in the terms of the men who created it." Now certainly the Cézanne painting of a few apples and pears was not produced by a disembodied ability to put paint on canvas: each of the countless decisions to choose *this* bit of paint and place it in *that* relation to the other bits on the canvas was a decision by the whole man, involving all his experience, thought, emotion, insight, and involving also the ideas about painting, the general ideas, and all the other things that had influenced him as a human being and artist. And certainly this was true of the Shakespeare sonnet from which I quoted a couple of lines. But the result in the end was an organization of elements of space and volume on the canvas, an organization of words on the page; and to know what was involved in the process is not the same thing as to experience the effect of the painting or the sonnet that resulted from the process; nor is it necessary or helpful in experiencing that effect. The effect is produced on one's mind by the organization of pictorial elements on the canvas, the organization of words on the page, and by nothing else; and one experiences it solely by looking at the one and reading the other. Similarly, whatever the biographical and historical influences involved in the process that produced the opening statement in the third movement of Beethoven's *Archduke* Trio, the result of the process was an organization of sounds with an effect which you can experience not by reading about the biographical and historical influences but only by listening to the organization of sounds in the statement.

To repeat: just as the way to understand a poem is to read it, and the way to understand a painting is to look at it, so the way—the only way—to understand a piece of music is to listen to it, and to keep listening.

This is also the way to deal with the difficulty that arises when you listen beyond the opening statement in a piece of music. A poem lies before you on the page; and you can read each line as slowly and as many times as you need for the rhythmed sound, the images, the overtones of sense and feeling to register on your mind. A painting hangs before you on the wall; and you can look at it as long as you need to take in all the details and their organization and be affected by them. But the sounds of a piece of music succeed each other in time—too quickly for your ear to catch some of the details or your mind to grasp them fully and relate them to others; with the result that instead of a coherent succession you may hear only a number of unconnected fragments. And the remedy for this is again to keep listening.

One way is to listen to the entire piece: with each hearing you will catch more of the details you missed and fit them into their places in what will become an increasingly coherent succession. Another way is to listen to the opening statement—of, for example, that third movement of the Beethoven trio—and then to a little more, repeatedly, until this additional passage is familiar and makes sense not only by itself but in relation to the first part; and to keep adding a little at a time to what you already know, until you know the entire piece.

If you want help—the help that will point out the details your ear may have missed, the large formal design you may not have been aware of—and if you want this help from a book, then you will have to do something that will cost more effort. For you will come up against a major difficulty for both the writer and the reader of a book about music—the difficulty of correlating printed word with living sound.

A statement about a passage of music which one's readers haven't heard can have no more real meaning for them than a statement about a line of poetry they haven't read or a detail of a painting they haven't seen. But whereas the writer can quote the line of poetry or reproduce the detail of the painting, he cannot provide the sound of the passage in the symphony. The only thing he can do is to help his readers to find it on a record, giving the passage in musical notation to make it easier to recognize and grasp. This isn't easy for the writer even when it is possible; and it calls for effort by his readers. But if the effort isn't made the statement is just words, which readers can repeat but without really knowing what they are talking about.

And so if you want to know more than you can discover by your own listening, you can skip ahead and read Chapters 24, 25 and 26 on musical procedures and forms; but then you will have to make the effort involved in hearing as you read. If that effort is more than the additional knowledge is worth, you can leave those three chapters unread and go straight on to the survey of music that follows.

3

Beethoven

Those who went on to read Chapters 24, 25 and 26 before this one will already have been made acquainted with some of the greatest works in our musical literature—Bach's *Passacaglia;* the Prelude to Wagner's *Tristan und Isolde;* Schubert's String Quartet Op. 29 and Piano Sonata Op. 78; Mozart's Rondo K.511 and Concertos K.453 and 482; and Beethoven's *Archduke* Trio, *Eroica* and Ninth Symphonies, his Piano Sonatas Opp. 109 and 111. And remembering how indiscriminately the word *great* is tossed about—how anything and everything presented on the radio is "great music"—I think it advisable to establish what I mean by the word when I apply it to those pieces by Beethoven and Schubert.

In his book on Beethoven, which I recommend as collateral reading, J. W. N. Sullivan discusses Beethoven's music as an expression, in successive works, of a developing personal vision of life—that is, of developing states of consciousness that were generated in him by his external experience, conditioned by his spiritual nature, and made explicit in the terms of his art. "In his capacity to express this content," says Sullivan, "Beethoven reveals himself as a great musical genius, and the content itself reveals him as a great spirit." And concerning this he observes further that "perhaps even Shakespeare never reached that final stage of illumination that is expressed in some of Beethoven's music."*

---

*J. W. N. Sullivan, *Beethoven—His Spiritual Development* (London, 1927).

This tells us not only what makes Beethoven's music great, but what makes the *Eroica* a greater piece of music than the First Symphony, and the Piano Sonata Op. 111 even greater than the *Eroica*. As against the First Symphony—the work of a young man confident, exuberant and untroubled in the exercise of his rich gifts—the *Eroica* is the work of one who has come to know catastrophe and suffering, and who in the blackest moments of his life has found in the resources of his own spiritual nature and creative powers the courage and strength to resist, to survive, to triumph (the heroism which the *Eroica* is concerned with is, then, as Sullivan points out, Beethoven's own). But as against this man for whom suffering is something to assert oneself against, the composer of the concluding movement of the Sonata Op. 111 is one who has come to the final realization of suffering as something to accept, in Sullivan's words, "as one of the great structural lines of human life," and who has attained "that unearthly state where the struggle ends and pain dissolves away."

Sullivan warns against a possible misinterpretation of what he says: Beethoven's music is not to be listened to as a sort of diary of daily events in his life. It tells us not his experience, but his attitude toward his experience; and not his immediate response to any and every happening of the day, but states of consciousness representing a lifetime of continuing perception and response to perception: the joyous exuberance and humor embodied in the Eighth Symphony, the exaltation communicated by the Sonata Op. 111, were not responses to the petty turmoil and wretchedness that filled Beethoven's daily existence at these times. Moreover, to Sullivan's warning I will add a reminder that we are concerned not with the joyous exuberance or the mystical exaltation itself, but with this as it is made explicit and communicated in the organized detail of the piece of music—and not just the detail of one piece of music but the constantly new and unique detail of each of a number of pieces.

The greatest Beethoven—greatest in what he says and in his use of his art to say it—is, then, heard in his last works: the last symphony, the last string quartets, the last sonatas and other pieces for piano, the *Missa Solemnis*. And we are concerned with the superearthly exaltation of his last years as it is embodied not only in the concluding movement of the Sonata Op. 111 but in the concluding movement of the Sonata Op. 109, the third movement of the Ninth Symphony. And not only these but the slow movements of the last quartets: on the one hand the expansively elaborating variation movements of Opp. 132 and 127; on the other hand the *Cavatina* of Op. 130 and the third movement of Op. 135, which exhibit the concentrated brevity of some of Beethoven's late writing (other examples of this brevity are the quietly reflective opening movement of the Sonata Op. 109, and some of the Bagatelles Opp. 119 and 126 for piano). Also the *Kyrie, Benedictus* and *Agnus Dei* of the *Missa Solemnis*. And other sections of the *Missa* in which, as in the final choral movement of the Ninth Symphony, the exaltation is carried to ever higher points of jubilant ecstasy.

We are concerned also with what lay behind the final illumination. For one thing, what is communicated by the *Arioso dolente* movement of the Piano Sonata Op. 110, the slow movement—tremendous in poignant expressive implications as in size—of the Piano Sonata Op. 106 (*Hammerklavier*). And for another thing, what is communicated by the grim opening movements of the Ninth Symphony, the *Hammerklavier* Sonata, and—in more concentrated fashion again—the Sonata Op. 111.

And we are, finally, concerned with those "strange seas of thought" in which—Sullivan says of the last quartets—Beethoven discovers "unsuspected islands and even continents," as we come to know them not only from some of the movements of the quartets but from the mystically introspective introduction to the *Benedictus* of the *Missa Solemnis*. And above all from passages in the *Diabelli* Variations for piano—Variation 20:

and the suddenly still and distant chords:

that follow the vehement fugue of Variation 32 and lead to the final apotheosis of Variation 33. These passages in the *Diabelli* Variations are perhaps the remotest points Beethoven's mind attained in the regions Sullivan speaks of.

And the Bagatelles for Piano Opp. 119 and 126, which I mentioned a moment ago, have not only the concentrated brevity, introspective remoteness and occasional strangeness of Beethoven's late writing for the piano—but in addition its occasional abrupt shifts of thought, feeling and style—all of which become especially remarkable in these pieces because their reduced scale makes for greater concentration, brevity and abruptness.

In all these his mind can be followed without difficulty; but the *Grosse Fuge* Op. 133 for string quartet and the concluding fugue of the *Hammerklavier* Sonata for piano many listeners find obscure and formidable.

A great spirit and great musical genius is heard also in those two tremendous movements of the *Eroica* Symphony that are presented in Chapter 25, and in its opening movement, a dramatic progression no less tremendous in its urgency, tensions and climaxes, its developing structure, and their cumulative power. And if that great spirit moves us with the range and force of the expressive content of the works of this period, the great musician amazes us with the profusion of musical forms embodying this content, their variety, and on occasion their innovations.

Thus what is expressed in the successive movements of the *Eroica* is expressed again in the Fifth Symphony, but with differences. The dramatic first movement is more grimly concentrated; and in later movements expressive content dictates an innovation in structure: the dramatically hushed conclusion of the scherzo movement leads in unprecedented fashion into the opening triumphant proclamation of the finale; and later in the finale the development breaks off at its height for a recapitulation of the hushed transition to the opening proclamation.*

*The effect of these innovations of Beethoven's is undone by editors of his scores who decide—as one did in the 1980s against the contrary evidence of the manuscript—that Beethoven really wanted the scherzo's opening and trio for basses and cellos repeated in classical fashion; and by conductors who piously observe the indication to repeat the opening proclamation of the last movement even though it violates harmonic sense to return to the tonic at a point where the music is already pressing forward into a new key. (Not only is the repetition harmonically disruptive, but it causes the material's reappearance near the end of the movement, for what becomes the third time, to seem wearisome.)

No less disruptive is the current practice of repeating the expositions of the first movements of the *Eroica* and Fourth Symphonies, and the exposition of the first movement and the beginning of the last in the Seventh Symphony. The purpose of these repetitions was not to give the movements balance and proportion, which repetition destroys, but to enable listeners in Beethoven's time to grasp material that would have seemed strange to them and been difficult to follow at first hearing. Today the music doesn't sound strange, and it is not necessary to repeat any of it for even a novice to get something from it. Brahms understood this and said as much: when a young musician expressed surprise at hearing him conduct his own Second Symphony without repeating the first movement exposition, Brahms's reply (which the musician reported to the twentieth-century Swiss pianist, Edwin Fischer, who wrote it down) was, "Formerly, when the piece was new to the audience, the repeat was necessary; today, the work is so well known that I can go on without it."

One conductor told me that his rule was to play repeats wherever the composer had inserted transitional measures that would never be heard otherwise. But I would say that the awkwardness of the transitional notes Beethoven inserted in the *Eroica*, their lack of any intrinsic value beyond their function of wrenching the music back to the home key, makes them something one does not *want* to hear, and demonstrates beyond any doubt that the repeat they introduce is not integral to the movement's structure but something grafted on to what was already complete in itself. The rule might almost be reversed: wherever a repeat is preceded by bad transitional music, the repeat is not to be played. But a better rule would be this: where the exposition is disproportionately brief in relation to the rest of the movement—as in the first movement of the Fifth Symphony, or the last movement of Mozart's *Prague* Symphony—it should be played twice if the composer provided that option. Where the exposition is expansive in relation to

Unprecedented too are some of the things that happen in the Piano Concerto No. 4. The audience assembled in Prince Lobkowitz's house in March 1807 for the first performance (with Beethoven himself at the piano) expected to hear first the usual orchestral introduction that would secure attention for the eventual entrance of the solo piano—instead of which it was the piano itself that claimed attention immediately with its spaciously meditative opening G-major statement, this surprise being followed by the surprise of the strings' B-major answer. And later came the extraordinary and unprecedented dialogue of orchestra and piano in the slow movement, leading to the piano's soliloquy, and to concluding hushed recollections of the opening dialogue—all of which make this brief movement one of Beethoven's most affecting utterances.

There is then the externally imposing, monumental Beethoven of the *Eroica* and Fifth Symphonies, who is heard also in the joyous Symphonies Nos. 4, 7 and 8; the wonderful late overture *Consecration of the House*, a work of outward exuberance but with a strangeness at times like that of the last Bagatelles; the breathtakingly energetic finale of the Quartet Op. 59 No. 3; the grandiose Piano Concerto No. 5 (referred to as the *Emperor*); the dramatic Piano Sonatas Opp. 53 (*Waldstein*), 57 (*Appassionata*), and 90, Violin Sonata Op. 47 (*Kreutzer*), Quartets Op. 59 No. 2 and Op. 95. And there is the lyrical, meditative Beethoven of the Piano Concerto No. 4, who is heard also in the Symphony No. 6 (*Pastoral*); the Piano Sonatas Opp. 54, 78 and 81a (*Les Adieux*); the beautiful *Andante Favori* for piano; the Quartets Op. 59 No. 1 and Op. 74 (*Harp*); the Variations for cello and piano on themes from Mozart's *Magic Flute;* the song-cycle *An die ferne Geliebte;* the exquisite song *Ich liebe dich;* and in several pieces of Beethoven's late choral music: the exalted and rapt Elegiac Song Op. 118; the impressive *Opferlied* Op. 121b; the charming *Bundeslied* Op. 122; *Calm Sea and Prosperous Voyage* Op. 112; and the incidental music for King Stephen Op. 117. (Of the other large works of this kind, the Violin Concerto Op. 61 would be regarded with less awe if the name of Beethoven were not attached to it:

what follows—as in the *Eroica*, or the first movement of Schubert's B-flat Piano Sonata—it should not be repeated. —*Ed.*

17

except for some beautiful pages in the development section, at the solo violin's second entrance, the first movement is feeble, platitudinous, diffuse; and much of the finale is silly. Even feebler are the Triple Concerto and Choral Fantasia.)

In addition there is the playful Beethoven who contrives little surprises and jokes. For example the opening theme of the finale of the Symphony No. 8 coasting along *pp* until it collides with the *ff* C sharp; the unexpected play with that C sharp in the coda, ending with the unexpected change of key; the two places where the full orchestra breaks off, and first the flutes and strings *p,* then the bassoon and kettledrum *pp* go chortling on. Or in the finale of the Piano Concerto No. 5 the episode in the development in which the piano takes off grandly with the imposing principal theme, but gets into a sort of tailspin of faster and faster passage-work that collapses into decisively final statements of the full orchestra—whereupon the horns enter quietly with a new key in which the piano takes off with the principal theme again, only to get into the same tailspin of fast passage-work that collapses into the same final statements of the orchestra—whereupon the oboe and bassoon enter quietly with still another key in which the piano takes off a third time, only to end up in the same way.

I mentioned earlier—as against the expansiveness of the *Eroica* Symphony—the concentration in the first movement of the Fifth; and other examples are the powerfully concise *Coriolan* and *Egmont* Overtures, the fiercely concise opening movement of the Quartet Op. 95. The slow movement of the Piano Concerto No. 4 is a more unusual and striking example of this concentration and brevity; another is the slow movement of the *Waldstein* Sonata, in which the opening statement returns with an added figure in the bass that builds up tremendous tension and power (if, that is, it is played that way). But there are also remarkable examples of expansiveness to take note of: the strange, quasi-improvisatory play of Beethoven's fancy in the Fantasy for piano Op. 77; the endlessly and delightfully inventive second movement of the Quartet Op. 59 No. 1; the second movement of the Quartet Op. 59 No. 3, with a strangeness in its poignancy that leads Sullivan to speak of its "remote and frozen anguish."

The first movement of Op. 59 No. 3 begins in fact with a slow introduction, mysterious and remote, which could introduce one of the last quartets. And this brings us to several other works in which there are intimations of what is to be heard in the music of Beethoven's last years: the *Archduke* Trio, whose wonderful slow movement I examine in detail in Chapter 25; the Piano Sonata Op. 101 with its tranquil and lovely opening movement and profoundly reflective slow movement; the Violin Sonata Op. 96 with its similarly tranquil and lovely but rather strange first movement and the powerful slow variation in the finale; the Cello Sonata Op. 102 No. 1 with its wonderful slow introductions to the two movements; the Cello Sonata Op. 102 No. 2 with its great slow movement—especially the middle section, and the return of the opening section with the cello's comments on the piano's statements.

Interesting in this connection is the Mass in C, with startlingly beautiful and expressive passages and powerful dramatic strokes, all on the small scale of an early try at something which when attempted again years later would come out with the sustained intensity, grandeur and exaltation of the *Missa Solemnis*.

And finally Beethoven's only opera, *Fidelio*, which in this country (but not in Europe) is generally considered one of his failures, but actually has some of the greatest and most effective dramatic music after Mozart's. Not only Leonore's famous *Abscheulicher! wo eilst du hin?* introducing her noble aria *Komm, Hoffnung,* but the wonderful quartet *Mir ist so wunderbar,* the Prisoners' Chorus, the affecting duet *Wir müssen gleich zu Werke,* the tremendous orchestral introduction to the dungeon scene and Florestan's *Gott! welch' Dunkel hier,* the affecting duet and trio and the dramatic quartet that follow, and the sublime *O Gott! welch' ein Augenblick!* at the end.

(A concert performance of the 1805 version of *Fidelio*—still called *Leonore* by Beethoven at that time—provided an opportunity to hear its diffuse, conventional and derivative writing, and enabled me, when I listened afterward to the 1814 version, to appreciate how unerringly Beethoven had operated at every point in the revision that produced this version's powerful concentration and conciseness of utterance and form. I heard in it none of the "stylistic inequalities" one scholar claimed were a result of the eight years that had elapsed between the two versions but only the great work of art that makes the later version the one to perform.)

Of the four overtures Beethoven wrote for the opera the *Leonore* No. 3, one of the most popular pieces in the orchestral repertory, has generally been thought of as the final perfected achievement of which the *Leonore* No. 2 is an earlier, imperfect version; but actually No. 2 uses much the same thematic substance in a completely achieved work that is in its own different ways fully as impressive as No. 3, with some details even more impressive. One of these is the prolonged activity of the cellos and basses at the end of the slow introduction—their progression, in the last two measures, from B natural to D flat, then back to B natural, and only then at last to the expected C of the beginning of the Allegro portion of the overture. Another is the more extensive development in this portion that reaches its climax in the off-stage trumpet-calls. And another is the omission of the recapitulation after the trumpet-calls, in accordance with a dramatic logic which the *Leonore* No. 3 sacrifices in completing the formal scheme.

As for Beethoven's early works, they begin with his attempts to write in the style and forms established and left to him by his illustrious predecessors. These attempts produced on the one hand fluent, characterless imitations like the Piano Trio Op. 11 and the Piano Quartet or Quintet Op. 16, but on the other hand works like the Serenade Op. 8 for string trio—in which the eighteenth-century delicacy, grace, loveliness and charm appear to represent something genuinely felt by Beethoven himself— and the engaging Trio Op. 1 No. 2. And also a long series of works in which his own voice makes itself heard with increasing insistence, authority and impressiveness.

That voice is heard in the imposing slow introduction to the Cello Sonata Op. 5 No. 2; in the vehement outbursts of the fast movements of the Symphony No. 1; in the introspective slow movement of the Piano Concerto No. 1; in the dramatic outbursts, contrasts and silences of the first movement of the Symphony No. 2, the elevation of its slow movement, the explosive exuberance of its scherzo and finale. And similarly in other

Great River of the Mountains

The Folklife Gallery

Center for Folklife, History & Cultural Programs
Crandall Public Library, Glens Falls, New York

Non-Profit
Organization
US Postage
PAID
Permit #511
Glens Falls, NY

The Folklife Center at Crandall Public Library
251 Glen Street, Glens Falls, NY 12801 www.crandalllibrary.org

Great River of the Mountains

Croswell Bowen, Carl Carmer, Margaret Bourke-White
on the upper Hudson River of the 1930s

Folklife Gallery • October 2009 – May 2010

Thursday, October 8, 5 to 7 pm Gallery Reception
7 to 9 pm Great River Revisited, illustrated talk
& book signing of "Great River of the Mountains" by Lucey Bowen

Thursday, October 15, 7 to 9 pm
North River, North Woods songs, stories,
poems & tunes by Dan Berggren & John Kirk

Thursday, October 22, 7 to 9
Tall Tales & Other Stories of the Adirondacks
by storyteller Bill Smith storyteller & fiddler Don Woodcock

Thursday, October 29, 7 to 9 pm
Old Adirondack Logging Films
narrated by historian Dick Nason & sponsored by Finch Paper

Front: Photo by Croswell Bowen, courtesy his daughter, Lucey Bowen, who has republished his 1941 book, *Great River of the Mountains*.
This series was produced by the Folklife Center & supported by the Folk Arts Program of the New York State Council on the Arts, a state agency.

works—some of the piano sonatas, some of the chamber music. In particular the String Quartets Op. 18, with their pages of engaging writing in eighteenth-century style, but also their pages in which Beethoven's individuality asserts itself: the affecting slow movement of No. 1; the graceful opening of No. 3 and its lovely slow movement; the impassioned opening of No. 4, its delightful Andante scherzoso in place of the usual slow movement, the engaging trio of its minuet movement, its bustling finale; the lilting first movement of No. 5, its charming minuet and fine trio, its energetic finale; and above all the humorous first movement, fine slow movement, intricately cross-rhythmed scherzo, and lovely slow introduction to the engaging finale, that make No. 6 one of the best of these early works.

And only Beethoven's voice is heard in several outstandingly fine works that we encounter at the end of this early period. The Piano Concerto No. 3, for example, is pure Beethoven in its powerfully dramatic first movement (e.g. the piano's first entrance: its three upward-rushing scales ending with the impact of cannon shots, which lead to its forceful proclamation of the principal theme of the movement), the expansively introspective slow movement, the dramatically eventful finale (e.g. the episode near the end of the development, in which the orchestra's fugato breaks off for the surprise of the piano's hushed A-flat octaves, which lead to the further surprise of the E-major statement of the principal theme—all in preparation for the piano's last return to the principal theme in its original key of C minor).

So with the Piano Sonata Op. 31 No. 2, characteristic in its imposingly dramatic first movement, poignantly lyrical slow movement, and dramatically eventful concluding perpetuum mobile. Also the Violin Sonata Op. 30 No. 3, equally characteristic in its energetic fast movements and gracefully wistful middle movement.

And so with the Piano Sonata Op. 31 No. 3, characteristic of the genially relaxed and lyrical Beethoven in its grace, warmth, good humor and bubbling high spirits. Also the Piano Sonata Op. 28, sometimes called *Pastoral* because of its quiet mood throughout, and much of it—especially the first and last movements—very lovely. The fine Thirty-two Variations in C minor. The *Eroica* Variations Op. 35, a piano work using the two initially insignificant bits of thematic material out of which Beethoven later built up the great finale of his *Eroica* Symphony, and one without the tremendous implications and impact of the symphony finale; but in it the variation procedure is already, for Beethoven, an expressive medium in which the emotion that operates through his technical resourcefulness and daring produces not only individual variations of lyric beauty and dramatic force, but in the end a work of large-scale structure and content. There are as well the Violin Sonatas Opp. 30 No. 1 and 24 ("Spring"). And the String Quintet Op. 29, of which every movement is an astonishing manifestation of Beethoven's matured powers.

Ludwig Van Beethoven (1770–1827)

4

Schubert

What Sullivan says of Beethoven I would say of Schubert: his music reveals him as a great spirit and great musical genius. I am aware of the generally held opinion that credits Schubert with lovely and affecting writing, but the writing of a lyricist without the powers of large-scale content and construction revealed in Beethoven's music—a lyricist whose large-scale works, then, are mere garrulously repetitive, structurally diffuse successions of lovely melodies. But in this instance, as in some others, I would say generally held opinion rests on nothing more authoritative than the unperceptive listening that started it and the inattentive listening that has kept it going—as you will prove to your own satisfaction if you listen attentively to what actually happens in the Schubert pieces presented in Chapter 25.

In the minuet movement of the Quartet Op. 29, for example, there is not only some characteristically beautiful writing, but—in that unexpected shift to C sharp minor—one of those miraculously achieved intensities of loveliness and expressive force that are characteristic also of Mozart and Berlioz. They are to be heard in breathtaking succession in the last quiet passage just before the end of Mozart's G-minor Symphony, and after the first two simple phrases of the English horn's serenade in the third movement of Berlioz's *Harold in Italy;* and they occur in similar succession in the scherzo movement of Schubert's posthumous

Piano Sonata in B flat, in the development section of the first movement, in the development of the first movement of the posthumous Sonata in A. And they are manifestations of powers that place Schubert with Mozart and Berlioz as one of the greatest of musical geniuses.

Similarly, the first movement of the Sonata Op. 78 offers not only, in the exposition, a characteristic example of Schubert's expansively meditative writing, but, in the development, an impressive example of the dramatic power that is no less characteristic—an example, in fact, of the iron-like power arising out of tranquil meditation that is so remarkable in Schubert. One of the most remarkable examples of this occurs in the slow movement of the posthumous Sonata in A: the recitative-like middle section that takes off quietly in a declamatory crescendo to a hair-raising climax. I can recall nothing like it anywhere in music.

And in the slow movement of the Quintet Op. 163 we hear the sublimity of other writing of Schubert's last year—most notably the opening pages of the posthumous Sonata in B flat, which communicate a final illumination such as we hear in Beethoven's last sonatas.

It is true that the first movement of the B-flat Sonata descends from the sublimity of its opening pages. But it rises again to the wonderful concluding reflections of the exposition, and to the later sublimities of the development which lead to those of the recapitulation of the opening pages. And the English critic D. F. Tovey is right in finding the weaknesses in works like this sonata to be "relaxations of their powers," and in contending that "neither Shakespeare nor Schubert will ever be understood by any critic or artist who regards their weaknesses and inequalities as proof that they are artists of less than the highest rank"; that "the highest qualities attained in important parts of a great work are as indestructible by weaknesses elsewhere as if the weaknesses were the accidents of physical ruin";* and that Schubert must be regarded, "on the strength of his important works, as a definitely sublime composer. It does not matter when, where, and how he

---

*Donald F. Tovey, "Schubert," *Essays in Musical Analysis* (London, 1935).

lapses therefrom: the quality is there, and nothing in its neighbor-
hood can make it ridiculous."*

That is the way to view the redundancies and diffuseness of
works like the beautiful Quartet Op. 161, Piano Trio Op. 100 and
Piano Sonata Op. 42. But on the other hand there are works in
addition to the Quintet Op. 163 and Sonata Op. 78—works like
the *Death and the Maiden* Quartet, the Piano Trio Op. 99, the
posthumous Piano Sonata in C minor and Sonatas Opp. 53 and
143, the last two symphonies—which do not demand such indulgence. What they do require is the realization that Schubert's
mind operates expansively, and this at all times—whether in an
extended progression of thought or a single statement, and
whether the utterance is tranquilly meditative or powerfully
dramatic. And the further realization that this expansiveness is
not slackness—that on the contrary it most frequently operates
with tension, and that the result then is highly effective large-scale
construction of Schubert's special kind.

Consider for example the best known of Schubert's instrumental works, the first movement of the *Unfinished* Symphony, in
which generally held opinion may have caused you to hear only
the occurrences of its famous melodies. I have said Schubert's
mind operates expansively; all the more remarkable therefore is
the fact that the single hushed opening statement of cellos and
basses is enough to achieve the purpose of the extensive slow
introduction of Haydn and Beethoven. The statement appears to
have only that introductory purpose, for it is heard no more in the
exposition: we hear next the melody of oboe and clarinet; and
noteworthy at this point is how, with the unhurried pace and calm
of the sustained melody, there is the movement, the momentum,
the urgency that Schubert creates with the figuration and plucked
notes of the strings. Noteworthy also is the fact that while the
melody itself is expansive its treatment is concise, carrying it
directly and quickly to a climax which breaks off for the sustained
note of bassoons and horns that is the pivot for one of Schubert's
extraordinary shifts of key. And noteworthy again is how, with

*Tovey, "Franz Schubert," *"The Main Stream of Music" and Other Essays*
(London 1949).

the quiet flow now of the famous melody of the cellos, there is the added movement and tension that Schubert creates with the syncopated accompaniment of clarinets and violas. Again the melody is expansive, its treatment concise, carrying it quickly to a climax which breaks off for last quiet reflections that bring the exposition to its close. And here we come to another demonstration of mastery: after an exposition concerned entirely with the woodwind and cello melodies it is the hushed opening statement of cellos and basses that returns now to be elaborated with increasing tension into a development of tremendous dramatic power; and noteworthy here is the way one of the climaxes breaks off repeatedly to recall the syncopated accompaniment of the cello melody. The recapitulation brings a return to the comparative calm of the woodwind and cello melodies, which has the effect of a resolution of the great dramatic conflict in the development; then the hushed opening statement of cellos and basses returns once more, to be elaborated this time into a powerful coda.

I cannot imagine anything further removed from the diffuseness and slackness generally attributed to Schubert than what is actually heard in this piece of music: the economy of its three themes, the conciseness of their treatment, the skill of their deployment in the formal design, the sustained tension from first note to last in this design—all of which adds up to one of the most remarkably compact and effective pieces of large-scale construction in the symphonic literature.

Nor is it diffuseness and slackness that we hear in the gigantic first movement of the Symphony No. 9, but rather an enormous energy, manifesting itself in an increased expansiveness of the themes and their treatment, a sustained momentum and tension—first in the solemn introduction, then in the animated exposition with its great pronouncement of the trombones over the unceasingly driving movement of the second theme, then in the development in which this driving movement builds up to tremendous climactic references to the trombone pronouncement, and finally, after the recapitulation, in the coda in which group after group of the orchestra joins the huge upward rush to exalted heights. Grandeur is what the expansiveness, momentum and tension produce; and grandeur continues to be the outstanding characteristic of the subsequent movements—above all the extraordinary whirling finale. We hear something like it in the finales of the Quartets Op. 161 and *Death and the Maiden;* but in the symphony the energy and momentum are breathtaking, and the reiterated opening notes of the expansive second theme over the unceasing whirl build up to tremendous pronouncements in the exposition, development and recapitulation, and to final sublimities in one of the greatest of codas.

I have been talking until now about the greatest of Schubert's large-scale instrumental works. Hardly less wonderful are the two movements of the uncompleted posthumous Piano Sonata in C major. This work, dating from 1825, is a product of matured powers; and what is astounding, therefore, is the high quality of the Sonata in B major Op. 147 that Schubert wrote at the age of twenty.

In addition there are large works of lesser stature which have beautiful pages—like the Piano Sonatas Opp. 120 in A major and 122 in E flat, which have Schubert's relaxed intimacy and sweetness in place of the power of some of the others; the Fantasia Op. 159 for violin and piano; the Octet Op. 166 for strings and winds, with many pages of wonderful writing and marvelous employment of the strings and winds in combination; the Quintet Op. 114 (*Trout*) for piano and strings. And there are engaging minor works like the *Rondo Brillant* Op. 70, and the early Sonata Op. 162 for violin and piano; the *Arpeggione* Sonata for cello and piano; the *Rosamunde* music for orchestra. Also there are the smaller-scale and more intimate examples of his mature writing for the piano, the *Moments musicaux* and Impromptus, most of them as affecting in their loveliness and melancholy as anything Schubert ever wrote, and the unfamiliar Allegretto in C minor, which is marvelous. Affecting in the same way is the *Andantino varié* Op. 84 No. 1 for piano duet, with its poignant theme that doesn't prepare us for the fascinating writing of the animated first three variations and the incandescent melodic invention of the fourth and last one. And other fine pieces in this category are the Rondo Op. 107; the *Marches caractéristiques;* the poignantly beautiful Fantasia Op. 103; and the Grand Duo Op. 140 (sometimes performed in Joachim's for the most part effective orchestration), which has a lovely second movement, a remarkable Trio in its Scherzo and an extraordinary quiet passage before its lively concluding measures.

There is Schubert's choral music: the early small-scale Mass in G, with lovely lyrical writing that expresses what Tovey calls Schubert's "fragrant piety," and occasional manifestations of impressive powers—most of them in the *Credo*, whose quiet closing section is especially remarkable. Similar lyrical writing is to be heard in much of the Mass in A flat, to which, however, the somber, powerfully expressive passage beginning with *"Et incarnatus est"* in the *Credo* is in striking contrast; the Mass in E flat, written in the last year of Schubert's life, also has impressively forceful and dramatic passages as well as lovely lyrical ones.

Schubert's first two string quartets are what the fifteen-year-old composer produced when—having heard Beethoven's quartets, and probably Haydn's and Mozart's—he tried his hand in this genre. And for someone expecting to find them no more interesting than Schubert's derivative first two symphonies, it is astonishing to hear in these quartets—in their musical ideas and manipulation of those ideas—the operation at an early stage of the same mind one hears operating more impressively in the works of his last years. One hears, that is, not only in the first two but in Nos. 4, 5 and 6 of the next year, melodic andantes that nobody but Schubert could have written; engaging minuets, with contrasting trios, that are equally individual; in No. 4 an extraordinary first movement elaborated out of the descending chromatic subject of the slow introduction; in No. 5 a finale with daring harmonic shifts and other surprises; in No. 6 an andante, with similar harmonic shifts in the development, that rises to moments of dark power. And in No. 8, which Schubert wrote when he was seventeen, as again in No. 9 a year later, one hears a leap forward in the increased power of the ideas and the expanded dimensions of the structures in which they are developed. (Nos. 10 and 11, however, are unimpressive.)

Likewise, for someone listening to the Sonata Op. 137 No. 2 in the expectation of hearing another imitative and inconsequential piece like the Sonata Op. 137 No. 1, it is astonishing to hear instead the extraordinary melodic and harmonic writing of the first movement; and one's interest is held by the subsequent movements that are less unusual. There are, finally, the songs. At a time when the instrumental works of Mozart and Beethoven—apart from the quartets—were eliciting from the seventeen-year-old Schubert only inconsequential imitations, a poem of Goethe could elicit such evidence of astonishingly matured imaginative and musical powers as *Gretchen am Spinnrade*. And this susceptibility to poetic stimuli, activating constantly more matured powers, resulted in a steady flow of songs throughout his life. It was a flow which included, inevitably, many that were less impressive than *Gretchen*. Conceding that "in his six hundred songs there is, no doubt, as Brahms said, something to be learnt from each one," Tovey points out that "*Erlkönig* and *Gretchen am Spinnrade* stand alone in four volumes of early work," and observes that "even in the later years there are songs . . . from which Brahms could have learned little but the fact that Schubert was always keeping his pen in practice, whether or not he had anything in his head at the moment."

But the flow also gave us some of our most treasurable pieces of music—the great song-cycles *Die schöne Müllerin* and *Winterreise*. The last songs later grouped under the title *Schwanengesang*—of which *Der Doppelgänger, Liebesbotschaft, In der Ferne, Abschied, Ihr Bild, Fischermädchen, Die Stadt* and *Aufenthalt* are outstanding. And single songs like *Auf dem Wasser zu singen, Nacht und Träume, Du bist die Ruh', Geheimes, Die Forelle, Totengräber's Heimweh, Der Tod und das Mädchen, Der Jüngling an der Quelle, Nachtviolen, Das Lied im Grünen, Der Musensohn, Erster Verlust, Im Abendroth, Lied eines Schiffers an die Dioskuren, Aus Heliopolis, Freiwilliges Versinken, An den Mond, Nähe des Geliebten, Das Geheimnis, Das Mädchen aus der Ferne, Der Pilgrim*, the great *Meerestille*, and *Vom Mitleiden Mariae* (whose spare, somber writing is like nothing I can recall in any other music of Schubert).

Other fine songs include, in no special order, *An die Musik, Horch, horch, die Lerch', Des Fischers Liebesglück, Seligkeit, Lachen und Weinen, Der Einsame, Wiegenlied* (the setting designated Op. 98 No. 2 or D.498), *Der Schmetterling, Am See, An die Laute, Dass sie hier gewesen, Der Wanderer an den Mond, Auflösung, Wanderers Nachtlied, Jägers Abendlied, An Sylvia, Die junge Nonne, Im Früh-*

ling, Wehmuth, Der Jüngling und der Tod, Der Hirt auf dem Felsen (with clarinet), the less familiar but lovely *Thekla*, and two unfamiliar early songs that are charming—*Die Entzückung an Laura*, and *La Pastorella*, with its bits of fioritura in Italian style.

Franz Schubert (1797–1828)

5

Mozart

From the towering and expansive immensities of Beethoven and Schubert we turn to music one of whose outstanding characteristics is its subtlety in the expression of powerful meanings. We hear in Mozart's music a melancholy, passion and intensity that some of his contemporaries found disturbing, but these powerful emotions expressed with an economy and conciseness analogous to what the mathematician calls elegance—manifestations of a keenness and precision of mind which only Berlioz exhibits in comparable manner and degree. And the English critic W. J. Turner considered Mozart to be the supreme classical artist precisely because in his music intensity and passion are crystallized in the clearest, the most beautifully balanced and proportioned, and altogether flawless musical forms.

Nobody has written with anything like Turner's wonderfully illuminating insight about the special qualities of Mozart's music and the ambiguities they create. For example about the "still, unplumbed melancholy underlying even his brightest and most vivacious moments." Or about the vital energy in which Turner doubts Mozart was exceeded by any other composer: the finale of Beethoven's Seventh Symphony, he contends, produces a bigger volume of noise, but not the quick, tense rush of Mozart's Overture to *The Marriage of Figaro*—the one being like the rumble of thunder, the other like the flash of lightning. "Its effect upon the mind," Turner says of the overture, "is out of all proportion to its impingement on the senses"—something that is true of all of Mozart's music.*

It may not be true for some listeners accustomed to the luxuriance and vehemence of Wagner and Strauss; but for others—after that luxuriance—the effect of Mozart's music is the greater for its economy and subtlety. For these listeners there is no need of waiting for Wagner and Strauss: they find Mozart completely adequate for every demand of the drama he is setting. They find this so when they listen to the orchestra's comments in Leporello's *Catalogue Aria* in *Don Giovanni:* to the discreetly mischievous detached notes of the violins, answered by cellos and basses, at the beginning; the eruptions of the violins and woodwinds, like bursts of laughter, a moment later; still later the suave phrase with which the violins punctuate *son già mille e tre;* after this the quiet ascending scale of cellos and basses, answered by the descending scale of violins, both like repressed laughter over *In Italia sei cento e quaranta;* and so on. Or the grandly impassioned and lamenting phrases of Donna Anna's *Fuggi, crudele,* the abrupt, energetic and bold phrases of orchestra and singer in Donna Elvira's *Ah chi mi dice mai:* what more modern music could place each character on the stage more effectively? Or Don Giovanni's *Là ci darem la mano:* could Wagner or Strauss have achieved anything as elegantly seductive? Or the solemn D-minor chords with which the overture begins; then the ominous dotted rhythm of the strings over which sustained woodwind chords lead to the poignant figure developed by the violins and interrupted by the vehement outbursts of the entire orchestra; then the powerful ascending scale passages, again over the ominous dotted rhythm that continues through the final measures which—first forceful, then quiet—lead to the Allegro portion of the overture: the Prelude to *Tristan und Isolde* does not establish the atmosphere for the drama to come, does not take possession of the listener's mind and emotions, more quickly and completely.

There are comparable things in *Così fan tutte:* in the first act the quintet *Di scrivermi ogni giorno!,* the trio *Soave sia il vento,* the

*W. J. Turner, *Mozart—The Man and His Works,* revised and edited by Christopher Raeburn (London 1938, 1965).

aria *Come scoglio;* in the second act the duets *Secondate, aurette amiche* and *Il core vi dono,* the aria *Per pietà,* the duet *Fra gli amplessi.* And in *The Magic Flute:* the ensembles involving the Three Ladies, the ones involving the Three Boys, the arias of the Queen of the Night, Tamino's *Dies Bildnis ist bezaubernd schön,* Pamina's *Ach, ich fühl's,* the trio *Soll ich dich, Teurer, nicht mehr seh'n?,* the fugato of Tamino and the Two Armed Men, Tamino's and Pamina's *Pamina / Tamino mein! O welch' ein Glück!*

But wonderful as all these are, they are surpassed by what is heard in *The Marriage of Figaro:* the three-hour outpouring of incandescent invention—miraculous in its varied loveliness, expressiveness, characterization, dramatic point and wit—that is one of the supreme wonders achieved on this earth by human powers. Nor do I mean only the vocal invention: *Figaro* surpasses the other operas in orchestral writing of the kind I have described in the *Catalogue Aria*—with its three-hour running fire of comment that creates the atmosphere of comedy in which even the serious things happen. And in this connection I will mention Tovey's observation that in the G-minor Symphony Mozart's musical language is, as it is in fact everywhere else, that of operatic comedy—by which Tovey doesn't mean that what is said in this language is humorous: one often, he says, finds the language of comedy the only dignified expression for the deepest feelings.* It is in this manner that they are often expressed by Mozart—the result being the ambiguity that is one of his outstanding characteristics, and of which an outstanding example is *Così fan tutte,* with its apparently farcical action for which Mozart wrote some of his most poignant and sublime music, and with things like the aria *Come scoglio,* whose apparent grand style sometimes invites the suspicion that it is parodying itself.

Nor—to get back to *Figaro*—do I mean only the vocal and instrumental invention of the arias. The work rises to its greatest incandescence in the climactic ensembles—the comparatively brief *Cosa sento!* trio of Act 1 and sextet of Act 3, the extended finales of Acts 2 and 4, of which the one of Act 2 is the supreme

---

*Donald F. Tovey, "Mozart—Symphony K.550," *Essays in Musical Analysis* (London, 1935).

achievement of its kind, and incidentally the supreme demonstration of the adequacy I spoke of a moment ago. Nothing could be simpler than

and nothing more modern and complex could express more effectively the Count's and the Countess's amazement at seeing Susanna step out from the cabinet. So with what follows: the bland irony of Susanna's *Signore! cos' è quel stupore?;* the atmosphere of wonder created by the orchestra for the Count's *Che scola!,* the Countess's *Che storia è mai questa,* Susanna's amused *Confusa han la testa;* a moment later the atmosphere of high comedy created by the orchestra for the Count's entreaties, the women's severe *Le vostre follie non mertan pietà;* still later the elaborate and menacing politeness of the Count's *Conoscete, signor Figaro, questo foglio chi vergo?* and the violins' impudent amusement behind Figaro's *Nol conosco;* the stolid stupidity in a state of excitement conveyed by the gardener's *Dal balcone che guarda in giardino,* burlesqued by Figaro's *Via piangione, sta zitto una volta;* and finally the suspense created for the Count's sparring with Figaro by the orchestra's long development of the figure

which swells to triumph for Figaro's *è l'usanza di porvi il suggello.*

The finale of Act 4 is another such succession, for whose conclusion—and the climax of the entire work—Mozart holds in reserve a last marvel. Its overwhelming effect, like that of anything else, comes partly from its context—where it is placed, what it follows. Three hours have been filled with the sorrow of the neglected Countess's *Porgi amor* and *Dove sono;* the agitated awakening emotions of Cherubino's *Non so più cosa son;* the enchanting playfulness of Susanna's *Venite, inginocchiatevi;* the longing of her *Deh vieni, non tardar;* the irony and menace of Figaro's *Se vuol ballare;* the mockery of his *Non più andrai;* the bitterness of his *Aprite un po' quegl' occhi;* the pompous malice of Bartolo's *La vendetta;* the ear-ravishing loveliness of the Letter Duet; the wit of Susanna's duets with Figaro, Marcellina, the Count; the comedy of the first-act trio, the third-act sextet, the great finale of Act 2, the finale of Act 4. Three hours have been filled with the orchestra's running fire of comment, which has continued to the last to create the atmosphere of comedy for even the serious happenings: even in the hush of amazement and wonder produced by the Countess's entrance the violins have softly chattered their amusement. But now at last there is an end to all this—a moment's silence; and when the Count begins his *Contessa, perdono* we hear music which speaks of the sublimity of human forgiveness—music which, after what has come before, is overwhelming. It becomes even more overwhelming when it is taken up by the entire group, and when it is carried to a point of superearthly exaltation. Then, in the silence which follows, solemn octaves of the strings gently ease us down to earth again—and to the bustle and fanfares of the final curtain of the operatic comedy. The passage lasts only a few minutes; but those three or four minutes, coming after the three hours, create the most wonderful moment I can recall in opera.

From the comedies of the last years of Mozart's short life (he died at thirty-five) we turn back to the *opera seria* he wrote at twenty-five—to *Idomeneo,* in which, says E. J. Dent in his illuminating book on Mozart's operas, we "see the young Mozart at his greatest heights." Dent speaks of the work's nobility and dignity of conception, its intense seriousness, the "monumental strength and . . . white heat of passion that we find in this early work of Mozart's and shall never find again;" and this turns out to be an accurate description of what we hear: the grandly impassioned gestures with which the overture begins, the continuing urgency of its so-called second subject in A minor, the breathtaking shift to C major; the powerfully expressive detail with which the orchestra points up the recitatives; the noble style of the beautiful arias; the dramatic use of coloratura style—most notably the descending staccato scale in Electra's final aria that suggests the laughter of a demented creature; the power of the great quartet, and of the chorus *O voto tremendo!*

For the rest there are two mature comedies to take note of first. One, the full-length *The Abduction from the Seraglio*, composed a year or two after *Idomeneo*, has some lovely and charming music in addition to the great bravura aria *Martern aller Arten*. The other, the one-act *The Impresario*, composed the same year as *Figaro*, has a delightful overture and superb vocal writing in its two arias and trio. And then there are six operas that Mozart wrote in his teens: *Ascanio in Alba*, which amazes one with the fifteen-year-old boy's completely assured handling of singers and orchestra in his own already fully achieved vocal and orchestral style; the charming *Bastien und Bastienne; La finta giardiniera*, whose overture has extraordinary rush and impact; *Il rè pastore*, of which the familiar aria *L'amerò, sarò costante* turns out to be the only piece in it of any magnitude, although the other arias are engagingly Mozartian; *Mitridate, rè di Ponto*, which the fourteen-year-old Mozart wrote during his stay in Milan to show—after he had heard a number of operas by other composers—what he could achieve in the genre, and which offers a large amount of formulaic recitative concerned with the formulaic drama, and occasional set pieces that astonish one with Mozart's assured operation in a melodic style already his own; and the uninteresting *Lucio Silla*. Uninteresting too is the later fragmentry *Lo sposo deluso*. Finally, there is Mozart's last opera, *La clemenza di Tito*, written for a coronation in the by then old-fashioned style of *opera seria*, which has impressive melodic writing in addition to its excessive amount of recitative.

I have called Dent's book illuminating; and nothing in it is more so than his observation that "the theater is the sphere in which Mozart is most completely himself; his concert works—concertos, symphonies, quartets and sonatas—are all fundamentally evocations of the theater." The truth of this statement is most evident in the concertos: the special circumstances which produced them made them the most explicitly dramatic in character of Mozart's instrumental works. And those circumstances also made them the most elaborately contrived, the richest in substance, the most complex in form, the most fascinating and exciting and in all ways impressive to listen to.

Mozart produced most of his greatest concertos for the occasions at which he presented himself to the public as the greatest musician of his time—exhibiting the capacities of the greatest performer, in music that exhibited the capacities of the greatest composer. He wrote a concerto as an actor might write a play for himself to appear in; and the form he produced was in effect the musical equivalent of a play. Listening to the opening movement of one of the piano concertos we first hear the orchestra perform with increasing suspense in anticipation of the moment when it bows itself from the center of the stage, so to speak, and the piano makes its first entrance, to hold attention for a while with graceful, lovely melodies, dazzling passage-work, exchanges with the orchestra, and eventually to work up to a brilliant exit, at which point the orchestra prepares for the piano's next entrance, and so on—the piano's last such entrance being made for the *cadenza* that exhibits the pianist's powers of improvisation, after which the orchestra brings the curtain down on the movement. And we hear similar dramatic alternation of orchestra and piano in the slow movement that presents the piano in Mozartian sustained vocal melody, the finale that often presents it in Mozartian high spirits.

The purpose of the form being to impress the listener, its fascination is, first, in what Mozart contrives for this purpose. But there is in addition a special fascination in the sense it gives of the immediacy of Mozart's presence: in the piano's every phrase of melody, every passage of brilliant figuration, every trill, every ornament, we are aware, almost as his own listeners were, of Mozart himself—showing everything he is capable of, attempting to impress, to dazzle, to overwhelm, and succeeding with an apparently inexhaustible flow of the unique poignant loveliness, the gaiety, and on occasion the power. These are the fascination of any one example of the form; but what is fascinating in one after another of the marvelous works is the seemingly unending variety of the invention with which Mozart fills out the same established scheme, goes through the same established series of steps in a way that is newly interesting and impressive each time, and on occasion—writing for an audience familiar with the established scheme—plays with this audience a little game of now doing what it expects and now surprising it with what it does not expect.

Thus we get the extraordinary first entrance of the solo violin in the concerto K.219 (Mozart was also an accomplished violinist): the orchestra finishes its introduction; we expect the violin to enter at the same lively pace; and instead it begins a breathtakingly beautiful and poignant slow melody which progresses through a half-dozen measures to a conclusion and a pause; after which violin and orchestra break the spell by resuming the original lively course of the movement. And on the other hand, at the beginning of the Piano Concerto K.271 we get the surprises that represent Mozart's love of fun: the orchestra begins imposingly, but before it can finish the piano jumps in to complete the statement; again the orchestra tries, and again the piano interrupts, after which the orchestra is allowed to proceed without further interruption to the final flourish, the final bow of its ritornello; but while it is still bowing the piano bursts onto the scene with a brilliant trill that leads into its opening statement.

The Violin Concerto K.219, which Mozart wrote at nineteen, the Piano Concerto K.271, which he wrote at twenty-one, are among the first great examples of the form; and from these and other early examples we learn that the difference between Mozart at twenty and Mozart at thirty is not, as we might suppose, the difference between Mozart immature and Mozart mature. In the Violin Concertos K.218 and 219, with their characteristic mingling of high spirits and poignant loveliness; in the Violin Concerto K.216, with its especially delightful first movement, its Andante movement whose long flow of sustained melody leaves one spellbound; in the Piano Concerto K.271, with another especially delightful first movement, one of Mozart's deeply affecting C-minor slow movements, and an exuberantly gay finale whose "rush" leaves one breathless—in these early works we hear the essential Mozart expressive content and Mozart form completely and astoundingly matured. What time brings is enrichment, elaboration, subtilization, which rise on occasion to sheer incandescence; that is the difference between the first movements of K.216 (1775) and K.271 (1777), and the first movement of the Piano Concerto K.453 (1784); between the slow movement of K.271, and the C-minor slow movement of the Sinfonia Concertante K.364 for violin and viola (1779); between the slow movement of K.216, and the Andante movement of the Piano Concerto K.467 (1785); between the finale of K.271, and the finales of K.466 (1785) and 488 (1786).

Enrichment, elaboration, subtilization, then, give us the later great examples of the form—the Piano Concertos K.450, 453, 456 and 459 (1784), K.466, 467 and 482 (1785), K.488, 491 and 503 (1786), and K.595 (1791). And incandescence gives us the individual movements and entire works, among those great examples, that are some of Mozart's supreme utterances in instrumental music.

Thus K.453 has a first movement that is one of the supreme examples of Mozartian instrumental high comedy—though one in which characteristically the gaiety is mingled with Mozartian poignancy. They are mingled right from the start, in the opening violin theme that begins with grace and elegance, continues with a poignancy the more intense for the exquisite contour of the embodying phrase, and is punctuated by mocking flutters of the woodwinds. A moment later the bassoon chortles on comically after the flourishes of the full orchestra stop, leading to another exquisitely contoured and poignant statement of the violins (at this point in the recapitulation Mozart contrives a couple of his little surprises and jokes: when the orchestra's flourishes stop it is not the chortling bassoon but the piano that continues them, leading not to that statement of the violins but to a sharply contoured theme which the piano itself stated in the exposition). And such alternations continue throughout the movement.

This first movement of comedy is followed by one of Mozart's most affecting and most extraordinarily organized slow movements. A poignant opening statement recurs several times, pausing each time before a long sequence of thought takes off from it; overlaid on this pattern of arrangement are alternations of orchestra and piano, and a cycle of keys; and after the piano's cadenza the woodwinds' last enunciation of the opening statement is completed, with sublime implications, by the piano. Then the finale: a genial theme and several variations, one of them suddenly hushed and ominous with its minor mode and syncopations; and a coda made breathtaking by the tempo, style, surprises and jokes of a Mozartian operatic-comedy finale.

In the seldom-played K.456 it is the Andante movement that is outstanding, with an extraordinarily beautiful and poignant theme in G minor that is elaborated in several impressive examples of Mozartian variation-writing.

K.466, one of the most frequently played, begins with what is perhaps the most powerful of Mozart's instrumental movements. The power of the hushed D-minor opening passage is an example of effect on the mind out of all proportion to the impingement on the senses: it is achieved by nothing more than the agitated syncopations of violins and violas, the quiet eruptions of cellos and basses, with not even one of the kettledrum-strokes that punctuate those eruptions in the orchestral outburst a moment later (not only kettledrums but trumpets are added to the orchestra in this work). In the second movement it is the interlude of sustained melody for the solo piano that is noteworthy—more so even than the stormy G-minor episode later in the movement. And then comes one of Mozart's incandescent perpetuum mobile finales, similar to the one in K.271, but its momentum this time unbroken by a minuet, and with a last-minute surprise in the coda: the theme

heard twice before in the movement, is now changed, extended, and unexpectedly answered by the horns' and trumpets'

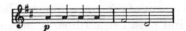

which becomes increasingly insistent in the crescendo that brings the movement to a close.

Trumpets and kettledrums contribute to the festive brilliance of the first movement of K.467, the gaiety of its finale; but they play no part in the extraordinary Andante in between. In this movement the orchestra makes a long opening statement of a succession of ideas, on which the piano then discourses in several sequences of thought that get to be excitingly eventful in the way that is so extraordinary: up above there is the calm of the melody as it proceeds with developing tensions and involvements; while down below there is the agitation of faster-moving accompanying violins and violas, the power of plucked bass-notes; and occasionally there are intensifying comments by the woodwinds. All these, working together, build up tension and impact that make this movement, for all its quiet, one of Mozart's most powerful utterances; and indeed with this power achieved in quiet it is one of the most extraordinary pieces of music he ever wrote.

In the first movement of K.482 festive opening proclamations claim attention for a rich flow of exquisite melodic invention; there is a similar flow of loveliness and humor in the finale; and in between is another of Mozart's most affecting and extraordinarily organized slow movements. Muted violins play a long and poignant melody in C minor; when the piano enters it is to play an elaborating and intensifying variation on this melody, reinforced at climactic moments by the orchestra's strings; the winds then enter with an engaging interlude in E flat major; the piano makes a second entrance with another variation on the opening melody, again reinforced momentarily by the strings; in a second interlude, this time in C major, the flute and bassoon, accompanied by strings, carry on a gracefully ornate dialogue; then the piano engages in a powerful dialogue with the full orchestra in another variation on the opening melody; after which orchestra and piano alternate in a coda that ends with a master-stroke: the concluding phrase of the first interlude, with the intense poignancy it acquires from being now in C minor.

In K.488 there is a return to an orchestra without trumpets and kettledrums for the flow of some of Mozart's most ear-ravishing and heart-piercing melodic invention in the first movement, another of his affecting slow movements in minor mode, and the supreme example of his incandescent perpetuum-mobile finales—the most breathtaking in its profusion of ideas, its momentum, its strokes of surprise and humor. The effect of these strokes comes, again, from their context; and Mozart expects us to remember how

etc.

proceeded and ended the first time, when he brings it back later in the movement and makes it proceed and end differently—i.e. prolongs it with changes of harmony that create increasing suspense before it suddenly leaps triumphantly into the clear with

piano

etc.

Similarly he expects our recollection of the previous two appearances of this blandly, suavely mocking statement:

etc.

to enable us to appreciate the effect of its unexpected last appearance near the end of the movement.

The large orchestra is heard again in K.491, contributing to the magnificence that is one of the outstanding characteristics of its first movement, another being its dramatic power—the power, for example, of the hushed C-minor opening passage of strings and bassoons and its forceful restatement by the entire orchestra a moment later; or of the forceful statements and the hushed concluding passage, again in C minor, after the cadenza. This movement towers above the engaging slow movement and the richly elaborated variation finale.

In K.503 too the first movement towers above the others by virtue of a grandeur and majesty that set it apart from other first movements. Thus it begins not with one of their immediately appealing opening themes, but, in the words of Tovey, "with a majestic assertion of . . . C major by the whole orchestra, with mysterious soft shadows that give a solemn depth to the tone."*

*Donald F. Tovey, "Concertos"—Foreword, *Essays in Musical Analysis* (London, 1935).

And these mysterious soft shadows of delicate woodwind textures after the initial radiance of the entire orchestra—the second time with a wonderful shift to C minor—are subtleties contrived for the eighteenth-century ear that may escape some listeners of today. Another such subtlety is created with a reiterated rhythmic figure, which in the opening ritornello is carried to a point where it is trumpeted forth on the note G and leads to C minor: when the orchestra trumpets forth those G's again at the beginning of the development, they are answered breathtakingly by the piano's reiteration of the figure on B, in a sudden shift to E minor that is the first of a series of such bold modulations.

Trumpets and drums are not suitable for the first movement of K.595, which also stands apart from the other concertos, and in fact from everything else, in its late-in-life calm (e.g. the opening statement of the violins, punctuated by the strange calls of the winds), with which it conveys intimations of agony that preceded calm (e.g. the poignantly altered repetition of the violins'

a few moments later)—so that as a piece of late writing by Mozart it has something like the character of a late work of Beethoven, or Schubert's Piano Sonata in B flat. Something of this character is heard also in the opening and closing sections of the Larghetto, which has in between an eventful, and in the end impassioned, interlude of sustained melody for the piano—one of the events being a breathtaking shift in key. But not in the finale, in which there is only lilting good humor, with moments of high spirits and fun.

And not, I will add, in another product of the last year of Mozart's life, the lovely Clarinet Concerto K.622—though the Mozartian poignancy makes itself heard in the lyricism and gaiety.

Writing about Schubert I referred to the last quiet passage just before the end of the finale of Mozart's Symphony in G minor K.550—a series of textures of sounds with miraculously achieved intensities of loveliness and expressive force. Hardly less wonderful is the analogous quiet passage soon after the beginning of that finale; and there is another series of such miracles about halfway through the first movement—the passage that leads to the return of the impassioned opening statement. These are incandescent moments in one of the most extraordinary examples of what Turner spoke about—one in which the utmost in passion and intensity is crystallized in the most exquisite of clear, beautifully balanced and proportioned musical forms. Its expressive content and form, in fact, not only set the G-minor apart from Mozart's other symphonies but make it another of the supreme wonders achieved by human powers.

The G-minor is the second of the last great group of three symphonies Mozart composed in approximately two months of the summer of 1788. Its intense melancholy, which is heightened by the clarinets he felt impelled to add later, may seem at first to be related to the desperate circumstances of Mozart's life at that time; but the loveliness of K.543—even though it pierces the heart as it ravishes the ear—and the festive majesty of K.551 that has caused it to be given the name *Jupiter* teach us not to attempt such correlations of works of art with the immediate circumstances of the artist's life.

There are flashing miracles again in the finale of K.543—e.g. the series of subtly altered statements of

that lead to the return of the opening statement of the violins. And in the finale of K.551 there is another of those extraordinary rushes of vital energy, expressing itself this time in contrapuntal manipulation of the several themes which Mozart carries to a jubilantly triumphant conclusion.

Of the same stature is the less frequently heard Symphony K.504 (*Prague*) (1786), with the grand opening gestures of a slow introduction that becomes powerfully dramatic before pausing for the brilliant Allegro; with an Andante rich in thematic ideas whose development is made eventful by bold shifts of key; and with a delightful concluding Presto.

Smaller in scale are the earlier movements of the seldom-played K.425 (*Linz*) (1783)—the imposing introduction leading to the brilliant Allegro, the lovely slow movement, the minuet movement. Unexpected, therefore, is the large scale of the finale, its richness of substance and elaboration.

The frequently heard K.385 (*Haffner*) (1782) has a powerful first movement elaborated almost entirely out of its opening statement, followed by a lovely and poignant Andante, a fine minuet movement, and another delightful concluding Presto.

The power of these later symphonies is something we don't find in the earlier K.338 (1780) and K.297 (*Paris*) (1778); but we do find a poignantly lovely Andantino in K.297, an especially lovely Andante di molto in K.338, framed by delightfully high-spirited opening movements and rushing finales.

And like the concertos the symphonies include early small-scale works, K.200 and 201 (1773–4) in which we hear the essential Mozart expressive content and form astoundingly matured: in K.200 the gaiety of the opening movement and rushing finale, the poignancy of the exquisitely contoured muted-violin melodies in the Andante, the pensiveness tinged with sadness in much of the minuet movement; and in K.201 the grace and wistfulness of the opening movement, the poignant loveliness of the Andante, the gaiety of the minuet (e.g. the comical punctuating flourishes of the winds) alternating with the exquisite poignancy of the trio; the high spirits of another rushing finale.

In Mozart's operas, concertos and symphonies we have heard the exquisite textures in which he combines the sounds of strings, of winds, of both strings and winds, of instruments and voices. You will find nothing to equal them (though Berlioz and Debussy will offer something comparable); and since string-quartet-writing is an art of texture you will hear in no other quartets the ear-ravishing use of the medium that you hear in the famous six— K.387, 421, 428, 458 (*Hunt*), 464 and 465—that Mozart dedicated to Haydn, and K.499, which is of the same period—1782–6. (The final three—K.575, 589 and 590, dedicated to the King of Prussia—are of lesser stature, though with some lovely writing.) Nor do they, of course, merely delight the ear: their expressive content, as always, touches the heart. And outstanding in these respects are the somberly powerful K.421, the now amusingly high-spirited, now deeply affecting K.458, the less frequently heard K.428 with its grave opening movement, its rich-textured Andante and comedy finale, and K.499 with its richly elaborated opening movement and slow movement, its lovely minuet, and another comedy finale.

But of greatest stature among the works of this category are two of the string quintets, K.515 and 516 (1787). The additional viola, by increasing the sonority and the richness of texture, contributes to the extraordinary power of the first movement of K.515; by darkening the instrumental color it contributes to the somber strangeness of the minuet and first part of the trio, the intensity of the middle part of the trio, the poignancy of the Andante. And the darkened instrumental coloring contributes, as does the key of G minor, to the effect of K.516, one of the best-known of these works, and unique in its expressive content: in no other work of Mozart do we hear such unrelieved melancholy as in the first movement, such poignancy in a minuet, this poignancy carried to such agonized intensity as in the slow movement; and nowhere does Mozart permit himself to speak with the anguish of the slow introduction to a finale whose apparent light-heartedness at first—incongruous after what has preceded it—is qualified as it continues.

Of the great string quintets that are heard less frequently than they should be, K.593 (1790) is especially notable for its deeply affecting slow movement and bustling comedy finale; K.614 (1791) for the unexpected high spirits of its delightful opening movement and finale; K.406 (1787) for its powerful opening movement and contrapuntal minuet movement in C minor, its poignant Andante.

K.406 is an arrangement of the earlier Serenade K.388 for winds, which has less expressive effect than the string quintet version but offers some of Mozart's beautiful writing for wind instruments, both solo and in combination. We hear more of this writing in the Serenade K.361 (*Gran Partita*), which has a very fine slow introduction, Adagio, and variation movement; and the brilliant Serenade K.375, which has wonderful details. Beautiful writing for strings and horns is to be heard in the charming Divertimentos K.247, 287 and 334—the second with an extraordinary Adagio in the style of a great vocal aria, the third with some wonderful details in the variation movement; for oboe, horns and strings in the engaging Divertimento K.251; for winds, horns, trumpets, and strings in the Serenade K.203, which has lovely Andante and minuet movements; and beautiful writing for three strings is heard in the Divertimento K.563, with its fine slow movement and extraordinary variations.

We hear writing for the oboe that is breathtaking in its vocal style and expressive intensity in the brief Adagio that is framed by charming Allegros in the Quartet K.370 for oboe and strings. And the larger-scale Quintet K.581 for clarinet and strings offers a flow of lyricism, characteristic in its poignant loveliness, that makes it one of Mozart's most beautiful works.

Concerning the Quintet K.452 for piano and winds I am in the awkward position of disagreeing with Mozart, who in a letter to his father pronounced it "the best I have ever written," since the opening Allegro, to my ears, is inane. But twice even in this movement—near the end of the exposition and the recapitulation—there is a succession of scale passages rushing up to sustained notes which create a texture with wonderful harmonic progressions; there are impressive episodes also in the slow movement; and there are of course wonderful textures of sounds of winds throughout. The piano is heard with clarinet and viola in the fine Trio K.498; it is heard with strings in the piano trios—of which K.496 is the best, and K.502 and 548 have beautiful slow movements— and in the piano quartets K.478 and 493—the second less immediately imposing in its themes, but rich in exquisitely wrought, and at times witty, detail. It is heard also in the sonatas for piano and violin, of which an early group includes the charming K.296, 301, 305 and 306, the impassioned K.304, the lovely K.378; and later ones include the powerful K.379, K.380 with its poignant slow movement, K.454 and 481 with their very beautiful slow movements, and K.526, the finest of the series, with one of the most charming of first movements, a grave, richly elaborated Andante that becomes wonderfully beautiful and deeply affecting, and one of the most brilliant and breathtaking of perpetuum-mobile finales.

For piano solo one of Mozart's finest pieces is the Rondo K.511 that I present in Chapter 25—unique in the chromaticism and expressive intensity of the exquisitely contoured principal melody and its recurring variants. And other late works of the same stature are the powerful Fantasia K.475 and Sonata K.457, which are sometimes played, as they were published, together; the Sonata K.576, with some of Mozart's most developed, most complex writing for the instrument; the fine Sonata K.570; the extraordinary Sonata K.533, remarkable in the large-scale and contrapuntal elaboration of the Allegro, the startling harmonic progressions that achieve the utmost in expressive intensity in the Andante (the earlier Rondo K.494, which Mozart published with this sonata as a concluding movement, is less interesting); the Adagio K.335 (really K.617a) for glass harmonica and Rondo K.616 for mechanical organ, both with striking modulations; the Adagio K.540; the Minuet K.355, a small but fine late piece (really K.594a); and another of Mozart's most remarkable works, the rhythmically intricate Gigue K.574. Other pieces of this period that are of lesser stature but engaging are the "Small sonata for beginners" K.545, the Sonata K.547a, Sonata movement K.400, and the Minuet K.498a. A little earlier are the magnificent Fantasia in C minor K.396; the Fantasia in D minor K.397, whose Adagio is a miniature example of declamatory vocal style; the Suite K.399, with its interesting and attractive Mozartian transformations of the styles of the movements of a Handel suite; the Rondo K.485, which is entirely and interestingly unusual in its procedures; and the Capriccio K.395, a strange piece unlike any other by Mozart, reminiscent of Bach, and implying a larger scale than its actual small one.

And still earlier are the fine Sonatas K.309, 330 and 333, the last with a good opening movement and a startling development section in the Andante; the powerful K.310; K.282, with its astonishing Adagio first movement; K.280, an excellent display piece; and the Sonatas K.332, 311, 283 and 279, of which the finales are good. Of the best-known Sonata K.331 I find the minuet movement more estimable than the opening theme and variations and concluding *Rondo à la turca*.

There are as well several sets of piano variations—K.179 on a minuet of J. C. Fischer and K.180 on a theme of Salieri, in which one hears the operation of matured powers; K.265 on *Ah, vous dirai-je, maman*, which has two impressive slow variations; K.264 on *Lison dormait*, with one of Mozart's wonderful syncopated and chromatic variations in minor and an extraordinary Adagio; K.352 on a march by Grétry, of which Nos. 4, 5 and 7 are outstanding; the unfamiliar variations K.353 on *La Belle Françoise*, a good work, especially in the slow variation; K.354 on *Je suis Lindor*, of which Nos. 4, 8 and 10 are outstanding; K.398 on *Salve tu* and K.455 on *Unser dummer Pöbel meint;* K.460 on *Come un' agnello*, which has good writing in the later pages; K.54 (actually 574a), a late work with a wonderful variation in minor mode; and the set of variations K.613 on *Ein Weib ist das herrlichste Ding*, which is fluent and pleasant and becomes impressive and powerful with the change to minor mode—at variation 6, the slow No. 7 and the elaborate No. 8.

In addition there are the fine Sonata K.448 for two pianos; the engaging sonatas K.381, 358 and 357 for piano four hands.

Other attractive pieces Mozart wrote as occasion demanded include the Concertone K.190 for two violins and oboe; the four Flute Quartets; the German and Country Dances—late works which have wonderful details; and the ballet music for *Les Petits Riens*. I would suppose that the Concerto K.191 for bassoon was written by Mozart as a display piece for some player he knew; and I would suspect also that it was an occasion for Mozart to amuse himself—not only obviously with the tootling and braying he gave to the solo instrument—but subtly with the comments he gave to the orchestra. Another such occasion was offered by a request for concertos for the French horn. In this instance, however, the results are unusually engaging in musical substance for this type of work; there is beautiful melodic writing in all four, even in the slightest of them, K.412; but what in addition makes K.447 the most impressive of them is the development section of the first movement, with its startling and dramatic shifts of key; and the smaller-scale K.417 also has wonderful pages in the development of its first movement. Three other engaging minor concertos are the Piano Concerto in E flat K.449, the Concerto for Two Pianos K.365 and the Flute Concerto in G K.313. (The Violin Concerto K.211, the Piano Concertos K.413, 414 and 415, and the Concerto for Three Pianos K.242 I find less interesting.) Charming also are the *Serenata Notturna* K.239 and the *Posthorn* Serenade K.320. And the *Haffner* Serenade K.250 (not to be confused with the later *Haffner* Symphony) that Mozart composed for a wedding in the Haffner family amazes one with its prodigal flow of invention suited to both the festive and the solemn aspects of the occasion.

Mozart's Masonic Music comprises three cantatas—*Dir, Seele des Weltalls* K.429, *Die Maurerfreude* K.471, and the *Kleine Freimaurerkantate (Laut verkünde uns're Freude)* K.623—and the Masonic Funeral Music K.477 for winds and horns. Listened to first, K.623 sounds initially like mere echoings of parts of *The Magic Flute;* but from K.429 one discovers that it is more accurate to say that those parts of *The Magic Flute* are in what might be called Mozart's Masonic style. K.429 is the best of the cantatas; but most impressive of all is the Funeral Music—a series of musical gestures of solemnity, grief and resignation, with occasional dramatic events provided by startling modulations.

Mozart also wrote a large number of songs, not all of which are as good as *Unglückliche Liebe, Abendempfindung, Der Zauberer, Das Veilchen, Das Lied der Trennung, An Chloë, Die Verschweigung* and the delightfully humorous *Die Alte.*

Most of Mozart's church music, finally, was written in his youth while he was in the service of the Archbishop of Salzburg; and an outstanding work of this period is the *Coronation* Mass K.317, written when he was twenty-three. It has several sections—the *Kyrie, Gloria, Benedictus* and *Agnus Dei*—which are very beautiful; but most impressive is the *Credo,* with an Allegro opening section that acquires tremendous power from its ostinato imstrumental figuration, then a change to Adagio for wonderful passages on the words *Et incarnatus est* and *Crucifixus etiam* and *passus et sepultus est,* and then a return to the Allegro with a lovely episode on *Et in spiritum sanctum.*

Once out of the service of the Archbishop he was kept busy by the instrumental works and operas with which he had to earn a living—too busy to be able to complete the *Mass in C Minor* that he began in 1782. But in its incomplete form it includes a magnificently powerful *Kyrie* with a lovely episode for solo soprano, and the wonderfully beautiful *Et incarnatus est.*

And death cut short his work on the *Requiem,* which was completed in accordance with his sketches and directions by his pupil Süssmayr. This work too has magnificently powerful sections like the *Kyrie* (with affecting passages for solo soprano), *Tuba mirum* and *Rex tremendae;* lovely ones like the *Recordare, Hostias, Benedictus* and *Agnus Dei;* and a *Lacrymosa* which takes its place with things like the Andante of the Piano Concerto K.467— what is extraordinary this time being the way the unceasing two-note violin figure builds up cumulative expressive force behind the affecting vocal parts.*

On a smaller scale are the early Mass K.192—interesting in the

*It is not known for certain how much of the *Requiem* was completed by Mozart, how much was only sketched by him and completed and orchestrated by Süssmayr, how much was actually composed by Süssmayr, and how much may have been completed, orchestrated or composed by an unknown third person, whose existence is surmised from portions of the score that are in a handwriting different from both Mozart's and Süssmayr's. The fact remains, however, that the "Süssmayr" version sounds more plausible and effective than anyone else's since. —Ed.

way its small scale compels Mozart to crowd an effective expressive stroke into almost every successive phrase of the *Credo,* and with beautiful sustained and developed writing for the soloists in the *Benedictus;* the *Vesperae Solennes de Confessore* K.339, of which the *Laudate Dominum* for solo soprano is only the most extensive and affecting of the occasional fine solo passages; the powerfully expressive *Kyrie* K.341; the sublime *Ave, verum corpus* K.618; the brilliant showpiece for soprano, *Exsultate, jubilate* K.165; and finally, the Mass K.139—an astonishing work, in whose brief sections the twelve-year-old Mozart writes in the various styles he has heard, but in a language unmistakably his own, and which he uses at times—in the *Qui tollis* and the *Crucifixus,* for example—with extraordinary power.

Even this long discussion of Mozart's music leaves undiscussed a large part of his enormous output that I have never heard, and some works, among those I have heard, that a busily engaged eighteenth-century musical craftsman turned out occasionally without inspiration or interest, and with no more inspiration or interest for us than for him. But the works I have dealt with—their use of the medium, and what they express through this use—make that busily engaged craftsman the most extraordinary musical artist who ever lived.

Thus we come to a paradox—that this genius died in poverty—about which it is worth adding a few observations as a corrective to some of the things you may have read or heard.

It is from Haydn, first, that we learn the truth about Mozart and his circumstances—from this passage in a letter to a friend in Prague, after the success there of *Don Giovanni:*

> If into the mind of every music-lover, but especially of the great of this earth, I could engrave the inimitable works of Mozart as deeply and with such musical understanding and such deep feeling as I experience them, then nations would compete to possess such a treasure within their borders. Let Prague hold on to the precious man—but also reward him; for without this the history of great geniuses is sad, and gives posterity little encouragement to further endeavor; for which reason, alas, so many promising talents are destroyed. I am angry that this unique Mozart is not attached to an

imperial or royal court! Excuse me if I get wrought up: I love the man too much.

From this we learn that the system of patronage did not offer everyone the opportunities and rewards that it did Haydn—that it allowed talent to perish, and not only talent but genius. For Mozart wrote much of his music, and much of his best, under conditions of wretchedness and strain created by poverty and debt; and his writing was cut short at the height of his powers by his death at thirty-five from privation and exhaustion. This has caused some composers and commentators, who explain in this way the indifference or dislike which much of today's music encounters, to take him as another instance of genius not being recognized in its own time. But from Haydn's letter we know that this was not so. The exhortation to Prague in the letter was prompted by the enormous success of *Don Giovanni* with the public there. And Mozart's appointment as imperial chamber composer shortly thereafter must be taken as an indication of his broad reputation and standing at the time, for Joseph II made the appointment even though he did not himself care for Mozart's music.

The truth is that the eminence of Mozart might be recognized even by those who found his music difficult or disturbing. That anyone could have felt this about it may appear incredible; but that is because the development of musical language and expressiveness has caused details of Mozart's vocabulary and grammar to lose for us much of the startling significance and impact they had for his contemporaries. To some of them his music was too complicated, and its melancholy—the black melancholy of a man who lacked the active, affirmative spiritual faith of Bach and Beethoven (but who Turner rightly observes was "deficient in nothing else")—was too unsettling.

The truth is also that as eminent a composer as Mozart might have bad luck with his patrons: when, for example, he did receive the court appointment from Joseph II, it was at a greatly reduced and wholly inadequate salary. As eminent a composer as Mozart might be unable to deal with his patrons efficiently: when he received a better offer from the King of Prussia, a sentimental appeal from the Austrian emperor sufficed to dissuade him from accepting it. As eminent a composer as Mozart might not know how to derive from a popular success like that of *Don Giovanni* in Prague the financial benefit that Handel or Gluck would have derived. As eminent a composer as Mozart, then, might die at thirty-five of privation and exhaustion, after producing works that as the embodiment of sensibility and feeling in tonal construction, and in their miracles of instantaneous loveliness and expressiveness, were unique and widely recognized as such while he lived.

Wolfgang Amadeus Mozart (1756–1791)

6

Haydn

Toscanini, excited once about a Haydn symphony he was going to play, exclaimed that he found Haydn more wonderful even than Mozart ("except of course," he added, "the G-minor—and the concertos"). What caused his face to register delight as he listened to a recording of the symphony was the method so well described by Tovey's statements that "the essential character of Haydn's form is dramatic surprise at the moment" and "nothing in Haydn is difficult to follow, but almost everything is unexpected."* It is a surprise achieved by variety—a moment-to-moment, point-to-point varying of melodic and harmonic direction, length of phrase, rhythmic grouping and accentuation, volume, orchestral activity, which calls for attentive point-to-point listening.

Here, for example, is the opening statement of the Quartet Op. 76 No. 2:

And here is how the repetition of this statement unexpectedly prolongs its third measure and does a little fooling around in the fifth and sixth before coming to a new conclusion in the seventh and eighth:

*Donald F. Tovey, "Haydn—Symphony No. 102," *Essays in Musical Analysis* (London, 1935).

For an example of this sort of thing in rich profusion and in a tempo that makes it easy to observe, listen to the introduction to the Symphony No. 104:

Listen, that is, to the dramatic surprise—after the radiantly sonorous opening call and answer—of the hushed statement of strings and bassoon in measures 3 and 4. Then the effect—after the C sharps at [a]—of the C natural at [b], and of what this C natural brings: the shift in key from D minor into F major. Then the effect—after the radiantly sonorous call and answer—of the changed hushed answer in measure 9. Then the effect—after the development of the first-violin figure with increasing intensity in measures 9, 10 and 11—of the sudden taking over of that figure by the cellos in measure 12 below sustained notes of the upper strings and flute, with increasing harmonic complexity that is resolved in measure 13. And then the startling effects—after the radiantly sonorous call, back in the key of D once more—of the hushed answer, of the note G instead of the expected A at [c], of the addition of the remote chord at [d], creating suspense that changes, with the harmonic progressions and the oboe comments in measure 16, to expectancy for the beginning of the Allegro portion of the movement.

This example of the packing in of detail to hold attention from one moment to the next illustrates Tovey's statement that "Haydn is a great master, with an eminent love of spaciousness, working on a very small scale."* And it illustrates another of Tovey's perceptive observations—that Haydn's forms become more subtle as his spirits rise. For what we hear in Haydn's instrumental music is a constant playing with the medium and with the listener's mind; and sometimes we hear this process raised to incandescence by his exuberance in the use of his powers for that purpose: on every page we get details which it amused him to contrive on Wednesday to startle his listeners, or hold them spellbound, or make them laugh, on Saturday. Thus the little surprises in the first two movements of the Quartet Op. 76 No. 2 leave us unprepared for the bomb that Haydn explodes in the minuet movement: a canon, with violins leading and lower strings following that make us laugh first with the unexpectedness of the procedure and then with some of the details of the progression. Or, in the Symphony No. 104, when the beautiful Andante movement has completed its formal cycle and we think it is about to end, it goes off on a wonderful wide-ranging digression. And a more obvious bit of musical fooling occurs at the end of the minuet: the silence when we are expecting another trill; and then a soft trill when we expect a loud one. Listening to such mischievously contrived details we are aware of the mind that is operating behind them—which is to say that the course of events in a Haydn symphony or quartet gives us the same fascinating sense of the immediacy of Haydn's presence and activity as we get of Mozart's from one of his concertos.

These are some of the fascinations of any one of the works; but to listen to one after another of the great last symphonies—the final group, Nos. 93 to 104, that Haydn wrote for his two visits to London, and some that preceded them—is to be astounded by the profusion and variety of invention from this inexhaustibly fertile mind.

*Donald F. Tovey, *op. cit.*

Astounding in the same way are an even larger number of the string quartets—the many fine works, the works with outstanding individual movements, and the ones that are incandescent. There are the six of Op. 1—engaging pieces for all their small scale and early style, with the playfulness and little surprises characteristic of Haydn, and with minuet movements that often astonish one with trio sections that provide the outstanding moments of the work. There are the six of Op. 2—also pleasant for the most part, but with individual movements that are more than that—e.g. the impressive first movement and Adagio of No. 4, the lovely trios of minuet movements in Nos. 1, 2, 5 and 6. The six similarly engaging quartets of Op. 3. And the six of Op. 9, whose substance and manipulation of substance resemble what Haydn carries to greater heights in the later works. The six of Op. 17, where his method of constantly playing with the medium and with the listener's expectations delights one in No. 6 and achieves outstanding movements in the others. Op. 20, of which Nos. 4 and 5 are among the outstanding examples of the genre, Nos. 1, 2 and 3 are very fine, and No. 6 is of lesser stature but moderately engaging. Op. 33, of which No. 3 (*Bird*), the best-known, stands out as one of Haydn's masterpieces, No. 2 is very fine, Nos. 1 and 4 have fine individual movements, and Nos. 5 and 6 are superb— No. 5 with its extraordinary Largo, its real Haydn Scherzo, its beautiful variation finale, and No. 6 with its highly elaborated first movement and impassioned Andante. Op. 42 is moderately interesting. Of Op. 50, Nos. 1 and 2 are not very interesting, but the other four are superb works.

The three quartets of Op. 54 are incandescent, the unusual and affecting slow movement of No. 2 being one of those that leave one spellbound—in this instance by the first violin's flights of impassioned florid utterance above the quiet statements by the other three instruments. In Op. 64, No. 5 is a fine work and Nos. 3 and 4 are superb. Of the three in Op. 74 No. 2 is incandescent and No. 3 is superb, also. All of the quartets of Op. 76 are fine works, but some offer especially notable examples of the Haydn method and its results: the fast movements of No. 1; the first movement, Andante and Minuet of No. 2; the beautiful first movement of No. 4, whose expansive opening theme has given the work the name *Sunrise;* the lovely first movement of No. 5. Of the two of

Op. 77, No. 2 carries to incandescence the method that delights one in No. 1. And there is the unfinished Quartet Op. 103, whose two movements are very fine.

That leaves the Quartet Op. 51, *The Seven Last Words of Christ on the Cross;* the writing in the seven slow movements is in Haydn's matured style, and that it doesn't engage my interest is difficult to account for; all I can do is report the fact.

And there are the String Trios Op. 53, which offer writing in which one hears the same unpredictable play of Haydn's lively and inventive mind as in his quartets.

The symphonies and quartets, the minor but engaging concertos for harpsichord in D, for trumpet in E flat and for cello in D, are only the best-known of Haydn's instrumental works. Recordings have latterly begun to make it possible to discover the stature and fascination of others that were almost never played in concerts up to now. There are the many trios for piano, violin and cello, of which the later ones are the best—Hoboken Nos. 12, 21, 23, 26 and 28 being outstanding—while the early ones are no more than pleasant to listen to. And there are the works for solo piano, most of them seldom performed.

Pianists, a notoriously unadventurous species, have been content to go on playing the extraordinarily beautiful and often amazing *Andante and Variations* in F minor (amazing not only in the beauty and expressiveness of the first section of the theme, but in what is done with it in the variations and the astonishingly wide-ranging coda), and at most the best-known Sonatas in E flat and D (Hob. Nos. 52 and 37). Fortunately, recordings (for as long as they have remained in the catalogue) have allowed us to hear some of Haydn's other piano pieces, like the fine Variations in C, the Variations in E flat (in which Haydn's elaboration of his brief theme becomes amazing), the good early Sonatas Hob. Nos. 19, 20, 23, 31 (which has an opening movement with the surprises of Haydn's late writing and an impressive slow movement), Nos. 32 and 34; and the even better later works like Hob. Nos. 40, 41, 42, 44, 46, 48, 49 (which is a marvel of the Haydn operation of constant melodic, harmonic and rhythmic surprise) and Nos. 50 and 51.

So, finally, with the choral and vocal works. We used to hear *The*

Creation, with its extraordinary representation of chaos that is amazing in its daring and power, its other passages that are wonderfully beautiful, and still others that charm us with their innocence and sweetness. And once in a great while there would be a performance of *The Seasons,* with its many lovely and charming pages, and some powerful ones in the *Winter* section. Now, through recordings, we know the cantatas *Berenice che fai* and *Arianna a Naxos,* written for Haydn's concerts in London; the *Te Deum*—buoyant and festive except for a poignantly expressive slow interlude; the engaging early and small-scale *Missa brevis in F* and *Missa brevis Sancti Joannis de Deo* (the "Small Organ Mass")—with their moving slow passages, such as the ones in the *Credo* dealing with the Crucifixion; the *Missa in honorem Sancti Nicolai* and *Missa in honorem BVM* (the "Great Organ Mass")—the latter an engaging, and at times moving, work on a scale large enough for an elaboration of its substance that makes it interesting. And we know in addition the later *Missa Sancti Bernardi de Offida* (*Heiligmesse*), the *Creation Mass,* the *Nelson Mass,* the *Theresienmesse,* the *St. Cecilia Mass,* and the *Missa in tempore belli* (*Paukenmesse*)—the last four of which in particular are impressive and often superb products of Haydn's fully matured powers.

And about those powers, their exercise and their development, there is this to say in conclusion. In the Esterhazy household, where Haydn spent thirty years directing the Prince's musicians in music which he composed for them, he was a servant who wore livery. But his service demanded of him the exercise of his talent, and provided him with the opportunity and the most favorable conditions for its development and fruition. However, it was not the opportunity and favorable conditions alone that produced Haydn's music, but these in conjunction with his talent, and the talent more than the opportunity and favorable conditions. Mozart produced his music under anything but favorable conditions (as did Schubert later); and on the other hand there were musicians in noble households who, under the same conditions as Haydn, did not write music with the same interest for us as his. Nor is the difference one merely of technique. He wrote in the same language as they—the common musical language of the period; and for the most part their music sounds like his. But on almost every page of his work there are things that lift him above them; and although in these things there is a difference in technical skill, this difference is only an external manifestation of the difference in what is being said.

One has to say on *almost* every page because there are works— some even, like the *Harmonie* and *Mariazell* masses, from the last years—that are less impressive than the rest. Furthermore, Haydn was a composer whose gifts were called into greater play by some forms than by others. The operas he wrote for the entertainment of Prince Nicolaus Esterhazy offer accomplished writing that is merely pleasant to listen to, culminating in finales that are similar to Mozart's but not their equal in quality and dramatic effect. Finally, Haydn was a composer whose art gained in inventiveness and subtlety over time. And of great importance in this regard was Haydn's encounter, in middle age, with the music of Mozart. In the relation between the two men and their contact with each other's work it was not only the younger who learned and absorbed from the older; Haydn's art gained something of the greater richness and subtlety of Mozart's. Thus it is that the early symphonies offer an occasional lovely slow movement or charming minuet or finale, but no first movement with the incandescent operation of powers of invention and development that one hears in the final Nos. 92 to 104. It is in Nos. 73 to 81 that one begins to hear the writing of a more accomplished composer and a harmonic daring and rhythmic freedom which he will carry to their greatest heights in the last series. And in the progression of the piano sonatas from early to late—i.e. from before 1776 to the early 1790s—one hears, as in the parallel progression of the symphonies, an unimpressive beginning and an increasingly impressive manipulation of increasingly impressive substance.

Franz Joseph Haydn (1732–1809)

7

Berlioz

By the criteria I applied to Mozart—use of the medium, and what is expressed through this use—Berlioz is another of the greatest musical artists. This estimate is not the generally accepted one you will find in the histories of music and appreciation manuals; it is however what I have discovered to be true from my listening to the music; and I propose to let readers of this book make the same discovery in the same way.

I suggest, then, listening to the song *Au Cimetière* from *Les Nuits d'été*—a setting of this poem by Gautier:

> Connaissez-vous la blanche tombe
> Où flotte avec un son plaintif
>   L'ombre d'un if?
> Sur l'if, une pâle colombe,
> Triste et seule, au soleil couchant
>   Chante son chant;
>
> Un air maladivement tendre,
> A la fois charmant et fatal,
>   Qui vous fait mal,
> Et qu'on voudrait toujours entendre,
> Un air comme en soupire aux cieux
>   L'ange amoureux.
>
> On dirait que l'âme éveillée
> Pleure sous terre à l'unison
>   De la chanson,
> Et du malheur d'être oubliée

Se plaint dans un roucoulement
Bien doucement.

Sur les aîles de la musique
On sent lentement revenir
Un souvenir;
Une ombre de forme angélique
Passe dans un rayon tremblant,
En voile blanc.

Les belles de nuit, demi-closes,
Jettent leur parfum faible et doux
Autour de vous,
Et le fantôme aux molles poses
Murmure en vous tendant les bras:
Tu reviendras?

Oh! jamais plus, près de la tombe,
Je n'irai, quand descend le soir
Au manteau noir,
Ecouter la pâle colombe
Chanter sur la branche de l'if
Son chant plaintif!

Listen to the first three vocal statements to the words

> *Connaissez-vous la blanche tombe*
> *Où flotte avec un son plaintif / L'ombre d'un if?*
> *Sur l'if, une pâle colombe, / Triste et seule, au*
> *soleil couchant / Chante son chant;*

Immediately striking is the exquisiteness of the vocal melody, of the underlying harmony (e.g. the changes beginning at *tombe*), of the instrumental color. And striking too is the freedom with which the melody moves, grows, takes form—freedom in relation to bar-line and meter; freedom in shape and length of phrase; freedom, then, from the conventional and expected regularities and symmetries. Even in the first statement the deployment of the four measures of vocal melody is irregular in relation to the bar-line (at *la*) and asymmetrical to the seven measures of instrumental accompaniment. In the next statement the melody is repeated, but with elaborating changes: not only the change in rhythm and contour (*un son*) and the exquisite change of F sharp to F natural (on the syllable *plain*), but the additional clause (*L'ombre d'un if*) that makes this statement asymmetrical in shape and length to the first. And in the third statement there are not only further elaborating changes in melody and rhythm but an additional clause that makes this statement asymmetrical to the second.

Clearly this is a progression in which nothing has been set down mechanically or perfunctorily; in which everything, on the contrary, exhibits the operation of a mind unceasingly attentive, active, creative—excitingly so in the placing of the occasional plucked bass-notes, which produce an effect out of proportion to their impingement on the senses. And about this there are two things to say. One is that this mind unceasingly active, which makes Berlioz fascinating to listen to, gives us music that can be described by Tovey's statement about Haydn: "Nothing is difficult to follow, but everything is unexpected." At one point after another the music moves in an unexpected direction, continues with something unforeseen, which turns out to be logical and right; and you will discover that Berlioz is in fact one of the great originals in music, whose thought, language and style are like no one else's before or after him. And the other thing to say is that in each decision to change this note in the melody or that chord in the harmony, to extend this note over the bar-line here or place that plucked bass-note there, we hear evidence that this active mind, as it fills in the musical canvas, so to speak, operates with an ear, a taste, a melodic gift, a harmonic sense, a magic with the orchestra—in short with musical powers—of a most unusual and distinguished sort.

We continue to hear the freedom and freshness of invention in the song's further statements. The melody (*Un air maladivement tendre*) repeats a figure of four quarter-notes against the three-quarter time marked excitingly by the plucked bass; then (*A la fois charmant et fatal*) it takes off, expanding freely over the bar-lines to a high point (*fatal*) from which it descends with exquisite inflections (*Qui vous fait mal* and *Et qui voudrait toujours entendre*); then (*Un air comme en soupire aux cieux*) it is quietly sustained as it rises to an exquisite inflection (*soupir aux cieux*) and conclusion (*L'ange amoureux*).

Now a new section begins (*On dirait que l'âme éveillée / Pleure sous terre à l'unison / De la chanson*): over more agitated eighth-notes in the strings the melody's groups of repeated A's are punctuated in exciting fashion by an irregularly placed and intensely poignant two-note chromatic figure of the woodwinds. This continues, with the addition only of an occasional plucked bass-note (*Et du malheur d'être oubliée / Se plaint dans un roucoulement*); but the conclusion (*Bien doucement*) is made suddenly exciting by quick repetition of the woodwind figure over plucked bass-notes. With increased agitation in the strings the melody (*Sur les aîles de la musique / On sent lentement revenir / Un souvenir*) rises with expansive freedom to a high point of intensity at which there are brilliant woodwind flourishes. Then (*Une ombre, une forme angélique / Passe dans un rayon tremblant*) the melody subsides, with the woodwinds continuing their poignant figure, and with the violins adding gleaming harmonics (at *tremblant*) which continue until the pause before the return of the opening section—this time to the words

Les belles de nuit demi-closes
Jettent leur parfum faible et doux / Autour de vous,
Et le fantôme aux molles poses / Murmure en vous tendant les bras:
"Tu reviendras!"
Oh! jamais plus, près de la tombe / Je n'irai, quand descend le soir / Au manteau noir,

It is here, at the beginning of the repetition of the opening statement, that we hear the most extraordinary manifestation of the powers I have mentioned. As the voice, below syncopated woodwind chords, begins its melody, violins and violas add a descending four-note comment, modified at each repetition with overwhelming expressive effect:

etc.

I doubt that anyone has ever produced a greater effect on the mind with so little impingement on the senses.

For the rest the opening statements are repeated with only slight changes until *Oh! jamais plus* etc., when the melody's four-quarter figure is repeated over one of Berlioz's enlivening pizzicato oscillations in the cellos, and an ostinato figure in the basses. And the melody itself changes at *Au manteau noir* for new concluding statements to the words

> *Ecouter la pâle colombe / Chanter sur la pointe de l'if*
> *Son chant plaintif!*

with the orchestra speaking poignantly before *Son chant plaintif,* with it, and after it.

If one were given nothing but this song to judge from one would have to say the man who wrote it was one of the greatest masters. Any of the other songs of *Les Nuits d'eté* would compel the same judgment; but I suggest listening further to *Sur les lagunes*—a setting of this poem by Gautier:

> Ma belle amie est morte:
> Je pleurerai toujours;
> Sous la tombe elle emporte
> Mon âme et mes amours.
> Dans le ciel, sans m'attendre,
> Elle s'en retourna;
> L'ange qui l'emmena
> Ne voulut pas me prendre.
> Que mon sort est amer!
> Ah! sans amour, s'en aller sur la mer!
>
> La blanche créature
> Est couchée au cercueil.
> Comme dans la nature
> Tout me paraît en deuil!
> La colombe oubliée

Pleure et songe à l'absent;
Mon âme pleure et sent
Qu'elle est dépareillée.
Que mon sort est amer!
Ah! sans amour, s'en aller sur la mer!

Sur moi la nuit immense
S'étend comme un linceul;
Je chante ma romance
Que le ciel entend seul.
Ah! comme elle était belle
Et comme je l'aimais!
Je n'aimerai jamais
Une femme autant qu'elle.
Que mon sort est amer!
Ah! sans amour, s'en aller sur la mer!

We shall see later on that one of Berlioz's most remarkable procedures is the repetition at intervals of an unchanged figure or note in the constantly changing context of the developing musical thought; and he does something of the kind in *Sur les lagunes:* the orchestra's powerfully somber three-note figure (in F minor) that establishes the atmosphere of the song in the very first measure recurs at intervals, punctuating the grief-laden vocal statements to the words

Ma belle amie est morte:
Je pleurerai toujours;
Sous la tombe elle emporte/Mon âme et mes amours.
Dans le ciel, sans m'attendre,/Elle s'en retourna;
L'ange qui l'emmena/Ne voulut pas me prendre.

In this opening section we hear again the unceasing creativeness producing the freedom and variety of melodic rhythm, shape and length, the unexpected shifts in direction caused, sometimes, by progressions in the harmony (e.g. before *Sous la tombe*). And the section ends with two statements that will recur as a refrain: the plaintive *Que mon sort est amer!*, followed by the passionate *Ah! sans amour s'en aller sur la mer!*

Now a shift to B flat major brings a momentary brightness in a new section which begins (*La blanche créature*) with tranquilly sustained loveliness, but continues with increasing intensity and poignancy (*Est couchée au cercueil;/Comme dans la nature*) that becomes heavy, dark grief (*Tout me paraît en deuil*). The momentum increases with the orchestra's activity: with the violin arpeggio that introduces *La colombe oubliée*, the two-note woodwind figures and plucked bass-notes that reinforce *Pleure, pleure et songe à l'absent*, in the crescendo of intensity that continues with *Mon âme pleure et sent/Qu'elle est dépareillée*. Suddenly there is a moment's silence; then again the refrain *Que mon sort est amer!/Ah! sans amour s'en aller sur la mer!* And again the somber three-note figure, which leads again to the opening musical statement—this time to the words *Sur moi la nuit immense*. The statement is again punctuated by the three-note figure, which leads now to one of the most wonderful passages in the song. The final C of the figure descends to C flat, which is repeated by the voice in the hushed *S'étend comme un linceul* over harmonic progressions on which it pivots to start the wonderfully beautiful and moving *Je chante ma romance/Que le ciel entend seul*. This leads to the climactic statements of the song:

> *Ah! comme elle était belle/Et comme je l'aimais!*
> *Je n'aimerai jamais/Une femme autant qu'elle.*

Again the three-note figure, which leads to the refrain. And then a last master-stroke: the three-note figure, previously heard only from the orchestra, is heard now from the voice.

After listening to these two songs you are in a position to understand my lack of awe for accepted opinion. For accepted opinion on Berlioz—in the music histories and appreciation manuals—credits him only with a gift for orchestral color and effect, and has it that he used gigantic orchestras to conceal the poverty and banality of his melody and harmony. Writing of "the musicians of the last century, from Berlioz to Strauss," one excessively esteemed historian spoke once of "orchestral scores which when dispossessed of their tremendous orchestral ornaments show an astonishingly meager invention and vague construction." And another wrote that the full orchestra was Berlioz's principal medium because of his preoccupation "with extreme and gigantic aims"; that he used "huge choral masses" for the same reason; that "he forged anew the poetry of *Faust* and *Romeo and Juliet* to his own ends, and monstrous works came forth, half oratorio, half symphony, half lyrical and half dramatic, all blazing with color"; that he similarly used liturgical texts, in the *Requiem* and *Te Deum*, for "a colossal musical exhibition and show of power." The composer of *Au Cimetière* and *Sur les lagunes* and the other songs of *Les Nuits d'été* doesn't seem to me to be preoccupied with extreme and gigantic aims or to be using dazzling orchestral effects to conceal meager invention; but what of the works that do use large orchestral and vocal forces? The answer happens to be given in one of Turner's critical articles that I encountered recently, written after his first hearing of the rarely performed *Requiem*. This is the work that is usually pointed to as the example of Berlioz's use of huge forces for extreme and gigantic aims; and Turner writes: "It is true that his Mass calls for sixteen kettledrums; it is true that he asks for four brass bands to be played north, south, east and west of the general body of chorus and orchestra. All these things in the hands of anyone but Berlioz would have resulted in incredible vulgarity; but Berlioz could not be vulgar." When the brass bands in the *Tuba mirum* "burst out into their antiphonal blazing coruscations," says Turner, "it is as though a thousand rockets had gone up over our heads and were bursting into flames"; but this, he adds, is only their first effect: "we soon discover that these extraordinary exhilarating pyro-technics are charged with meaning, the flames are not mere flames but *expressive, imaginative,* full of poetic significance."*

It is good to have this answer to the idea of large means being connected with extreme and gigantic aims. That idea is true of some artists, but not of all; it is true of some painters, for example, but not of every painter who chooses to apply oil paints to a large canvas rather than a pencil to a small sheet of paper; it is equally not true of every composer who chooses to write for an orchestra rather than a string quartet; and, as Turner testifies, it isn't necessarily true even of a composer who elects to write for an orchestra with sixteen kettledrums and four additional brass bands: when that composer is a Berlioz he uses such large forces with the same precision, and for as legitimate artistic ends, as small ones. The impression of the *Requiem* given by the histories

*W. J. Turner, "A Musical Cataclysm," *Musical Meanderings* (London, 1928).

and music appreciation manuals is of the additional four brass bands blaring away uninterruptedly and blatantly for two hours; whereas actually they are used in only a few sections, and where they do play with full power, as in the *Tuba mirum*, they do not merely blare away but operate with imaginative purpose and effect; in addition to which—and this is something Turner doesn't speak of—they don't always play with full power. Indeed the most impressive evidence of Berlioz's integrity in the matter is the discretion and taste with which he uses them in the *Lacrymosa:*

Introduced and accompanied by an explosively agitated orchestral figuration the tenors begin a beautiful melodic passage in nine-eighth time which moves with Berlioz's characteristic freedom of rhythm, shape and direction; when the sopranos and altos repeat the passage the tenors continue with a counterpoint that is similarly free; and the next repetition by the basses is enriched and given exciting momentum by similar counterpoints of women and tenors, reaching a climax that subsides into a new and quiet section. In this, altos and tenors sing a brief figure that is commented on by the basses—the figure and comment being derived from the opening section. They continue and develop with increasing intensity to a conclusion; then comes a section (*Pie Jesu, Domine, donna eis requiem*) of tranquilly sustained melodic loveliness and exquisite harmonic progressions. From this there is suddenly a return to the explosive orchestral figuration and the tenors' nine-eighth melody of the opening; and it is here that Berlioz begins to use the four additional brass bands: in each nine-eighth measure the third group of three eighths is reinforced by a note or chord from one after another of the four bands—the effect of these cries of the brass being indescribable. And in the repetitions of the melody that effect is heightened: with the repetition by sopranos and altos the brass chords from one after another of the bands are fuller and are intensified by kettledrum-rolls; with the repetition by the basses each reinforcing chord is played by all four bands together with thunderous rolls of kettledrums and bass drums. The momentum and excitement are tremendous; and again the climax subsides into the quiet discussion of figures derived from the opening section, carried on this time in three vocal parts instead of two, hence with greater intricacy of rhythm and texture, and with wonderful comments from the woodwinds. And this time the section ends with a crescendo to a climax in which the additional brass bands join in a tremendous unison proclamation of the nine-eighth melody by chorus and orchestra.

As precisely—and on occasion as exquisitely—wrought are the sections that do not employ the additional brass bands: the radiant *Sanctus;* the *Hostias,* which uses, in addition to strings, only flutes and trombones, but these with astounding originality and impressiveness; the *Quaerens me,* for chorus without any orchestra at all. And of these the most remarkable is the *Offertorium:*

This is one of the great examples—great in scale and effect—of the procedure Berlioz used in *Sur les lagunes:* the repetition at intervals of an unchanged figure or note in the constantly changing context of the developing musical thought. The orchestral part is a fugal development of the long opening statement—a development made increasingly rich and exciting by the constantly fresh and unusual elaborating ideas and figurations that are heard with the successive entries of the statement, but also by the episodes into which the fugal progression digresses: the expansive melody to which the progression rises twice; the poignant quiet melodic passage of the violins that follows this expansive melody the second time, dying out gradually for the next fugal entry; the climax to which this entry rises almost immediately. And throughout all these developments and episodes the chorus repeats at intervals its plaintive

Until the end, when the fugal progression gradually dies out and the orchestra becomes silent, the chorus continues alone with its plaintive figure and also stops, and then something breathtakingly unexpected and beautiful happens: a succession of entries of the chorus's figure, wonderfully changed from minor to major, and accompanied by sustained notes of the winds, create an expanding ethereally radiant texture for the final words; after which the chorus's figure is the *Amen.*

Another remarkable example of the same procedure is the second movement of the symphony *Harold in Italy*—the *March of Pilgrims Singing Their Evening Prayer*. Over a marching bass we hear one of Berlioz's exfoliating melodic progressions with exquisite inflections and unexpected turns that pivot on, and are enriched by, equally unexpected and exquisite moves in the underlying harmony, and are further enriched by the subtly contrived instrumental colors. In this instance the progression is a succession of developing statements, alternately from violins and violas, each taking off from the same beginning but moving unpredictably each time to a different concluding note that is answered by a magical note of the horn with exquisite murmurings of the woodwinds—the magic of the horn note being that it seems to be a different note each time but actually is the same note sounding wonderfully different in the different contexts (something not to be achieved without the powers Berlioz is alleged not to have possessed).

After the fourth such statement the further development of the melodic idea is carried on by cellos, basses and bassoons in alternation with violins and woodwinds, while the solo viola plays the melody it plays in each movement. All this produces a texture with great rhythmic intricacy and increasing intensity, in a crescendo to the point where the opening series of statements begins again, proceeding for a time as before, but then, after the third statement, moving unexpectedly to new conclusions, each punctuated by the magical horn note. Then—over the continuing march of the basses, and with accompanying arpeggios from the solo viola—comes the *canto religioso;* after which the march returns briefly and dies out in the distance.

The other movements are no less remarkable in their different ways. In the third, *Serenade of a Mountaineer of the Abruzzi to His Mistress,* we hear first some preliminary pastoral pipings; then the English horn begins the serenade with two statements of a simple tune that don't prepare us for the sudden succession of ear-ravishing melodic inflections, harmonic progressions and instrumental colorings. And in the finale, *Orgy of Brigands,* we hear an activating play with dynamics, orchestral sonority and rhythmic grouping and accentuation that is like a tossing about of thunderbolts.

Those titles of the movements of *Harold in Italy* make the work a piece of *program music*—which I would define as music whose generalized expressive meaning is linked to specific visual images, ideas or incidents. A march, with a middle section in a style with religious connotations to our ears, is made a *March of Pilgrims Singing Their Evening Prayer;* music with pastoral connotations, and a lilting tune, are made a *Serenade of a Mountaineer of the Abruzzi to His Mistress;* exciting play with dynamics, orchestral sonority and rhythmic grouping and accentuation is made an *Orgy of Brigands.*

As in the case of music with only generalized expressive meaning, the interest of program music is not in the images or ideas or incidents themselves but in their musical embodiment. And not only the interest but the value: Berlioz's *Harold,* his *Symphonie fantastique,* his *Romeo and Juliet*—like Mozart's *Figaro* and Schubert's *Nacht und Träume*—are as good as the music he put into them; and that music, like Mozart's and Schubert's, is not less good for its connection with the literary meanings that stimulated Berlioz's musical imagination and enlarge our musical experience.

The stimulation of Shakespeare's poetry gives us, in Berlioz's *Romeo and Juliet,* a work whose central sections are the supreme, the incandescent achievements of his powers. These sections follow a number of preliminaries: first an instrumental *Introduction,* an Allegro fugato depicting *Strife—Tumult* and breaking off for imposing pronouncements of trombones and bass tuba that constitute the *Intervention of the Prince;* then the *Prologue,* in which a small mixed chorus tells the story that will be told in the later sections of the symphony—of the quarrel between the two families, of the Capulets' ball (the orchestra breaks in with a little of the brilliant ball music that we will hear later), of Romeo in the Capulet garden, Juliet on her balcony, their avowals of their love (the orchestra plays a little of the impassioned music of the *Love Scene* that we will hear later); then *Strophes,* a fervent comment sung by the solo contralto, followed by the chorus's description of the dreamy Romeo being chaffed by his friends, including Mercutio, whose exquisite *Queen Mab* Scherzetto is sung by the solo tenor and chorus (note the characteristic writing for woodwinds);

after which the chorus (to music we will hear later in *Juliet's Funeral Procession*) tells of death and the reconciliation of the two families.

This brings us to the first of the sections of the symphony proper that I spoke of a moment ago. Melancholy statements of the violins represent *Romeo Alone,* and lead to one of the great Berlioz melodies: a poignant two-measure statement by oboe and clarinet that is repeated, each time with changes in harmony, orchestration and texture that increase its intensity, to the point where violins and woodwinds take off on one of those Berlioz progressions in constantly unexpected directions and with heart-piercingly exquisite inflections. The sharp rhythm of the ball music, heard as though from a great distance, breaks in for a moment but dies out for the lovely oboe melody of Romeo's *Melancholy.* Then the sharp rhythm breaks in again in a transition to the rhythmically activated orchestral brilliance of *Concert and Ball—Great Festivity at the Capulets'.*

And now comes one of those supreme, incandescent sections, the *Love Scene,* which Toscanini once characterized as the most beautiful piece of music in the world, for reasons that are evident from the start. Strings *pppp* and flutes *pp* create the enchantment of *Capulet's Garden Still and Deserted,* leading to breathtaking distant notes of a horn *pp* and last exquisite comments by the violins; then we hear the young Capulets, on their way home, singing reminiscences of the ball music over a wonderfully beautiful comment of the strings. Their singing dies out in the distance; and the music concerned with the balcony scene begins: murmurings of muted lower strings over which are heard sighs of the English horn and clarinet, and, later, exclamations of the unmuted violins which increase in intensity, then subside and break off for agitated figures of the strings that introduce the mournfully impassioned melody of the muted cellos (reinforced by a horn):

p canto espress

In this melody one hears, unquestionably, the voice of Romeo; and concerning it there is a comment to make which applies to everything that follows. The expressive content of the section is unmistakable: declarations, avowals, the *premiers transports, premiers aveux, premiers serments* described in the *Prologue;* and these are conveyed in musical terms of the most exquisite delicacy which not only characterize the emotions of the young lovers but reveal the delicacy of feeling of Berlioz himself. One can say of this section what Turner said of the *Requiem*—that it provided an opportunity for vulgarity, but Berlioz could not be vulgar.

The murmurings of muted strings, sighs of English horn and clarinet, exclamations of violins are heard again, and lead to a more intensely impassioned statement of the cellos' melody. This subsides into the woodwinds' agitated

which is interrupted twice by declarations of the cellos:

And these, the second time, lead to another exquisitely inflected and heart-piercing melody:

and to this statement:

which keeps returning after numerous episodes, some impassioned, some quiet and lovely, like

and (much later)

Eventually there is a last impassioned reference to the cello melody; this is followed by an agitated passage that works up to a point of great intensity at which it breaks off abruptly: the enchanted night has reached gray dawn, and the last halting, fragmentary references to [1] and last sighing exclamations with which the piece ends.

The *Love Scene* is followed by the orchestral magic of the *Queen Mab* Scherzo—the magic which at once evokes the world of the subtitle *The Fairy of Dreams* with the play of alternating woodwinds and muted strings leading to a rush of muted violins. The rush subsides; the preliminaries are repeated; and eventually the rush becomes the theme of a continuing section, with woodwinds first contributing mere glints of light and later alternating with the strings in the rush and chatter. This first section ends on a sustained trill of the violins, which continues in the next section as an accompaniment to the melody of flute and English horn—an accompaniment to which are added gleaming violin harmonics and, a few measures later, the exciting darting about of the violas in references to the rushing theme of the first section. That first section returns, but only briefly; then distant horns are heard in a new section, their statements punctuated by comments of strings and woodwinds. There is a hush, in which kettledrum-beats begin a crescendo that leads to a blazing up of the entire orchestra; this breaks off for a tremolo of violas *ff,* which drops to *pp* for evocative chords of muted strings and woodwinds; then another section begins: an ostinato of the clarinet over gleaming notes of the harp, which gradually draws additional instruments into a crescendo to a point of breath-taking orchestral splendor. This breaks off for a brief return to the first section; then, suddenly, there is a slowing down, a dying out of the exciting activity, the beginning of the end of the dream: a passage of wonderfully evocative hushed chords of muted strings, then of strings alternating with woodwinds, then string chords punctuated by silvery notes of antique cymbals, leading to staccatos of woodwinds, of plucked strings, of harps and strings, and a pause on a sustained note of the cellos; and then a last rush that brings the extraordinary piece to an end.

No less extraordinary in its own way is the section that follows, *Juliet's Funeral Procession,* which is another great example of the procedure we observed in the *Offertorium* of the *Requiem,* with the chorus repeating its plaintive *Jetez des fleurs!* on the reiterated note E at intervals during the fugal march and the melodic episode played by the orchestra, and then the violins repeating the plaintive E's at intervals as the fugal passage and melodic episode are sung by the chorus.

Extraordinary too is the next section, *Romeo in the Vault of the Capulets:* the opening Allegro agitato e disperato, the sudden silence and solemn antiphonal chords of brass, woodwinds and strings; then, over lamenting figures of muted violas and cellos punctuated by heavy accents of basses, the grandly sustained melody of Romeo's *Invocation,* dying out for a passage in which tentative phrases of the clarinet, recalling the sighs of the beginning of the *Love Scene,* alternate with increasingly agitated exclamations of the low strings in *Juliet's Awakening,* leading to the orchestral outburst of *Delirious Joy, Despair,* which breaks off for the tearing, shattering details of *Last Agonies and Death of the Two Lovers.*

Astonishing, therefore, after all this creativeness and originality, is the conventional grandiloquence of the finale.

Romeo and Juliet is only the greatest of the works of Berlioz that we owe to the susceptibility of his powers to the stimulation of poetry. At the age of twenty-six he produced *Eight Scenes from Faust*—including the beautiful *Easter Hymn* and *Peasants' Chorus*, the striking *Rat Song* and *Flea Song*, the hauntingly lovely *King of Thule Ballad* and *Romance of Marguerite*. These were retained in *The Damnation of Faust* seventeen years later, with the additional music including things as beautiful and impressive as the opening scene, the choral scene introduced by Mephistopheles's *Voici des fleurs* (note, among other details in the exquisite orchestral writing of the concluding *Dance of the Sylphs*, the activity of the harps), Mephistopheles's *Invocation* and *Serenade*, the *Minuet of the Will-o'-the-Wisps*, the trio.

Still later his love of Virgil resulted in the opera *The Trojans*. Its greatness is different from that of the *Love Scene* of *Romeo and Juliet* and the second and third movements of *Harold in Italy:* of the incandescently beautiful writing that overwhelms one in those early pieces there are only a few major examples in *The Trojans*—the septet in Act 4 *Tout n'est que paix* and duet *Nuit d'ivresse* concerned with the peace and enchantment of the African night, the effect of whose exquisite vocal writing is heightened by such orchestral details as the reiterated C of the flute, the change from this to the alternation of C and D flat, and every now and then the heavy punctuating beat on the bass drum; the wonderful passage with Mercury's repeated *Italie!* that ends the act; and the *Royal Hunt and Storm* that begins it, with its lovely opening section and the marvelously altered repetition of this section at the end. Throughout, in the later three acts concerned with the tragic involvement of Dido and Aeneas, there is the quietly beautiful vocal writing characteristic of Berlioz's later years; but much of the time, even in these acts, as in the earlier two concerned with the fall of Troy, one hears only an accomplished use of the Berlioz idiom in the service of the text. And the greatness one is aware of here is that of the arrestingly individual musical mind operating in, and commanding attention with, the use of the idiom with assured mastery and complete adequacy to the text's every demand.

Berlioz's last opera, *Beatrice and Benedict,* with a libretto adapted from *Much Ado About Nothing*, disappoints the expectations created by its overture; indeed the overture, it turns out, has the music of the outstanding pages—Beatrice's affecting aria *Il me souvient le jour du départ* and the delightful finale—of this late work, whose orchestral writing has some of the earlier fascinating liveliness and brilliance, but whose vocal writing hasn't the heart-piercing loveliness and expressive power of the great melodies of *Romeo and Juliet* and *The Damnation of Faust*.

However an earlier opera—*Benvenuto Cellini*, whose libretto Berlioz fashioned not from poetry this time but from parts of Cellini's *Autobiography*—is from first to last a demonstration of the riveting operation of Berlioz's distinctive mind, as in the incandescent comic trio in the first act, and the orchestral introductions that prepare one's mind for each scene.

Of the orchestral music not discussed so far there is first of all the *Symphonie fantastique*, in which, if you forget the program, with its march to the scaffold and witches' Sabbath, you will hear music that is beautifully imagined and written—e.g. the waltz in the second movement to which Berlioz gives such elegance and distinction. Less familiar is the *Symphonie funèbre et triomphale* for wind band, of which I find the opening *Marche funèbre* more affecting than the *Oraison* and *Apothéose*. Then there are the overtures: the most frequently heard is the brilliant *Roman Carnival*, a concert piece for whose opening section Berlioz salvaged the theme of Cellini's big first act aria after the failure of the opera. Played less often are the brilliant overture to the opera itself and the one for *Beatrice and Benedict;* and only rarely are there performances of the *King Lear* and *Corsair* overtures—whose relation to their titles is obscure and less important than the working of the Berlioz mind that is intensely interesting in both, especially in their opening sections. Of the remaining two—the early *Les Francs-juges* and *Waverly*—much of the former sounds like an exercise in Berliozian orchestral rhetoric without expressive point, while the latter has astonished me with symmetrical melodic banalities which it is hard to believe could have been set down, even in his immaturity, by the composer with the original and unpredictable mind that is heard in the later pieces.

In the same way, it is hard to believe that *Herminie,* the uninteresting cantata that Berlioz, while a student at the Paris Conservatoire, submitted in 1828 in his third unsuccessful attempt to win the *Prix de Rome,* was written by the same man who a year later submitted in his next unsuccessful attempt the astounding *La Mort de Cléopâtre,* whose very first impassioned orchestral measures proclaim what is evident throughout, though most impressively in Cleopatra's invocation *Grands Pharaons* over the orchestra's powerful bass ostinato—that this is not a fumbling of unmatured gifts but an operation with absolute assurance in a style completely individual and completely formed.

Of the remaining vocal and choral music there is first the *Te Deum.* Listening to it after the *Requiem* one is aware that it doesn't rise to the heights of the *Requiem's Lacrymosa* and *Offertorium* but offers an operation of the Berlioz mind similar to what one hears in the *Requiem's* earlier sections—that is to say, this is one of the works in which Berlioz employs large forces with unfailing discretion and taste, whether in the quiet writing filled with characteristic subtle marvels, or in the brilliantly and grandly sonorous passages which culminate in the final *Judex crederis* with its extraordinary ostinato phrase that is built up to a great climax.

The oratorio *L'Enfance du Christ,* written in the same period as *The Trojans,* has suitably quiet writing for a small orchestra, chorus and vocal soloists; much of Part 1 is in a mellifluous nineteenth-century oratorio style; but we begin to hear the Berlioz mind in fascinating operation in the Overture of Part 2, and in the music it introduces: the lovely *Shepherds' Farewell to the Holy Family* and the wonderfully beautiful *Repose of the Holy Family.* And there are moving and beautiful passages in Part 3: the Narrator's description of the journey to Saïs, Joseph's appeals for refuge, the trio for flutes and harp, the concluding vocal passage.

And, finally, there are the three lovely pieces Berlioz wrote at different times for chorus and orchestra—*Sara la baigneuse, Méditation religieuse* and *La Mort d'Ophélie;* and three superb independent solo songs—*La Captive, Le Jeune pâtre Breton* and *Zaïde.*

Certainly, in Berlioz's case as in every other composer's, it is possible for someone to know and understand the music and decide that one doesn't care for it. But the actual situation is that many have listened to the music in the expectation of hearing the poverty of invention they have read about, and as a result have heard only what they expected to hear; and that others have listened without such preconceptions, but with habit, and have found it difficult to gear their minds to music so different in every way from the music they were accustomed to. That situation calls for additional listening with ears and mind open to the particular distinctive and unusual things Berlioz has to say. And such listening will, I think, lead most people to the conclusion that his music is some of the most beautiful and moving that has come down to us.

Hector Berlioz (1803–1869)

8

Bach

At this point I would like to turn back to Bach. I present one of his best works—the organ *Passacaglia* in C minor—in detail in Chapter 24. But before I speak of other great works of his, I will make a general observation about his entire output. Or rather—having recently found my point formulated very effectively in one of W. J. Turner's articles—I will let him make it for me.

Quoting C. Sanford Terry's description of the fifty-three cantatas Bach composed between 1736 and 1744 as an "unflagging cataract of inspiration in which masterpiece followed masterpiece with the monotonous periodicity of a Sunday sermon," Turner calls it nonsense and contends that "this 'monotonous periodicity' was exactly what was wrong with a great deal of Bach's music." Bach, he says, "had arrived at the point of being able to sit down at any minute of any day and compose what had all the superficial appearance of being a masterpiece. It is possible that even Bach himself did not know which was a masterpiece and which was not, and it is abundantly clear to me that in all his large-sized works there are huge chunks of stuff to which inspiration is the last word that one could apply." What makes it difficult to evaluate the music correctly, says Turner, is Bach's virtuosity; but while the prodigious technical skill may interest and amaze the academic musician "with the score in his hands and his soul long defunct," for Turner it is valueless "unless . . . it is as expressive as it is accomplished."*

*W. J. Turner, "A Note on the B Minor Mass," *Music and Life* (London, 1921).

This seems to me an excellent description of the essential fact about Bach—that one hears always the operation of prodigious powers of invention and construction, but frequently an operation that is not as expressive as it is accomplished.

The occasion for Turner's remarks was a performance of the *B-Minor Mass*, which is generally regarded as a towering masterpiece from first note to last, but in which I have, like Turner, come to hear only in certain portions what he describes as "those really creative moments which are popularly called inspired." For me they are the second *Kyrie*, the *Gratias agimus*, *Qui tollis* and *Cum sancto spiritu* of the *Gloria*, the *Et incarnatus est* and *Crucifixus est* of the *Credo*, the *Sanctus*, and the *Dona nobis pacem*, all for chorus; and only one aria, the *Et in spiritum sanctum* for bass. But you may find other portions genuinely expressive and moving that Turner and I do not.

Similarly you may be moved by more than what I find moving in the *St. Matthew Passion:* chiefly the chorales, the big opening and closing choruses, the great chorale-fantasia *O Mensch, bewein' dein' Sünde gross* that ends Part 1; also some of the accompanied recitatives of the soloists, but only very few of their arias—the tenor's *Ich will bei meinem Jesu wachen*, the soprano's *Aus Liebe will mein Heiland sterben*, and the alto's great *Erbarme dich*, one of Bach's most inspired moments. Or the *St. John Passion:* again the chorales, the magnificent opening chorus, some of the recitatives and ariosos, and the alto's aria *Es ist vollbracht*.

So with the smaller choral works. The Cantata No. 4, *Christ lag in Todesbanden*, is for me one of Bach's great utterances; but in some of the other cantatas, the *Magnificat*, the *Christmas Oratorio*, the *Easter Oratorio*, it is almost entirely the choral portions, and particularly the chorales, that I find beautiful and moving, rarely one of the arias; and most of these smaller works that I have heard I have, like Turner, found to be mechanical exercises of Bach's technical skill. But here again you may discover more than Turner and I.

Begin, then, with Cantata No. 4 *Christ lag in Todesbanden*, Cantata No. 140 *Wachet auf, ruft uns die Stimme*, which has superb choral passages but less interesting writing for the soloists, Cantata No. 1 *Wie schön leuchtet der Morgenstern*, which has beautiful choral writing and moderately engaging arias, Cantata No. 56 *Ich will den Kreuzstab gerne tragen,* which has interesting writing for both the chorus and the single soloist, Cantata No. 147 *Herz und Mund und Tat und Leben,* which has the well-known chorale *Jesu, Joy of Man's Desiring (Jesus bleibet meine Freude),* and Cantata No. 68 *Also hat Gott die Welt geliebt,* which has the aria *Mein gläubiges Herze.* To these add the motet *Jesu, meine Freude,* one of Bach's greatest works, the beautiful sacred songs *Bist du bei mir** and *Warum betrübst du dich?* (from the *Anna Magdalena Bach Book*) and *Komm, süsser Tod* (No. 42 in the *Schemelli* collection), and the chorale *Vater unser in Himmelreich* (from the collection of chorale settings for Bach's son Carl Philipp Emanuel). Then go on if you wish to the other choral works: the oratorios, the *Magnificat,* the Passions, the Mass in B Minor, some of the other cantatas. (The often-performed secular *Coffee Cantata* and *Peasant Cantata* I advise against; they are not without moments of humor, but on the whole are quite dull.)

And so with the instrumental works—in particular the ones that result from Bach's setting himself gigantic tasks and problems on which to exercise his skill. One of these is the *Clavierübung* (perhaps best translated as "Keyboard-Study"—*study* being used in the same sense as when a finished painting is titled a "study," and not in the sense of *études* or exercises). This is a collection of keyboard music comprising the six partitas, *French Overture, Italian Concerto* and *Goldberg Variations* for harpsichord or clavichord, and the Prelude in E flat, a number of chorale-preludes, the Fugue in E flat and four duets for organ. In his notes for a recording of the entire collection the harpsichordist and scholar Ralph Kirkpatrick once contended that what he translated as the "keyboard practice" of the title is to be taken "in the sense of an exercise, an activity of the spirit," and cited Bach's own statement that the various pieces had been composed "to delight the spirit of music-lovers." But Bach's way of exercising the spirit was to exercise his craftsmanship; and some of the results offer more to delight an interest in the skillful use of technique than to delight the spirit.

All six partitas are no doubt fascinating to anyone interested in their "astonishing assimilation of French, Italian and German

---

* Scholarly opinion today is that *Bist du bei mir* was only copied out by Bach, not composed by him. —*Ed.*

keyboard styles"; but as a mere music-lover I find only No. 1 in B flat, and to a lesser degree No. 3 in A minor, interesting to listen to simply as music. Similarly, the *Italian Concerto* and *French Overture* may excite some listeners with Bach's "[appropriation] to the harpsichord [of] prevailing French and Italian orchestral styles of the preceding fifty years"; but listening to the music I am excited only by the slow movement of the concerto. Again, the organ pieces may interest some people with the elaborately organized "mathematical and symbolic structure" that Bach erects out of the chorales to illustrate the basic tenets of Lutheran doctrine; but what interests me as music is the magnificent opening prelude and only a few of the chorale-preludes—the closing fugue being impressive as a piece of fugal construction. The four duets may be "the most highly concentrated two-voice music that Bach ever wrote"; but I find them dull. And while everything in the *Goldberg Variations* may sound like "unsurpassable invention" to some ears, I hear examples of mechanical use of the variation procedure as well as things as wonderful as the three slow variations in minor mode.

Similarly, the *Well-Tempered Clavier*, with its forty-eight preludes and fugues in the twenty-four major and minor keys, includes pieces as charming as the Prelude No. 3 of Book 1, the Prelude No. 12 and Prelude and Fugue No. 15 of Book 2; as quietly poignant as the Preludes Nos. 12, 16 and 23 of Book 1 and No. 14 of Book 2; as impressive and affecting as the Prelude No. 8, Fugue No. 12 and Preludes and Fugues Nos. 4 and 22 of Book 1, the Fugue No. 9 of Book 2. But it also includes many examples of competent construction that are, for me, not interesting pieces of music.

Again, *The Art of Fugue*—Bach's last work, which he left uncompleted—contains some of his most magnificent music (which I suggest your hearing a fugue or two at a time). But of the collection of contrapuntal exercises on a theme of Frederick the Great entitled *The Musical Offering* I find only a few of the canons and the concluding six-voiced ricercare similarly impressive.

Listening to the three sonatas and three partitas for unaccompanied violin, the six suites for unaccompanied cello, one is aware of Bach's success with the difficult problem he set himself, of contriving for the instrument a melody that would imply its underlying harmonic progressions between the occasional chords. But one is aware also that solving this problem was not equivalent to writing great or even enjoyable music. Or at any rate it is what I am aware of: I hear an operation that is genuinely creative and expressive only in the great *Chaconne* of the Violin Partita No. 2 in D minor and the superb Prelude of the Violin Partita No. 3 in E; elsewhere I hear only Bach's craftsmanship going through the motions of creation and producing the external appearances of expressiveness. And I suspect that it is the name of Bach that awes listeners into accepting the appearance as reality, into hearing an expressive content which isn't there, and into believing that if the content is difficult to hear, this is only because it is especially profound—because it is (so one note-writer would have had us believe) "the passionate, yet untroubled meditation of a great mind" that lies beyond "the composition's formidable technical frontiers."

I might add that the formidable technical frontiers this writer referred to are the difficulties for the present-day violinist or cellist caused by the fact that the pieces were written for performance on an instrument with a flat bridge and finger-board on which the notes of a chord could be produced on the several strings simultaneously, as they cannot be on the present-day instrument with curved bridge and finger-board. Violinists or cellists who play on modern instruments have to break or arpeggiate the chord, and to distend the melodic phrase to fit the arpeggiated chord in; and the sonatas are among the accepted test-pieces with which they demonstrate their technical and musical powers to the public—the powers that in this case enable them to create continuity in the distended phrases, to do this with an appearance of ease, and—if they are great musicians—with eloquence in the playing. But whether the works are performed on present-day instruments or on the ones Bach wrote for, I suspect that it is the eloquence in the playing that listeners mistake for eloquence in the music.

Among the six sonatas for violin and clavier No. 3 in E major is, for me, one of Bach's finest instrumental works; and there are interesting movements in No. 1 in B minor, No. 2 in A major, and No. 5 in F minor. But the sonatas for flute and clavier and sonatas for gamba and clavier I find uninteresting.

An outstanding work for solo clavier is the Toccata in C minor; another is the Capriccio *On the Departure of His Most Beloved Brother,* the various movements of which astonish one with what they manage to achieve in form and expression operating on so small a scale—e.g. the poignancy of the little passacaglia, the high spirits and humor of the little fugue. Other good ones are the Toccatas in D major and E minor, the Fantasy of the *Chromatic Fantasy and Fugue.* The French Suite No. 5 in G major and English Suite No. 3 in G minor have several moderately enjoyable movements; the others I find uninteresting.

Of the *Brandenburg* Concertos No. 3 in G major is for me the most impressive; Nos. 2 in F and 4 in G are also enjoyable; No. 1 in F has an impressive slow movement; No. 5 in D is only moderately interesting; No. 6 in B flat is completely boring. (The *Brandenburg* Concertos exist in two forms—as Bach composed them originally in Weimar and Cöthen, and in the more familiar versions with the changes he made when he copied them a few years later for the Margrave of Brandenburg. One basic difference between the two is that, except for No. 1, they were written originally not as orchestral works but as chamber music for single players; and in addition there were differences in instruments. In the original version of No. 2 a treble recorder was used in place of the flute, and a horn (Bach specifies *"tromba o vero corno di caccia"*) in place of the trumpet; in No. 4 two *"flauti d'echo"* (which today may be approximated by high-ranging sopranino recorders) in place of flutes or lower-ranging recorders. And in the first movement of No. 5 there is a harpsichord cadenza of 19 bars in place of the elaborate one of 65 bars that Bach substituted in the Brandenburg version. The horn in No. 2 works well; the sopranino recorders in No. 4 do not, for my ears; and overall I prefer the Brandenburg versions.)

Of the four suites for orchestra the best-known No. 2 in B minor has charming dance movements; No. 3 in D major has some others, and in addition the famous melody known as *Air for G String;* No. 4 in D has a fugal section in the opening movement and a Bourrée that are fine; No. 1 in C is for me another boring piece.

Of the concertos for one or more solo instruments the D minor for clavier (or violin) is one of Bach's greatest instrumental works.

In the two fast movements the seemingly inexhaustible flow of inspired invention becomes breathtaking; and in the wonderful slow movement a grave opening statement by the orchestra is repeated in different keys as a sort of ground-bass that provides structural coherence for the ornate and wide-ranging melody of the solo instrument.

Another great work is the Concerto in D minor for two violins, with an endless progression of melody in the slow movement that makes it possibly the loveliest piece of music Bach wrote. And the Concerto in A minor and the slow movement of the Concerto in E for violin are also fine.

The other concertos, to my ears, are uninteresting.

That leaves the important category of works for organ— important because the organ was Bach's most immediately personal medium, through which he expressed what was strongest in him: his religious feeling and his feeling for musical architectonics. These give us the great *Passacaglia* in C minor (582) that I present in detail in Chapter 24; they give us also the great preludes and toccatas with fugues—the Toccata, Adagio and Fugue in C (564), the Toccata and Fugue in D minor (565), the Fantasia and Fugue in G minor (542), the Preludes and Fugues in A minor (543), B minor (544), C minor (546), the Prelude (with a fugue that is impressive as construction) in E minor (548) and the magnificent opening Prelude in E flat (552 No. 1) of Book III of the *Clavierübung* (part of what used to be called *The German Organ Mass*).

They give us other fine works like the impressive Allabreve in D (589), the Fantasia in C minor (562), the Prelude and Fugue in F minor (534), the fine Prelude (with a less interesting fugue) in C (545), and the fine *Dorian* Toccata (with an impressively constructed fugue) in D minor (538); and enjoyable works like the Preludes and Fugues in D (532), C minor (537) and G minor (535), the engaging (but repetitious) Toccata (with an uninteresting Fugue) in F (540), the independent Fugue in G minor (578— called the *Little G minor*), the pleasant Pastorale in F (590), the Trio Sonatas Nos. 5 in C major, which has a fine opening movement but uninteresting subsequent movements, and 6 in G major, which has only a fairly good opening movement. And inevitably they give us accomplished pieces of construction that are impressive as tonal engineering but not as expressive communication—examples being the fugue of the *Dorian* Toccata and Fugue in D minor (538), the Prelude and Fugue in C (547), the fugue (*Wedge*) of the Prelude and Fugue in E minor (548), and the concluding *St. Anne* Fugue in E flat (552 No. 2) of Book III of the *Clavierübung*.

So with the chorale-preludes—the meditations on the texts and melodies of the Lutheran chorales. They include such fine and moving examples as *Ich ruf' zu dir, Herr Jesu Christ* (639) and *Wenn wir in höchsten Nöten sein* (641) of the *Orgelbüchlein* (Little Organ Book); *Herzlich tut mich verlangen* (727), *Vater unser im Himmelreich* (737) and the brief *Liebster Jesu, wir sind hier* (731) of the *Miscellaneous Chorale-Preludes; Komm' Gott Schöpfer, heiliger Geist* (667), *An Wasserflüssen Babylon* (in three versions, of which the best-known are 653b in five parts and the last one, 653, in four parts) and *Jesus Christus, unser Heiland* (665) of the *"Great Seventeen"* chorale-preludes (a collection formerly referred to inexactly as the last *Eighteen*); three of the longer and more elaborate of the chorale-preludes in Book III of the *Clavierübung: Kyrie, Gott Vater in Ewigkeit* (669), *Wir glauben all' an einen Gott* (680) and *Aus tiefer Not schrei ich zu dir* (686); four of the short pieces (for manuals without pedal) from that collection: *Kyrie, Gott Vater in Ewigkeit* (672), *Christe, aller Welt Trost* (673), *Kyrie, Gott heiliger Geist* (674) and *Vater unser im Himmelreich* (683). And such supreme utterances as *O Mensch, bewein' dein' Sünde gross* (622) of the *Orgelbüchlein* and *Nun komm' der Heiden Heiland* (659) and *Schmücke dich, o liebe Seele* (654) of the *"Great Seventeen."**

*Others I like are:
Of the *"Great Seventeen"*—*Herr Jesu Christ, dich zu uns wend'* (655), *O Lamm Gottes unschuldig* (656), *Nun danket alle Gott* (657), second versions of *Jesus Christus Unser Heiland* (666) and *Nun komm' der Heiden Heiland* (660), two versions of *Allein Gott in der Höh' sei Ehr* (662 and 664), and the merely engaging *Von Gott will ich nicht lassen* (658); the independent chorale-prelude *Vor deinen Thron tret' ich* (668—revised later with little change as *Wenn wir in höchsten Nöten sein*, 668a); of the *Orgelbüchlein*—*In dich hab' ich gehoffet, Herr* (640), *Wer nur den lieben Gott lässt walten* (642), *Gelobet seist du, Jesus Christ* (604), an earlier version of *Vater unser im Himmelreich* (636), *Christum wir sollen loben schon* (611), *Mit Fried' und Freud' ich fahr' dahin* (616), *Christus, der uns selig macht* (620), *Da Jesu, an dem Kreuze stund'* (621), *Christ lag in Todesbanden* (625), *Erschienen ist der herrliche Tag* (629), and the strange and moving *Das alte Jahr vergangen ist* (614); and the merely engaging

It remains to say something about the practice of transcribing Bach's organ music for other instruments, although that practice is less common now than formerly. Since Bach himself made some of his clavier concertos into violin concertos, or a concerto movement into a choral movement of a cantata, there would seem to be no reason against merely orchestrating one of his organ works. And good reasons can be offered for it: the desirability of making the work known to many people who would not hear it played on the organ; the advantage of having the strands of the contrapuntal texture stand out more clearly by means of different orchestral colors than they can be made to do by organ registration. But those good reasons don't include a reason that has been offered in the past: the orchestral transcription isn't needed to fulfill completely a conception only partly fulfilled in the original organ version. The notion that the composer of two hundred years ago—or even three or four hundred—who didn't have the Philadelphia Orchestra to write for worked in an agony of frustration is as incorrect as the analogous notion would be about the painter of that period: the composer's mind operated in the terms of the musical instruments, language, style and forms available to him, and fulfilled its conceptions completely in those terms. That certainly was true of Bach writing for the organ; it was no less true of Bach writing for the unaccompanied violin. He could have written the *Chaconne* for an orchestra; he could have rewritten it for orchestra after writing it for unaccompanied violin (as in fact he made the Prelude of the Sonata No. 6 into a piece for organ and orchestra, the Prelude to the Cantata No. 29); but since he did neither it is clear that he conceived of the piece entirely in the terms provided by the unaccompanied violin and was entirely satisfied with the fulfillment of his conception in those terms.

This is not to say that the works must never be translated into the terms of another medium. Bach did an enormous amount of

---

Valet will ich dir geben (735) and *Ein' feste Burg ist unser Gott* (720) of the Miscellaneous, and *Wachet auf, ruft uns die Stimme* (645), the best of the Schübler chorale-preludes.

But these among a large number of pieces which sound like routine products of the accomplished and busy craftsman. —*B.H.H.*

such transcription himself. But when Bach himself makes a violin concerto out of his clavier concerto, a cantata prelude out of a sonata movement for unaccompanied violin, we hear the same mind, personality and feeling operating in the new work as in the old; and this undoubtedly would be so if he were himself to transcribe one of his organ works for the orchestra of today. What his own orchestral transcription of the work would demonstrate is that a composer's instrumentation is no less an integral part of his art than is a painter's color, his way of scoring no less an expression of his feeling than is his way of writing melody and harmony. This means that even a Schönberg, applying orchestral color to the lines of Bach's texture with precision and subtlety that express his fastidiousness and taste, gives the music the impress of his own mind and feeling. The others—Stokowski, Ormandy, Elgar, Respighi—call to mind a remark of Ernest Bloch about Richard Strauss: "Debussy is like a painter who looks at his canvas to see what more he can take out; Strauss is like a painter who has covered every inch and then takes the paint he has left and throws it at the canvas"; and such transcribers give us Bach with the impress of their own vulgarity. Stokowski's orchestrations and performances, in particular—with their lurid phrasing, their tonal heaving and billowing—give us not the religious feeling and structural power that are Bach's, but the feverish, orgiastic excitement that was Stokowski's.

As for piano transcriptions, polyphony employing the two keyboards and pedals and the varied registration of the organ is not easily or always adequately transferred to the single keyboard and single tone-color of the piano. The need for reconstruction has sometimes provided an excuse for making a work a piece for the display of pianistic virtuosity; it led Busoni to think the work out anew in pianistic terms, and in some instances not only to expand the original textures into imposing piano sonorities but even to add measures here and there which completed the thought in his own mind. There is on the one hand, then, Busoni's thunderous harmonization of Bach's *Chaconne* for unaccompanied violin, and on the other his simple, and for me acceptable, transcriptions of the Toccata, Adagio and Fugue in C major (564), the Preludes and Fugues in E flat (552) and D major (532) and the chorale-preludes *Ich ruf' zu dir, Herr Jesu Christ* and

Nun komm' der Heiden Heiland; and an additional reason for accepting them besides their simplicity is that the contrapuntal textures, which often are unclear when the works are played on the organ, are clear when they are played on the piano. Acceptable also is Dame Myra Hess's effective piano arrangement of *Jesu, Joy of Man's Desiring.*

Johann Sebastian Bach (1685–1750)

9

Other Music of the Eighteenth Century

We have been concerned thus far with the work of a few major figures among the composers of the music that falls within the normal range of our interest—European music of the past three or four centuries. There remains for us to explore the large amount of great or moving or enjoyable music produced by their contemporaries, their predecessors, their successors.

Thus, in the early part of the eighteenth century there is the music of Bach's contemporaries—Handel, Vivaldi, Domenico Scarlatti, Couperin, Rameau; and later in the century the music of the contemporaries of Haydn and Mozart—Gluck, Bach's son Carl Philipp Emanuel, Boccherini. The music historians would insist that these are not the only eighteenth-century composers worth your attention: they object to the practice, in the concert hall and the appreciation course, of having a period represented by a few outstanding figures and neglecting the other composers who they insist produced equally good music; and they contend that this has resulted in our knowing only a small part of the masterworks of the past.

Well, since the 1950s recordings have provided the opportunities to hear a great amount of music that previously wasn't performed or recorded; and some of it has indeed proved to be music we had been the poorer for not knowing. But most of the newly revealed masterworks have been products of the well-known outstanding figures rather than of their obscure contemporaries: in eighteenth-century music I can recall a couple of charming quartets by Stamitz and Richter, a couple of arresting symphonies by Brunetti; but the works of major stature that come to mind are Couperin's *First Tenebrae Service,* a couple of Carl Philipp Emanuel Bach's symphonies and a few of his sacred songs, Haydn's masses and some of his unfamiliar quartets. It is true, as the historians contend, that many others besides Haydn used the musical language and style of his time; it is not true that these others produced with them music as good as his: the historians' difficulty is their inability to tell when a language and style are being used in a work of great art, and when they are merely being used, period.

As a matter of fact there are works in which even the great masters use the language and style of their time uninterestingly. They are among the things on records that could have been left unrecorded. And we can leave them unheard.

But we do want to hear the magnificent and joyous choruses and beautiful solos of Handel's *Messiah;* the dramatic and imaginative writing, mostly for chorus, of his *Israel in Egypt;* his *Samson* (one of his finest works); the ear-ravishing lyricism of his *Acis and Galatea;* the similar writing in *Alcina, Tamerlano* and *Ariodante* (which have fine arias and duets in a context of a great amount of recitative that gets to be tedious), in *Semele* (which includes much that is attractive in addition to the well-known *Oh sleep, why dost thou leave me?* and *Where'er you walk*), and in *Julius Caesar, Solomon, Theodora* and *Atalanta* (the last of which includes one of the loveliest of his arias, *Care selve*). We want to hear parts of *Xerxes* (the familiar *Ombra mai fù* with which it begins), *Joshua, Saul,* and *Belshazzar* (in which the writing that is expressively adequate in the first act comes to exciting life in the second). But *Jephtha,* Handel's last oratorio, is not the crowning achievement of matured powers that one expects; rather it is a mere going through the motions of his style that comes to life only in Jephtha's anguished second-act aria, *Open thy marble jaws*—with its clipped phrases and powerful harmonic progressions—and in a few of the later recitatives and arias.

We want to hear as well Handel's *Dettingen Te Deum,* the *Ode for St. Cecilia's Day, L'Allegro ed il Penseroso,* the *Chandos Anthems,* and two superb early works—the *Roman Vespers* and *Dixit Dom-*

inus. The fine instrumental writing of the *Water Music* and *Royal Fireworks Music* (the latter in the version with the strings Handel added for concert performance), the unfamiliar and outstanding Hornpipe in D and Overtures in D and B flat, the Concerto for Orchestra called *Alexander's Feast,* the Concerti Grossi of Op. 6 (which are more impressive than those of Op. 3), the Concerto No. 3 for oboe, the Concertos for strings and winds (which are largely instrumental reworkings of popular sections of Handel's oratorios), the Sonatas for solo instrument and figured bass Op. 1 (of which the best-known of the six intended specifically for violin—Nos. 13 and 14—are outstanding). And we want to hear some of Handel's harpsichord suites—in particular the outstanding No. 8 in F minor of Book One.

We want to hear the poignantly lovely writing of Vivaldi's *L'Estro armonico* and *Il Cimento dell' armonia e dell' invenzione* (of which Nos. 1 to 4 are the well-known *The Four Seasons*), some of his miscellaneous concertos, the sonatas for solo instruments (of which No. 5 of those for cello and figured bass is outstandingly beautiful), and some of his church music. We want to hear some of the engagingly melodious works of Corelli, Bonporti, Leclair, Galuppi, Nardini, Benedetto Marcello, Pergolesi, Tartini and Veracini, as well.

We want to hear Alessandro Scarlatti's charming madrigals, songs and instrumental music; and Domenico Scarlatti's harpsichord sonatas—fascinating and exciting in their endless invention, their harmonic daring, their increasing complexity and subtlety of texture, rhythm and harmony as the series progresses, the power of some of the ones in slow tempo, the verve and brilliance of some of the ones in fast tempo, which utilize the sharp, biting, flashing sounds of the instrument for their effect. We want to hear not only the charming harpsichord pieces of Couperin (Louis as well as François) but François Couperin's *Pièces en concert* for viola da gamba and figured bass, his impressive motet *Audite Omnes,* his secular songs, and his *Three Tenebrae Services*—extended vocal declamations which are made remarkable by their unique style and expressive force. We want not only Rameau's harpsichord pieces, but his *Concerts en sextuor*—arrangements for strings of the *Pièces de clavecin en concert* for harpsichord—which have some of this composer's loveliest music; also his ballet music *Les Indes galantes*, and parts of some of his operas.

We want to hear not just Orfeo's familiar aria *Che farò senza Euridice*, but the other beautiful and affecting music of Gluck's *Orfeo ed Euridice*—notably Euridice's exquisite *E quest' asilo* and the wonderful sustained melody of Orfeo's *Che puro ciel;* also the operas *Iphigénie en Aulide* and *Iphigénie en Tauride*—of which the latter has the loveliness and nobility of the more familiar works, but also occasional harmonic progressions and uses of wind-instrument color that are strikingly unusual and dramatic. And we want to hear the charming music for the ballet *Don Juan.* (Much of Gluck's opera *Alceste*, however, is less impressive than its best-known aria, *Divinités du Styx.*)

We want to hear the beautiful organ music of Walther. The few engaging instrumental pieces from the enormous output of Telemann. And the works of Carl Philipp Emanuel Bach that exhibit the operation of a mind excitingly individual, daring and dynamic—the symphonies, sacred songs, some of the solo keyboard music, and a *Magnificat* with a number of impressive fast movements (the opening *Magnificat anima*, the *Deposuit potentes*) and beautiful and touching slow movements (the *Quia respexit*, the *Et misericordia ejus*, the *Suscepit Israel*).

Of Boccherini we want to hear not the Cello Concerto in B flat "edited" in the nineteenth century by Grützmacher (actually a work by Grützmacher himself, made out of thematic materials from five genuine Boccherini concertos which he freely altered and provided with accompaniments, tuttis, harmonization and orchestration of his own) that cellists continued to play even after Boccherini's own B-flat Concerto was discovered and published—but the Cello Concerto in D, which turns out to be a better example of the individual operation of the Boccherini mind than even the genuine Concerto in B flat; also the quartets (especially Op. 6 No. 1, which has perhaps the most extraordinarily lovely and affecting of his slow movements), and the quintets, trios, and symphonies—all of which are engagingly and at times excitingly individual in invention and procedures.

And from the end of this period we want to hear the astonishing vocal and orchestral writing in Cherubini's opera *Medea*, the lovely choral writing in his C minor and D minor *Requiem*s, and the writing for stringed instruments in the six quartets—the latter being works which leave one amazed by the endlessly varied invention of a mind as lively as Haydn's in an idiom entirely his own.

Carl Philipp Emanuel Bach (1714–1788)
Luigi Boccherini (1743–1805)
Francesco Bonporti (1672–1749)
Gaetano (Caetano) Brunetti (1744–1798)
Luigi Cherubini (1760–1842)
Arcangelo Corelli (1653–1713)
François Couperin ("Le Grand") (1668–1733)
Louis Couperin (1626–1661)
Baldassare Galuppi (1706–1785)
Christoph Willibald von Gluck (1714–1787)
George Frideric (Georg Friederich) Handel (1685–1759)
Jean-Marie Leclair (1697–1764)
Benedetto Marcello (1686–1739)
Pietro Nardini (1722–1793)
Giovanni Battista Pergolesi (1710–1736)
Jean-Philippe Rameau (1683–1764)
Franz Xaver Richter (1709–1789)
(Pietro) Alessandro Scarlatti (1660–1725)
Domenico Scarlatti (1685–1757)
Carl Stamitz (1745–1801)
Giuseppe Tartini (1692–1770)
Georg Philipp Telemann (1681–1767)
Francesco Maria Veracini (1690–1768)
Antonio Vivaldi (1678–1741)
Johann Gottfried Walther (1684–1748)

10

Music of Earlier Centuries

It isn't very many years since music, in the concert hall and the appreciation course, began with Bach and Handel, and everything before them was dark and unknown except for the distant gleams of Palestrina and—a few centuries beyond—Gregorian chant. Gradually this situation changed—as small record companies, with the encouragement of music historians (musicologists, as these scholars are called) sought out repertoire not recorded by the large companies—and the public learned there was a great deal more in those early centuries, though again not as much as the musicologists claimed.

The musicologists, intent on establishing the value of their explorations and excavations, but reasoning in a world of concept thousands of miles from the facts they are digging away in, have produced one of their pat schematizations: not only, they say, has each period had *its* music, produced by *its* creative energies, and satisfying *its* esthetic needs, but since human creative energies must be presumed to have been equal in all periods, it follows that the music of the tenth or eleventh or twelfth century was the equal of the painting and architecture, and the equal also of the music of the eighteenth or nineteenth century. And so we have had one of these men introducing some recordings of keyboard pieces from 1350 to 1700—most of them insignificant in ideas, structure, and even mere size—with the pronouncement that "the music in this album is not 'ancient music,' stale, dusty, and at best a curio for historically minded snobs. It is no more 'ancient' than Rembrandt's painting or Gothic cathedrals."

Actually, human creative energies have not been equal in all periods, or in all the arts of any one period. We find no important or even interesting poetry in England from the death of Chaucer in 1400 to the publication of Wyatt's poems in 1557; we find only minor poets between Pope and Blake; we find no painting of any consequence in the eighteenth- and nineteenth-century Germany that produced the music of Bach, Haydn, Mozart, Beethoven, Schubert, and other great composers whom we have still to investigate.

Moreover, the music of an early period that satisfied *its* esthetic needs will not always satisfy ours today—or those of every listener of today. You may, then, not be moved by the meaning of the single, subtly inflected melodic line of Gregorian chant (plainsong). But you might want to know what it sounds like; and repeated hearings may cause the subtle inflections to mean more than they do at first (myself, I have found the antiphonal Ambrosian chant, with its greater intensity embodied in its more florid style, more significant and exciting). And so with the other music presented in this chapter: some of it may require repeated hearings; and even then you may conclude that not all of it is for you.

While many of the examples of the first types of polyphonic music do no more than satisfy our interest in how the music of the ninth, tenth or eleventh century sounded, there are, as early as the twelfth and thirteenth centuries, pieces which the ear of today finds esthetically effective. And there is no question about the effectiveness for our ears of some of the more developed polyphony of the fourteenth and fifteenth centuries—of Dufay, Dunstable, Machaut, Isaac, Ockeghem, Obrecht, de La Rue, and Josquin des Prés.

Nor is there any such question, in the first part of the sixteenth century, about the effectiveness of the magnificent motet *O crux splendor* of Willaert. Or later in the same century of the powerful *Tenebrae factae sunt* of Ingegneri; or of the magnificent pieces that Andrea and Giovanni Gabrieli wrote for performance by three or four choirs, brass, strings and organ in St. Marks, Venice; or of the fine madrigals of Marenzio.

Palestrina's beautiful, but to my ears unchanging, vocal polyphony is to be heard in the famous and lovely *Missa Papae Marcelli,* the *Missa Assumpta est Maria, Missa brevis* for four voices, *Missa Aeterna Christe munera,* and the *Oratio Jeremiae Prophetae,* as well as in the motets *Sicut cervus desiderat, O bone Jesu,* and the outstanding *Super flumina Babylonis.* Lassus's works include the remarkably beautiful motets *Omnes de Saba venient, Salve Regina Mater misericordiae, Tui sunt coeli, Alma redemptoris Mater,* and a work of his that I find to be the most impressive and affecting in my experience—the sixteen musical statements of his Penitential Psalm VII. Victoria's Responsories *O vos omnes* and *Tenebrae factae sunt* are two magnificent examples of the dark intensity characteristic of his writing, others being the Masses *O quam gloriosum, O magnum mysterium* and *Missa Quarti toni,* the *Requiem Mass* for four voices (i.e. in four parts) of 1605, the motets *O quam gloriosum, Gaudent in coelis, Ave Maria* and *Ascendens Christus,* the several *Laudi,* the *Tantum ergo,* and the *Vere languoris.*

There is no question either about the power of some of the madrigals of Gesualdo, though in the last of them it is achieved by harmonic progressions that are amazingly bold and strange even to our ears today. (Listening to all six books, one discovers that what the earlier ones offer is beautiful writing in the traditional style, with only a few pieces in the fourth book exhibiting the beginnings of his later idiosyncratic writing. Likewise his sacred music—the Responsories, the motets—exhibits less of the harmonic strangeness of the final madrigals.)

There is even greater variety of beauty and expressive power in the works of Monteverdi. You might begin with the madrigals of Book VII—extraordinarily beautiful and varied pieces for one, two, three, four, or six voices with various instrumental accompaniments—or Book VI, with the famous *Lagrime d'amante al sepolcro dell' amata.* Then the *Vespers of 1610.* And then his moving and expressive operas (or *favoli in musica*), *L'Orfeo* and *L'Incoronazione di Poppea.*

These early operas are for the most part written as recitative-like arioso supported by a harmonized bass line or *continuo.* The harmonization and instrumentation of this bass line must be done by the musician of today in accordance with what is known about the style of the music and its performance in Monteverdi's time [consequently, it may sound different from one recording to another]. I find it moving in *L'Orfeo* and *Poppea*, but tedious in Monteverdi's *Il Ritorno d'Ulisse*. More of this kind of expressive arioso, leading to occasional melodic pieces which are very beautiful, may be heard in the opera *Euridice* by Monteverdi's contemporary Peri, and in *La Calisto* by Cavalli, the best-known of the seventeenth-century composers of *dramma in musica* who followed them.

Of the music of the German composers of this period there are the *St. John* and *St. Matthew* Passions, *Weinachts-Historie* (*Christmas Story*), and other sacred music of Schütz; the organ music of Scheidt; the instrumental music of Praetorius. Somewhat later there are Froberger, whose Variations on the popular air *Auf die Mayerin* has one variation that is astonishing in its powerful chromatic writing; and Rosenmüller, whose *Nunc dimittis* and *In te Domine speravi* for solo voice have expressive florid writing that is moving and beautiful, and whose *Die Augen des Herrn* and *Confiteor tibi Domine* for chorus are equally impressive in their different ways. And after these there is Pachelbel—worth hearing not just for his *Canon*, but for his harpsichord pieces and for his organ music: the engaging fugues, the simple, strong choral-preludes *Jesus Christus unser Heiland* and *Wie schön leuchtet der Morgenstern*, the more involved and very beautiful *Warum betrübst du dich* and *Ein' feste Burg*, the latter with a majestic second part that is very imposing. And there is in France in the same period Lully, whose *Miserere* for chorus and soloists— among other works of his—has beautiful and moving passages.

We find some of the most beautiful and affecting music of the sixteenth and seventeenth centuries in the works of English composers—notably the superb *Mass for Four Voices*, the *Mass for Five Voices*, the lovely motets and madrigals, the fine instrumental and harpsichord pieces that make Byrd a major figure in this great period of English music. Also the works of his contemporary Dowland, among whose many lovely and affecting songs—in his four books of *Songs or Ayres* and his collection *Lachrimae, or Seaven Teares*—are *I Saw My Lady Weep, Shall I Sue, Sweet, Stay*

Awhile and *Can She Excuse,* and two that are especially fine: *Weep You No More, Sad Fountains* and *Sorrow, Stay.* And at the beginning of this period there is the sacred music of Tallis, whose mass *Puer natus est,* motets *Lamentations of Jeremiah, Suscipe quaeso Domine, Salvator mundi,* and the forty-part motet *Spem in alium* are outstandingly beautiful, as is his harpsichord piece, *O Ye Tender Babes.*

Other English composers of the time who produced lovely songs and madrigals and fine instrumental pieces are Parsons, whose song *Pandolpho* is particularly fine. Wilbye, whose outstanding madrigal *Lady, When I Behold* has wonderful harmonic progressions. Bull, whose *In Nomine* and Pavana for harpsichord are magnificent. Morley, who wrote charming songs and an *Agnus Dei* that is especially beautiful. Gibbons, who produced beautiful motets, anthems and madrigals (including *The Silver Swan*), and an extraordinary harpsichord piece, *The Lord Salisbury his Pavin.* Weelkes, whose many madrigals include the outstanding *Happy O Happy He, Draw on, Sweet Night, Weep, Weep Mine Eyes, I Always Beg, Oft Have I Vowed,* and one— *Thule, the Period of Cosmographie*—with rich textures and unusual and wonderfully expressive harmonic progressions. Tomkins, who in addition to his fine madrigals wrote two especially good pieces for harpsichord: *The Perpetual Round* and *Fortune My Foe.* Robert Johnson, who wrote the poignant and moving madrigal *Defiled Is my Name.* And Farnaby, who wrote a fine "setting" of a Pavana by Johnson.

And with all these there are many others—Fayrfax, Taverner, Newman, Randall, Holborne, Tye, White, Sheppard, Greaves, Edwards, Vautor, Campion, Rosseter, Ford, Bartlet, Pilkington, Dering, Jenkins, Locke—too numerous to list in detail.

We come in this way to another great figure, the last in English music—Purcell. His individuality and power are strikingly evident in the famous *Fantasia in Five Parts on One Note,* one of the Fantasias for strings, all superb pieces, in whose slow sections we follow a mind that moves in strange, daring and at times startling ways—as it does also in the *Chacony* in G minor for four viols and the Pavane that is often played with it. The chaconne's reiteration of a ground-bass (see Chapter 24) is a favorite procedure with

Purcell (as in fact with his English predecessors)—one that he uses with impressive effect not only in instrumental but in vocal pieces. Thus, the phrases of *When I Am Laid in Earth* in the opera *Dido and Aeneas* succeed each other over the repetitions of a ground-bass. And so with *O Let Me Ever, Ever Weep!* and *Next Winter Comes Slowly* in *The Fairy Queen,* a work that is overwhelming not only in the profusion but in the expressive range of its superb writing. And on the other hand *The Cares of Lovers* from his *Masque of Timon of Athens* and the independent songs *I Love and I Must* and *Tell Me Some Pitying Angel* are three magnificent and breathtaking examples of Purcell's powerfully expressive florid vocal style. There is as well the *Ode for St. Cecilia's Day*—a fine piece, characteristic in the boldness of its harmonic progressions as well as in the florid vocal writing that Purcell makes so exciting.

The other varieties of his writing are to be heard in the songs *Fairest Isle* from *King Arthur* and *I Attempt from Love's Sickness to Fly* from *The Indian Queen*—two lovely examples of simple melody; the lovely sacred duet *Close Thine Eyes;* the extraordinary dramatic scene *In Guilty Night (Saul and the Witch of Endor);* the two sets of Trio Sonatas for two violins and continuo (the second set of which contains the lovely *Golden Sonata*); the harpsichord music and other instrumental pieces; the *Music for the Funeral of Queen Mary* for brass and choir, the anthems *Remember Not Lord Our Offenses, Man that Is Born of Woman* and *Thou Knowest Lord the Secrets of Our Hearts* (called *"Funeral Sentences"*); the *Te Deum, Jubilate Deo* and other sacred music.

Finally in this survey there is Blow, whose *Ode on the Death of Mr. Henry Purcell* is both charming and touching. The music of his opera *Venus and Adonis,* composed for the entertainment of Charles II, is excellent too, and the words of the unknown librettist are very entertaining today.

John Blow (1649–1708)
Dr. John Bull (1562 or 63?–1628)
William Byrd (1543–1623)
Pietro (Pier) Francesco Cavalli (1602–1676)
John Dowland (1563–1626)
Guillaume Dufay (c. 1400–1474)

John Dunstable (c.1390–1453)
Giles Farnaby (c.1563–1640)
Johann Froberger (1616–1667)
Andrea Gabrieli (c.1510–1586)
Giovanni Gabrieli (c.1553–1612)
Carlo Gesualdo (c.1561–1613)
Orlando Gibbons (1583–1625)
Marc' Antonio Ingegneri (c.1547–1592)
Heinrich Isaac (c.1450–1517)
Robert Johnson (c.1583–1633)
Josquin des Prés (Desprez) (1440–1521)
Orlando di Lasso (Lassus) (1532–1594)
Jean-Baptiste Lully (1632–1687)
Guillaume de Machaut (c.1300–1377)
Luca Marenzio (1553 or 54?–1599)
Claudio Monteverdi (1567–1643)
Thomas Morley (1557 or 58?–1602)
Jacob Obrecht (c.1450–1505)
Johannes Ockeghem (c.1410–1497)
Johann Pachelbel (1653–1706)
Giovanni Palestrina (1525–1594)
Robert Parsons (1530–1570)
Jacopo Peri (1561–1633)
Michael Praetorius (1571–1621)
Henry Purcell (1659–1695)
Johann Rosenmüller (1619–1684)
Pierre de La Rue (c.1460–1518)
Samuel Scheidt (1587–1654)
Heinrich Schütz (1585–1672)
Thomas Tallis (1505–1585)
Thomas Tomkins (1572–1656)
Tomás Luis de Victoria (Vittoria) (1548–1611)
Thomas Weelkes (1576–1623)
John Wilbye (1574–1638)
Adrian Willaert (c. 1490–1562)

16th–17th-Century English Composers—mentioned:

John Bartlet (fl. 1606–1610)
Thomas Campion (1567–1620)
Richard Dering (Deering) (c.1580–1630)
Richard Edwards (1524–1566)
Robert Fayrfax (Fayrefax, Fairfax) (1464–1521)
Thomas Ford (c.1580–1648)
Thomas Greaves (fl.1604)
Antony (Anthony) Holborne (fl. 1584, d.1602)
John Jenkins (1592–1678)
Matthew Locke (1621 or 22?–1677)
(William) Newman (fl. 1538)
Francis Pilkington (1570–1638)
William Randall (d. c.1604)
Philip Rosseter (c.1568–1623)
John Sheppard (c.1515-1560)
John Taverner (c.1490–1545)
Christopher Tye (c.1505–1572)
Thomas Vautor (fl.1600–1620)
Robert White (c.1538–1574)

11

Brahms

People change for us as we ourselves change in time; the things they said come to make more sense or less; and works of art, which are personal communications of a special kind, also change in significance and value for us. From which it follows that for someone to think less than he once did of certain pieces of music, as I have come to do of certain works of Brahms, is not to be guilty of unnatural behavior, of an enormity beyond comprehension. It probably will happen to you with one composer or another. And the reason it happened to me with Brahms is something to talk about here, because it has to do with the nature of his music.

For many years Brahms's music was for me, every note of it, the greatest of all. Until one day, as I was playing through the slow movement of the Cello Sonata Op. 99 at the piano, I suddenly was aware of hearing not real creative activity but the pretense, the pose of such activity—the pretense of feeling in synthetically contrived themes that were being manipulated by formula to fill out the pattern of the movement. And having heard it here I began to hear it in other works.

I recall a broadcast of a performance of the Piano Concerto No. 2 by Toscanini and the NBC Symphony with Horowitz as soloist. Sounds came through my radio that were evidence of attentive, purposeful activity by Brahms, Toscanini, Horowitz, the orchestra, the audience; but what also came through powerfully was the impression that this was the activity of people under a spell continuing to go through a long-established ritual that was without reality or meaning—performers and listeners going through the motions of esthetic response to a piece of music in which the composer went through the motions of esthetic creation. Anyone not under this spell, anyone able to listen freshly to the agitated statements of the piano that broke in on the quiet opening of the first movement, would, it seemed to me, perceive that they were the noisy motions of saying something portentous that really said absolutely nothing; and listening further he would discover that the entire movement was a succession of such attempts at now one such effect and now another.

Tchaikovsky's comments on Brahms have been quoted as an illustration of one composer's inability to understand and justly appraise the work of another; but actually composers have sometimes written about other composers with the special insight of the practitioner of an art; and when Tchaikovsky criticizes in Brahms's music the conscious aspiration to something for which there is no poetic impulse, the striving for something that must be unstriven for, the conscious attempt at Beethoven's profundity and power that results in caricature of Beethoven, and the operation, for these purposes, of the technical mastery that produces "so many preparations and circumlocutions for something which ought to come and charm us at once"*—when Tchaikovsky speaks of all this he is describing what is plain to hear in the works that Brahms wrote, as he himself expressed it, with the consciousness of the tramp of Beethoven behind him.

The superb song *Botschaft* exhibits the genuine emotional impulse and musical gift of a lyricist, a creator of small forms; the *Variations on a Theme of Haydn* is one of the fine works the small-scale artist produces when he employs his technical skill to say the one small thing a number of different ways, and creates a large form by writing a continuous series of small ones. On the other hand the opening movement of Brahms's first published work, the Piano Sonata Op. 1, exhibits the labored and bombastic proclamations, the stretches of arid manipulation, that are the results of the small-scale artist's attempt to write greater than he

*Rosa Newmarch, ed., *The Life and Letters of Tchaikovsky* (London, 1906).

feels and to produce with technique what doesn't issue from emotional impulse. Similar striving for portentous utterance and similar arid manipulation are exhibited by the opening movement of the Piano Concerto No. 1, which grew out of Brahms's first attempt at a symphony after hearing Beethoven's Ninth; by the opening movement of the Symphony No. 1 that he did produce after twenty years' labor with the tramp of Beethoven behind him; by the other concertos; by the *Tragic Overture*, which is gloomy about nothing of great consequence; by the pretentious chamber music (of which the Sonata Op. 108 in D minor for violin and piano is the best of the lot, and the Cello Sonata Op. 99 possibly the worst); by the dull *Alto Rhapsody* for solo voice and orchestra; by the pretentious and dull *Four Serious Songs* (*Vier ernste Gesänge*) for voice and piano; by the even more pretentious and prodigiously dull *German Requiem* (*Ein Deutsches Requiem*); and by the other choral works. Nor is the sentimentality that is a characteristic of Brahms which Tchaikovsky fails to mention— the cloying saccharine sweetness of many of the slow movements, the archness of many of the scherzo movements—easier to endure.

As a matter of fact the cloying sweetness and archness are heard also in small-scale works—some of the songs, the uninteresting *Liebeslieder Walzer*, most of the Intermezzos and Capriccios and other small pieces for piano that are, to my ears, arid artifice dipped in treacle. And as a matter of fact a few examples of large-scale operation come off for me—the finale of the Symphony No. 2, the second and final movements of the Symphony No. 3, and all but the third movement of the Symphony No. 4, whose concluding passacaglia is one of Brahms's finest essays in variation form.

These few symphony movements, then, the *Variations on a Theme of Haydn* (in its original orchestral version), the enjoyable *Academic Festival Overture*, the sets of piano variations on themes of Handel and Paganini and the lesser ones on an original theme Op. 21 No. 1 and on themes by Schumann, the Capriccio Op. 76 No. 2, and some of the songs—notably *Botschaft, Sapphische Ode, Minnelied, Die Mainacht, Sonntag, Ständchen, Meine Liebe ist grün, Das Mädchen spricht, Immer leise wird mein Schlummer* and *Der Tod das ist die kühle Nacht**—these are the music of his that I have continued to hear with belief and pleasure. But the rest, which is only the pretence of artistic creation to my ears, may be the real thing to yours; and yours are making the decisions for you.

Johannes Brahms (1833–1897)

---

*Other good songs are *Von ewiger Liebe, Vergebliches Ständchen, In stiller Nacht, Vor dem Fenster, Der Gang zum Liebchen, O kühler Wald, Dein blaues Auge, Geheimnis, Am Sonntag Morgen, Wie Melodien zieht es, O liebliche Wangen, (Der) Jäger, Therese, An die Nachtigall, Treue Liebe, Wir wandelten,* the charming *Auf dem Schiffe* and the equally charming *Geistliches Wiegenlied* for voice, viola and piano, the unpretentious and attractive early songs of Opp. 3, 6, 7 and 19, the less elaborate among those of Op. 32, and Brahms's skillful settings of a large number of engaging German folksongs. —*B.H.H.*

12

Wagner

In the preceding chapter I spoke of my impression of the musicians and audience at a performance of Brahms continuing, under a spell, to go through a long-established ritual. And it is interesting to find an English critic, Richard Capell, writing in the 1920s about Wagner's success in imposing on the world his own idea of his work as a prophetic mission, in having the music-dramas presented in a darkened theatre "more austere than many cathedrals" and to an audience—formerly a prominent part of the spectacle—that was now " a dark and huddled anonymous throng assisting almost clandestinely at the enacted mysteries." No European music before Wagner's, said Capell, had worked "this quasi-hypnotic spell"; and although esthetic fashions had changed there still remained great numbers of "these 'perfect Wagnerites' who religiously adore many things in Wagner which in detachment could only be considered as incoherent, tautologous, morally reprehensible, or even dull."*

Capell was writing as an admirer and enjoyer of Wagner, but one with the detachment that made him aware of what he termed the "radical falsity" of the libretto of the *Ring* tetralogy—"that the simple barbarians of the old saga are endowed by Wagner with a new consciousness and a manner of expressing themselves which are by no means simple—and all the while they retain their

---

*Richard Capell, *Opera* (London, 1930, 1948).

antique savagery of action. Wotan's cunning and Siegfried's brutal prowess were all very well before these persons took to heroising themselves, but then they became unpardonable." Thus, the Siegfried who robs Brünnhilde of the ring is "a symbol and an ideal, a demi-god, a savior. He is Siegfried, Wagner's 'ordained man of the future'—and he is nothing but an ordinary looting *soudard*. Similarly, Wotan, 'the substance of the Intelligence of the Present,' turns out to be the substance of a fraudulent army contractor."

Now I once had occasion to remark to myself—concerning a performance of *Das Rheingold* that initiated a matinee *Ring* series for perfect Wagnerites at the Metropolitan—that the famous long-sustained opening E flat from the orchestra pit "cast a spell over the people who crowded the auditorium to capacity, a spell under which the visual and aural presentation of a story about mighty beings symbolized to them mighty significances." But, I added, to "one listener whom the E flat did not place under this spell . . . no mighty significances were conveyed by what he saw and heard." And I will add now that none were conveyed to me by the subsequent music-dramas of the *Ring* tetralogy. For me, then, it isn't only the libretto that doesn't work; it is also the music. I am aware of the prodigious musical powers operating in those scores, and the wonderful moments they achieve here and there (to say nothing of the wonderful pages in the other works we shall come to in a moment). But I find that the endless narrative declamation, the endless bombastic proclamation, the endless literal illustration of words and action (of which the *Ride of the Valkyries* is only the worst example), and the occasional tawdriness and cheapness (notably in the final scenes of *Siegfried* and *Götterdämmerung*) are as unendurable as the philosophical posturings and the equally pretentious and laughable verbal jargon of the texts (e.g. *Winterstürme wichen dem Wonnemond*, or *Starke Scheite schichtet mir dort*, or *Schweigt eures Jammers jauchzenden Schwall*).

Fortunately, some of the good moments can be heard without all the rest in the form of the most commonly encountered concert excerpts—notably *Dawn* and *Siegfried's Rhine Journey*, *Siegfried's Funeral Music*, and *Brünnhilde's Immolation* from *Götterdämmerung*, some of whose orchestral writing is marvelous, and the later parts of Acts One and Two of *Die Walküre*. But again you may find the things I dislike in the entire operas convincing and impressive; and you will act in accordance with your findings, not mine.

The Prelude to *Tristan und Isolde*, on the other hand, from its very first statement, does cast its spell over me—despite which I manage, at its conclusion, to remember to skip the next half-hour or so of boring declamatory narration, explanation and argument to the point where the music of the Prelude returns as Tristan and Isolde drink the love potion. King Marke's fifteen-minute reproach near the end of the second act is something else I skip; but most of the music in this act is marvelous in its luxuriant tonal beauty and expressiveness, rising to sheer incandescence in the duet, beginning with *O sink hernieder*. In the Prelude to Act 3 we hear one of Wagner's most wonderful pages—wonderful as a musical evocation of the desolate scene and the wounded Tristan's bodily illness and sickness at heart that will be revealed when the curtain rises. And after Kurwenal's conversation with the shepherd and his first exchanges with the awakening Tristan we come to the powerful music of Tristan's delirium, which rises to the climax of his curse of the potion, and ends with the exquisite passage *Wie sie selig*.

Though Tristan and Isolde are—compared with the characters of the *Ring*—human beings, even they are somewhat dehumanized and monumentalized in Wagner's music-drama (the music, says Capell, "is accompanied on the stage by rather more than life-size gestures of actors who, no matter how gifted, never can avoid bringing to mind the Siegesallee statuary"). But Wagner's only comedy, *Die Meistersinger von Nürnberg*, is, for once, concerned with characters who are, act like, and are involved in the situations of, real human beings—with the exception of Beckmesser, who is a caricature, and as such a major and deplorable defect in the work. It is true that, as Capell puts it, "for the pint pot of this comedy Wagner poured out music in quarts and gallons"; but if Wagner is characteristically long-winded in the work, he is also uncharacteristically genial and sunny—except with Beckmesser, in whom he is revenging himself on the Viennese critic Hanslick—which is to say that the exhaustingly garrulous outpouring includes a large amount of extraordinarily lovely music. Formerly the only thing one could do was arrive in the first imtermission: one missed the good moments in Act 1, but was fresh for the beautiful passages in Act 2—the gay opening dance, the entrance of Pogner and Eva, Sachs's monologue *Was duftet doch der Flieder*, his conversation with Eva, her *Geliebter, spare den Zorn*, the watchman's song, Sachs's cobbling song, and the quiet closing pages after the riot. And after these one still wasn't too exhausted for the lovely things in Act 3—the affecting Prelude, Sachs's monologue *Wahn! Wahn!*, Walter's description of his dream, Eva's *Meister, 's ist nicht so gefährlich*, the ensuing scene of Sachs, Eva and Walter, the baptism of Walter's song, the quintet, the charming dances and songs of the apprentices, the crowd's *Wach auf* in greeting to Sachs, Walter's song. Now, with the entire opera on records, one can listen to an act at a time.

Parsifal was presented by Wagner, and still is accepted by the perfect Wagnerites, as a work of religious character; but I find this sensualist's exaltation of chastity decked out in religious mumbo-jumbo repellent, and would expect a religious person to find it offensive. In addition, the long dull stretches in the music reveal an astonishing enfeeblement of the powers of invention and manipulation that are so prodigious in the earlier works. But in the radiant closing pages of the lovely *Good Friday Spell* we hear his language marvelously enriched and subtilized—e.g. the ascending scale of clarinet, bassoon and horn in the seventh and eighth measures from the end.

For the rest, of the early works the most mature is *Lohengrin*, with some fine pages in addition to the Prelude to Act One that testify impressively to the gifts Wagner began with. It is interesting how much of the writing is still in the old operatic style he was to leave behind, though there are also beginnings of his later declamatory style. *Tannhäuser* is an earlier product of Wagner's musical gifts in which they do not yet operate as interestingly as in *Lohengrin* a few years later (and the stylistically incongruous and heavily Teutonic *Bacchanale* he inserted afterwards is ludicrous). The Overture is as much as I find worth listening to in *Der fliegende Holländer* (*The Flying Dutchman*), and that is more than I find in *Rienzi*. The juvenile operas *Die Feen* and *Liebesverbot* may be deferred indefinitely.

In addition to the music-dramas and operas there are the five Wesendonck songs, of which *Im Treibhaus* uses the thematic material of the Prelude to Act 3 of *Tristan und Isolde* in a piece of extended vocal declamation that is in its own way as wonderful as the Prelude.

The purely instrumental works include the *Siegfried Idyll*, a delicate and charming, if also repetitious and diffuse, piece Wagner fashioned out of some of the better themes of the final scene of *Siegfried* to celebrate the birth of his son; and the early *Faust Overture*, which is hardly adequate to its subject but not bad to listen to.

Everything else—the early Symphony, the marches, concert overtures and piano pieces, and the endlessly boring and deservedly unfamiliar early piece for men's chorus and orchestra, *Liebesmahl der Apostel*—may be safely ignored.

Richard Wagner (1813–1883)

13

Verdi

Verdi, unlike Wagner, did not spin vast ad hoc fantasies about the past and future of art to rationalize his own present practice, but simply addressed himself to the task of setting a libretto to music as well as he knew how; he set to music not philosophically pretentious dramas about gods and heroes of Teutonic mythology, but melodramas about passionate Italians and Spaniards; for his dramatic purpose he did not weave leitmotifs into hour-and-a-half progressions of continuous *melos,* but produced series of clearly outlined melodic structures. All this was enough to make him an object of condescension for some; and they found additional reason for condescension in the vulgarity to which they attributed his popularity.

There are, certainly, crudities and vulgarities in Verdi's early exercises of his powers; but one thing to say about this is Francis Toye's observation that the occasional vulgarity of *Il Travatore* is "a by-product of the vitality and passion without which there can be no great art."* Another is that the powers, operating with vitality and passion, give us in *Il Trovatore* such wonderful melodic structures as Leonora's *Tacea la notte placida* and *D'amor sull' ali rosee,* the Count's *Il balen,* Manrico's *Ah! sì, ben mio;* and their composer is not someone to condescend to.

Moreover, even in the still earlier *Macbeth* we get in the vocal

*Francis Toye, *Verdi—His Life and Work* (New York, 1946).

and orchestral writing of the *Sleepwalking Scene* an astounding manifestation of the art which later—developed, enriched, subtilized—fills in moment after moment in *Otello* with sustained invention of marvelously wrought details of melody, harmony, figuration and orchestration—such as the orchestral passage leading from Desdemona's *Splende il cielo,* at the end of the choral episode early in Act 2, to her *D'un uomo che geme;* or the developing violin figure and harmonic progressions of Otello's *Dio! mi potevi scagliar* in Act 3. And the man who wrote the chorus's song around the fire, Iago's drinking song, and the duet of Otello and Desdemona, in Act 1; the duet of Otello and Iago, and especially Iago's *Era la notte,* in Act 2; the duet of Otello and Desdemona, Otello's *Dio! mi potevi scagliar,* the trio of Iago, Cassio and Otello, and the final ensemble, in Act 3; Desdemona's *Willow Song* and *Ave Maria,* in Act 4—this man is an artist to whom nobody may condescend.

The art that is incandescent and robust in *Otello* shows a further refinement and subtilization in *Falstaff,* in writing that is all lightness and fluent grace and transparent texture. The writing is largely point-to-point invention for the words; and some of this invention—for example, the opening uproar—is only the product of an experienced artist's resourcefulness; but much of it—for example Falstaff's interviews with Dame Quickly and Ford in the second scene—is a succession of marvels of subtly contrived expressive point, wit and loveliness, whose very subtlety may require repeated hearing for full appreciation. Moreover, the point-to-point invention includes vocal writing as lovely as Dame Quickly's *Un angelo che innamora* in her first scene with Falstaff, or Mistress Ford's *Ogni più bel giojel mi nuoce* in her first scene with him, but for the most part also as brief—the two duets and two arias of Nanetta and Fenton being the only examples of extended lyricism. And one thing in *Falstaff* is new: the poignant autumnal quality of much of the music of the last act—for example, Falstaff's *Ber del vin dolce* after the innkeeper has brought him the wine; and the orchestra's phrases accompanying his arrival at Herne's Oak. This music conveys to us for once the emotion of Verdi himself—the emotion, that is, of a man nearing the end of his life.

As for the other operas, we hear in the best-known of the early ones conventions and formulas of the period to which Verdi's powers give artistic validity and impressive effect. In *Rigoletto* the outstanding example of this is the famous quartet, in which freshly attentive listening enables us to appreciate the individualized writing for the four characters in the dramatic situation that makes it one of the most remarkable ensembles in opera. In *La Traviata* it is Violetta's *Ah! fors' è lui*, with its concluding efflorescence into florid passages that are not mere vocal exhibitionism of the period but an expression of the intensity of her emotion about her meeting with Alfredo, as the florid passages in the following recitative *Follie! Follie!* and aria *Sempre libera* are expressions of her feverish decision to reject love and pursue pleasure. In both operas, moreover, we hear other manifestations of Verdi's powers: in *Rigoletto* not only the Duke's *Quest' o quella*, his *Parmi veder le lagrime,* Gilda's *Caro nome,* their *E il sol dell' anima,* but the tremendous Prelude and the extraordinary first duet of Rigoletto and Sparafucile; in *La Traviata* not only Violetta's *Addio del passato,* her duet with Germont, her *Parigi, o cara* with Alfredo, but the music of the parties in Violetta's and Flora's homes that continues as a background of feverish gaiety for the poignant dialogue and dramatic incidents in the foreground. And in *Rigoletto* there is the *Zitti, zitti* chorus, with a delicacy that foretells the ensembles in *Falstaff;* in *La Traviata* the Preludes to Acts 1 and 3, whose divided violins are an example of the increasingly elaborate and refined orchestral writing we hear with the beautiful melodic invention in *Un Ballo in maschera* and *Simon Boccanegra.*

It is this orchestral writing that, with the exquisite vocal writing, gives us the *Nile Scene* of *Aida.* And it is the harmonic richness and imaginative instrumental invention of the supporting orchestral writing in *Don Carlo* that combines with the refined idiom, the flexible phraseology of the heart-piercingly beautiful and expressive vocal parts to cause its best pages to rank with the writing in *Otello* as one of Verdi's supreme achievements. These great pages include the duets of Carlo and Elisabetta in Acts 2 and 5, the duet of Rodrigo and King Philip in Act 2; the entire scene which begins with the King's soliloquy *Ella giammai m'amò* and continues with the confrontation of the King and the Grand Inquisitor, the confrontation of the King and Elisabetta, the quartet of these two with Eboli and Rodrigo, and Eboli's *O don fatale;* and they include the tremendous orchestral introduction of the final scene and Elisabetta's *Tu che le vanità,* a vocal utterance whose melodic grandeur is heard nowhere else in Verdi.

It must be added that one wants to hear the opera with the original 1867 first act that Verdi eliminated entirely in his drastic revision of 1882–83. And one wants to hear that first act with the powerful orchestral prelude and the brief opening scene of the peasants' encounter with Elisabetta in the forest of Fontainebleau that Verdi had been compelled to cut even before the opera's première, that he never published, and which Julian Budden characterized in his book on Verdi's operas as "arguably the most valuable of the passages" lost at that time. But one wants to hear the other four acts in Verdi's revised versions for the sake of the incandescent new writing he added later—in one instance in place of the much less effective writing of the original—even though performing the later edition entails the loss of a few numbers of less magnitude that Verdi omitted from it. (It might be well to add here that the revised *Simon Boccanegra* and *Macbeth* are to be preferred over the originals for the same reason.)

Moreover, one wants to hear the opera in Italian, not in French. True, for the Paris Opera Verdi set the libretto in French; but in Budden's words, "Certainly he never imagined that it would be performed outside France in any other language than Italian," which was "still in most theatres the accepted lingua franca of opera"—the language in which, a few months after the Paris première, it was performed in London. True also, Budden considers a performance in French preferable: "Words and music fit better together; the drama in every situation leaps out with far greater force"; but in reality, even at the close range provided by a recording, one often hears not the sense of the words as they are distended by the music to which they are sung, but only their sound. And to my ear it is the sound of the Italian words that fits better than the sound of the French with Verdi's music—specifically the sound of *Io vengo a domandar grazia alla mia Regina* that fits better than *Je viens solliciter de la Reine une grâce* with what Verdi has Carlo sing to Elisabetta in their second-act duet.

Finally, of this middle group there are also *I Vespri Siciliani,* whose overture's very first phrases seize one's mind with the power that operates throughout the work, and *La Forza del destino.*

What was said a moment ago about the best-known of the early operas may be said also of the less familiar of them: it is interesting to hear almost from the beginning the Verdi powers operating within the conventions of the style of the period, impressively for the most part, and now and then with originality and distinction. (The two exceptions, in which these powers do not operate, are *Ernani,* which except for the aria *Ernani, involami* is uninteresting, and *I Lombardi,* of which nothing is as impressive as the trio that is all most music-lovers have known until recently.) In most of the operas before *Rigoletto—I Due Foscari, Alzira, Attila, Aroldo, I Masnadieri, Il Corsaro*—one hears the operation of unmistakable gifts that will later produce the great writing they do not produce at this stage.

Nabucco, one of the first of these, was Verdi's first major success, the work that made him a national celebrity and the new eminent figure in Italian opera. And listening to it on records, undisturbed by the stage action that is hard to bear with today, one appreciates the new and powerfully expressive character of the writing for voices and orchestra produced by the new mind operating within the old style and form that Verdi is working in at this early point in his creative life. Likewise, *Un Giorno di regno,* Verdi's one comic opera before *Falstaff,* and this one an attempt at the *opera buffa* of Rossini and Donizetti, also surprises one with the writing that his gifts make effective and interesting.

Of the more familiar *Luisa Miller* the first two acts offer merely competent writing, except for the tenor aria *Quando le sere al placido;* but the third has writing that is powerfully expressive and distinguished. And in *Stiffelio* one already hears, after a surprisingly weak overture, Verdi's powers, which are interesting merely as such part of the time, at other times achieving impressive writing—in particular, occasional orchestral writing that is astonishing by turns in its harmonic progressions or its accompaniment figurations or its instrumentation.

As for the non-operatic works, the same matured powers, the same enriched and refined art, the same taste and honesty that produce the later great operas help this dramatic composer of genius to write the superb and moving *Requiem*. And the extraordinary final manifestation of those matured powers is the *Te Deum* for chorus and orchestra, which Verdi composed in his eighties, five years after *Falstaff*, and which is perhaps his most overwhelmingly beautiful single piece of writing.

The *Te Deum* is one of four works assembled under the title *Four Sacred Pieces*. While it is the finest of them, the *Stabat Mater* also offers beautiful choral and orchestral writing, but in a more diffuse progression; the *Laudi Alla Vergine Maria* is a piece of lovely *a cappella* writing for women's voices that nevertheless I find only mildly interesting; and the *Ave Maria* is a strange-sounding but impressive *a cappella* contrapuntal exercise around a *scala enigmatica* that interested Verdi.

There is also an earlier unfamiliar and beautiful *Ave Maria* for solo soprano and strings.

And there is, finally, his one string quartet, in E minor, which he wrote during a hiatus in rehearsals for *Aida,* and in which he amused himself, and charms us, with an exercise of the mastery in instrumental writing and the subtle harmonic sense that we hear in the later operas. Just as in an opera Verdi seizes one's mind with what he has the orchestra play before the curtain rises, he seizes it in the Quartet with the impassioned opening statement, and then holds it with what he goes on to contrive in his weaving of the texture of the four strands of string sound—impassioned in the first movement, charmingly graceful in the next one, lighter and presaging the writing in *Falstaff* in the third, and offering strokes of surprise and humor in the finale.

Giuseppe Verdi (1813–1901)

14

Tchaikovsky

Tchaikovsky is another popular composer who has been regarded with condescension for which we hear no justification in
his music. Listening to one of his ballet scores—*Swan Lake, The
Sleeping Beauty, The Nutcracker* (the entire score of each, not just
the usual excerpts)—listening, that is, to the canvas, so to speak,
being filled in with detail, we hear in the operation a wonderful
precision and taste in the use of the entire complex of musical
line, color, texture and mass. And we hear also this mastery of the
medium serving dramatic and imaginative powers of a high
order—the powers revealed for example in the ominous figure
that interrupts the opening melodic passage of *Swan Lake* and is
developed with increasing tension over plucked bass-notes and
sustained brass-notes; or in the music at the end of Act 1 of *The
Nutcracker,* and the Prelude to Act 2, which convey so marvelously the world of a child's dream.

Listening to Toscanini's, Cantelli's, Maazel's or Abbado's performances of the *Pathétique* Symphony we hear the music, as it
proceeds in strict accordance with Tchaikovsky's directions in the
score, take shape as something contrived with the same feeling
for the complex of musical line, color, texture and mass; and we
hear also the dramatic power it has when given these correct and
beautifully integrated plastic proportions. We are then able to
perceive the effect of the more usual performance that exagger-
ates every crescendo and decrescendo, every acceleration and

retardation (to say nothing of the additional changes of tempo and volume Tchaikovsky doesn't request in his score) and makes every *p* a *ppp*, every *f* an *fff*, in the overemphasis that is traditional in playing Tchaikovsky. We are able, that is, to perceive the distortion of the shape of the work, the consequent falsification of its meaning. It is the traditional overstatement in performance that converts drama and intensity into the melodrama and hysteria for which Tchaikovsky is looked down upon. And this overstatement has become the criterion by which mere statement is judged inadequate for failing to impart to the music "its essential feverish excitement"—which is as though some actor's ranting in Shakespeare had become the criterion by which the correct delivery of the lines were judged inadequate.

Tchaikovsky's music has been treated in this way because of the knowledge about his neurotically disordered personal life; and he provides part of the answer to the contention that knowledge of a composer's life is necessary for complete understanding of his music—a plausible contention until we think of some of the actual cases. On the one hand not one statement of Schubert has been reported to us that reveals the insights communicated in his greatest works; on the contrary, it is from the music that we infer the probability of these insights in the man. And on the other hand it is Berlioz's extravagances of behavior and utterance that are responsible for the ideas about "monstrous works" in which he carried out "extreme and gigantic aims" that people would not have got from mere listening to the works themselves. So with Tchaikovsky: it is, among other things, the neurotic self-accusations of incompetence and insincerity that are responsible for the ideas about the defects and the insincerity of his music that people would not have got from mere listening to the ballet scores, the operas *The Queen of Spades* and *Eugene Onegin,* the Overture-Fantasia *Romeo and Juliet,* the *Manfred* Symphony, and even the intensely subjective Symphonies Nos. 4, 5, and 6 (*Pathétique*).

What is to be heard instead in almost everything he wrote is his spontaneity of feeling and utterance, his unforced dramatic power, his extraordinary feeling for the musical medium and his ability to work with it to superb effect. Together with the subjectivity of the last three of his six symphonies, of which the *Pathé-*

tique is the best of the series, there is an idiosyncratic innovative expansion and modification of the traditional sonata-form structure in the first movements of Nos. 4 and 5 for the involvements of their tremendous musical drama. In *Manfred,* much of whose thematic material is as good as any of Tchaikovsky's (the work stands, in order of composition, between the Fourth and Fifth Symphonies), there is some of his best—that is, among other things, his most impersonal and restrained—symphonic writing, notably in the powerful first movement, the most impressive of the four and musically the most difficult to bring off, and in the technically very difficult second movement.

After these impressive achievements of Tchaikovsky's matured powers, the three early symphonies amaze one—No. 3 most of all—with occasional writing that could also be the superb orchestral invention of Tchaikovsky's maturity. This is especially astonishing to hear in No. 1 (*Winter Dreams*), composed nine years before the others. In No. 2, called *Little Russian* because of its use of Ukrainian folk songs, the first movement substituted in 1879 for the one composed in 1872 has some of Tchaikovsky's beautiful melodic writing but in a context of sonata-allegro manipulation and hubbub that is only moderately interesting; but the movements that follow offer characteristic writing that even in this early period is fascinating in its filling out of the musical canvas in the second movement, engaging in the third, and impressively skillful in its lengthy elaboration of the ideas of the finale. But it is No. 3 that astounds one right at the start with the slow introduction that could be taken for Tchaikovsky's later writing, and after that with the *alla tedesca* second movement, the Andante and the Scherzo; and the impact of these is not lessened by a first movement development and a finale that are less interesting than the rest.

Of the four Suites for Orchestra, the Divertimento in No. 1 and the Theme and Variations in No. 3 are outstanding examples of the superb invention in some of the movements of these works, achieved with taste and precision in the use of the entire complex of musical line, color, texture and mass. No. 1 has in addition a strangely somber Introduction which is followed by a Fugue that is more interesting than most of Tchaikovsky's fugues; and No. 4, *Mozartiana,* is his skillful orchestration of several piano pieces by

Mozart, including the extraordinary Gigue K.574 and the fine Variations on *Unser dummer Pöbel meint*. Another engaging Tchaikovsky piece is the Serenade for Strings Op. 48.

And there are the tone-poems. A few years before Tchaikovsky produced the synthesis of the dramatic elements of Shakespeare's *Romeo and Juliet* in a sonata-form structure that is one of his orchestral masterpieces, he produced the more simply structured *Francesca da Rimini*, whose stormy beginning (with its wonderfully evocative opening chords) and closing sections frame the superb melodic invention of its central section concerned with the passion of the two characters in Dante's poem. Tchaikovsky's *The Tempest* has passages of effective and beautiful writing, but in its entirety achieves nothing, in relation to the Shakespeare play, comparable with his *Romeo and Juliet*. *Hamlet* is another inadequate musical embodiment of its subject, and not very interesting to listen to for itself. Uninteresting, too, is the even later *Voyevode*.

For the rest, the Overture *1812*, the *Marche Slave*, the *Capriccio Italien* are things you can neglect.

As for the instrumental music, a regrettably neglected work is Tchaikovsky's Piano Concerto No. 2, whose musical substance, aside from the concerto fireworks, is much superior to that of the ubiquitous No. 1—a high point being the elegantly impassioned melodic episode for piano alone in the first movement. There are also the fine single completed movement of the Piano Concerto No. 3; the Concerto for Violin, a very good work; the *Méditation* Op. 42 No. 1 that was originally intended to be the Violin Concerto's slow movement; the *Variations on a Rococo Theme* for Cello and Orchestra, which has pages of superb Tchaikovskyan writing; the *Grand Sonata* Op. 37 in G for Piano, which has an impressive first movement that is in fact grand in style—holding the attention it commands with its proclamatory opening—and other movements that offer additional manifestations of Tchaikovsky's powers of invention for the piano; and the set of piano pieces, most of them charming, called *The Seasons* (or *The Months*), which includes the familiar Barcarolle *June*. On the other hand, the *Concert Fantasy* Op. 56 for Piano and Orchestra is a very inferior work which deserves its obscurity.

The Trio for Violin, Cello and Piano is a fine work, but too long. The Sextet *Souvenir de Florence* and the three String Quartets, on the other hand, are surprisingly uninteresting—except for the lovely *Andante Cantabile* movement of the first Quartet, Op. 11, and the *Andante funèbre e doloroso* movement of the third, Op. 30, especially the strikingly unusual writing in its opening section.

Of Tchaikovsky's many operas the best-known are the comparatively early *Eugene Onegin* and the next-to-last one, *The Queen of Spades* (or *Pique Dame*). *The Queen of Spades,* with its melodious arias and beautiful orchestral writing, is Tchaikovsky's most impressive opera. However, the *Maid of Orleans* (or *Jeanne d'Arc*), which makes Joan's execution the consequence of a love affair with the Duke of Burgundy, and of which her aria *Adieu, forêts* is the most familiar part, has characteristically accomplished and effective lyrical and dramatic writing in the style of its predecessor, *Onegin. Mazeppa* provides an opportunity to hear the operation of Tchaikovsky's impressive powers in expressive vocal arioso and the continuous orchestral writing that is its supporting and commenting context; and a further growth of Tchaikovsky's powers in this genre is revealed by *The Enchantress* (or *The Sorceress*). Astonishing, therefore, is Tchaikovsky's last opera, the one-act *Iolanta,* a work composed at the same time as his score for *The Nutcracker*—i.e. at the height of his powers—which is strange to hear and difficult to account for, not only with its libretto that fascinated Tchaikovsky but makes no more acceptable sense in *its* way than the texts of some of the operas of Verdi and Wagner do in *their* ways, but with its music that is pleasant to listen to but which, with the exception of the tenor's aria that is the work's most impressive passage, rarely attains any resemblance, in mastery of the medium and expressive eloquence, to the great writing of Tchaikovsky's we are familiar with. Finally, there are fragments of an early unfinished opera, *Undine,* a duet from which turns out to be Odette's supported Adagio in Act II of *Swan Lake.* And *Tcherevichky* (*The Little Shoes,* or *The Slippers*—Tchaikovsky's later revision of an earlier work, *Vakula the Smith*), of which I presume the few excerpts I heard are not the music Gerald Abraham said "ranks with the best Tchaikovsky ever wrote."

As for Tchaikovsky's other vocal music, his *a cappella* settings of texts by Pushkin, Lermontov, other Russian writers and himself are enjoyable. And his songs, though unfamiliar to the musical public that knows the instrumental music so well, are masterpieces that should be in the standard repertory with those of Schubert, Schumann and Wolf: while they are traditional in their melodic style and structure, one hears in each—in Tchaikovsky's writing for the voice, in the contexts he writes for the piano—the same extraordinary powers of expressive melodic invention and dramatic imagination as in his ballet scores, orchestral suites and symphonies.

In summation, then, it is a composer's works that we are concerned with and evaluate, not the circumstances under which they were produced; and by the evidence of the great works I have mentioned Tchaikovsky was a superb artist. Nor was he less so for having produced other works inferior to them.

Peter (Piotr) Il'ych Tchaikovsky (1840–1893)

15

Musorgsky

One article of Turner published in 1924* that is of particular interest for us today opens with the statement that "the beginning of any live, intelligent interest in any art is the desire to know an artist's work in its pure, unadulterated state as it finally left the hands of its creator." It may seem obvious that one wants to know a painting as its creator painted it, not as it was repainted by someone else, and that the same is true with any other work of art. But it must be equally obvious that Turner had a reason for making his statement—the reason, in fact, that many works of art are presented to us *not* in their pure, unadulterated state as they left the hands of their creators.

Turner cited examples from poetry: Swinburne had exposed editors' alterations of the texts in various editions of Shelley; Sampson's accurate edition of Blake, Grierson's of Donne, had revealed the similar editorial tampering with their poems in previous editions. And the situation in music, he said, was even worse: not only had editors and performers taken even greater liberties with the originals, but there were few critics with the knowledge required to expose them, and even the objections that were made occasionally were ignored. Turner's explanation of this was "the generally lower intellectual integrity of men of music

*W. J. Turner, "The First Duty of a Musician," *Variations on the Theme of Music* (London, 1924).

as compared with men of letters," to which I would add the generally lower intellectual sophistication and understanding where music is concerned: those who understand that one mustn't change someone else's painting or poem don't understand that one mustn't change the harmony or texture of someone else's music.

And so we had the many nineteenth-century "editions" of music of earlier centuries in which the editors, not knowing or caring what the music was intended to sound like, "corrected" it to make it conform to nineteenth-century ideas of what music should sound like. We had Gevaert's "edition" of Haydn's Cello Concerto in D, which in addition to re-orchestrating the work cut half the recapitulation out of the first movement. Or Leonard's "edition" of Corelli's *La Folia,* which should have been called Leonard's *La Folia* since that was what it really was. Or Grützmacher's "edition" of the Boccherini Cello Concerto in B flat, which was actually a work by Grützmacher himself, whom the statement in the preface of the Eulenburg score of the genuine concerto, which had been discovered in the Dresden Library, accused of combining "wantonly altered parts of [the original] with such from other works of Boccherini and Orchestra Tutti of his own . . . ." Ironically, even the discoverer of the genuine Dresden Concerto in B flat, when preparing the work for publication, could not forbear to "improve" Boccherini's orchestration. Moreover, those "editions" were the ones cellists continued to play and record until recently, though correct editions were available. And in this we see the "lower intellectual integrity of men of music" that Turner spoke of.

But a contributing cause is the lower intellectual sophistication and understanding I spoke of, which is to be seen in this mixture of sense and nonsense in Edmund van der Straeten's *History of the Violoncello:*

> . . . Very meritorious was Grützmacher's activity as an editor of classical works which had been practically lost, especially such rare treasures as the concertos by Haydn, P. E. Bach, Boccherini, sonatas by Duport, Geminiani and others. Unfortunately he treated these masters with little reverence as regards the text of their compositions, and in various cases he pieced together "sonatas" from about

half-a-dozen original compositions and edited them as if they appeared in their original form. In the case of the six solo sonatas by Bach, he went so far as to edit a "concert edition," in which he crowds additional chords, passages and embellishments, distorting these great and fine works in the most unpardonable manner. Yet for all that, we must be thankful for the many works which he has rescued and made accessible. . . .

Nonsense, since what Grützmacher made accessible was not the great works but his falsifications of them, which kept the true works from becoming known. Which brings me to the subject of this chapter. The occasion for Turner's article was the announcement that the piano-and-voice arrangement that Musorgsky himself made of his opera *Boris Godunov* for publication in 1874 was to be published again, after having been out of print for many years. What had been performed since 1896 and available in published form was Rimsky-Korsakov's revision, in which he corrected what he considered to be "the fragmentary character of the musical phrases, the harshness of the harmonies and modulations, the faulty counterpoint, the poverty of the instrumentation, and the general weakness of the work from the technical point of view," which he contended had been responsible for its failure when it had been produced in 1874. It would always be possible, said Rimsky, to publish a "musicologically accurate edition"; he was satisfying the immediate "need of an edition for performances, for practical artistic purposes, for making [Musorgsky's] colossal talent known"— purposes which he claimed were in fact achieved by his revision. For after he became chairman of the Society of Musical Gatherings in St. Petersburg in 1896, he said, "there sprang up in the Society the idea of a stage production of *Boris Godunov* in my revision." The success of this production led to one by Mamontov's company in Moscow with Chaliapin, after which as part of Chaliapin's repertory the Rimsky revision was produced at the imperial Mariinsky Theater in St. Petersburg in 1904 and came to Paris in 1908 in the Diaghilev production that carried the work to Western Europe and America. And Rimsky's claim to have in this way "[made] Musorgsky's colossal talent known" to a world that otherwise would not have known it is accepted to this day.

But what led to the republication of Musorgsky's original work in 1924 was the loudly proclaimed discovery of some French critics that Rimsky, far from making Musorgsky's talent known, had concealed it with his corrections. In the famous words of Jean Marnold, "Rimsky-Korsakov cuts . . . one, two or three measures as serenely as he cuts fifteen or twenty. At will he transposes a tone, or a half-tone, makes sharps or flats natural, alters modulations. He even corrects the harmony. During the tableau in the cell of Pimen the liturgical Dorian mode is adulterated by a banal D minor. The interval of the augmented fifth (a favorite device of Musorgsky) is frequently the object of his equilateral ostracism. . . . From one end of the work to the other he planes, files, polishes, pulls together, retouches, embellishes, makes insipid, or corrupts. . . ."* Imagine the analogous things being done to a painting or a poem: you will see what violation of the integrity of another artist's work Rimsky-Korsakov was guilty of; and you will see also that it was one which no painter, no poet would commit or be allowed to commit.

Nor is it true that Rimsky's revision, or any other edition "for performances, for practical artistic purposes," was necessary. It is Rimsky himself who, in *My Musical Life,* tells us of *Boris Godunov*—i.e. Musorgsky's own revised 1872 version—being produced in St. Petersburg in 1874 "with great success," and of its continuing to be performed once or twice each year until 1882, when, "the Lord knows why, productions of the opera ceased altogether, although it had enjoyed uninterrupted success." Concerning the reasons which only the Lord knew, Rimsky writes that "there were rumors afloat that the opera had displeased the imperial family; there was gossip that its subject was unpleasant to the censors"; but he says nothing about any practical difficulties that made necessary "an edition for performances, for practical artistic purposes." Musorgsky's original would have been as practical to produce in 1896 as in 1874; and if it had been produced in 1896 it would presumably have repeated its success of 1874–1882. And if it *had* been produced by the Society in 1896 instead of Rimsky's revision it would have taken the same subsequent

---

*Jean Marnold, "Nicolai Rimsky-Korsakov et Boris Godounoff," *Musique d'autrefois et d'aujourd'hui* (Paris, 1911). The essay first appeared in 1908 in the journal *Le Mercure de Paris;* the translation may be Haggin's own. —*Ed.*

steps as the revision in becoming the version the world would know today.

The real reason for what Rimsky did was very different from what he claimed, and much less to his credit. Musorgsky was one of the two great originals of the nineteenth century (Berlioz was the other), with stature and powers that triumphed over his insistence on learning solely by doing; Rimsky, on the other hand, was a minor talent who tells us he needed the help of codified practice in harmony and counterpoint for "new living currents to flow into my creative work." What was original and powerful in Musorgsky's writing was to Rimsky's ears, therefore, error which he tried persistently and unsuccessfully to get Musorgsky to change. And having been unable to get Musorgksy to change it when alive, he proceeded to change it himself when Musorgsky was dead.

Nor is it true that "there sprang up in the Society the idea of a stage production of *Boris Godunov* in my revision." The idea "sprang up" in Rimsky; and in another man there would have "sprung up" the idea of a production of Musorgsky's original work. By using the opportunity to produce his revision instead, Rimsky succeeded not, as he claimed, in making Musorgsky's work known to the world, but in keeping it from being known to most of the world to this very day. For though he argued plausibly that whenever the world disapproved of what he had done it could return to Musorgsky's original score, which he had not destroyed, actually once the revision had taken root everywhere in opera houses, in singers' repertories, in people's minds, then routine and inertia combined with lack of conscience and understanding to keep it from being dislodged for Musorgsky's original. And we come here to what is more extraordinary even than what was done to poor Musorgsky's work—namely, the way people's minds have operated in relation to what was done to it.

Thus, for years it has been the accepted belief that Rimsky's changes had enabled a work that had failed in its original form to be performed with success. That belief goes back to Rimsky's statements in justification of his revision; and it has continued, amazingly, in the face of his own testimony to the contrary: the passage in *My Musical Life* in which he says Musorgsky's *Boris* was produced in 1874 "with great success" and continued to be performed "with uninterrupted success" until 1882. Even the compilers of the documentary material in *The Musorgsky Reader* quoted and accepted the statement in Rimsky's *My Musical Life* that the revision satisfied the "need of an edition for performances, for practical artistic purposes," but did not quote the passage which revealed there had been no need of such revision for that purpose.

Thus, too, with the republication of Musorgsky's score in 1924 it was possible for people, by playing through it, to discover that everything was wonderfully right and nothing called for correction, and at the end to be left overwhelmed by what they had heard achieved with such originality, power and absolute assured mastery. And some did. But there were others of whom one could say what Tovey said of Rimsky himself—that they were incapable of "telling a blunder from a stroke of genius or feature of style."* And you will find them declaring today that a hearing of Musorgsky's original demonstrates how much it gained from the editing of a man properly schooled in his craft—which amounts not just to saying that something like Rimsky's *Le Coq d'or* is good of its kind, but to setting it up as the good by which the kind of a *Boris Godunov* must be judged deficient. Imagine that Van Gogh's work had been tidied up by some academician, or even by someone like Sargent; and imagine anyone contending that the restored Van Gogh originals demonstrated how much they had gained from the tidying up—contending, in other words, not merely that Sargent was good for what he was, but that his good was the good for Van Gogh.

Moreover, if it *had* been discovered that someone had re-painted Van Gogh's or any other painter's work, there would have been no debate over whether the work was more effective with the changes or without them, and whether therefore they should be retained or removed: it would have been taken as a matter of course that they had no validity and the original work must be restored. But in the case of *Boris* we find the celebrated English critic Sir Ernest Newman writing that the difficulty with *Boris* is one of having to choose not merely between Musorgsky's

---

*I have not discovered the source of this comment by Tovey. —*Ed.*

own two versions, each complete and with merits of its own, but from these two and Rimsky's, since it too is "a good practical proposition" in the theater.* We have had European opera companies producing Musorgsky's original and going back to Rimsky's revision because it "sounds better." I have had a man who conducted the Musorgsky original at Covent garden insist that the change back to the Rimsky version there had been a good thing because it had induced the London public to listen to a great work it had stayed away from before, and have been unable to get him to understand that this was as though a museum had induced the public to like an El Greco painting by having someone touch it up to make its forms and colors more conventional—that what the London public had listened to was no more Musorgsky's great work than the prettied-up painting would be El Greco's.

Even the most accurately perceptive and clearest-minded English critic of his time, Gerald Abraham, in his notes for an HMV and RCA Victor recording of the Rimsky version, recognized that by applying to *Boris* an art whose "essence . . . is brightly tinted transparency, clear-cut harmonies, and part-writing realized in primary orchestral colors" Rimsky "imprinted his own personality over the entire work," but went on nevertheless to call this result "a fascinating posthumous collaboration of two very different but very fine musical minds." One would have expected Abraham to recognize the obvious disparity and incompatibility of the mind that expresses itself in Rimsky's "brightly tinted transparency, clear-cut harmonies, and part-writing realized in primary orchestral colors," with the mind that produces the somber power of *Boris;* and one would have expected him not to want the imprint of a mind like Rimsky's on a work like Musorgsky's.

Even perceptive critics like Desmond Shawe-Taylor and Edward Sackville-West, acknowledging in 1951 that "most students and scholars agree in condemning Rimsky's well-intentioned alterations," found that "Nevertheless, it is possible to feel, after frequent hearings and examinations of both versions, that the case against Rimsky has been overstated," and that the differ-

*I have not discovered the source of Newman's observation, either. —*Ed.*

ences in the *Farewell and Death of Boris* "are comparatively small."* Equally surprising was Andrew Porter's statement more than twenty years later that his hearings of the various musical texts used at different times in the Covent Garden staging of *Boris*—including not only Musorgsky's and Rimsky's but a combination of the two—had "prompted no hard, unqualified conclusions" as to which should be used, instead of the conclusion one would have expected of him, that only Musorgsky's could legitimately be used.**

Moreover, only a minority of opera house directors and conductors—Toscanini, amazingly, not among them—has understood, first, that no matter how effective, the Rimsky recomposition of Musorgsky's work was impermissible, and, further, that the effectiveness Rimsky achieved was not the effect Musorgsky intended. What, for example, Rimsky's orchestral brilliance made more effective was the Coronation scene as *he* perceived it, not the scene as Musorgsky perceived it, whose drab orchestral coloring was to convey his perception of the coronation of Boris as no more a genuine occasion for the down-trodden Russian people's shouts of joy than his refusal of the throne in the first scene had been a genuine occasion for that people's visibly coerced pleas to him to accept it.

Thus it was that although Musorgsky's original had been known since 1924, and the full orchestral score had been available since 1928, the Rimsky version continued to be given at the Metropolitan until 1953. In that year Rudolf Bing was persuaded by the conductors Fritz Stiedry and Max Rudolf, his musical advisors at that time, to produce Musorgsky's own work; but having no understanding in the matter he accepted Stiedry's contention that Musorgsky's orchestration needed strengthening to give it carrying power in a theater as large as the old Metropolitan—something I could have disputed, since I had had no difficulty in hearing it in the Academy of Music when Leopold Stokowski had performed the original *Boris* in Philadelphia in 1929. And with these occasional Rimskyisms in the orchestra-

---

*Edward Sackville-West and Desmond Shawe-Taylor, *The Record Guide* (London, 1951).
**Andrew Porter, *"Boris Redivivus,"* in *The New Yorker*, December 30, 1974; reprinted in *Music of Three Seasons* (New York, 1978).

tion the public heard a little less than the entirety of Musorgsky's own work. But worse was to come a few years later, when in 1960–61, with Stiedry gone and Erich Leinsdorf advising Bing, this version was replaced by one coarsened and vulgarized by Shostakovich's re-orchestration and partial recomposition of the work. And when, still later, the singer Nicolai Ghiaurov in 1968 made it a condition of his participation in a new staging of *Boris*, Bing announced a return to the Rimsky version. The conductor Rafael Kubelik was one of the few who understood; and having performed Musorgsky's own revised 1872 version in Munich, he reinstated it at the Metropolitan for a new production in 1974.

Thus it was, also, that should you have wished to hear the original *Boris* on records you would not have found any of it before 1956 or the complete opera until 1978. In 1953, in the very year that the Metropolitan at last produced Musorgsky's original, HMV in England, making its first complete recording of the work, recorded the Rimsky version; and an English reviewer thought this was justified by the fact that the Rimsky version was the one most people knew—which was like arguing against publishing the accurate texts of Shelley's poems because most people knew the inaccurate ones. Thus it was, also, that Columbia in the United States, which at the time had the recording rights for the Metropolitan's productions, decided not to record its production of the original *Boris*, leaving it to Victor to make available the Book-of-the-Month Club's Metropolitan Opera Record Club recording of parts of the 1956 Metropolitan performance, selected with poor judgment and sung in disturbingly poor English. [Other recordings of the Rimsky version followed, notably one by von Karajan, who staged and recorded Rimsky's *Boris* with Ghiaurov in Salzburg in 1966. As for Stokowski, who had conducted Musorgsky's original in concert in 1929, only a year after the full score was published, evidently the composer's own version was something to make a pilgrimage to only while it was in the news, for he never performed it again. Instead he put together what he called a "Symphonic Synthesis"—highlights for orchestra in a scoring of his own—and played and recorded that several times. And when, in 1951, he recorded vocal excerpts from the opera itself he used Rimsky's version, not Musorgsky's.]

Rimsky-Korsakov's injury to Musorgsky was not just that he

made his falsification rather than Musorgsky's own work what most of the world knows as *Boris Godunov* to this very day; it was also that he gave the world the idea of Musorgsky as a clumsy dilettante. This has caused some people, when they have heard Musorgsky's own work, to hear only a dilettante's inept crudities. But I contend that to hear *Boris* as it was actually written is to be moved not only by the moment-to-moment invention as such, but by its demonstration of extraordinary powers operating with an incandescent adequacy for every dramatic point they are called on to deal with. They are the powers which, for example, transform the brutal four-note ostinato figure accompanying the bailiff's entrance in the first scene into the lamenting ostinato figure of the introduction to the St. Basil's scene, and which then give us the Simpleton's song and the chorus's plea for alms. And I believe that if we had only this scene to judge by, or only the scene of Boris's death, or only the final scene in the forest of Kromy, we would have to say the man who produced it was a great master. It doesn't matter that much of the scene in Pimen's cell is boring, or that much of the scene in Marina's garden is tawdry: they don't alter the quality of what is heard in the two scenes of the Prologue, the scene in Boris's apartment, and above all the three scenes of the last act.

This brings us to the work's one difficulty, presented by the fact that Musorgsky's own score exists in two versions—the one completed in 1869 and the revision of it completed in 1872. And in this connection, a distinction must be made between the changes in the 1872 version that Musorgsky made to satisfy the imperial opera administration that had rejected the 1869 version, and the changes that represented his own second thoughts. It was to satisfy the opera administration that he added the two Polish scenes, with a female character, Marina, for the false Dmitri to be romantically involved with; it was his own second thoughts that impelled him to rewrite much of the act in Boris's Kremlin apartment, to compose the new scene in the forest of Kromy as the opera's new conclusion, and—making room for the additional scene—to omit the scene before the cathedral of St. Basil, transferring its episode of the Simpleton tormented by the boys to the Kromy scene.

Recognizing that Marina is a fifth wheel in the essential dramatic action, and recognizing also the musical inferiority of the Polish scenes, listeners should feel free to skip them. But conductors, recognizing the musical quality and dramatic importance of the St. Basil scene, should restore it, and with it—transferred back from the Kromy scene—the episode of the Simpleton tormented by the boys. Which doesn't rule out a concert performance of the more somber 1869 version of the act in Boris's apartment, or its inclusion as an extra selection on a record, to satisfy interest in what Musorgsky produced originally.

What is amazing about *Boris* in addition to the music itself is the fact that the first version was completed by a man of thirty, the second by a man of thirty-two, who had had no formal, professional musical education, and who, it is relevant to note, had had an onset of delirium tremens at twenty-six. But what is perhaps even more amazing about his next opera, *Khovanshchina,* whose writing takes off from that in the St. Basil and Kromy scenes in *Boris,* is that it was produced in the later years of this man's life— years of steady personal disintegration and dissipation, of increasing sordidness and disorder in his daily existence, in which nevertheless his mind managed to carry on, in some inner refuge, a disciplined creative activity that put together, bit by bit, richly elaborated works like *Pictures at an Exhibition,* the *Sunless* song-cycle, *Songs and Dances of Death* and *Khovanshchina.*

But with effort concentrated on the rescue of *Boris,* there hasn't been an awareness that the *Khovanshchina* we have heard is also a product of Rimsky's rewriting. Paul Lamm, who gave us the edition of the original Musorgsky texts of *Boris,* produced a similar edition of *Khovanshchina* in 1931. In his preface Lamm says Musorgsky left the work completed in piano and vocal score with these few inconsequential exceptions: he didn't produce either of the conclusions for Act 2 that he discussed in letters; he left only the vocal parts of the scene of Marfa and Andrei in the last act; and he didn't place a double bar at the end of the final chorus, which may mean that he planned something further. Lamm also informs us that some years later the scene of Marfa and Andrei was harmonized in accordance with Musorgsky's practice elsewhere by B. W. Assafiev, who also orchestrated the portions of the work Musorgsky left unscored.

But at the time of Musorgsky's death, someone had to put *Khovanshchina* in order and complete it; and Rimsky-Korsakov, who did this, also inflicted on it the same damaging "correction" as on *Boris*. First, cuts: Rimsky justifies his having "eliminate[d] certain passages which . . . were musically weak" by the fact that Musorgsky himself had begun to cut the work, and by the purpose of "making the work suitable for stage performance"; but what was permitted to Musorgsky was not permitted to Rimsky, and the work would have been made suitable for stage performance by an edition of the complete text that allowed each producer to decide for himself how much to use. Moreover, as it happened, a Vanguard record years ago offered two excerpts from Musorgsky's original version that I thought were magnificent music; and not surprisingly all of the first and part of the second were among the passages Rimsky had eliminated because he found them musically weak.

Next, and worse, Rimsky says he "had occasion here and there to put a little order into the choral parts, and to retouch the solo parts now and then, as they were written somewhat unevenly by Musorgsky himself"; but Musorgsky's writing needed no such putting in order or retouching, and the real reason for Rimsky's tampering with it was simply that he liked it better his way, and having been unable to get Musorgsky to change it when alive he changed it himself after Musorgsky's death. And the changes—in melody, harmony, key and rhythm—are more numerous and substantial than Rimsky's words "a little order" and "retouch" convey.

Because Rimsky published his revision it was the version that had to be used in performance for fifty years, after which opera-house routine and inertia combined with lack of understanding and conscience to keep it from being replaced by the Musorgsky original when this was published in 1931. Hearing Rimsky's *Khovanshchina* again recently, after many years and without the Lamm score, I was struck by the Musorgskyan character and expressiveness that the music retains even as adulterated by Rimsky—in particular the expressive power of the arioso writing in which so much of the dramatic dialogue proceeds. But that power would be even greater with the adulteration removed.

The writing in *The Fair at Sorochinsk*, as against *Boris* and

Khovanshchina, is that of a comedy, and is a distillation from Ukrainian melody, with (in Musorgsky's words) "shades of nuance and idiosyncrasies characterizing the musical outlines of the Little Russian language." Most important, it is the work of Musorgsky's last years, the product of fully matured powers which operate with absolute and impressive assurance in the engaging melodic writing and the superb recitative. Musorgsky left this opera almost completed in piano and vocal score, with a few parts orchestrated; and several composers have at various times completed and orchestrated it. Concerning a present-day version by the composer Vissarion Shebalin, Lamm tells us that he scrupulously "[based] his work, wherever possible, on Musorgsky's own material and song-jottings," and similarly orchestrated the opera in accordance with Musorgsky's own practice in the few orchestrated parts he left.

The writing in the scenes for the opera *Salammbô* that Musorgsky began to write in 1863 and left uncompleted in 1866 is similar in idiom and expressive power to the writing in *Boris;* and in fact one chorus develops the principal musical idea of Boris's first monologue in the Kremlin scene, and another uses one of the ideas of Boris's farewell to his son. Musorgsky orchestrated only three of the scenes and left the others in piano-and-voice form with a few indications for instrumentation; four of the choral pieces have been transcribed, orchestrated and altered by Rimsky-Korsakov.

[Of the uncompleted opera *The Marriage* (1868) only the first act is by Musorgsky.]

Regardless of what some have said about Musorgsky's ability to write for orchestra, his contemporaries were unanimous about his powers as a pianist, especially in dramatically and pictorially imaginative invention such as we hear in *Pictures at an Exhibition.* For many years I knew this work only in Maurice Ravel's orchestral transcription, which I took for granted was more effective than the original for piano—accepting too uncritically the prevailing idea of the time that the orchestra did everything better. And I retain a vivid recollection of my amazement when at last I heard the original played, and discovered how completely achieved an imaginative creation it is. In this work of his maturity—it is dated 1874—Musorgsky writes at every point, in every detail of melody, harmony and figuration, with the unfailing assurance of a man who is absolute master of his style; and in his musical translations of *Goldenberg and Schmuyle, Catacombs,* and *Con mortuis in lingua morta* he writes as a musical artist of the highest rank.

Moreover, listening with knowledge of the piano original I was now able to appreciate fully not only the imaginative insight and skill exhibited in Ravel's orchestral equivalents of Musorgsky's writing for the piano, but his artistic rectitude in restricting himself to those equivalents, which made his version almost unique among such orchestral translations. I had thought the use of the saxophone for the melody of *The Old Castle* was the one exceptional instance of a desire to shock; but when the passage was played on the piano, there, to my amazement, was the timbre that called for the saxophone. Even one departure from Musorgsky's piano score turned out to have an explanation: the notes C, D flat, B flat, B flat of the rich Goldenberg's outburst of arrogantly abrupt dismissal at the end of *Goldenberg and Schmuyle,* in the Lamm edition published in 1930, were changed to C, D flat, C, B flat in the Ravel transcription. It was some years later that I found this substitution of C for Musorgsky's B flat in the published piano version available to Ravel in 1923—the version edited for publication (in 1886) by Rimsky-Korsakov, for whom the B flat had been a Musorgsky crudity that he corrected with the C. And with knowledge of Musorgsky's and Ravel's achievements I could appreciate fully how badly the piece had been defaced by its other transcribers and arrangers—Stokowski, Vladimir Horowitz, Lucien Caillet and Harold Bauer—who took Rimsky's idea of Musorgsky as a dilettante as an excuse to do with his music what Rimsky had.

For the rest, Musorgsky's only major orchestral piece is *Night on Bald Mountain,* of which the composing and scoring were finished in 1867, but which was not published as Musorgsky first wrote it until 1968, and of which, for more than a hundred years, only a later Musorgsky revision "orchestrated" by Rimsky was performed. The two versions are like two different works—one offering Rimsky's fine-sounding and effective reworking of Musorgsky's writing, the other the daringly original and powerful writing of Musorgsky's 1867 piece.

There are in addition several unfamiliar smaller pieces, among them two for orchestra and untouched by Rimsky—an attractive but derivative and therefore uncharacteristic Scherzo in B flat, composed by the nineteen-year-old Musorgsky in 1858; and a Triumphal March *The Capture of Kars* composed in 1880.

Finally, Musorgsky's high-level creative achievements include some of his songs: notably the seldom-heard *Sunless* cycle, with perhaps the finest examples of his fully developed style of subtly inflected vocal declamation, and the better-known *Songs and Dances of Death*. But the cycle *The Nursery*, and his individual songs—among them *Cradle Song, The Magpie, Night, Little Star, The Ragamuffin, On the Dnieper, Pride, Ballade, King Saul, The Flea* and *The Classic*—also reveal how sensitized his writing for voice and piano is to the words of the texts.

Modest Musorgsky (1839–1881)

16

Other Music of the Nineteenth Century

In contrast to Brahms who produced bad music in the attempt to write greater than he felt, Chopin made a great art of writing small poetic pieces for the piano. I speak, I should say, of the music scraped clean of a hundred years' encrustation of performers' affected, mannered phrasing that has made it seem sentimental and morbid. Even so my use of the term *great* may be questioned—though I don't think there would be any question about the art exhibited in the richly elaborated style of writing and its employment of the resources of the piano, or in the beautiful and subtle invention of pieces like the Impromptu Op. 36, the Nocturne Op. 27 No. 2, the *Berceuse* (with some of Chopin's most exquisite writing), the Barcarolle, some of the Mazurkas—the art exhibited most strikingly perhaps in the Preludes and Etudes, in each of which a piano figuration exercising the hand in a particular segment of piano technique provides the terms with which Chopin creates a piece of music as exquisitely thought and formed as any other. But I think *great* is correctly applied to the works in which there are not only beauty and subtlety but magnificence and power—the Nocturne Op. 48 No. 1, the Polonaises Opp. 44 and 53, the Sonata No. 2 (whose opening movement reveals Chopin's innovative mastery of sonata-allegro form), the Sonata No. 3, the Concerto No. 1, the Ballades Nos. 1 (an astounding early achievement) and 4, the Polonaise-Fantaisie Op. 61. These, in contrast to his innumerable exquisitely wrought small pieces, offer writing that is structurally and expressively large in scale. What his matured powers achieve in the rarely performed Ballade No. 4—the succession of elaborations of its initial ideas—make it not only the most extraordinary and impressive of the four Ballades but one of the two finest of all his large-scale works—the other being the Polonaise-Fantaisie. As for the other works of Chopin's maturity, for solo piano there are the Fantaisie Op. 49—one of the great works, the Fantaisie-Impromptu Op. 66, the Scherzos and Waltzes, the *Andante Spianato and Grand Polonaise* Op. 22 (of which the lovely Andante is the most interesting part), a fine posthumously published Sostenuto in E flat, the rarely heard Bolero and Tarantelle, and the Concerto No. 2—less uniformly beautiful than No. 1, but with a lovely slow movement that contains an unusual episode of powerful declamation. And there is the seldom-heard Sonata Op. 65 for Cello and Piano, in which the operation from the very first phrases is that of a mind distinguished and reserved, and which requires more than one hearing for full appreciation of the rich detail, the organization, and the beauty of the first movement— the most impressive of the four.

The showy *Allegro de Concert* Op. 46 for piano and orchestra, and the Rondo Op. 73 for two pianos, I find uninteresting.

Of the piano pieces he composed between the ages of seven and sixteen the interesting ones are those—beginning with the Polonaise in D minor he wrote when he was twelve—in which one first hears his characteristic ornamented melodic style, used effectively but without the later enriching harmonic subtlety. Surprisingly, the unfamiliar Sonata No. 1 Op. 4 that he composed when he was sixteen is not only uncharacteristic but uninteresting except for its Minuetto. But the Mazurkas in G major and B flat, Waltzes in C, Polonaise in B flat (*Adieu*), and Rondo *à la Mazur* written in the same period are recognizably Chopin's. And the pieces that followed up to 1831—*Souvenir de Paganini*, Mazurkas in G and D, Polonaise in G flat, Waltzes in E and E minor, a *Lento con gran espressione* in C sharp minor—reveal Chopin operating with complete assurance and power in his individual style.

And there are, finally, the posthumously collected songs that Chopin wrote between the ages of eighteen and thirty-five, whose melodies are in the simple folksong-like style of those in some of his mazurkas, and whose piano parts also are simple, with none of the florid passages of Chopin's writing for piano solo.

We hear another richly elaborated style of writing for the piano used with superb effect by Schumann in his sets of imaginative pieces for solo piano—*Papillons, Carnaval, Kinderszenen,* the *Fantasiestücke* Op. 12; parts (the episodes in fast tempo, fewer of the sentimental ones in slow tempo) of *Kreisleriana* and *Davidsbündlertänze;* the remarkable *Vogel als Prophet* from *Waldszenen;* the bravura *Toccata;* the Variations on the name *Abegg.* And we hear it in some of his large-scale solo works—the *Études symphoniques,* the Sonatas Opp. 11 and 22, the Fantasia Op. 17, and the Piano Concerto.*

And this writing for piano contributes much to the effect of some of the finest songs we have—all of the *Dichterliebe* cycle, which is Schumann's towering masterpiece; parts of *Liederkreis* Op. 39 (*Mondnacht* and *Waldesgespräch* especially, but also *Auf einer Burg, Zwielicht, Frühlingsnacht* and the two versions of *In der Fremde*); parts of *Myrthen* (*Der Nussbaum* and *Du bist wie eine Blume* especially, but also *Die Lotusblume, Frühlingsnacht* and *Widmung*); and, among the single songs, *Aufträge, Loreley, Der Hans und die Grete* (No. 1 of *Der arme Peter*), *Alte Laute, Ständchen, Die Kartenlegerin,* and others that are not the incandescent writing of *Dichterliebe* but the interesting operation of the same mind—*Das verlassene Mägdlein, Die Waise, Die Blume der Ergebung,* and *Frühlingslied.* Less valuable are the songs of the

* It might be added that the composer of these pieces is entitled to have his second thoughts about them accepted by performers. In the familiar second edition of *Davidsbündlertänze,* Schumann added a number of repeats and made a few minor changes in harmony, chord-writing, and directions for performance. And listening to the earlier one I am not persuaded, as some players are, that his revisions were damaging, and that the first version is the right one to play. So with the first, manuscript version of the concluding movement of the Fantasia: it ends with a repetition of the passage from Beethoven's song cycle *An die ferne Geliebte* with which Schumann ended the first movement; and not only do I find it understandable that Schumann later should have decided to have the dreamlike concluding movement maintain the style of its flow to the end, but listening to the original version I feel that Schumann's decision to remove the passage by Beethoven produced an ending better suited to what it ends. And by the same reasoning I must regret the inclusion by some players of the five variations that Schumann decided to omit from the published edition of the *Études symphoniques.* —*B. H. H.*

Frauenliebe und -Leben cycle (though their poor quality may be concealed by singing that is as deeply affecting as Lotte Lehmann's used to be); *Liederkreis* Op. 24 (the earlier and less interesting of the two cycles with that name); and the mellifluously sentimental duets (with the exception of the vivacious *Unterm Fenster*).

I find Schumann's other writing inferior: the remaining piano pieces; the works for solo instruments with orchestra; the setting for solo voices, chorus and orchestra of passages from Goethe's *Faust;* the orchestral music (though there are some beautiful pages—the introduction of the Symphony No. 4 and the second and third movements in which this introduction recurs, the slow movement of the Symphony No. 2, and parts of the *Manfred* Overture). Of least consequence is the chamber music—with the exception of the popular and enjoyable Piano Quintet and the Piano Trio Op. 80. Negligible, too, are a number of feeble works of various kinds that convey the mental deterioration and failing artistic powers of Schumann's later years.

What Schumann's songs begin, Hugo Wolf's continue—which is to say that Wolf's writing for the piano, in a style more developed even than Schumann's, contributes even more to the effect of the song, and indeed is often so integrated with the vocal part as to provide the context essential to its continuing sense. Wolf's susceptibility to the stimulation of poetry led him to write almost nothing but songs, and was responsible for what is so remarkable about them—the vocal writing that is like an extension of the words around which the music shapes itself as it points up their meaning. This is true of all the songs; what is true only of some is that the progression which is so remarkably integrated with the poem is in addition a moving or attractive piece of music.

Among the best, then, are: from the Spanish Songbook—*Nun wandre, Maria, Die ihr schwebet, Ach, des Knaben Augen, Herr, was trägt der Boden hier, In dem Schatten meiner Locken* and *Auf dem grünen Balkon;* from the Italian Songbook—*Nun lass uns Frieden schliessen, Auch kleine Dinge, Und steht ihr früh, Gesegnet sei, Und willst du deinen Liebsten sterben sehen, Du denkst mit einem Fädchen mich zu fangen, Ihr jungen Leute* and the ironic *Du sagst mir dass ich keine Fürsten sei;* of the Mörike songs—*Lebe wohl, In der Frühe, Fussreise, Auf einer Wanderung, Auf ein altes Bild, Gebet* and *Zum neuen Jahr;* of the Goethe songs—*Phänomen, Anakreon's Grab* and Mignon's *Kennst du das Land?;* of the Eichendorff songs—*Verschwiegene Liebe* and *Heimweh;* of the Keller songs—*Wie glänzt der helle Mond;* and of the other single songs—*Andenken* and *Frohe Bottschaft.*

The vocal writing in Wolf's one completed opera, *Der Corregidor,* shapes itself around the German words to point up their sense in the same fashion; and it is writing I enjoy more in the opera than in many of the songs. Wolf also produced two good works for string quartet—a seldom-played Quartet in D minor, composed between the ages of eighteen and twenty-four, whose style is remarkably individual, engaging and interesting, and also remarkably unrelated to what one hears in his songs; and the charming and better-known *Italian Serenade* (of which he made a skillful orchestral version as well). Of less interest is his only major work for large orchestra, the symphonic poem *Penthesilea.*

In Mendelssohn we have another minor master who—working on a small scale of emotion and texture—produced the magical overture and the other exquisite pieces for *A Midsummer Night's Dream,* the delightful *Italian* Symphony, the charming and graceful *Scotch* Symphony (with an especially good scherzo and finale), the Violin Concerto (with an especially fine opening movement), the Octet for strings, and three fine overtures: the imaginative *Fingal's Cave* (or *Hebrides*), *Ruy Blas,* and *Fair Melusine*—the last with an exquisite opening section. Mendelssohn's other works—the symphonies, the overture *Calm Sea and Prosperous Voyage,* the piano and organ pieces, the insipid oratorios, the chamber music, most of the songs (though one, *Neue Liebe,* is charmingly reminiscent of the music for *A Midsummer Night's Dream*)—I find inconsequential.

Contemporary with Mendelssohn, Chopin and Schumann was Liszt, whose compositions, however, in whatever form and by whatever title, I would neglect—the piano pieces, most of them a characteristic mixture of the pretentious, the pianistically showy, and the pretty-pretty; the appallingly tasteless transcriptions of Schubert's songs and "paraphrases" of the music of others; and the bombastic orchestral and choral works—including the *Faust Symphony*, whose first movement's few impressive details and second movement's few lovely ones aren't enough to make one willing to endure the long-winded banality and grandiloquence of the rest.

And at the opposite pole from Wolf—a composer mostly of concentrated small pieces—is Bruckner, whose symphonies reveal a yearning for monumental utterance without any capacity for the sustained thinking that must go into large-scale form— without even Brahms's ability, by the exercise of technical skill, to achieve the mere external appearance of a continuous musical progression. Bruckner's principle of large-scale construction seems to have been to keep shoveling in chunks of material until the desired huge dimensions had been reached, making no connection between the details and sections of a movement other than the one he imposed arbitrarily of succession in time. And the quality of these details and sections—the attempts at momentous profundity by a mind capable only of dull commonplace, the laboring after tenderness and warmth—make his symphonies unendurable. However, in his sacred music—in the *Te Deum* especially, and in the Mass in E minor (but not in the uninteresting Mass in D minor)—where the substance of the music comes out of what Bruckner feels deeply about the meaning of the words, and where this substance forms itself around the structure of the text, he produces fine-sounding, effective writing and impressive, moving works.

In opera Bellini exhibits his extraordinary gift for melodic writing in the purely lyrical *La Sonnambula*—in the beauty and the expressive poignance and eloquence of Elvino's *Tutto è sciolto* and Amina's *Ah, non credea mirarti*—and in his last opera, *I Puritani*, which exhibits his developed powers not only in the melodic writing that attains its highest point in the arias *A te, o cara* and the even greater *Qui la voce*, but also in its dramatically meaningful orchestral writing—e.g. the details of the passage from Elvira's *Morte!* to Arturo's *Credeasi, misera!*—and in the ensemble writing that elaborates points of climax most impressively in the finale of Act 1, and in the climactic ensemble initiated by *Credeasi, misera!* in the last act.

Though the early *Il Pirata* doesn't attain the level of these later works, it reveals Bellini as an accomplished practitioner of the style of his period who at times enobles that style—for example in the opening sextet of the first-act finale, Imogene's replies to Ernesto in their second-act duet—especially the wonderfully changed music for the passage beginning with *ma qual s'ama un uom sepulto*—and her aria *Col sorriso d'innocenza* near the end. *Norma* I find less interesting than either *I Puritani* or *La Sonnambula,* but it has the beautiful arias *Teneri figli* and *Deh! Non voleli vittime,* the duet *In mio mano,* and what is perhaps the finest, and certainly the most famous, of Bellini's melodic structures, the aria *Casta diva. Beatrice di Tenda* and the unfamiliar *I Capuleti e i Montecchi* are lesser works. Bellini also wrote an interesting Oboe Concerto—with characteristic melodic writing and a charming polonaise—and a number of attractive songs.

Donizetti, too, reveals himself as a superb melodist—in the tragic *Lucia di Lammermoor,* in his masterpiece of operatic comedy, *Don Pasquale,* and in the comic *L'Elisir d'amore.* For *La Fille du régiment,* another comedy, Donizetti doesn't provide writing as good as that of *Don Pasquale* and *L'Elisir;* but his lyrical gift produces two beautiful arias for the title role, and there is a charming trio in the second act.

This is to speak only of the best-known works. Since the 1950s, when Maria Callas created new interest in the operas of Donizetti and Bellini with her singing of their difficult vocal parts, works unheard for decades have been revived for particular singers and recorded. Some of the unfamiliar operas of Donizetti have turned out to be merely products of his efficient use of his style, as *Roberto Devereux* does in all but the beautiful and subtly phrased melodic writing of Elizabeth's *Vivi, ingrato* at the beginning of the last scene. But on occasion they have offered the operation of his impressive powers in vocal and orchestral writing which has astonished one with the imaginative freedom, the affecting expressiveness, the dramatic force of his invention.

Lucrezia Borgia is one of these. Except for the *Brindisi*—a set piece in bravura style for its special purpose, and the least valuable music in the opera—the characters sing melodic writing of high musical quality, with intensifying florid elaboration at cadences, that amazes one with its Verdian dramatic force in the second-act confrontation of Lucrezia, her husband and her son, and moves one with its expressiveness in the concluding duet of Lucrezia and her son—the aria of the dying Gennaro in this scene being the finest piece in the opera.

The early *Anna Bolena* is another work of this kind—whose impressive quality and freedom of vocal and orchestral writing accounts for its having been the opera that established Donizetti as a composer in Italy. *Maria Stuarda,* though not as powerful as *Lucrezia Borgia,* continues the interesting features of that earlier work—the occasional replacement of recitative by stretches of dramatically expressive arioso, the use of the orchestra to comment expressively on the vocal melody. *Gemma di Vergy* and *La Favorita* are both characteristic—the first in the powers that operate with assurance to provide the dramatic action with expressively moving music; the second in several outstandingly beautiful melodic structures besides, among them the tenor aria *Spirito gentil.* Donizetti's one-act *melodramma giocoso, Il Campanello di notte farsa,* offers—in addition to a large amount of uninteresting recitative—several vocal pieces in serious, mock-serious and comic styles that are quite good—the beginning of the final trio being especially impressive. But in *Linda di Chamounix,* though one is struck repeatedly by details of developed orchestral writing that one doesn't expect to hear in an Italian opera produced in 1842, one is not struck by outstanding examples of Donizetti's melodic writing.

As with Donizetti and Bellini, so with Rossini. It was not very long ago that the public's acquaintance with Rossini encompassed *The Barber of Seville* and a few overtures, of which even *The Barber* was enjoyed but not highly respected. Since the 1950s, recordings have enabled the public to hear other works that have revealed Rossini as a composer of far greater talent and achievement than he had been credited with. In operatic comedy *La Cenerentola* turns out to have even more impressive lyric, comic and bravura-style writing than *The Barber*—with the florid passages sometimes breathtaking in their controlled extravagance. *L'Italiana in Algeri* and *Il Turco in Italia,* written just before these, exhibit a youthful freshness of invention in the lyric, comic, and florid bravura styles that will rise to incandescence later; but though his melodic style doesn't yet achieve the great writing of the arias of *The Barber* and *La Cenerentola,* he is already capable in *L'Italiana* of the delightful comic writing of the duet *Se inclinassi a prender moglie,* the quintet *Ti presento di mia man,* the ensembles of the first-act finale; and in *Il Turco* of the several fine concerted numbers and of Fiorilla's lovely simple song *Se il zefiro si posa.* And *Le Comte Ory,* Rossini's last comedy—which was followed by his last opera, *William Tell*—exhibits, in place of the earlier bravura writing, a delicacy and grace, a refinement of melody, harmony, orchestration and texture, that are surprising and delightful.

Comedy appears to have been Rossini's major gift, but listening to *William Tell,* the serious work with which he chose to end his career as composer of opera, one is impressed by the assurance and effectiveness with which he writes for characters and situations so different from those of his comedies. Concerning Matilda's second-act aria *Selva opaca* Berlioz observed correctly that "Rossini has . . . written few pieces as elegant, as fresh, as distinguished in their melody, and as ingenious in their modulations as this one . . . the immense merit of the vocal part and the harmony [being matched by the] style of accompaniment." And the passages which follow this one—the duet of Matilda and Arnold, the trio of Tell, Walter and Arnold, the choruses of the three cantons—deserve Berlioz's description of them as the marvel that follows marvel.*

William Tell is Rossini's major serious opera, but in the earlier *Otello* one is impressed right at the start by the power of the slow opening section of the overture (and surprised by the Allegro section, which is in the absurdly unsuitable style of his comedies— the opera's one example of Rossinian carelessness), by the orchestra's expressive support of the vocal parts, and by the melodic beauty and the dramatic force of much of that vocal writing itself—the writing for Desdemona, the florid writing for Otello and Rodrigo, some of it rising to sensational points in the high tenor range. *L'Assédio di Corinto* also has some superb writing, as does *Semiramide,* a work in which every character sings in every situation in an extreme florid vocal style not for expressive effect

---

*Hector Berlioz, *"Rossini's 'William Tell,'"* *Gazette Musicale de Paris*—I, 1834; reprinted in *Source Readings in Music History,* Oliver Strunk, ed. (New York, 1950).

but for spectacular vocal display. *La Donna del lago* is distinguished, also, but the refinements and subtleties in this work—which for one musicologist constituted an important demonstration of the powers as a composer of serious music that he contended were what impressed Rossini's contemporaries more than his gift for comic opera—are in reality more impressive in the comedy *Le Comte Ory.*

As for the earliest works, the amazingly precocious Rossini could, at the age of twenty-five, write the serious music of *Elisabetta, regina d'Inghilterra* with assured competence, but not the dazzling incandescence of his writing in *The Barber* a year later. Likewise in *Mosè in Egitto* he operates as an accomplished composer in a style in which he produces on the one hand, for the scenes concerned with religious conflict, writing that has dignity and solemnity but not grandeur, and on the other hand, for the scenes concerned with human emotions, writing that only rarely—for example in Sinaide's aria near the end of Act Two—rises above the routine to an approximation of what he achieved in *William Tell.* Rossini's early conventional writing is to be heard as well in *Armida* and *Tancredi* (which seems not just conventional but uninteresting), and, surprisingly, in the comedy *La Scala di seta,* whose familiar Overture is as delightful as the others while the unfamiliar little opera itself turns out to be far below the later works in quality and quite dull.

Among his non-operatic works there are the twelve-year-old Rossini's six Sonatas for two violins, cello and bass, in which it is astonishing to hear the operatic style of his maturity—for example in the amusing details in the opening movement of No. 3 and the grandly sustained operatic cantilena in the middle movement. There is the comparatively late and only recently reassembled comic cantata for fifteen voices, *Il Viaggio a Reims,* which Rossini wrote for the celebration of the coronation of Charles X in 1825 and withdrew after the few performances of that occasion, but parts of which he used in 1828 in *Le Comte Ory.* And there are the many small vocal and instrumental and piano pieces—some slight, some humorous, some exquisite—that Rossini wrote in the years after *William Tell* in which he produced no more operas.

The kind of engaging melodies in those little vocal and instrumental pieces aren't expressively suitable for certain of the texts to which they are applied in the late *Petite Messe solenelle,* however—the soprano solo to the words of the *Crucifixus* being only the most absurd example of this incongruity. But the work also has several sections that are more suitable and impressive— the *Gloria,* the *Cum Sanctu Spiritu,* the *Et Resurrexit* (though even this last ends with a grossly inappropriate treatment of the final line *In unum Deum credo*); and the expressiveness of the attractive melodic writing is enhanced occasionally by unusual harmonic progressions. (For the first performance in a private home Rossini wrote the instrumental accompaniment for two pianos and harmonium; later, in anticipation of public performance, he scored it for full orchestra; and the orchestral version, not the less effective "original" version, is the one that should be performed.) The less familiar *Missa di Gloria* is, like the *Requiems* of Mozart and Verdi, an effective setting of the sacred text in the normal musical language and style of Rossini's other music. And there is superb writing in the *Stabat Mater,* notably in the last four sections.

Meyerbeer, less gifted than Rossini, and whose music is encountered less often today than it was in the nineteenth and early part of the twentieth centuries, was nevertheless the man who succeeded Rossini in Paris as the most celebrated opera composer of his time. His best-known operas, *Les Huguenots* and *Le Prophète,* are the works not of a great writer but a craftsman skilled in providing the varieties of music for the situations, actions and spectacle of a "grand opera"—writing that is effective for its every purpose, agreeable to listen to, and at times moving. They include music for the spectacular singing that was one of the features of productions at the Paris Opera, and these works were part of the standard repertory in which the legendary singers Bernard Shaw wrote about were heard at Covent Garden and the Metropolitan Opera before the 1920s. Today the occasional complete recording provides an opportunity to hear the skillful way Meyerbeer filled out the five-act structure of these works of his period around the arias and duets familiar now almost exclusively from the records made by those great singers of the past—Hempel, Destinn, Jörn, Slezak, Caruso and the others.

More engaging are the products of a French minor master,

Bizet—his opera *Carmen* (in its original form with spoken dialogue, which adds greatly to the dramatic effect, as against the version in which the dialogue was replaced by the recitatives of Guiraud); his music for *L'Arlésienne;* the suite from *La Jolie Fille de Perth;* his Symphony in C; *Jeux d'enfants* for two pianos; and a strange and fascinating solo piano piece, titled *Variations chromatiques,* which nobody would guess was written by the composer of *Carmen.*

Another French minor master of fascinating originality of mind and style is Chabrier—not in the *España* by which he is known almost exclusively, but in the *Dix Pièces pittoresques* for piano (four of which he made into the *Suite pastorale* for orchestra); the *Trois Valses romantiques* for two pianos, especially the affecting No. 3; the smaller-scale *Marche joyeuse* and *Fête polonaise;* and the skillfully fashioned and enjoyable comic opera, *Le Roi malgré lui.* However, while Chabrier's one-act operetta, *Une Éducation manquée,* has a few pretty tunes, one hears the distinctive Chabrier mind and matured skill operating only in the final duet.

Among the good works of another minor French composer, Lalo, are his *Symphonie espagnole* and Overture to *Le Roi d'Ys* (the Concerto for cello is not interesting). And I have had much enjoyment from Delibes's music for his ballet *Coppélia.* On the other hand most of Fauré's suave and pretty music remains something I don't respond to. The little I do care for doesn't include his opera, *Pénélope,* which offers expertly devised orchestral and vocal writing that achieves statement of the sense of the words and action and nothing more—not the writing that a Gluck or a Berlioz would make moving in addition. But parts of Fauré's incidental music for *Pelléas et Mélisande* are exquisite and hauntingly lovely, the *Nocturne* in *Shylock* is marvelously, unexpectedly expressive, and his *Requiem,* too, is not only beautifully contrived, but, in its quiet way, deeply felt.

The slight, facile works of Saint-Saëns may be left unheard. As for Franck, like Brahms he is most enjoyable when he is least pretentious—in the *Variations symphoniques* for piano and orchestra, and in the symphonic pieces *Les Éolides* and *Psyché* and the String Quartet (though these last three suffer from Franck's repetitive long-windedness). A few other works have good portions as well: the *Morceau symphonique* from his *Rédemption,* the Prelude and Chorale of the *Prelude, Chorale and Fugue* for piano, the second movement of the Symphony in D minor, the introduction to the first movement of the Piano Quintet and its middle movement, and parts of the Sonata for violin and piano. The quiet portions of Franck's Three Chorales for organ also contain some exquisite writing; but even this is repetitious, and in addition there are the bombastic proclamations and affirmations that are hard to take. Moreover, an observation by Tovey—"The saintliness of Franck shines nowhere more brightly than where his music is most *mondaine"*—describes a combination of qualities that you will hear occasionally as well (in the sweet choral portions of *Psyché,* for example) and may not like even in the best works.

The somber opening measures of Gounod's best-known opera, *Faust,* arouse expectations that are disappointed by the mellifluous tunefulness of most of the work that follows. And while Nicolai's *The Merry Wives of Windsor* has a place in history as the source of the musical style of the German operetta, its facile tuneful writing exerts no other claim to our attention. Much better than either of these are Thomas's *Mignon* and Humperdinck's *Hänsel und Gretel.* And Peter Cornelius's *The Barber of Baghdad,* not often performed, turns out to be an engaging German counterpart of Italian operatic comedy, exhibiting his gift for words, which produces amusing German equivalents of Italian patter, his gift for the music that makes the words work effectively, and his ability to write charming melody for the serious moments.

As for operetta, a recording of Johann Strauss II's *Die Fledermaus* a number of years ago by a group of superb Vienna State Opera singers enabled me for the first time to hear the music with the German words that fit so perfectly in sound, in sense, in atmosphere; for the first time to hear the words and music sung in a way that is possible only for people who have been hearing and singing them all their lives; and for the first time, as a result, to understand the love in Germany and Austria for what is in fact a masterpiece of its genre. Strauss's *Gypsy Baron,* though not another *Fledermaus,* has some characteristically charming and lovely music, too. *One Night in Venice* impresses me as being of even lesser stature, though parts of it are engaging.

What is true of Strauss's operettas is true also of those written by the remarkably gifted French composer Offenbach: *La Vie Parisienne, La Périchole,* [and *La Belle Hélène*] are in the special style of a particular French theatrical genre, using characters, situations and ways of thinking, behaving and joking from the French life of its period; and their delightful melodies, amusing lyrics and skillful orchestration are best heard performed by French artists completely familiar with the genre, the life it satirizes, and its style of performance, and who can, moreover, enliven the works with the rhetorical heightening characteristic of the expansive and intensified French style of stage speech.

The Russian nationalists associated with Musorgsky achieved nothing of the stature and power of his works; but the engaging things they did produce are exemplified by Borodin's opera *Prince Igor,* which contains the superb *Polovtsian Dances,* and by his piece *In the Steppes of Central Asia,* but not by his symphonies (the Borodin method of repeating a few attractive themes in a number of different keys doesn't produce much of a symphony) or his quartets. Light but pleasant are Ippolitov-Ivanov's *Caucasian Sketches,* of which I like best *In a Mountain Pass.* More substantial are Rimsky-Korsakov's *Capriccio espagnol, Russian Easter* Overture, and three of his operas: *The Snow Maiden,* the best-known *Le Coq d'or,* and the early *May Night*—which is made enjoyable by its varied writing alternately for the two young lovers, the low-comedy characters out of Gogol, and the fantastic water-sprites. (*Scheherazade* and the *Antar* Symphony are boring.) And earlier there are Glinka's operas *A Life for the Tsar* [and *Russlan and Ludmilla*] and his fine songs.

Even more impressive products of this kind are those of the Czech nationalists. The vein of lovely and richly harmonized melody that we hear in Dvořák's superb *Slavonic Dances* Op. 46 (and in the lesser *Slavonic Dances* Op. 72) provided much of the substance for his chamber music and symphonies. The most impressive works are the Symphony No. 9 (*From the New World*), the *Symphonic Variations* Op. 78, the *Carnival* Overture (whose

quiet interlude is one of the composer's loveliest and most affecting pieces of writing), and the String Quartet Op. 51. Others that
are enjoyable are the Symphonies Nos. 7 and 8 (it is interesting,
moreover, to hear how the Brahmsian details in the Symphony
No. 7 are worked into the flow of engaging writing that is
Dvořák's), the *American Suite* Op. 98b, the suite called *Legends*
Op. 59, the unfamiliar *Czech Suite* Op. 39 (which turns out to be a
much more attractive piece in his nationalist style than the more
familiar bland Serenade for Strings Op. 22), the String Quartet
Op. 96 (*American*), Piano Trio Op. 65, Piano Quintet Op. 81, and
the fine *Gypsy Songs* Op. 55. The other small-scale works are less
interesting; and the *Stabat Mater* illustrates a defect of some of his
large-scale pieces—that each section begins with an impressive
idea that is dwelt on at what becomes excessive length. The
opening movement of the Piano Concerto in G minor, Op. 33, is
one of those, and in the later movements even the substance is
unattractive.

A nationalist source of inspiration similar to Dvořák's fur-
nished Smetana with the melodious substance of his delightful
operatic comedy *The Bartered Bride,* his enjoyable string quartet
From My Life, and two of the symphonic poems in his cycle *Má
Vlast: From Bohemia's Meadows and Fields*—with a magnificent
opening and other lovely pages—and the beautiful *Die Moldau*
(the other pieces in the cycle have only occasional effective
moments).

Finally, at the beginning of the nineteenth century there is
Weber, a minor figure contemporary with Beethoven and Schubert. In the complete opera *Der Freischütz* we hear, in addition to
the well-known overture and arias of Agatha, the other melodic
passages that delighted Berlioz with their freshness, and the
Wolf's Glen scene that was strikingly original in Weber's time and
retains its dramatic power today. In *Oberon,* too, we find a number
of fine pieces in addition to the well-known overture and the aria
Ozean, du Ungeheuer; but these occur at intervals in an enormous
amount of spoken dialogue (German) of a preposterous play.
[Likewise with *Euryanthe.*]

The fresh and individual voice is heard in Weber's symphonies,
also, but speaks more interestingly and impressively in the piano
concertos, the *Konzertstück* for piano and orchestra, the *Invitation*

to the Dance for piano solo (more often played in Berlioz's orchestration), and in the four piano sonatas—especially in the grace and elegance of the lyrical No. 2, parts of the dramatic No. 3, and the wide-ranging No. 4 (one understands Schumann's terms "special" and "melancholy" applied to this work but not the programmatic meaning—a struggle of reason against insanity—which Weber's pupil Benedict claimed to have received from the composer himself). And Weber's voice is heard as well in the beautiful melodic writing in his works for clarinet—the Concerto No. 1, the Grand Duo Concertante Op. 48, Quintet Op. 34, and Seven Variations Op. 33.

Vincenzo Bellini (1801–1835)
Georges Bizet (1838–1875)
Alexander Borodin (1833–1887)
Anton Bruckner (1824–1896)
Emmanuel Chabrier (1841–1894)
Frédéric (Fryderyk) Chopin (1810–1849)
Peter Cornelius (1824–1874)
Léo Delibes (1836–1891)
Gaetano Donizetti (1797–1848)
Antonin Dvořák (1841–1904)
Gabriel Fauré (1845–1924)
César Franck (1822–1890)
Mikhail Glinka (1804–1857)
Charles Gounod (1818–1893)
Engelbert Humperdinck (1854–1921)
Mikhail Ippolitov-Ivanov (1859–1935)
Edouard Lalo (1823–1892)
Felix Mendelssohn (-Bartholdy) (1809–1847)
Giacomo Meyerbeer (1791–1864)
Carl Otto Nicolai (1810–1849)
Jacques Offenbach (1819–1880)
Nikolai Rimsky-Korsakov (1844–1908)
Gioachino Rossini (1792–1868)
Camille Saint-Saëns (1835–1921)
Robert Schumann (1810–1856)

Bedrich Smetana (1824–1884)
Johann Strauss II (1825–1899)
Ambroise Thomas (1811–1896)
Carl Maria von Weber (1786–1826)
Hugo Wolf (1860–1903)

17

Richard Strauss

We come to the end of the nineteenth century and the beginning of the twentieth—to Richard Strauss, Mahler, Debussy.

The powers that operate with youthful vigor and exuberance in Strauss's tone-poems *Don Juan* and *Till Eulenspiegel* exhibit matured refinement and sheer incandescence in *Don Quixote*. This is his masterpiece—inspired in its invention; unflawed by a single Straussian excess or error of taste; every note in the complex texture really counting for something; every detail making its programmatic point brilliantly. So profuse is the programmatic detail, and so subtly achieved at times, that much of it will be caught only by the musically trained listener familiar with the score or capable of reading it as he listens; and other listeners need to have it pointed out to them. This is difficult to do in a book; but here are some of the important things to listen for.

Strauss subtitles the work *Fantastic Variations on a Theme of Knightly Character,* and describes it further as an Introduction, Theme and Variations, and Finale. It makes its points, then, by applying the variation procedure to themes which characterize Don Quixote, Sancho Panza and Dulcinea; and much of the substance of the work is derived from the high-spirited statement of flute and oboe with which the Introduction begins:

This leads to a statement of the violins that will play an important part:

a statement conveying a grace that is a little stiff-jointed and absurd, and whose conclusion:

conveys the fact that things are distorted in the Don's mind. Next a statement of the violas, derived from [1]:

which rambles on until the oboe enters with Dulcinea's theme:

This is interrupted by excited martial calls of muted trumpets over gigantesque mutterings of tubas and string basses that contribute to the absurdity; and now all the thematic substance continues to be heard in an increasingly involved and dense texture representing the Don's increasing confusion of mind, and reaching its conclusion in several loudly proclaimed discordant chords and a final loud and empty note of the trumpets and trombones that tell us his mind has cracked and he has lost his reason.

We are now formally introduced to the chief characters of the musical narrative. First, in the words of the score, "Don Quixote, the knight of melancholy countenance," wonderfully delineated by a theme derived from [1] and [4], in minor instead of major, and played by the solo cello, which represents the Don in this work:

He is described further by [2] and [3].

Then Sancho Panza, who is as wonderfully delineated by a new theme from the bass-clarinet and tenor-tuba, which, with the solo viola, represent him in the work:

And the solo viola adds a few marvelously contrived examples of his homely platitudes.

And now the two set out in the first variation of their musical journey—the Don jogging along in the solo cello, Sancho in the bass-clarinet, with the image of Dulcinea (flute, oboe, muted violins) eliciting chivalresque thoughts from the Don ([2] from the solo cello) to an accompaniment of down-to-earth mutterings by Sancho ([S] from bass-clarinet and solo viola). Suddenly they stop: a slowly circling progression by clarinet, bassoon, violins, violas describes the circling of the distant windmills. The Don (solo cello) gallops to a closer point and stops for another look: the windmills continue their circling. Convinced now that they are giants, he gallops up to give battle: there is a crash, a harp glissando; and a sustained note of the solo cello tells us the Don lies prostrate, while the windmills continue their circling. Gradually he revives.

And he is off again in the second variation. A vigorous martial variant of [D] pauses before what the Don thinks is an army, despite Sancho's frantic remonstrances ([S] from the woodwinds) that it is a flock of sheep, whose bleatings are now heard. Again the vigorous martial statement, which tells us of the Don's attack; then piteous cries from the scattering sheep; and once more the vigorous martial statement, now proclaiming the Don's victory.

[S] from the bass-clarinet and tenor-tuba opens Variation 3, which is an argument about the life of chivalry, with Sancho expressing doubts and the Don affirming belief. A series of brief exchanges, with [3] from the first desk of first violins repeatedly expressing the Don's growing impatience with Sancho's persistent objections, leads to an extensive statement by Sancho (solo viola) of all his nuggets of homely wisdom. Eventually the Don interrupts angrily ([3] from the violins), quieting down for an affirmation of his belief which becomes impassioned, reaches a great climax, and ends on a sustained chord of finality—only to have Sancho venture another doubt ([S] from the bass-clarinet), which the furious Don silences ([3] from the violins).

And they set out again in Variation 4, jogging along until they see some pilgrims approaching, in whom the Don sees a band of ruffians. He attacks; there is a crash; and a sustained note of the low strings tells us he lies prostrate while the pilgrims recede into the distance. Sancho utters mournful cries ([S] from the bass-clarinet, tenor-tuba and solo viola); when the Don (solo cello), begins to revive, the exuberant bass-clarinet and tenor-tuba express Sancho's joy.

In Variation 5 the Don, at night, keeps vigil in extended declamation of the solo cello, in the course of which his thoughts of Dulcinea make him giddy (harp glissandos, tremolos of the other instruments).

Resuming their journey in Variation 6 the two meet a peasant girl mounted on an ass (parody of Dulcinea's theme from the oboes, with punctuating strokes of the tambourine). She is, says Sancho, Dulcinea transformed by an enchanter. The Don is indignant ([2] from the solo cello); Sancho insists (solo viola).

In Variation 7 the soaring aloft of [2] (strings) and [4] (horns), the glissandos of the harp, the rolls of the kettledrums, the chromatic scales of the flutes, the rushing and whistling of a wind machine all combine to describe the Don—seated on a wooden horse and fanned by a huge bellows—imagining himself riding through the air, while the note D held throughout by the string basses tells us he never leaves the ground.

Next, in Variation 8, a lilting barcarolle ([2] transformed by solo violin and oboe, with the notes of [D] spaced out by English horn, trombone and strings) gives us the episode of the ride in the boat which capsizes. The notes of [D] plucked by the strings suggest the struggling to shore; then [D] *religioso* from flutes, clarinets and horns constitutes a little prayer of thanksgiving.

Galloping off again in Variation 9 the Don meets two monks (two bassoons engaged in a dry-as-dust theological wrangle) whom he takes for magicians and puts to flight—only to encounter, in Variation 10, a fellow-townsman disguised as a knight, who defeats him in a joust and exacts the penalty that he return home.

And now the finale, which depicts the dejected Don plodding homeward, then his last reflections (solo cello's sustained melody derived from [1]) and peaceful death (solo cello's expiring octave-drop to its final note).

Of Strauss's other tone-poems the earlier *Tod und Verklärung* and *Also sprach Zarathustra* are inferior in musical substance; the later *Ein Heldenleben* has pages of superb writing (the love scene, the hero's works of peace, the conclusion) and other pages of Strauss's worst. As for the still later *Sinfonia Domestica*, *Eine Alpensymphonie* and *Metamorphosen* (an endless manipulation of a couple of themes in an apparent progression that never really moves an inch), they are only three examples of the deterioration in the later Strauss—a deterioration in the quality of his musical ideas until eventually there were no ideas at all, with no diminution in the prodigious technical virtuosity and garrulous facility, so that although genuine creative activity stopped, the production of endless pages of empty tonal luxuriance went on almost to the day of his death.

This deterioration is heard also in the later operas—in *Elektra* (whose horrors I find unconvincing except for the scene of

Elektra and Orestes, one of Strauss's best pieces of operatic writing), in *Die Frau ohne Schatten*, in *Ariadne auf Naxos*, and in the vastly overrated *Der Rosenkavalier*. Most of this opera is, to my ears, an expertly made hubbub of sounds with no musical significance in themselves and none in relation to the words and action they carry; of the rest the Princess's first-act monologue and the third-act trio are enjoyable enough but seem to me not equal to the demands of the texts; and the one moment of inspired creation and beauty is the second-act *Presentation of the Rose*, with its first exchanges of Octavian and Sophie.

It is the earlier opera *Salome* that offers passages of impressive power achieved by the enormously complex writing—notably the final scene. But it offers others in which the complexity gets to be a luxuriance out of control of artistic purpose or taste. And it offers also the appalling *Dance of the Seven Veils*.

For the rest, the suite *Le Bourgeois Gentilhomme* is inferior late Strauss with amusing touches; *Aus Italien* and the Sonata for Piano and Violin are inferior early Strauss; the early *Burleske* for piano and orchestra is more engaging.

In addition, some of the songs are lovely—*Ständchen, Freundliche Vision, Die Nacht, Traum durch die Dämmerung, Ruhe meine Seele, Zueignung, Wiegenlied, Befreit, Hat gesagt—bleibt's nicht dabei, Ach Lieb' ich muss nun scheiden* and *Heimkehr.* (Others that are attractive are *Meinem Kinde, Das Bächlein, Das Rosenband, Winterweihe, Wozu noch Mädchen, Heimliche Aufforderung* and *Allerseelen*).

Richard Strauss (1864–1949)

18

Mahler

It is with Strauss that one can begin to speak of gigantic means and aims; and even more with Mahler. The aim was expressed once in Mahler's statement: "For me 'symphony' signifies using all the means of available technique to construct a world for myself"; and the means are the huge orchestras, choruses and vocal soloists, the enormous formal structures in which they are employed. But the employment of the huge orchestras is not the opulent daubing of Strauss; rather it resembles Berlioz's practice in the fastidiousness, precision and originality of its use, frequently, of now only these few instruments and now only those few to produce contrapuntal textures as clear as they are complex. Mahler's use of the orchestra is in fact only one part of an entire operation that resembles Berlioz's in the fact that nothing in the music is perfunctory or mechanical: if an instrument plays or an inner voice moves, the activity is never a routine instrumental doubling or filling in of texture, but always something done with attention, thought and purpose. And this evidence of a mind always working—working, moreover, in unexpected, individual, original and fascinating ways—holds interest even through one of Mahler's long-winded twenty-minute symphony movements.

The best introduction to Mahler, I think, is the Symphony No. 4, whose expansively relaxed and genial earlier movements lead to a gay final movement for soprano that is one of Mahler's best pieces of writing: a setting—now hauntingly poignant, now engagingly merry—of *Das himmliche Leben* from Arnim and Brentano's collection of German folksong poetry, *Des Knaben Wunderhorn (The Youth's Magic Horn)*. The work thus illustrates one outstanding fact about Mahler—that his musical imagination was rooted in the Bohemian folksong he heard in his youth. Much of his creative energy went, as a result, into the writing of songs—the settings of poems from *Des Knaben Wunderhorn* that he grouped together under that title, the settings of these and other poems in *Lieder und Gesänge aus der Jugendzeit (Songs of the Days of Youth)*, *Das Klagende Lied (Song of Lament*—an early and immature work that I would recommend skipping), *Lieder eines fahrenden Gesellen (Songs of a Wayfarer)*, the individual settings of poems by Rückert (notable among them his great one of *Ich bin der Welt abhanden gekommen*), and his setting of translations of Chinese poems *Das Lied von der Erde (Song of the Earth)*.

And another result was the close relation of his vocal and instrumental writing: the folksong-like character of much of his instrumental lyricism; the introduction of actual song into movements of several of the symphonies. Thus, the dramatic and brooding first movement of the Symphony No. 2 *(Resurrection)* is followed by an engaging *Ländler;* this by a gigantic Scherzo which is an orchestral reworking of Mahler's song *Des Antonius von Padua Fischpredigt;* this by a song, *Urlicht*, in which the contralto sings that "man lies in greatest need," but that God "will light my way to eternal blissful life"; and this by a setting of Klopstock's *Resurrection Ode*, sung by the soprano and chorus. And in the Symphony No. 3, two vocal movements lead to another consoling conclusion, this one for the orchestra alone, and Mahler's most sublime utterance.

It is these works that I find accessible and at times moving, not the excessively lugubrious *Kindertotenlieder (Songs on the Death of Children)* and not the ranting later symphonies, in which Mahler's symphonic writing, which embodies his philosophical views and emotional responses to the world and human existence, begins to do so in ways that are repetitious and unattractive. Whereas in the Symphony No. 4 we hear the Mahler who set the naïve and gay poems of *Des Knaben Wunderhorn*, in his last works we hear the tormented, sick-at-heart, world-weary Mahler, filled with thoughts of imminent death, who set the poems of *Kinder-*

MAHLER

totenlieder. The final song of *Das Lied von der Erde,* composed between the Eighth and Ninth Symphonies, is in fact a song of farewell to this earth; and we find ourselves again in the expressive world of that song in the very first measures of the Symphony No. 9, the beginning this time of a slow instrumental movement whose opening section of farewell keeps recurring in alternation with sections of conflict, and whose conclusion after a half-hour is reminiscent of the *"ewig . . . ewig . . ."* at the end of the song. But as I listened to the symphony again some years ago, I found the operation of the Mahler rhetoric all too predictable this time; and it was difficult not to be impatient when Mahler—as though unable to believe he had said his say adequately—started the section of farewell still another time to say it again. I had the same reactions to the similar long slow movement that ends the work. (In between are an engaging *Ländler* and an unattractive *Burleske* which are like last recapitulations of what was said in all the earlier *Ländler* and *Burlesken.*) And I was left feeling that in these two movements Mahler falls far short of what he achieves in the concluding Adagio of the Symphony No. 3. And hearing No. 10 (the first movement that Mahler lived to orchestrate himself, the remainder that he completed in short score and that others have orchestrated convincingly on the basis of his notations and sketches) I recognized the difference between the earlier Mahler diffuseness produced by an active, inventive mind and the later diffuseness that is most of the time a mere filling in of the huge canvas with endless repetitions of empty gestures and lifeless mannerisms—e.g. the endless repetition of uninteresting and unattractive material in the opening Adagio.

And so with the other later symphonies: they don't work for me as the earlier ones do, though I am aware of beautiful moments: In No. 5 there is the fine Adagietto. No. 6 has a lovely Andante and a characteristic scherzo—both characteristically long-winded—but in the first movement and finale there is a straining for portentous utterance that isn't achieved, for me, and the long-windedness is beyond my endurance. There is little I find attractive in the Symphony No. 7, in which one hears the individual Mahler mind, but operating strangely, endlessly. However, in No. 8 (the so-called "Symphony of a Thousand"), a setting for orchestra, choruses and solo singers of the hymn *Veni Creator*

Spiritus and the final scene of Part Two of Goethe's *Faust,* I can appreciate the quiet writing—the marvelously wrought textures that reveal Mahler's fine ear, his fastidious taste, in melody, harmony and orchestral color. There are several such passages in the hymn; and Part Two, which goes on too long, begins with the most extraordinary writing of the work—the orchestral introduction and opening chorus.

And so, finally, with *Das Lied von der Erde:* it has been a surprise to me to find that I care less than before for much of the vocal writing; but I am more aware of, and fascinated by, the use of now these few instruments of the huge orchestra and now those few in writing—notably in *Der Einsame im Herbst* and *Von der Schönheit*—that is unfailingly original, clear, precise, fastidious and distinguished—this being what holds interest even through the lugubrious twenty-five-minute final song.

In fact even in the earlier symphonies not everything is uniformly impressive. The second and third movements and the fourth movement's *Urlicht* are what I find fascinating and moving in the Second, not the first movement—of which the arresting opening promises something important, but in fact merely keeps repeating the unfulfilled promise—and not the last movement's grandiloquent concluding proclamations. Much of No. 3—apart from the extensive episodes for solo post horn in the third movement, which are hauntingly beautiful, and the sublime finale—I find uninteresting: the shifting from one thing to another and the attempts at portentous utterance in the thirty-three-minute-long opening movement, the arch writing at times in the second and third movements.

However, the First Symphony is engagingly youthful and fresh, for all its characteristic changes of mood. That is, listening to it again I am aware of how even in this early work the cheerful opening movement is darkened by the powerfully wrenched, anguished exclamations near its conclusion, and of how similar alternations of light and dark occur in the subsequent movements—in particular the recurring Mahlerian frenetic outbursts in the finale that give way in the end to quiet recollections of the first movement and to Mahlerian grandiloquent affirmations.

Gustav Mahler (1860–1911)

19

Debussy

The fastidiousness and precision and originality that Mahler exhibits in his use of the orchestra we hear in even greater degree in Debussy's music, and not only in the orchestration but in the melody and harmony. Debussy is another of the great originals; and he exhibits his originality not only in a substance quite different from that of the music we have been considering until now, but in equally different procedures, and in the completed entities which these procedures result in—entities without the kind of continuity of melody, development and structure we have been hearing. In one of Debussy's mature works we hear a substance of evocative fragments of melody, figuration, harmony and instrumental color; and a fitting together of such fragments in a progression with coherence and cumulative effect.

The originality of substance and procedure begins to show itself in the varied play with the flute theme in the opening section of Debussy's first major orchestral piece, the *Prélude à L'Après-midi d'un faune,* and in the similar closing section; while the expansive melody of the middle section reminds us of the astonishingly conventional and sugary idiom of the music that preceded this piece—such as the *Arabesques* and *Suite bergamasque* for piano.

But there are no such reminders in *Nuages,* whose thematic fragments and precisely achieved subtleties of orchestral coloring evoke marvelously, from the first measures, the still atmosphere of the scene of clouds moving across the sky. (*Nuages* is one of three pieces in the *Nocturnes* for orchestra, *Fêtes* and *Sirènes* being the others.) As for those orchestral subtleties, note the opening two measures of clarinets and bassoons alone, then the addition of an oboe, then its withdrawal; note then the entrance of the English horn, the addition of flutes and horns, then of the chord of the muted violins *pp* (with clarinets and bassoons), and with this the kettledrum roll *ppp;* note in that violin chord:

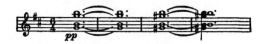

the change from G natural to G sharp, then the change from chord to simple octave.

We have here the beginnings of the method that exhibits its matured development in the rich, complex textures of *La Mer, Ibéria* (particularly its second movement), and the smaller-scale *Gigues* and *Rondes de printemps* (*Gigues, Ibéria* and *Rondes de printemps* constitute the *Images* for orchestra). This evocative orchestral invention of Debussy—subtly evocative, that is, of the sights and sounds of the natural world—has seemed to me to reach its highest point in the second movement of *La Mer.* But I now think this is equalled by the aural image of spring in *Rondes de printemps:* though the progression is less clearly outlined and coherent than in *La Mer,* the invention in this piece is even more profuse and more complex in texture.

The same matured orchestral style is to be heard in the opera *Pelléas et Mélisande;* and it is in fact the superb orchestral writing that I find effective and impressive in the work, not the tenuous vocal declamation. Nor do I find this declamation more interesting in Debussy's songs.

As astonishingly original in the light of its conventional and sugary antecedents is the style of writing for the piano that we hear fully matured in *Soirée dans Grenade* and *Jardins sous la pluie* of *Estampes,* in *L'Île joyeuse,* in *Reflets dans l'eau, Hommage à Rameau* and *Poissons d'or* of the *Images* for piano, and in a few of the Preludes—*La Cathédrale engloutie, La Sérénade interrompue, La Puerta del vino.* The various elements of that piano style are elaborated in the *Études*—pieces ostensibly exercising the hands in the playing of thirds, fourths, sixths, and so on—some of which I find interesting only for their elaboration of that style (as in fact I do some of the pieces with titles) but a few of which—concerned with thirds, octaves, eight fingers, chromatic steps—are in addition engaging and impressive as pieces of music. And *Doctor Gradus ad Parnassum, The Snow is Dancing* and *Golliwog's Cake-Walk* of *Children's Corner* are charming.

Of the chamber music the early Quartet, though not one of Debussy's best works, has a second and third movement that are exquisitely wrought and lovely; but the late sonatas for cello and piano, for flute, viola and harp, and for violin and piano offer what to my ears is style carried to a high point of refinement and subtlety, but with little or no content; and the same might be said of the orchestral piece *Jeux*. For the rest, the First Rhapsody for orchestra and solo clarinet, the incidental music to *Le Martyre de Saint Sébastien*, the early Symphonic Suite *Printemps, En blanc et noir* for two pianos, and *La Damoiselle élue* for soprano with orchestra are uninteresting, as is the third of the *Nocturnes* for orchestra—*Sirènes*, with women's chorus—though I am aware of the subtle peripheral activities of the orchestra (*Fêtes*, the second of the *Nocturnes*, is more enjoyable). As for *La Boîte à joujoux*, the moment-to-moment invention, in Debussy's delicate and tenuous ironic style, is so closely tied up with the many incidents of a children's ballet as not to provide a satisfyingly coherent musical experience when listened to by itself.

Claude Debussy (1862–1918)

20

Music of the Twentieth Century I

BERG, SCHÖNBERG, WEBERN, BARTÓK
HINDEMITH, STRAVINSKY

The originality I have referred to in the work of certain composers was something incidental to their achievement of the works of art their minds were concentrated on. With the twentieth century we come to originality—in melody, harmony, rhythm and form—that was consciously striven for, and that was carried to the point where some composers were no longer in communication with the general music public. And so we come to the problem of modern music and the arguments about it.

On the one hand some have contended that the situation is an old one—that the great composers of the past were obscure to *their* contemporaries—and have argued from this that the music which the public has trouble in understanding today is as good as the music it had trouble in understanding in the past. Mozart has been cited as one composer who starved to death for lack of appreciation; but his great contemporary Haydn flourished handsomely, and actually Mozart's difficulty was not the public's failure to recognize his greatness, which it did recognize, but his own lack of skill—whether he was dealing with a French duke who didn't pay him for his daughter's lessons, or an Austrian emperor who paid him only half the salary he had paid Gluck, or a manager who paid him only half the customary fee for an opera, or a publisher who paid him nothing for some quartets—his lack of skill in manipulating the musico-economic machinery of the period to convert the public's appreciation into the money that would have kept him from dying of poverty and overwork at thirty-five. Beethoven also has been cited: the difficulties his contemporaries had with his last quartets have been offered in support of the contention that he too died in want for lack of understanding of his music; but actually he did not die in want, and not only the financial support he received from his noble patrons but the sums he was paid by publishers who competed for his works are evidence of the lifelong contemporary recognition of his greatness even by those who had trouble with his last quartets at first hearing. Schubert is still another who is alleged to have starved to death for lack of recognition; but actually, though he was always poor, it was not privation but an earlier venereal disease that weakened his body's resistance to the typhus of which he died; and he died at the point where his music, which had been appreciated from the start by those who knew it, was beginning to be sufficiently known and recognized for publishers to ask him for works (in the year of his death the Vienna correspondent of the Dresden *Abendzeitung* referred to "the inspired Schubert" whose "name already resounds from all lips"); so that if he had lived he probably would have been able in a few years to command adequate compensation for what was published. The scurrilous attacks on Wagner have been cited as evidence of his contemporaries' inability to understand his music; but he was no less warmly defended, and the Bayreuth Festspielhaus is merely the surviving concrete evidence of the enormous interest, recognition and support that his work commanded in his own lifetime.

On the other hand some have contended, correctly, that the situation is new, but have gone on with further contentions that are incorrect. The American composer Aaron Copland, in his excellent book *Music and Imagination,* quotes from an address at Harvard University some years ago in which E. J. Dent pointed out that "in the days of Handel and Mozart nobody wanted old music; all audiences demanded the newest opera or the newest concerto, as we now naturally demand the newest play and the newest novel," and asked why in music today we demanded the old and were hostile to the new. One reason, said Dent, was the excessive reverence for the classics, which he suspected began in England at the Handel commemoration of 1784 (Germany apparently didn't count). And another reason was the change in public. "In Handel's day there was in all European countries an inner ring of cultivated connoisseurs who were the direct patrons of the composers," whereas "the bourgeois public of the nineteenth century had no tradition of connoisseurship . . . and it had no sense of patronage." This was Dent's formulation of the myth of the golden age of eighteenth-century patronage. The fact was patronage by an aristocracy of birth and rank; the myth converts this into patronage by an aristocracy of mind, spirit and taste; and similarly it converts the change from the eighteenth-century aristocratic to the nineteenth-century bourgeois public into a change from an educated, cultivated and enlightened public to an uneducated, uncultivated and unenlightened one. Actually eighteenth-century patronage of music was part of the ritual of aristocratic existence; and you need only read Mozart's letters to learn that the ritual was practiced by many aristocrats of birth and rank who lacked aristocracy of mind, spirit and taste. Actually too the musico-economic set-up of direct patronage for the creation and performance and hearing of music was replaced largely by the nineteenth-century set-up of the public concert and generally distributed printed editions; and in this set-up the new bourgeois public included people who attended concerts under no other compulsion than their interest in the music—the enlightened interest of the educated, cultivated people many of them were. This public listened to the old music which the new widely distributed editions made it possible to perform; but it listened also to the music that was newly composed; and it continued to listen to both old and new all through the nineteenth century and into the twentieth. If therefore at that point it began to be hostile to the new, the reason cannot have been excessive reverence for the old; it must have been rather the particular nature of those new works of Schönberg, Webern and the rest— the experiences they offered the ear, mind and spirit, as against the experiences that had been offered by new music until then.

But on this point, Copland, in an earlier book called *Our New Music,* advanced another argument. In that book he undertook to describe and explain the changes in expressive content and extensions of vocabulary in modern music, in order to remove from the reader's mind the "fantastic notions" with which he said "newspaper writers and radio commentators who ought to know better" had misrepresented modern music and prejudiced the public against it—to remove, that is, the notions that the music lacked emotion and melody, that it was over-complicated in rhythm and ugly in harmony. In this way he undertook to make it possible for the reader to recognize in the emotion that was merely changed in quality and intensity, in the melody, harmony and rhythm that were merely enriched, the things that made Schönberg and Webern "*our* music," as natural and acceptable to our ears, as interesting and significant to our minds, as people a hundred and two hundred years ago found *their* music.

And the argument about the extension of vocabulary was stated somewhat differently by Gerald Abraham in his excellent book *This Modern Music,* which provided an admirably clear explanation of the extensions of vocabulary and syntax in the music the public had found incomprehensible. As in the case of a foreign language, Abraham contended, one could not understand modern music merely by listening to it, but had to learn its vocabulary and grammar—though the converse was no less true, that "no amount of knowledge of the why and wherefore of [the] musical speech will make that language your own, as natural to you as Bach's or Wagner's, without a great deal of keen listening practice." But children learn their native language by ear long before they study its grammar; and I know from personal experience that foreign languages are best learned in the same way: after a few months in Vienna, as a boy of ten, I spoke German without having seen a grammar. And this is even more true of music, which, as Abraham himself observed in another connection, "has no sense outside itself": the internal coherence of the progression of sounds is conveyed directly by, and on the other hand apprehended directly from, the sounds themselves as heard. That was how I learned to understand the simplest musical vocabulary and syntax in earliest childhood long before I learned anything about chord progressions; it was how I extended that vocabulary and syntax later to include Debussy, Ravel, early Stravinsky (to *Le Sacre du printemps*), Prokofiev, Bloch. And when that way no longer worked—when in the twenties I began to hear music by Schönberg and others that conveyed no sense to me—I found that no amount of reading of explanations of vocabulary and syntax caused the music to begin to make the sense it had not made. So it has continued to be. When, a few years ago, I began to enjoy some of the later works of Stravinsky I had previously found arid and ugly, it was as a result of listening—listening, it is true, with help, but the help of Balanchine's ballet choreography for the works, not of the incomprehensible explanations by the Stravinskyites or Stravinsky himself. Similarly, when I found Schönberg's *Erwartung* expressively effective, the expressive effect was something imposed on my mind directly by the progression of sounds that I heard for the first time; whereas the principle of organization that Abraham pointed out in a passage of Schönberg's *Five Piano Pieces* still doesn't work for me as a principle of coherent sense in the progression of sounds as heard. And this is true not only of me but of the general public.

Which brings us back to Copland's argument. When the public rejected Schönberg and Webern it didn't do so under the influence of the critics' misrepresentation of them; it acted on the basis of its own direct experiences of the music; and the critics merely described the experiences they had shared with the non-professional, non-writing listeners. To this day the countless explanations like those by Copland and Abraham haven't induced the public to hear in Schönberg and Webern "*our* music," as natural and acceptable to our ears, as interesting and significant to our minds, as people a hundred and two hundred years ago found *their* music. But readers of mine have reported finding in Bartók the meaning I have said I don't find—which is to say that where the public has come to accept a composer, there too it has acted on the basis of its own direct experiences of the music.

And so you will act: with twentieth-century as with earlier music my experiences and judgments are offered subject to confirmation by your own ears and mind. I must report that Alban Berg's musical idiom is one that conveys no coherent musical sense to me in the self-contained structures of his instrumental works—the Violin Concerto, the *Lyric Suite*, the Piano Sonata Op. 1—or even with the words of his cantata *Der Wein* (of more interest are his *Seven Early Songs*). But the powerfully moving words and situations of the nightmarish drama of *Wozzeck* are given enormously enhanced expressive force by the distorted vocal declamation and discordant orchestral comment, which make the work one of the monuments of the operatic literature. And you are free to find the instrumental works as meaningful as the opera. *Wozzeck* is concerned with pitiful human beings who involve one with them emotionally. Berg's *Lulu*, on the other hand, is concerned with depraved human beings by whom one is repelled; and whereas in *Wozzeck* one hears discordant writing that heightens the expressive effect of the powerfully moving words, in *Lulu* one hears exacerbated vocal writing which has no expressive relation to the unmoving words, and an extreme of discordant orchestral writing which has no relation to the dramatic situation and action. To my ear, then, *Lulu* is not the masterpiece that others accept it as being. But you are free to find that it is.

And so with Schönberg: the endless rambling in the early, tonal works—*Gurrelieder, Transfigured Night (Verklärte Nacht)*—makes as little coherent sense to me as the sounds my ear finds hideous in the later more advanced works—*Pierrot Lunaire*, the First and Second String Quartets, the String Trio, the Serenade Op. 24, the Piano Pieces Opp. 11 and 25, the Five Pieces for orchestra Op. 16, the songs, the First Chamber Symphony, the Violin Concerto, the *Music to Accompany a Motion Picture,* and the opera *Moses and Aaron.* I am aware that tremendous powers are operating in the later music, including the mental power and personal force one was aware of in the bitterly and angrily twisted things Schönberg used to say about his music and the public's attitude, but that these powers operate in the service of an extreme eccentricity and perversity in the music as in the statements. The statement, for example, establishing only two categories of concertgoers—those who want easily digested entertainment (and don't like his music) and those "who want to be elated if it hurts" (and who do like his music), and omitting the more important category of people who don't want easily digested entertainment and are willing to work for their elation, but whose work brings them no elation from the distorted musical elements in Schönberg's music.

Three works by Schönberg stand out as exceptions: his monodrama *Erwartung* is in a style which, to my ears, resembles that of Berg's *Wozzeck* and has a similar nightmarish expressiveness. It is the first advanced work of Schönberg that has had any expressive effect for me. His Second Chamber Symphony is marvelously scored. And so are his transcriptions of two of Bach's chorale-preludes for organ and his *St. Anne* Prelude and Fugue in E flat major. (However, the Concerto for String Quartet and Orchestra that Schönberg made out of Handel's Concerto Grosso Op. 6 No. 7 by reworking and elaborating its substance in his own terms will be acceptable only to those who accept Schönberg's own music; to my ears it is horrible.)

So with Webern: there are on the one hand his early and traditional Passacaglia Op. 1, richly scored for a large orchestra, his marvelously contrived orchestration of the six-voiced Ricercare of Bach's *Musical Offering*, and his Six Pieces Op. 6 for orchestra, which, since it is a still early, transitional work, exhibiting only the beginnings of the distinctive Webern style, offers actual phrases, some of them stated with wonderfully calculated subtle orchestral coloring, and sometimes producing a moving expressive or atmospheric effect. Effective in the same way are the Five Movements (*Fünf Sätze*) Op. 5 for string quartet. But then there are the Symphony for Small Orchestra Op. 21, the Five Pieces for orchestra Op. 10, the Concerto Op. 24, and the Variations Op. 30, which are in the fully developed Webern style of wisps of sound in fragments of phrases that make no coherent musical sense to my ears. Of one of these—Webern's Symphony for Small Orchestra—Paul Rosenfeld once wrote: "To be sure, the fragile little piece is unconventional in its form. This is most slender and lightly indicated. The very volumes of the score are made up of the tones of [the individual instruments], emitted for the most part singly and separately in Indian file. There are scarcely any chords. The passages for the *tutti* are instantaneous, and little instrumental polyphony occurs. Indeed, in form the Symphony resembles a Cézanne water-color, with its hair-line indications of essential contours. Etc., etc." I don't deny the fragility, the slenderness, the volumes and all the rest. What I deny is that a little squeak followed by a little whistle followed by a little toot followed by a little squeak again is like the hair-line indications of essential contours in a Cézanne water-color—in other words, that it faintly suggests a more substantial content. From such music I get nothing.

I get nothing from the first movement of Bartók's Concerto for Orchestra, either, and the third merely goes through the gestures of an elegy, for me; but the other fast and light movements I find quite engaging—the *Allegretto scherzando* movement with its grotesquerie, the headlong finale, and above all the *Intermezzo interrotto*, which I find unique in the music of Bartók I have heard in its subtly wrought loveliness of sound and expressive content. Likewise with his opera, *Bluebeard's Castle:* we are informed that Béla Balasz's libretto has made of the Bluebeard story something on the high philosophical and psychological level of what Shaw made of the Don Juan legend. If this is achieved in the original Hungarian text it doesn't survive translation into English— mostly "Give me the key" answered by "Judith, do not ask me," with, each time one of the doors is opened, an attempt at high-flown language that falls flat on its face. The words, then, create no dramatic interest in the hour-long opening of the seven doors; nor does Bartók's vocal writing impart to them any musical interest. What *is* interesting is the orchestral part—interesting, for one thing, in its unexpected luxuriance, but also in the dramatic effectiveness of its masterfully contrived sonorities.

Bartók's last work, the Concerto for Viola, is, like some other late works of his, a mixture: a first movement in a musical language I don't understand, but with an accessible and lovely close, an equally accessible and beautiful slow movement, and an engaging finale using folksong-like material. To Bartók's researches into the folk-music of his country we owe also the fine *Hungarian Folk-Tunes* and *Rumanian Folk-Dances* for violin. The third movement of his Violin Sonata No. 1 begins with material derived from folk-dance that is understandable and impressive, but the first two movements and a *grazioso* episode in the third are in an idiom which makes no musical sense to me. Similar harshly dissonant, powerful, and skillful treatment of folk material is heard in the two Rhapsodies for violin and orchestra and the Rhapsody No. 1 for cello and piano. Of the *Deux Images* for orchestra, No. 1 is luxuriantly atmospheric, except for a harshly dissonant episode, and in No. 2 dissonance achieves grotesquerie and grimness, with an episode of distorted lyricism. In the same way, some of the étude-like piano pieces from his *Mikrokosmos* are engaging, others not.

However, I find the whole of Bartók's *Music for Strings, Percussion and Celesta* to be a work put together with impressive craftsmanship which doesn't make the musical sense for my mind that it made for Bartók's and makes for some other listeners'. This is equally true of the Violin Concerto, the Sonata for unaccompanied violin, *Contrasts* for violin, clarinet and piano, and the hideous score for the ballet *The Miraculous Mandarin*. As for the string quartets, except for the obvious humor of the Burletta movement of the last one, my mind finds no path in the regions of musical thought in which Bartók's mind travels in these works.

With Hindemith there was no difficulty in understanding the harmonically sour and emotionally dry works that he kept grinding out for many years with enormous technical efficiency, but there was, for me, no pleasure in listening to them such as I have had recently with parts of *The Four Temperaments*—the third section of the theme, and certain sections of the variations, especially the Phlegmatic—which are in a lush, sensuous, and conventional idiom strangely different from the more normal sour, acrid idiom of the other parts I do not care for (except as soundtrack for Balanchine's wonderful choreography). Hindemith's *Symphonic Metamorphoses on Themes of Weber* is also in the changed, astonishingly conventional and sensuous idiom of his later music, which raises questions about the earlier sourness and aridity; the third movement *Andantino* is quite lovely, and the other movements are engaging. The ballet *Noblissima Visione* I find uninteresting; and further hearings have not made me care more than I did at first for *Mathis der Maler*. The Sonata for viola and piano Op. 11 No. 4 is an early work, much of it conventionally melodious and pleasant, with only an occasional hint of the unattractive procedures of the arid works that followed. Of these the String Quartet Op. 22 has occasional impressive pages, and you are free to enjoy the other pieces of its kind.

Among the century's experimenters and innovators who have proved to be fruitful artists Stravinsky stands out as the towering figure. I mentioned that I have only recently enjoyed some of his later works; I should add that there are some I still don't like, but also that there is one—the ballet score *Le Baiser de la fée* (1928)— that I enjoyed at first hearing. What I liked were things it had in common with his earliest masterpiece, the ballet score *L'Oiseau de feu* (1910); and for some years I failed to perceive what it had in common with the later works I disliked.

One striking thing about *L'Oiseau de feu* is how beautifully it is wrought: we hear, for example, a use of the orchestra as precise and fastidious, to achieve coloring often as delicate and subtle, as Debussy's—the most beautiful example being the transition from the Berceuse to the Finale. And there is the mosaic-like fitting together of substance, instead of its development, that we noted in Debussy. But there is no resemblance to Debussy in the bold, raw dissonance at the end, or in the reiteration of dynamic syncopated figures that builds up tension and excitement in the *Infernal Dance*. And it is the further exploitation of this dissonance and rhythm that we hear in the music for one of the great artistic masterpieces of the century, the ballet *Petrushka* (1911), and that achieves the overwhelming power of the ballet score *Le Sacre du printemps* (1913).

In addition to being beautifully wrought *L'Oiseau de feu* is unusual, for Stravinsky, in its direct expressiveness. And both of these things are true of *Le Baiser de la fée*, but in even greater degree: *Le Baiser*, for me, is Stravinsky's most beautiful score, with an expressiveness that has a wider range than that of *L'Oiseau* and is more touching in the lyrical episodes of the boy and his bride, more powerful in the dramatic episodes of the boy and the fairy. And two other beautifully wrought and directly expressive ballet scores are the genial *Apollon Musagète* (1928)— whose expressiveness is very touching throughout, but especially in the hauntingly beautiful coda—and the grave and haunting *Orpheus* (1947).

On the other hand we hear in *Le Baiser* the tension-producing syncopations and ostinatos characteristic of Stravinsky's abstract works, like *Danses Concertantes* (1942) and the *Symphony in Three Movements* (1945). And *Le Baiser*, finally, throws light on a practice of Stravinsky that has been misunderstood—his use of themes and styles of composers of the past. At the beginning of the village scene of *Le Baiser* we hear repeatedly a fragment of Tchaikovsky's piano piece *Humoresque*—but only this fragment, and worked into a context of Stravinsky's own. This is the way he uses the other bits of thematic substance of Tchaikovsky in *Le*

Baiser; and it is the way he uses the substance and styles of other composers. It is analogous to the old practice of writing variations on another composer's theme: Brahms writing variations on a theme of Paganini wasn't imitating Paganini but writing music of his own that resulted from letting his mind play with Paganini's theme; and Stravinsky has given us music of his own that has resulted from letting his mind play with themes and styles of composers of the past.

Stravinsky did something of the kind, with certain differences, when he composed music "after Pergolesi" for the Massine ballet *Pulcinella* (1919–20); and in notes for a recording Robert Craft amplified the "after": the melodies are Pergolesi's; the original forms of the pieces are sometimes unchanged, sometimes expanded or remodeled; the harmonies are recomposed by Stravinsky, though much of the time on Pergolesi's bass line; the instrumentation is entirely Stravinsky's. And this play of Stravinsky's mind with Pergolesi's materials works out into one of Stravinsky's most attractive scores.

I say "play"; and sometimes—in *Pulcinella* especially—it sounds as though it *is* for fun; but in *Oedipus Rex* (1927) we hear in the arias a manipulation of the old styles to achieve not the melodic beauty they achieved originally but a harshly austere and monumental utterance suited to this drama of man pursued and destroyed by implacable destiny.

Stravinsky's opera *The Rake's Progress* (1951) offers more of the fascinating play of his mind with forms of the past—this time with the eighteenth-century styles and forms he used in his setting of the play, in writing that ranges from the brilliant fanfares and processional music, the arias in sustained and often lovely melodic style of the earlier scenes, to the grave and affecting music of the last two. This brilliant tour de force has its failures—some of the writing for the voice that is like Stravinsky's writing for instruments, and therefore unvocal and unattractive. But it has also its astonishing successes—notably the brothel scene, with Tom's beautiful and touching aria *Love, too frequently betrayed,* the powerful churchyard scene, and the moving Bedlam scene, with Anne's lovely lullaby and the chorus's grave comments.

In Stravinsky's earlier opera, *Le Rossignol* (1909–14), it is the first act that has what little good music there is in the work; even here what is offered as the bird's song is Stravinskyan artifice which creates no believable illusion, and all the writing in the later acts is exceedingly thin and ineffective.

Of the other stage works, the delightful and witty score for Balanchine's *Jeu de cartes* (1936) stands out above the rest. *L'Histoire du soldat* (1918) is one of those pieces I have not liked on previous occasions, but recently I have been amused by the Soldier's March, the Royal March, and a little of the Ragtime (there is too much of it). *Les Noces* (1917) for voices and orchestra I remember being an effective soundtrack for Bronislava Nijinska's tremendous ballet years ago, but I get nothing from the piece's endless reiterations by themselves. And what a friend characterized as the "whimsy-whamsy" of *Renard* (1916) doesn't work for me any better.

However, I have come to enjoy some of Stravinsky's instrumental music that I didn't enjoy before. Not the Duo Concertante (1932) for violin and piano, an expertly contrived but, for me, unattractive piece; and not the *Suite Italienne* (1933) for cello or violin and piano—Stravinsky's transcriptions of several pieces from *Pulcinella*, which are much less effective than the original orchestral versions. But the Violin Concerto's (1931) wryly parodistic classical references include an aria in an amusing exaggeration of grandly florid style, though there is a good deal else that is unattractively ugly. I enjoy some passages of the Piano Concerto (1923–24) now that I didn't when I first heard it in the twenties; but I still don't like it as much as some of the subsequent works in which he used the same method with increasing elaboration and expertness—the engaging *Capriccio* (1929) for piano and orchestra, and the Concerto (1935) and Sonata (1944) for Two Pianos. Less successful is the Ebony Concerto (1945) that he put together with all the Stravinsky precision for the Woody Herman Orchestra, and in which bits of jazz melody and rhythm are subjected—unsuitably and pointlessly, I would say—to the Stravinsky ostinato treatment. Of the compositions for solo piano, there are the *Four Études* (1908)—masterfully contrived trivia, of which the fourth is an amusing burlesque *Souvenirs d'Espagne*—and the early and parodistic Eight Easy Pieces (1914–17) for Piano Four Hands. The Sonata No. 2 (1924) and Serenade in A (1925) I find uninteresting.

Two engaging neo-classical pieces are the *Dumbarton Oaks* Concerto for winds (1938) and the Concerto in D for strings (1946). The Symphony in C (1940) for full orchestra is another example of his accessible and enjoyable style of that period, and characteristic in its exciting ostinatos and tensions. Enjoyable too are his skillful arrangement for small orchestra (1941) of the *Bluebird* pas de deux from *The Sleeping Beauty*, which has some of Tchaikovsky's most inspired invention; the engaging *Circus Polka* (1942); the early *Scherzo fantastique* (1908); the less consequential Four Norwegian Moods (1942), which contain rhythmically involved Stravinskyan manipulations of simple materials; and the amusingly parodistic *Ragtime* (1918) for eleven instruments. The first movement of the Septet (1953) has engaging passages, and the passacaglia in the second movement is wonderfully made, but the third movement is altogether unattractive. The Octet (1923) for winds and brass is interesting only in the finale. And the Symphonies of Wind Instruments (1920) I continue to find as ugly as I did when Stokowski first played it in the twenties.

Like Verdi in his *Requiem*, Stravinsky writing music to religious texts can write only as he writes at all times—as a composer of dramatic music; in the *Symphony of Psalms* (1930), then, there are again in the first and last movements the dramatic ostinatos, which are again exciting, and which impart this dramatic excitement to the sober Latin words; the fugal middle movement I still find horrid. As for the astringency and fastidiousness of his Mass (1948), I find most of it arid; the exceptions are the Hosannah, which is the only section with any relation, for my ears, to the meaning of the words, and some passages of effectively austere sonorities in the Credo and Agnus Dei. I find very little of the Cantata (1952) moving or attractive, either. But in Stravinsky's *In Memoriam Dylan Thomas* (1954)—a setting of Thomas's *Do Not Go Gentle into That Good Night* for tenor and string quartet, with a dirge-like prelude and postlude for trombones in alternation with string quartet—the instrumental portions and several of the vocal phrases are very moving, and the fitting of note to note is fascinating throughout.

This brings us to Stravinsky's last compositions. Stravinsky's successive works have given us the results of the play of his mind on whatever musical material—whatever style of this or that composer or period—he happens to have been interested in at the moment; and parts of the ballet *Agon* (1953–57) sound like the result of his late interest in the serial, "atonal" writing of Berg, Schönberg and Webern. But while my hearings of this piece have made me aware of the operation of impressive powers in the making of it, they have given me little pleasure from the result. Likewise with *Threni* (1958), a setting of the First, Third and Fifth Elegies of the Jeremiad: I can hear that the putting together of the sounds is done with fastidious precision and mastery; but only in a very few instances—the music for the word *Perii* in the line *Inundaverunt aquae,* the words *No timeas* in the line *Appropinquasti in die,* the entire concluding statement *Converte nos*—is the resulting musical object, for me, a moving expressive communication; and in very few others is it attractive or interesting merely for the way it is made and sounds as an object. And the same applies to most of the other works of this period—the *Canticum Sacrum* (1955), *Movements* (1959), *The Flood* (1962) and *Requiem Canticles* (1966).

I expect these late compositions would be without coherent meaning for me even if I could understand Stravinsky's explanations of them, since I have found repeatedly that the principle of organization of a work of this kind did not turn out to be a principle of coherent sense in the progression of sounds as heard. Thus, for Stravinsky, looking through the lenses of his practice, his attitudes, his interests of a "doer" in his art (as he referred to himself), *Movements* is made interesting and valuable by the doing in it—by the fact that "every aspect of the composition was guided by serial forms, the sixes, quadrilaterals, triangles, etc. The fifth movement . . . uses a construction of twelve verticals. The gamma and delta hexachords in this movement are more important than the A and B, too. Five orders are rotated instead of four, with six alternates for each of the five, while, at the same time, the six work in all directions, as though through a crystal."* All this, for him, makes *Movements* as interesting and valuable as the doing in *Le Baiser de la fée* makes that piece; and there are other people, certainly, who will feel the same. "When I compose something I use the language of music, and my statement in my grammar will

*Igor Stravinsky, *Memories and Commentaries* (New York, 1959).

be clear to the musician who has followed music up to where my contemporaries and I have brought it"; and certainly, for those who have been able to follow music to that point, both the piece itself and Stravinsky's description of it will be equally intelligible. But for non-doing listeners who have not been able to follow music to where Stravinsky and his contemporaries have brought it, *Movements* may make no musical sense and Stravinsky's description of its construction may be unintelligible.

Béla Bartók (1881–1945)
Alban Berg (1885–1935)
Paul Hindemith (1895–1963)
Arnold Schönberg (1874–1951)
Igor Stravinsky (1882–1971)
Anton Webern (1883–1945)

21

Music of the Twentieth Century II

OTHER COMPOSERS OF THE
TWENTIETH CENTURY

Gerald Abraham points out in *L'Oiseau de feu* elements derived from Rimsky-Korsakov and other Russian predecessors of Stravinsky;* but we hear also what the mind of Stravinsky made of them. Similarly one hears in Prokofiev's *Scythian Suite* (*Ala and Lolly*) things which suggest the possibility that the man who wrote this music about pagan Scythia in 1914 knew the music Stravinsky had written about pagan Russia the year before; but we hear also that these things, if they do represent the influence of *Le Sacre du printemps*, are part of the personal and individual way of writing that Prokofiev exhibits in this and other early works. And it is in fact some (not all) of these early works—the Violin Concerto No. 1, the Piano Concertos Nos. 1 through 3, the *Visions fugitives* for piano, the Piano Sonatas Nos. 1 through 4, the *Scythian Suite* for orchestra, the ballet score *Chout*, the Symphony No. 1 (*Classical*), the operas *The Gambler*, *The Love for Three Oranges* and *The Flaming Angel*—that are the most engaging by virtue of the astonishing imaginative and musical powers that operate with youthful freshness and exuberant creative energy.

Not that fine works aren't produced later by the more experienced composer—notably the superb score for the ballet *The Prodigal Son* (more impressive in its original form and expressive

---

*Gerald Abraham, "The Music of Yesterday and Today—Later Nationalist Tendencies," *A Hundred Years of Music* (London, 1938, 1949).

context as a ballet than as reworked into mere movements as part of the Symphony No. 4). And even when, after Prokofiev's return to Russia in 1927, what appears to be operating in some works is the developed craftsmanship that could grind out lifeless imitations of his earlier writing on demand, there are also occasional exceptions—the Symphony No. 5, unusual and impressive in the sustained and involved construction of its first and third movements; the Violin Sonata Op. 80, with an impressive opening movement, and an Andante and a lyric episode in the finale that are very lovely; the String Quartet No. 2, with a beautifully lyrical slow movement based on a Caucasian love song, and a superb finale; parts of the Piano Sonata No. 6—the Allegretto second movement, the involved and dissonant middle section of the third movement; and parts of No. 7—the even more involved and dissonant middle section of the second movement, the explosion of motor energy in the ostinato finale.

Peter and the Wolf is amusing the first and second times, but when you know the story and begin to concentrate your attention on the music you may find that there isn't enough for such concentrated attention; and there is even less in the Suite from Lieutenant Kije. For the rest—the other symphonies, concertos and sonatas, the String Quartet No. 1, the Quintet for winds and strings, the Sinfonia Concertante, the Sonata Op. 94 (in its original form for flute and piano, whose sonorities make this version more attractive than the more familiar one for violin), the small piano pieces, the ballets Le Pas d'acier, Romeo and Juliet and Cinderella, the opera War and Peace, the cantata Alexander Nevsky—I find less interesting.

Of the works of other Russian composers of the period, Scriabin's Piano Sonata No. 3 is more arresting than some of Prokofiev's later ones. But in Rachmaninoff's piano concertos the best thing is what his incisive, dramatic style of playing (and that of one or two other pianists after him) makes of music written for that purpose. Beyond the single indulgence of his own or Van Cliburn's performance of the Concerto No. 3, the best of the series, you should waste no time on the exciting ways in which Rachmaninoff says something of little importance in the other concertos, the Rhapsody on a Theme of Paganini, the orchestral works, or the trashy Preludes for piano. Nor should you waste any time on the compositions of Khachaturian, Kabalevsky and the others. Worst of all, by far, is Shostakovitch. The point often made about him—that his is an example of a distinguished and promising creative gift perverted and stunted by government pressures in Stalinist Russia—was undermined by the émigré Russian composer, Nicholas Nabokov, who told in an article in *Harper's* in the 1940s* of his own first impressions of Shostakovitch's early works—that they were skilful but not particularly new or imaginative. And when Shostakovitch's opera *Lady Macbeth of Mtsensk* was given in New York (first in the original version and later in the somewhat revised version called *Katerina Ismailovna*) I noted that in this early work, as in later ones, he operated with a resourceful fluency that for many people was enough to make him an important composer; but that it was a resourceful fluency in writing that was not original—whether it was the undistorted lyricism he adopted for Katerina's lament, or the jeering and grimacing of his natural inclination, in which I heard a reworking of some of Prokofiev's writing by as low-grade and vulgar a mind and taste as had ever communicated itself to me through an artistic medium.

What followed—the appalling ballet *The Golden Age*, the symphonies from the Fifth on, the later chamber music—was crude, derivative, inane, banal and pretentious. But what had preceded—the First Symphony, the early chamber music, the piano pieces—had differed from the later works only in that those were made even worse by, first, Shostakovitch's attempts at profundity, then by the required simplifications and bombastic affirmations of the Stalin years, and finally [by the composer's growing sardonic bitterness]. These qualities of the music represented not only pressures or their absence but the personal resources that were involved with Shostakovitch's articulateness in his medium—the inner core of qualities, emotions, insights which in a great artist governs the flow of sounds (or words or paints), eliminates what is superfluous, what is imitative or derivative, and produces a style, a form, a content which are concentratedly, homogeneously individual. In my opinion, then, in Shostakovitch's case political pressures did not turn a good composer into a

*Collected in *Old Friends and New Music* (New York, 1951).

191

bad one: the music was bad from the start and had in it the promise of continued badness; and the political pressures only made it worse.

Sibelius I class as something of an indulgence. A hundred years from now, I am aware, the world may hear in the Fourth Symphony what Sir Ernest Newman heard—"a convulsive effort on Sibelius' part to build without the least fragment of mortar, bogus or real, . . . a kind of Cyclopean architecture, block being laid on block without any other join than the surfaces of the materials themselves." But it is also possible that it will hear in those pretentious snorts of the brass, those ominous drum-rolls, those wild cries of the woodwinds, a bogus mortar of stylistic mannerisms with which Sibelius pads out a few thematic fragments into a symphony movement.

Believe your own ears, then, if they don't hear in this piece the greatest of all the symphonies—the stark, austere work of a man who said that while other composers gave the world champagne he gave it cold, clear water, and a work for whose significance one has to penetrate deep below the surface. Believe them when they hear in that abrupt ending of the second movement an ostentatious gesture of strict matter-of-factness and unpretentiousness; when they hear in that lush theme of the third movement, in its last statement, a devastating revelation of Sibelius's craving for champagne, while with the strangely meandering woodwinds and other such "starknesses" in the movement he pretends to a stern addiction to cold, clear water. I am not saying that the champagne is wrong, but on the contrary that it is the thing to enjoy in Sibelius, that there is less of it in the Fourth Symphony than in the others, and that this makes it inferior to them, not—as the Sibelius cultists would have it—the one that towers above the rest in massive strength.

Take instead the Symphony No. 7, which is Sibelius's best in spite of its inadequacies as a symphonic structure that are more apparent with each hearing (Sibelius's first title for the work, Fantasia Sinfonica, was the correct one); or No. 5, which is also good; but take them for what they are—music which is excellently put together by a man with nothing profound to say but with a remarkable feeling for his medium and ability to use it effectively for what he does have to say; music which, then, on its unprofound level, is fine-sounding and enjoyable. Take in that way the delicately poignant *Swan of Tuonela*, the *Festivo*, an early and very enjoyable light piece in which one is astonished to hear, somewhat misplaced, the dramatic explosions of the brass and other stylistic mannerisms of his symphonies, and possibly the first movement of the Violin Concerto. But don't take the Symphonies Nos. 1 and 2, in which the same thing is said as in Nos. 5 and 7, with less refinement of method; the dull Symphony No. 3; the pretentiously sterile No. 4; the collection of mannerisms called No. 6; the symphonic poems; the songs and small instrumental pieces; and above all the incidental music to plays.

Nielsen's symphonies, about which the English began to talk a while back with similar solemnity as about Sibelius's, are a Danish version of the same thing—not an imitation, but similar to Sibelius's Fifth, for example, in their fluent use in large and dramatic forms of material that is engaging in its folk-like character and its regional flavor.

A personal and individual way of writing, somber and impassioned, is heard in the music of Ernest Bloch—extraordinary for its period in the richness and depth of the emotion from which it proceeds, the richness of the highly individual idiom and the expansiveness of the forms in which the emotional impulse makes itself musically articulate. Bloch's finest work is the comparatively early Quintet for piano and strings; and there are impressive pages also in the Violin Sonata No. 1, the Viola Suite, the early Hebrew Rhapsody *Schelomo* and the later and finer *Voice in the Wilderness*, both for cello and orchestra. The even later String Quartet No. 2 exhibits a refinement and subtilization of the idiom of those earlier works, and its slow portions offer some of the most beautiful writing Bloch did. Effective also are the first movement of the Violin Concerto, the three pieces for cello and piano called "From Jewish Life," and *Baal Shem* (Three Pictures of Chassidic Life) for violin and piano, of which *Vidui* and *Nigun* contain impressive examples of Blochian declamation, while *Simchas Torah* is less consequential.

Of the String Quartet No. 3, however, I like only the Adagio and the one or two slow episodes in the other movements; Nos. 4 [and 5] turn out to be even more disappointing than No. 3; the Concerto Grosso is one of Bloch's least significant works; and the late *Concerto symphonique* gives the impression of mere style without impulse, kept going at wearying length by technique.

Other writing that is highly individual is that of the Czech composer Janáček, whose style takes off from Dvořák's and Smetana's but is made modern and powerful by dissonance in his special harmonic language. This is heard most impressively in his *Slavonic* (or *Glagolitic*) *Mass*, but impressively in certain other compositions as well—in two of the operas: in *Jenůfa*, an early, dramatic work whose vocal arioso and idiomatic orchestral context are powerfully communicative, as they are not in some of Janáček's other operatic writing, and which surprises one with occasional beautifully wrought lyrical passages; and in the later *Cunning Little Vixen*, a fable whose words are sung in recitative-like phrases that fit into a continuous flow of distinctive, attractive and expressive orchestral writing. And, among the instrumental works, in the late Sinfonietta, whose folksong-like substance is quite engaging in the third and fourth movements, and whose fifth movement builds up an impressive conclusion with its unusual number of brass instruments; in the early *Idyll* for strings; and in the early *Lachian Dances*, genuine Moravian folksongs which are given added interest and effect by Janáček's idiosyncratic, strange harmonic contexts.

His other works I find less communicative—in particular the other operas: *Katya Kabanová*, in which the dramatic dialogue proceeds for the most part in arioso with no expressive relation to the words or to the continuous flow of powerful and often dissonant orchestral writing: *The Makropoulos Affair*, a Moravian forerunner of Berg's *Lulu*, in which the lack of relation between the orchestral writing, vocal recitative and words is exacerbated by discontinuity of musical thought; and *From the House of the Dead*, whose style ranges from declamatory arioso to mere detached ejaculation, which is powerful and grim and may be effective in support of action seen on a stage but is monotonous when listened to by itself. Uninteresting also are Janáček's chamber music and later piano pieces, his more conventional-sounding narrative song-cycle, *The Diary of One Who Vanished*, and the inferior orchestral suite, *Taras Bulba*.

In England Elgar is considered a great composer, and he was esteemed even by so extraordinarily acute a music critic, in his youth, as Bernard Shaw. But even in England there has been a dissenting minority, one of whom, E. J. Dent, created enormous excitement some years ago by calling Elgar's music rhetorical and vulgar; and delighted to have my own judgment confirmed I go on to some of the other English composers.

For sheer gorgeousness of sound there is nothing like Delius's music; but one work after another is the same gorgeousness under one title after another, with the only difference that in the later works the gorgeousness is further enriched, elaborated, subtilized; and with the lack of clarity of definition in the idiom there is lack of clarity of definition in the form. Try *Brigg Fair* first, since it is not only as beautiful as any, but gains from being in the highly vertebrate form of theme and variations. The experience may satisfy your interest completely; or it may give you a desire for more—the beautifully wrought intermezzo *Walk to the Paradise Gardens* (the one interjection of eloquence in the opera *A Village Romeo and Juliet*); *In a Summer Garden*, a long piece of exquisite impressionistic writing; *Summer Night on the River*, a shorter piece of such writing; *Appalachia;* the closing scene of *Koanga;* the prelude to *Irmelin;* and the first two of the *North Country Sketches*. The early *Paris* has some beautiful quiet writing at the beginning and end, but gets to be rather tawdry in between. And to get pleasure from the monotonously amorphous Violin Concerto, the Piano Concerto, the orchestral pieces *Hassan* and *Eventyr*, the songs, or *A Mass of Life* you would have to like Delius in the strangely intense way that some people like Bruckner or Sibelius.

On the other hand, you will probably enjoy Vaughan Williams's beautiful Fantasia on a Theme of Thomas Tallis and his lovely Mass in G minor. His Fantasia on the English folksong *Greensleeves* and the Suite *English Folksongs* are also engaging works. I care less for his early and late symphonies; and in the Symphony No. 4 he appears to have decided to catch up with the times—with results that are noisily uninteresting.

As for Walton, the point to be made is that neither in his early masterpiece of musical parody, *Façade*, nor in the works he produced subsequently when he set himself to be a serious composer, did he operate with original materials. In *Façade* he used various styles of popular and folk-music; in the serious works a melange of what he had heard in the concert hall. But whereas in *Façade* he impressed on the borrowed materials a personal wit, in the serious works he exhibited only an increasing expertness in their assimilation and manipulation. It is an expertness which often succeeds—i.e. makes the synthetic operation sound like the real thing—as it does in *Belshazzar's Feast*, for which Walton adapted existing musical resources to the Biblical text with technical mastery, fastidiousness and impressive effect; also in the Partita commissoned for the Cleveland Orchestra's fortieth anniversary, with its two fast movements of engaging orchestral hubbub and engaging Siciliana, in the Symphony No. 1, in parts of the Violin and Viola Concertos, and in the choral and orchestral portions of the opera *Troilus and Cressida*. Nevertheless, *Façade* seems to me Walton's most successful achievement as a composer.

England's outstandingly gifted composer in the twentieth century was Benjamin Britten; but his impressive gifts included an extraordinarily resourceful craftsmanship which, like Bach's, could on occasion operate on its own in a mere going through the motions of creative activity that produced a mere appearance of a musical operation—an appearance of saying something when nothing really was being said—the worst example being his opera *The Rape of Lucretia*. But in parts of *Albert Herring* one hears real and effective invention for the situation—in what, for example, Britten invents for Lady Billows's grand announcement to Albert of his election to be King of the May, for the festivities and fun at the coronation party, for the dirge in the last scene. And from first to last in *A Midsummer Night's Dream* the music establishes the atmosphere of the scenes, points up Shakespeare's words, and works with superb effect with and for the play on its three levels: the unreal supernatural level of Oberon and Titania (established by the counter-tenor voice of Oberon, the coloratura style of

Titania), the real human level of the lovers, the low-comedy level of the artisans. It is Britten's finest work.

Peter Grimes also has writing in which the resourcefulness operates freshly and creatively in the service of real imaginative effort for the dramatic purpose. It is, I remember from the production I saw, music which effectively carries and points up the happenings on the stage; but it is, I find now, music which much of the time has, beyond its dramatic usefulness, no intrinsic quality to make it interesting to listen to by itself—the quality, for example, that melody might have and that the actual recitative and arioso don't have. However, the Four Sea Interludes and Passacaglia are impressive.

Other Britten works that are real creations are *Les Illuminations* for soprano or tenor and strings, the Serenade for Tenor, Horn and Strings, the cantata *St. Nicolas,* his imaginative and attractive settings of English folksongs, and *The Young Person's Guide to the Orchestra*—an ingenious set of variations and concluding fugue on a theme of Purcell. I find some of Britten's arrangements in *A Ceremony of Carols* effective and beautiful, too, but some—e.g. *In Freezing Winter Night*—too elaborate and clever.

The rest you can safely neglect: the boyhood trifles he made into *A Simple Symphony;* the clever resourcefulness of the Variations on a Theme of Frank Bridge, the *Sinfonia da Requiem,* the Nocturne for Tenor, Seven Obbligato Instruments and Strings, *Phaedra,* the songs. Also the other operas—*Billy Budd,* in which exuberant resourcefulness unrestrained by a sense of fitness produces Billy's florid singing in his duet with the old sailor but proves inadequate to the musical requirements of some of the later dramatic situations—e.g. Captain Vere's thoughts after the killing of Claggert (in the revised two-act version I hear only one piece of effective music—Budd's monologue before dawn of the day of his execution, a sustained melodic flow in a style suggesting folksong that is hauntingly lovely); *The Turn of the Screw,* which offers uninteresting "modern"-style vocal and instrumental sounds that have no expressive relation to the words and action; and *Death in Venice,* whose writing doesn't convey the subtleties embodied in Mann's prose narrative and is of no real musical interest in itself.

That leaves the *War Requiem*. It begins with some of Britten's most superbly effective invention—the powerful two-note opening phrases for the orchestra to which the chorus sings *"Requiem aeternam dona eis."* But then the boys' chorus enters with writing for *"Te decet hymnus"* that says nothing at all, and the solo tenor with writing that does no more for Wilfred Owen's poem *What passing-bells for these who die as cattle.* And thereafter there is the same alternation of now and then a passage of impressively effective writing, and more often a passage that is a mere craftsman's spinning of notes.

The most widely known English composer after Britten is Sir Michael Tippett; and in the face of the published belief of so excellent a musician as Colin Davis that the opera *The Midsummer Marriage* is "a musical outpouring unique in the history of English music" I must report that my ears hear nothing in it of the slightest musical interest; and the same might be said of the endless manipulation of meaningless substance in Tippett's Symphony No. 2.

In twentieth-century France there has been little music of consequence apart from Debussy's. Certainly not the elaborately contrived trivialities of Ravel—though if either of Koussevitzky's Boston Symphony recordings of Ravel's *Daphnis et Chloé* Suite No. 2 is ever reissued, that one work would be worth having just for those miraculous performances; and the pianist Webster Aitken once made me see that Ravel's piano music, which cannot provide musical experiences of any value by the expressive or evocative power of its content, does provide the player and some listeners with exciting experiences of a different, non-musical kind by the effectiveness of its exploitation of the resources of the instrument.

Most of Poulenc's music has no appeal for me, either; but parts of his Concerto for Organ, Strings and Tympani are engaging; and the music in popular styles which carries the buffooneries of his early opera *Les Mamelles de Tirésias* is enjoyable, too. At one time the melodic arioso of Poulenc's second opera, *Dialogue des Carmelites,* and the orchestral writing that introduces, supports and comments on the action, seemed accomplished and suitable as a setting of the Bernanos play—about a fear-ridden girl of the French nobility who finds the courage to ascend the scaffold with the other nuns of her Carmelite order. Hearing it again some years later, however, the mellifluous writing had less interest for my ear and appeared to do very little for the dramatic action. And while the forty-five minutes of fragments of recitative and arioso in his last opera, *La Voix humaine*, constitutes a tour de force for its solitary singer—in the character of a woman at one end of a telephone line, who tries desperately and unsuccessfully to hold on to her lover at the other end—for the listener the work becomes boring after the first few minutes. As for Honegger's opera, *Jeanne d'Arc au Bûcher*, I would say the subject of Joan is one for the treatment—at once simple and monumental—it got in the great Dreyer film years ago, not for the inflated rhetoric of the Claudel text and Honneger's complementary mood- and background-music of the kind and quality one hears in films.

On the other hand, the Serenade for Small Orchestra by Jean Françaix, which Balanchine used for his ballet *À la Françaix*, is very engaging. Perhaps Satie's ballet scores *Parade, Les Aventures de Mercure* and *Relâche* would likewise, if heard with their ballets, reveal what the English musician and writer Constant Lambert admired in them, but it doesn't appear when they are heard by themselves. And Satie's piano pieces, to me, reveal a gift for extremely funny titles and comments but not for the music to go with them. Milhaud's expertly contrived music I have found uninteresting, apart from the effective but misplaced jazz elements in certain of his scores (e.g. *La Création du monde*) and his sonorous arrangements of the music of Couperin. Finally, there is Boulez, who is, with all his extraordinary musical and intellectual gifts, an eccentric in his thinking and composing whose music—*Le Marteau sans maître, Pli selon pli, Doubles*—has made no sense to me at all.

The major Italian operatic composer after Verdi was Puccini.*

---

* Boito, the only significant Italian musical figure between Verdi and Puccini, was a man of literary skill and ideas but no creative power in music; *Mefistofele*, the work by which he is remembered as a composer, demonstrates his ability to use the resources of his period competently, but the few moderate successes in that use—notably Margherita's *L'Altra notte* and some of her later phrases to Faust in

Jose Iturbi I think it was who said of himself that he was not the best pianist in the world but not the worst, and Puccini is supposed to have felt that way about his operas. One senses it in the music. There is no strutting about, no declaiming by gods, but ordinary human emotions expressed in a stream of melody; no pretentiousness, no inflation, no bombast, but directness, honesty and great technical skill. *Madama Butterfly* was the first opera that I heard at the Metropolitan, with Geraldine Farrar, still lovely to look at and listen to, in the title role, and Arturo Toscanini conducting. The attractions of Puccini and Miss Farrar continued strong for several years. Even when the tug at the heart-strings in the third and fourth acts of *La Bohème* had come to feel a little strong, the lighter moments in that opera still seemed delightful. However, other things became more interesting to me, and a performance of *Madama Butterfly* in the mid-1930s was the first I had heard in at least fifteen years. It was an extraordinary experience to recognize details as they appeared, to recall how this or that melody had intoxicated me twenty years before, and to be unaffected by it now. As a detached observer I could still note that the writing was fluently melodious and suave and expertly handled, but the intervening years had brought the recognition that Puccini's music is superficial in a way that Verdi's is not. And today Puccini's operas impress me as the worst kind of trash.

The even lower-grade operas of Leoncavallo (*I Pagliacci*), Mascagni (*Cavalleria Rusticana, L'Amico Fritz, Iris*), Giordano (*Andrea Chénier, Fedora*), Cilea (*Adriana Lecouvreur*), Ponchielli (*La Gioconda*), Zandonai (*Francesca da Rimini*) and Montemezzi (*L'Amore dei tre re*) you can skip as well. Busoni's music has its cult, but for reasons that are not discernable in his opera *Dr. Faust*—to my ear the writing of a highly accomplished composer able to make elaborate gestures of saying the portentous things he doesn't really have to say (and not in his trashy piano music, either, or in most of his piano transcriptions, some of which are quite the most tasteless specimens of the genre that I can recall).

Among more recent Italian composers one of the better is Luigi

---

in the prison scene—count for little beside the major failure, the ineffective music for the opera's principal character. —B.H.H.

Dallapiccola; I would suppose Berg's idiom to be one of the sources of the language of Dallapiccola that I find impressive in the *Marsia* Suite for orchestra, and that provided forceful musical underlining of another nightmarish drama in the opera *The Prisoner*. A good instrumental work is the *Cinque frammenti di Saffo*. Another is the *Tartiniana* for violin and orchestra, in which Dallapiccola does what Stravinsky has done so many times—i.e. lets his mind play with thematic substance from the music of another composer—and in which Dallapiccola's application to Tartini's themes of his own devices of manipulation, his development of them in his own language, achieves writing that is fascinatingly put together, impressive, and at times moving. However, some other works of his have offered only a variety of ingenious combinations of sonorities which are not a medium of expressive communication to me or attractive to the ear merely as combinations of sonorities.

If you wish to explore the individual products of some of the lesser twentieth-century composers, you might begin with Vittorio Rieti's pleasant *Suite champêtre*. Most of the writing of Martinů provides successive examples of this composer's ability to spin out nothing much to nothing much more, but his Piano Concerto No. 4 (*Incantation*), while it does not say anything of great consequence, is enjoyable to listen to and at times impressive in its toccata-like play with sonorities and effects. Lutoslawski's Concerto for Orchestra is more powerful and interesting; but two later pieces of his, *Funeral Music* and *Venetian Games,* convey no expressive meaning to me. Werner Egk's early Quattro Canzoni has none of the extemely unattractive and ineffectual writing of his opera *The Inspector General*, but instead popular Italian melodic and rhythmic styles manipulated in harmonically dissonant and orchestrally elaborate contexts, with results that retain some of the attractiveness of the popular materials and add the attractiveness of some of the treatment they are given; Gottfried von Einem's Piano Concerto Op. 20 also offers cleverly effective manipulation of traditional materials, and his resourceful eclectic writing in *Das Stundenlied* is an effective musical context for the Brecht words. In von Einem's effective opera *The Trial,* based on the Kafka novel about a man destroyed by a relentlessly hostile world for reasons and in ways beyond rational comprehension, the music gives expressive force not to particular incidents or words but to the terrifying situation, and it does this not with the vocal writing but with the powerful orchestral commentary—the effect of the work, for me, being that of a long orchestral crescendo which reaches a shattering climax in the last scene.

Finally, there is in addition some unprofound and enjoyable music that has presented no difficulties to anyone's ears and mind: the slight works in which de Falla uses the piquant Spanish idiom with twentieth-century sophistication and fastidiousness—his Suite from *The Three-Cornered Hat*, the *Seven Spanish Popular Songs*, the Dance from *La Vida breve*, the Suite from *El Amor brujo*, and the *Nights in the Gardens of Spain* (but not the harpsichord Concerto); Albéniz's *Ibéria;* a few engaging songs by the Cuban composer, Joaquín Nin; Dukas's amusing *Sorcerer's Apprentice;* Enesco's Rumanian Rhapsodies; Respighi's brilliant orchestrations of some of Rossini's small vocal and instrumental pieces in *La Boutique fantasque* and *Rossiniana,* and his own *Fountains* and *Pines of Rome, The Birds,* and *Ancient Airs and Dances* (but not his dreadful *Roman Festivals*).

Isaac Albéniz (1860–1909)
Ernest Bloch (1880–1959)
Arrigo Boito (1842–1918)
Pierre Boulez (b. 1926)
Benjamin Britten (1913–1976)
Ferruccio Busoni (1866–1924)
Francesco Cilea (1866–1950)
Luigi Dallapiccola (1904–1975)
Frederick Delius (1862–1934)
Paul Dukas (1865–1935)
Werner Egk (b. 1901)
Gottfried von Einem (b. 1918)
Sir Edward Elgar (1857–1934)
Georges Enesco (1881-1955)
Manuel de Falla (1876–1946)

Jean Françaix (b. 1912)
Umberto Giordano (1867–1948)
Arthur Honegger (1892–1955)
Leos Janáček (1854–1928)
Dmitri Kabalevsky (1904–1987)
Aram Khachaturian (1903–1978)
Ruggero Leoncavallo (1857–1919)
Witold Lutoslawski (b. 1913)
Bohuslav Martinů (1890–1959)
Pietro Mascagni (1863–1945)
Darius Milhaud (1892–1974)
Italo Montemezzi (1875–1952)
Carl Nielsen (1865–1931)
Joaquín María Nin (b. 1908)
Amilcare Ponchielli (1834–1886)
Francis Poulenc (1899–1963)
Sergei Prokofiev (1891–1953)
Giacomo Puccini (1858–1924)
Sergei Rachmaninoff (1873–1943)
Maurice Ravel (1875–1937)
Ottorino Respighi (1879–1936)
Vittorio Rieti (b. 1898)
Erik Satie (1866–1925)
Alexander Scriabin (1872–1915)
Dmitri Shostakovitch (1906–1975)
Jean Sibelius (1865–1957)
Sir Michael Tippett (b. 1905)
Ralph Vaughan Williams (1872–1958)
Sir William Walton (b. 1902)
Riccardo Zandonai (1883–1944)

22

American Music

Virgil Thomson once observed in a review of a work by Howard Hanson that Hanson had written lots of music, which made him a real composer, but that the music was as standardized in expression as it was eclectic in style, which made him not a real creator. I would say this of a great many other American composers, past and present—among them Edward MacDowell, Samuel Barber, Gian Carlo Menotti and George Rochberg. And I would go further and say that some Americans haven't really created anything even in music that has *not* been standardized and eclectic. I felt this about Roy Harris, Henry Cowell, Walter Piston, Wallingford Riegger and David Diamond, whose music was heard a great deal at one time; about Carl Ruggles and Charles Ives, whose music has aroused interest by not being heard (nowadays it is axiomatic that every work of Ives that had to wait fifty years for its first performance is a shamefully neglected masterpiece by a composer of genius); and I feel it about William Schuman, Roger Sessions, John Cage, George Crumb, Charles Wuorinen, Steve Reich and others whose music is heard a great deal nowadays.

But the stamp of real creative power is, I think, unmistakable in the music of Griffes—in the early *Roman Sketches* for piano (of which the familiar *White Peacock* has been orchestrated) that he wrote in a language and style derived from French impressionistic piano music of the turn of the century; in most of the *Poem* for flute and piano—which is to say all but the dance in the middle; and in the later Piano Sonata, in which he struck out in a new language and style related to the "modern" tendencies of his time, producing a work that is impressive by the authoritative manipulation of the materials rather than effective as musical communication. (*The Pleasure-Dome of Kubla Khan* for orchestra is less consequential than these others.)

The best works of Loeffler, Griffes's near contemporary—*Poem, The Death of Tintagiles* and the *Pagan Poem,* all for orchestra—are those of a minor master, almost excessively fastidious in emotion and workmanship. The *Pagan Poem,* which used to be played a great deal in the 1920s, impresses one today as lacking continuity and coherence; but one still enjoys the effective writing, the loveliness of individual bits of material.

Of more recent instrumental music Harold Shapero's *Symphony for Classical Orchestra* has impressed me with the creative power I have been talking about. It is evocative of the past but stamped with the impress of Shapero's mind in the way some of Stravinsky's works are that hark back to earlier forms; and it is like Stravinsky's also in the assured mastery of the operation and the engaging result. And creative power is heard in Alexei Haieff's Piano Concerto—in the building up of sustained tension with explosive ostinato figures in the manner of Stravinsky but with ideas of his own that make it a work as individual as it is arresting. Several of Haieff's *Five Pieces for Piano* and *Four Juke Box Pieces* are engaging, too. But his expert manipulation of rhythm, sonority, and texture in his Quartet No. 1 communicates nothing to me except in the brief and lovely final movement.

In Elliott Carter's music I am able to appreciate the impressiveness, the highly developed competence and originality, of the enormously complex objects he creates, but I must report that listening to what goes on in them is, for me, like listening to what goes on in a conversation in a foreign language I don't know, and that I do not find them enjoyable or interesting simply as sounds. Similarly in Alan Hovhaness's *Khaldis,* a concerto for piano, four trumpets and percussion, as in several of his piano pieces, he has fashioned a musical language for himself out of Armenian and other Asiatic sources—a language I can recognize as a medium of expressive communication for him, though it is for me as exotic as its sources; I am, then, emotionally uninvolved, and listening on the outside, so to speak, I can only note this piquant sonority here, this striking effect there.

As for Ives, the great to-do about the originality that showed itself in his use of this or that revolutionary procedure many years before Schönberg and others seems to me to be about what is unimportant: the important thing is what music Ives produced with whatever technique he used. In the Symphony No. 2, then, one hears occasional lovely writing, especially in the slow portions; but one hears it in a progression that rambles on, shifting from one thing to another in one tempo and another, with no integration and no cumulative effect. And the best of Ives's music is fitful and eccentric in that way.

But some of Ives's music is like the Symphony No. 3, none of which registers on my mind as coherent and meaningful musical thinking. And other pieces are like *The Unanswered Question* in that they offer a big idea and little music—strings in the back playing quiet chords which represent the conventional life that goes on and on, while a trumpet on one side repeats a phrase which asks if this is what life is good for, and increasingly agitated exclamations of flutes on the other side make futile attempts at an answer. And still others are like the Symphony No. 4, which offers a bedlam Ives thought of as embodying "the searching questions of 'What?' and 'Why?' which the spirit of man asks of life," and "the diverse answers in which existence replies."

The outstanding American composer of serious music, then, is Aaron Copland. The creative power I have been talking about was evident in Copland's engaging *Music for the Theater* when it was first heard in 1925. And it remained so even in the unattractive, inaccessible works, written in an austere, highly dissonant "modern" idiom, that came after *Music for the Theater*—notably the stony *Piano Variations* of 1930. But one was glad to have this creative power manifest itself agreeably again in the lovely ballet score *Billy the Kid* (1938), one of the first of a series of such ballet and film scores written in a simpler and more attractive idiom—*Music for Radio* (1937), *Music for the Movies* (1942), *Rodeo* (1942), *Appalachian Spring* (1944)—which continued to be more engaging than the occasional symphonic, instrumental and chamber works he went on writing in his dissonant style—the Sonata (1941) and Fantasy (1957) for piano, the *Short Symphony* (1933—the Symphony No. 2, later rewritten as the Sextet for string quartet, clarinet and piano), the Symphonic Ode (1927–29, and revised in 1955), and *Connotations* (1962). (As for *El Salón Mexico* (1936), Copland said he hoped to have put in something of the spirit of the Mexican people that he felt in the popular tunes he had heard. However, with his treatment of the languorous tunes—which put them into a rhythmic straitjacket and poured harmonic acid over them—I would say he put into the work the spirit not of the Mexican people but of Aaron Copland.)

Copland's opera *The Tender Land* (1954 and later revised) seems to me the finest of the works he wrote for a wide audience—his largest and most richly filled-out canvas, so to speak. One is struck first by the loveliness achieved with the assured mastery one is always aware of in Copland's operation; then by the variety of expression and its unfailing adequacy for the dramatic purposes, the power when this is called for; and in the end by the rich profusion of the invention and elaboration. (It must be added, however, that Horace Everett's libretto makes of an incident in the life of a simple rural family something high-flown that I for one cannot believe in; one should perhaps listen to the last scene of *The Tender Land* in the way one listens to *Il Trovatore;* but there is the difficulty that what is unbelievable in *The Tender Land* can't, because of its immediacy in time and place and its English words, be put out of mind as easily as what is unbelievable in *Il Trovatore*.)

Earlier I spoke of Copland's attempt, in a book he published in 1941,* to persuade us that music like Schönberg's in Europe or his own *Piano Variations* here, when rightly heard and understood, was as natural and acceptable to our ears, as interesting to our minds, as people a hundred years ago found their music. In that connection it is interesting to note that in 1938 Copland had written the first of his ballet and film scores which Arthur Berger, in his excellent book on Copland, tells us represented his decision to stop writing esoteric abstract works for a small special public and write instead music that would interest the large general music public—a decision implying recognition that music like

---

* Aaron Copland, *Our New Music* (New York, 1941).

Schönberg's in Europe or Copland's *Piano Variations* here was *not* as natural and acceptable to our ears, as interesting to our minds, as people a hundred years ago found their music.

In opera the distinguished creative achievements other than Copland's *The Tender Land* have been Virgil Thomson's *Four Saints in Three Acts* and *The Mother of Us All*. Thomson, whom I seldom find successful with autonomously organized instrumental pieces is often brilliantly successful with music organized around words—specifically the words of Gertrude Stein, which he uses in these two works. By separating and differentiating the repetitions of a Gertrude Stein verbal sequence Thomson's music articulates them, gives them point and even sense, imparts to them its own structure and climax, and achieves something unique, delightful, and often very funny. Some of the humor consists in skillful musical pointing up—by the high-lighting of a group of words, the placing of it in relation to its context—of Stein's surprises and irrelevancies of juxtaposition; and Thomson adds occasional incongruities of his own contriving between words and music—words of little or no sense or weight, musical style and structure of great emotional import and weight. But when such music is given to words like the "led, said, wed, dead" sequence in *Four Saints* the result is very moving. However, in Thomson's last opera, *Lord Byron*—a late setting of a feeble libretto by Jack Larson—I hear vocal writing that is mostly a mere shapeless doodling of notes to carry words to which it has no expressive relation, frequent bizarre-sounding orchestral contrivance with no relation to what is being sung, and excruciatingly discordant choral writing with no justification I can discover and no precedent in Thomson's earlier operas. To these failures of powers is added a failure of judgment: the choice—as the vocal medium of the work's darkly passionate protagonist—of a high light tenor voice, employed much of the time in its cruelly taxing highest range.

Of Thomson's other vocal music *Capitals, Capitals* is like a preliminary tryout of his method of setting Gertrude Stein words, in which the words and their musical treatment haven't enough variety and richness to hold interest for more than two or three of the work's twenty minutes. And Thomson's *Stabat Mater* is written in a French vocal style that I don't care for even in the original. Among Thomson's successful instrumental pieces is the fine score for the ballet *Filling Station,* his bland and at times amusingly parodistic *Synthetic Waltzes* for two pianos, the Cello Concerto—a good-humored piece that characteristically repeats rather than develops its engaging hymn tunes—and the *Acadian Songs and Dances* from his music for the film *Louisiana Story.*

Having said that Thomson's and Copland's are the only distinguished American operas, perhaps this is the place to speak of the thinking that has gone into some of the others. Leonard Bernstein, coming to the final sequence in the excellent *Omnibus* television talk in which he described what the music in an opera does with the drama, found the real meaning of the *grand* in grand opera to be the way the music magnifies and crystallizes emotion—to the point, he added, of making words almost unnecessary. Opera reaches its highest state, he said, when the music is so communicative that the merest general knowledge of the dramatic action provides us with the key to rich apprehension. Citing as an example the end of *Tristan und Isolde,* he pointed out that we don't have to understand every word Isolde sings to feel her exaltation. We have to know, said Bernstein, that—Tristan having died in her arms—Isolde stands over his body, ecstatic, mystically united with him, transfigured through love. And that is all we have to know for Wagner's music to do what every great work of art does—namely to create a special world of its own, into which we enter, and from which we emerge enriched and ennobled.

It was good to have this stated, and stated so well to so many people, for if it is the music in an opera that causes the drama to take place in the enriching and ennobling special world of the work of art, then it is the music that makes an opera valuable, worth performing and worth listening to, or makes it none of these. Good music translates even dramatic absurdity into a *Trovatore,* a *Rigoletto,* an *Aida;* poor music cannot make anything of a good drama but a poor opera.

I stress the primacy of the music because the tendency—of the American composer, the American public and most American critics—has been to make the drama primary, so that an interesting dramatic idea has won acceptance for music of little or no intrinsic value or dramatic force. The most spectacular successes of this kind in recent years have been won by the works of Menotti. I have already indicated that the music is derivative in a profusion of styles ranging from contemporary down to Puccini and even lower; and I listened to *Amahl and the Night Visitors,* as I have in fact listened to Menotti's other operas, with incredulous amazement—finding it difficult to believe I was really hearing these sugary, trashy tunes, that they could even have occurred to anyone operating as a serious composer today, that he could not have been too embarrassed to let anyone else hear them, and that other people could have considered them worth publishing to the world. But a lot of people like Puccini and worse; and the other reason for Menotti's success—his success even with sophisticated and professional listeners—is his choice of dramatic subjects whose development powerfully engages the audience's interest and emotions—so powerfully, in fact, that the audience is misled into thinking its interest and emotions are being powerfully engaged by the music, whereas actually the most striking fact about *The Consul* is the expressive inadequacy of the mellifluous melodic idiom for the moments of dramatic climax that it expands in the arias and ensembles. The same is true of *The Medium* and *The Old Maid.* But in *The Last Savage* I am struck by the loss of the former fluency of his trashy invention, and the discrepancy at point after point between the evident attempt and the feeble achievement even in his own terms.

And so with the operas of other American composers—Carlisle Floyd, Lee Hoiby, Douglas Moore, Hugo Weisgall, Vittorio Giannini, Jack Beeson, Robert Ward and above all Marc Blitzstein: all have relied on what happened on the stage to capture and hold attention, and have carried the stage action with music which in no instance has had the impress of an original creative mind. In Blitzstein's proletarian period his texts about the class struggle concealed from many listeners—including professional ones who should have known better—the feebleness and flatness which they would have heard in the music if their emotions had not been engaged and their judgments had not been confused by words about unions and vigilantes. (The intellectual level of his opera *The Cradle Will Rock* is indicated in the episode in which Mrs.

Mister, the wife of the owner of the steel company, bustles in to tell the minister, the Reverend Salvation, that her husband has told the President that the country must have war for its profits and the President has obeyed his orders, after which she gives the Reverend Salvation a roll of bills, and he steps into the pulpit and preaches a war sermon. To call this dated today is to imply that it was valid in 1937.)

Blitzstein made a further claim to attention in one work after another with some feature that was novel, daring and provocative of controversy. (With his string quartet the talk was all of the three movements written *Largo, Largo, Largo* and achieving differentiation through texture instead of pace.) I cannot conceive of sounds being feebler and flatter, sounds having less of the significance and effect they were intended to have, than the sounds which I heard during the first act of *No for an Answer;* but the act had its duet in which the boy sang "Fra-a-a-ancie, ta-ta-ta-ta-ta," which was clever and amusing and covered Blitzstein's inability to write music for the emotions of a couple in love—or in fact for any serious emotions or situations whatever. And later the distractions were the great plays of O'Casey and the popular ones of Hellman that he adapted for his own purposes—the unsuitable purposes, as it turned out, of American musical comedy. Not that there would have been anything wrong in Blitzstein's writing musical comedy; on the contrary, it was what he should have written, because it was what he had a gift for. But one's enjoyment of his good comic songs in *Juno,* for example, was lessened by the recollection of what had been in the original play—O'Casey's *Juno and the Paycock*—at each point, and by the thought of what a monstrous idea it had been to turn the great play into a series of musical-comedy jokes.

This brings us to another idea with no justification in reality—that the distinctively American opera will evolve from the American musical. It was in connection with Blitzstein's *Regina*—his setting of Lillian Hellman's melodrama *The Little Foxes*—that Leonard Bernstein first stated his belief that, with its increasing use of the technical devices of opera—the use, for example, of the device of double soliloquy in Rodgers and Hammerstein's *South Pacific*—the American musical comedy was becoming the American opera. This left out of account what seems to me the decisive factor in the matter—namely, the expressive connotation of the musical substance to which the technical devices are applied: if the musical setting of the text employs the language of serious music, the resulting expressive communication is that of opera; if it employs the language of musical comedy, the resulting expressive communication is that of musical comedy. And this is true no matter how many technical devices of opera are introduced: when the device of double soliloquy is used with substance in the language of serious music in the second-act duet of Sophie and Octavian right after the presentation of the rose in *Der Rosenkavalier,* the result is opera; when this device is used with substance in the language of musical comedy in *South Pacific,* the result is musical comedy. Nor does the musical comedy become opera when its musical language is used in the setting of a serious or profound book or play, as in Kurt Weill's *Lost in the Stars,* derived from Alan Paton's *Cry, the Beloved Country,* or Blitzstein's *Regina* or *Juno.* The result is, rather, musical falsification of the play.

Gershwin's career as a serious composer represented the further fallacious idea that, since he was an outstanding writer of distinctively American show tunes, he was the man to write the distinctively American symphony and opera, and those show tunes were the thing to make them out of—which was like saying the Austrian symphony or opera had to be made by Johann Strauss II out of his waltzes. If Johann Strauss had acted on this idea he would have produced works like Gershwin's Piano Concerto and *Porgy and Bess,* which are filled with characteristic show music that communicates exactly what it would communicate in a musical show—but pieced together in the required formal patterns with derivative and inconsequential connective material in the idiom of serious music. And *Porgy* represents the additional fallacy, that because the American Black has contributed to the amalgam of Broadway show music, Broadway show tunes are the right musical medium for any drama about Blacks: we have, then, life in Catfish Row expressed in tunes like *Summertime* and *Bess, You Is My Woman Now* that one might have heard sung by white singers in a Gershwin musical, and that don't acquire any meaning connected with Blacks in Catfish Row when they are sung by Black singers in *Porgy and Bess.* In addition we have these tunes alternating with even more glaringly incongruous material in styles borrowed from grand opera—like the recitative in which Catfish Row Blacks sing such facts as that they will have to get up at five o'clock the next morning. It is the principals' songs, then, and some of the choral passages that are the work's valuable music, not the ineffective arioso dialogue (spoken dialogue like that of Chabrier's opera would have been better for *Porgy*).

(The fallacious thinking responsible for *Porgy and Bess* is responsible also for what has been called an "American folk opera"—Kurt Weill's *Down in the Valley.* Here it is folksongs that are the right musical medium for any play about rural folk; so that we have the rural characters of *Down in the Valley* singing their anguish and terror and other powerful emotions in expressively unrelated American folk melodies separated from their own texts. And as if this weren't enough, when the man about to be hanged thinks with desperate longing of his girl, or she thinks similarly of him, each breaks into what in actual style—including Robert Russell Bennett style of orchestration—is a leading tenor's or soprano's number in a Broadway musical.)

Only in *An American in Paris* does Gershwin invent delightfully imaginative non-show-music material, in addition to the superb blues in the middle. In this piece he also is able to integrate his material in a coherent form; and it is for me his one unqualified success as a serious composer. Concerning the Piano Concerto I will add that, while the whole idea in the first movement of producing the sequence of exposition, development and recapitulation of sonata form with show music material was wrong, some of the episodes Gershwin produced from his themes in the process are superb. And so too is much of the material in the two Rhapsodies—the flow of attractive invention that leads to the simple and grand big tune in *Rhapsody in Blue,* the *Second Rhapsody*'s big tune itself, one of Gershwin's most gorgeous creations, a sinuous progression with extensions and developments that are made exciting by startling harmonic shifts. Enjoyable, too, are Gershwin's actual musical shows—*Oh, Kay!, Girl*

Crazy, Of Thee I Sing, Lady Be Good, Tip Toes, Primrose—in whose overtures the charming songs are built up and elaborated impressively.

Gershwin's *Oh, Kay!* is an example of what might be called the classical form of the American musical—in which the book was nonsense devised to provide the principals with occasions for their songs and dances. That form continued for some time, giving us *Jamaica,* in which nothing happens except the excuses for the brilliant lyrics of E. Y. Harburg and the songs of Howard Arlen that make these lyrics work so effectively, *Music in the Air,* with some of Jerome Kern's loveliest music, and others with wonderful music by Vincent Youmans and Irving Berlin.

But there have been other musicals with changes. Some of the changes have merely made the musical a better musical, by having the lyrics and songs take off from situations in a book that makes sense, as in Lerner and Loewe's *My Fair Lady,* Jerome Kern's *Show Boat,* Cole Porter's *Kiss Me, Kate,* and Rodgers and Hart's *The Boys from Syracuse* and *Pal Joey.**

Other changes in the musical, however, have had the purpose of making it something else, more worthy and important—of helping it become the American opera. This has given us Frank Loesser's *The Most Happy Fella,* with its quasi-operatic setting of the entire text of its book derived from a serious play; and Leonard Bernstein's score for *West Side Story,* with its mixture of serious and popular idioms, its application to them of the elaborate technical and specifically operatic devices that Bernstein contends are changing the musical to opera.

Most of the music of *West Side Story* I don't find interesting to listen to (though Stephen Sondheim's lyrics and Bernstein's intricate music make "America" a brilliant song). But its effectiveness as theater illustrates a significant fact about Bernstein the com-

---

*The Rodgers and Hart musicals are, moreover, in a special style, one of whose characteristics, it seems to me, is the deceptive appearance of simplicity and innocence. This is usually created by the music as one begins to hear it; then, as the phrase rounds itself out with the line of the lyric, the music underscores the witty point of the words and one gets the impact of the unsuspected wicked force behind the dead-pan innocent simplicity—as in "Couldn't sleep . . . and wouldn't sleep . . . Until I could sleep where I shouldn't sleep" in "Bewitched" from *Pal Joey.* —B. H. H.

poser. In an interview following a broadcast of his *Age of Anxiety* Symphony some years ago Bernstein described the conflict in the life of someone who was both a composer and a conductor. The composer, he said, was an introverted person with a strong inner life; the conductor was always dealing with various large groups of people, and thus leading a mostly external life. I found it difficult to imagine the composer of the work I had just heard as an introverted person with a strong inner life: like his other music it had given me the impression of the composer in Bernstein being as much an extrovert as the conductor—the impression, that is, that the composer, like the conductor, lacked an inner discipline, a controlling sense of measure, and that the poor quality of the ideas, the sprawling forms, were a result of this lack, which left the creative process one of everything going out with nothing held back. And the years since then haven't changed the operation, but have only made worse what goes out instead of being held back—e.g. the *Kaddish* symphony, in which the basic Norman Corwin style of vocal rhetoric is infused with a vulgarity of Bernstein's own, giving the words an awfulness that forbids quotation, and in which the music is largely a suitably raucous, but hardly more bearable, ranting in the dissonant idiom of the day.

It is his work for musical shows that seems to me the most successful of the numerous Bernstein operations. In this genre too he is not an original creator: in *On the Town* and *Wonderful Town* he only uses the standard materials of Broadway show music enjoyably; in *Candide* he uses every musical style *except* that of Broadway show music in writing that is brilliant in the way it gives effect to Richard Wilbur's witty lyrics; and in *Trouble in Tahiti* he demonstrates conclusively that his gifts operate most successfully for comedy: his serious music for this play about a disenchanted suburban couple is highly accomplished; but it is the gift for mimicry and parody, which he had applied with such brilliant results to the styles of Italian opera in the song "Glitter and Be Gay" in *Candide,* that operates here in the service of a sense for effective theater—placing on the omnipresent television screen of today a dance-band trio of a girl and two boys who periodically croon into the mike in three-part harmony their background commentary on the mornin' sun that kisses the windows, kisses the walls, of the liddle white house, the liddle white house in Scarsdale, kisses the driveway, kisses the lawn, kisses the newspaper at the front door, of the liddle white house in Highland Park . . . the liddle white house in Shaker Heights . . .

Harold Arlen (b. 1905)
Samuel Barber (1910–1981)
Jack Beeson (b. 1921)
Irving Berlin (1888–1989)
Leonard Bernstein (1918–1990)
Marc Blitzstein (1905–1964)
John Cage (b. 1912)
Elliott Carter (b. 1908)
Aaron Copland (1900–1990)
Henry Cowell (1897–1965)
George Crumb (b. 1929)
David Diamond (b. 1915)
Carlisle Floyd (b. 1926)
George Gershwin (1898–1937)
Vittorio Giannini (1903–1956)
Charles Tomlinson Griffes (1884–1920)
Alexei Haieff (b. 1914)
Howard Hanson (1896–1981)
Roy Harris (1898–1979)
Lee Hoiby (b. 1926)
Alan Hovhaness (b. 1911)
Charles Ives (1874–1954)
Jerome Kern (1885–1945)
Charles Martin Loeffler (1861–1935)
Frank Loesser (b. 1910)
Frederick Loewe (b. 1904)
Edward MacDowell (1860–1908)
Gian Carlo Menotti (b. 1911)
Douglas Moore (1893–1969)
Walter Piston (1894–1976)

Cole Porter (1891–1964)
Steve Reich (b. 1936)
Wallingford Riegger (1885–1961)
George Rochberg (b. 1918)
Richard Rodgers (1902–1979)
Carl Ruggles (1876–1971)
William Schuman (b. 1910)
Roger Sessions (1896–1985)
Harold Shapero (1920–1985)
Virgil Thomson (1896–1989)
Robert Ward (b. 1917)
Kurt Weill (1900–1950)
Hugo Weisgall (b. 1912)
Charles Wuorinen (b. 1938)
Vincent Youmans (1898–1946)

PART TWO

23

Criticism

The comments of Berlioz on *Selva opaca* from *William Tell* that I quoted in my discussion of Rossini occur in the long essay on *Tell* that Berlioz wrote for the *Gazette musicale de Paris* in 1834 and that is reprinted in Strunk's *Source Readings in Music History*. I consider this one example of the formal criticism Berlioz wrote for French periodicals and newspapers well worth the price of the entire volume; but at the very least it is worth a visit to the library; for I know no better introduction to the writing of the greatest of music critics. And remembering again how indiscriminately the word *great* is tossed about, I will establish what I mean when I apply it to Berlioz's criticism.

What I mean is much the same as what I meant when I applied it to Beethoven's music. Not only does one find in Berlioz's criticism the critical perception that is the absolute essential in such writing; not only does one find this perception formulating itself with literary brilliance and delightful gaiety and wit. In addition one finds—behind all the literary brilliance and gaiety—that perception dealing rigorously with the work of art before it; and with this integrity in relation to the material there is an intensity, a passion, a greatness of spirit in the operation that bring tears to my eyes whenever I read the writing.

These personal qualities appear most vividly of course in the

For full titles and publication details of the books discussed in this chapter, see below: *Bibliography*. —*Ed.*

personal writing—the *Memoirs,* the letters. Consider for example the letter in which Berlioz tells his father of his determination to become a composer:

> I am willingly swept away toward a magnificent career (one can apply no other term to a career in the arts) and not toward my ruin; for I believe I will succeed, yes, I believe it: the matter is no longer one for considerations of modesty; to prove to you that I am leaving nothing to chance I think, I am convinced that I will distinguish myself in music, every outward sign points to it; and in myself the voice of nature is stronger than the strictest decrees of reason. I have all imaginable odds in my favor if you will back me; I won't need to give lessons like so many others to be sure of a living; I possess some fields of knowledge and elements of others, of a kind that will enable me one day to deepen them; and certainly I have experienced passions strong enough for me not to make mistakes whenever there will be need to represent them or give them voice [make them speak].
>
> If I were condemned mercilessly to die of hunger in the event of failure (this would not lessen my persistence, I assure you) your arguments at least and your anxiety would be more justified; but that is not the case, and on the lowest estimate I am convinced that I will be able one day to have an income of two thousand francs; but let us say only fifteen hundred francs, I will live even on this sum; let us say only twelve hundred, I would be satisfied, [and?] even if music were to bring me nothing. In short I want to make a name for myself, I want to leave on earth some traces of my existence; and such is the strength of this feeling, which has within it nothing but what is noble, that I would rather be Gluck or Méhul dead than what I am in the prime of life.
>
> That is the way I think, that is what I am, and nothing in the world will be able to change me; you could withdraw all help from me or force me to leave Paris, but I don't believe that, you wouldn't want in this way to make me lose the best years of my life, and break the magnetic needle which you cannot prevent from obeying the attraction of the poles.
>
> Farewell, my dear papa, reread my letter, and do not ascribe it to some excited impulse, never perhaps have I been more calm. I embrace you affectionately as well as Mama and my sisters.
>
> Your respectful and affectionate son,
> *H. Berlioz*

I share Turner's doubt that one can read this without being moved, and especially moved if one knows what came of those confident hopes—if one has read Berlioz's own account in his *Memoirs* of the experiences that lead him to write twenty years later:

> . . . I end . . . with profuse thanks to sacred Germany where the worship of art has kept itself pure; to you, generous England; to you, Russia, who saved me; to you, my good friends in France; to you, lofty hearts and minds of all nations whom I have known. I was fortunate in knowing you; I have, and I will faithfully keep, the most precious memory of our relations. As for you, maniacs, stupid mastiffs and bulls, as for you my Guildensterns, my Rosencrantzes, my Iagos, my little Osrics, serpents and insects of every kind, "farewell my . . . friends"; I despise you, and I hope not to die before I have forgotten you.

The *Memoirs*, then, is something to read because it is a remarkable and superbly written personal document. But also it is valuable for the incidental observations on music one encounters in it.

In addition to his formal music criticism, some of which he collected in the volume *À Travers Chants*, Berlioz wrote feuilletons—imaginative, ironic, witty, and often very funny. Of these he published two collections, *Les Soirées de l'orchestre* (usually translated as *Evenings in the Orchestra*) and *Les Grotesques de la musique*. The first, *Evenings in the Orchestra*, has an unusual and amusing framework: the author spends a number of evenings in the orchestra pit of an opera house; and when a worthless opera is performed the members of the orchestra read, tell stories or talk about music, providing the opportunities for Berlioz to introduce his articles. Though the volume includes pieces of serious criticism, like the long study of Spontini or the report on music in London, its contents are mostly the lighter, sometimes extravagantly fantastical or satirical, but always perceptive writings, like the pieces on the art of the claque, the life cycle of the opera tenor, the miseries of being a critic.

À Travers Chants and *Les Grotesques de la musique* have not been translated into English as of this writing. Of the English translations of the others, the nineteenth-century Holmes version of the

Memoirs, edited and extensively retranslated by Sir Ernest New-man in 1932, does not conform to the French words in every instance but even so gives a better equivalent in English of Berlioz's vivid and impassioned French than David Cairns's translation of the 1960s, which—by adhering even less to Berlioz's words, order of words and sentence structure—has him writing in the unimpassioned manner of a well-bred Londoner. Humphrey Searle's *Berlioz: A Selection from His Letters* offers better choices of letters and better translations than Jacques Barzun's collection *New Letters of Berlioz 1830–1868*. Charles E. Roche's original 1929 translation of *Evenings in the Orchestra* is preferable to the prissy urbanity of Barzun's later revision of it. And by the time you read this there may be others.

For music criticism comparable with Berlioz's—the finest written in English, and some of the finest in any language—read the concert reviews and articles of Bernard Shaw. You may be surprised to hear that he did such writing; but the fact is you will do better to read what he said about a performance at Covent Garden in 1890 than what you will find in a newspaper about a performance at the Metropolitan today—or for that matter what Shaw himself said later about world events. He was not a great spirit; but the music criticism he wrote in his early thirties reveals a genial and attractive human being astonishingly different from the perversely unpleasant and silly world-figure of later years. And it reveals him, at that early period, using vast resources of literary brilliance, fun and wit in the service of a distinguished critical perception and taste in music that is an additional agreeable surprise to someone familiar only with the later Shaw who concerned himself almost exclusively with politics and sociology. In his method of operation as a critic, then, Shaw resembles Berlioz; and what makes him a great critic is an integrity like Berlioz's in relation to his material—the fact that behind all the brilliance and fun and wit the critical perception and taste deals rigorously with what is before it. And the result is a flow of comment on the daily events of those distant musical seasons that is still some of the most discerning, the most instructive, the most enjoyable you can read in any language.

You are not likely to be interested in the performance of Boito's

Mefistofele that Shaw wrote about on May 29, 1889; but it provided the occasion for his observation that Gounod's *Faust* was "a true musical creation, whereas Boito has only adapted the existing resources of orchestration and harmony very ably to his libretto"—which embodies an instructive distinction you will find useful when you listen to much of the new music written today. And relevant to some opera productions you may see today is Shaw's remark that "the house likes Boito's prologue, in spite of the empty stage and the two ragged holes in a cloth which realize Mr. Harris's modest conception of hell and heaven."

In no newspaper today are you likely to encounter the accurate perception and good sense of Shaw's comment after a performance of Brahms's *Requiem*. The audience's delusion that "Brahms is a great composer, and the performance of this masterpiece of his an infinitely solemn and important function" was, he says, "not confined to those who, having found by experience that good music bores them, have rashly concluded that all music that bores them must be good. It raged also among the learned musicians, who know what a *point d'orgue* is, and are delighted to be able to explain what is happening when Brahms sets a pedal pipe booming and a drum thumping the dominant of the key for ten minutes at a stretch, whilst the other instruments and the voices plough along through every practicable progression in or near the key, up hill from syncopation to syncopation, and down dale from suspension to suspension in an elaborately modernized manner that only makes the whole operation seem more desperately old-fashioned and empty." And adding that Brahms seems to have thought he could produce more remarkable effects than Beethoven by keeping his pedal-points going even longer than Beethoven's, Shaw observes that while the academics like this sort of thing the genuine musician dislikes nothing more than "an attempt to pass off the forms of music for music itself, especially those forms which have received a sort of consecration from their use by great composers in the past"—which neatly exposes Brahms's classicism for what it is.

Nor on the other hand will you find anything more perceptive on Verdi than what Shaw wrote after Verdi's death—his insistence, for example, that there was no evidence in a single measure of his last three operas that Verdi had heard a note of Wagner, but evidence instead that he had heard Mendelssohn and Bee-thoven, whose music "is the music of a Germany still under that Franco-Italian influence which made the music of Mozart so amazingly unlike the music of Bach. Of the later music that was consciously and resolutely German and German only . . . of the music of Schumann, Brahms and Wagner, there is not anywhere in Verdi the faintest trace. In German music the Italian loved what Italy gave. What Germany offered of her own music he entirely ignored." This is still the answer to those who even today will have it that the writing in Verdi's last operas represents the influence of Wagner.

The gaiety of Berlioz and Shaw is not in W. J. Turner: even his irony, however intense, is quiet. He writes with a poet's precision of statement, in the expression of a poet's insights. Those insights give us the illuminating statements about Mozart; they also enable him to make this astonishing observation after Toscanini's con-certs in London in 1935—that as he had sat watching Toscanini he "was suddenly reminded of Berlioz's remark: 'Do you think I make music for my pleasure?' I am certain that it is not a pleasure for Toscanini to conduct, but rather that he suffers. It is because of his extreme musical sensibility and intense concentration. Here lies the essence of his superiority." Astounding, because it was written fifteen years before an afternoon on which Toscanini said: "Conducting is for me great suffering. When I am alone with the score I am very happy; when I am on the podium I am always afraid. I am afraid the horn will be late, the clarinet will not play correct. . . ."

Turner, with the same dislike of Brahms the serious composer as Shaw's, expresses it in different terms. Explaining why he rates the *Haydn Variations* and the final passacaglia movement of the Fourth Symphony highest in Brahms's work, he says it is because in his variation-writing Brahms is not "being a poet (in the Aristotelian sense) or a great creator; he is merely being a musician"—that is, a craftsman. "I do not like Brahms when he goes forth to battle. . . . Brahms was much too earnest, and to be earnest is always to be ridiculous, since it is given only to the elect, the few supremely great—a Beethoven, for example—to be not earnest but serious. . . . But Brahms when he is being entirely natural and self-forgetful, when he is not at all obsessed by the tramp of Beethoven behind him . . . then he is a truly great and inspired musician."

There were four collections of Turner's reviews and articles: *Music and Life, Variations on the Theme of Music, Musical Meanderings*, and *Facing the Music—Reflections of a Music Critic*. His other books included *Music—An Introduction to Its Nature and Appreciation* and critical biographies of Mozart, Beethoven and Berlioz.

Of the writing of other English critics Gerald Abraham's in the 1940s and 1950s is worth looking for in the library; and a collection of David Cairns's critical writing of the 1950s and 1960s, *Responses*, includes some—about Beethoven's *Fidelio*, Verdi's *Falstaff*, Mozart's *Idomeneo*, Schubert's large-scale works—that is as good as I have ever read. Its high value derives from the fact that Cairns manages not to do what other writers usually do when they have occasion to hear music, which is to listen with minds filled with the generally accepted ideas about it, and therefore to hear what those ideas lead them to expect to hear. But I must add that some of what he says—for example about the greatness of Tippett's opera *A Midsummer Marriage* and Elgar's First Symphony—is contradicted for me by what I hear in the music.

Worth reading, too, are the articles of the great nineteenth-century Viennese critic, Eduard Hanslick, which are fluent, graceful, urbane and witty, but in the formulation of judgments which reveal great knowledge and understanding and thorough preparation (e.g. by study of the scores of new works) in support of excellent critical perception that is in close contact with the music. Like most critics—and most people—he is out of phase with certain minds and their manifestations in art: the composers of program music, the mature Wagner, Bruckner. But if this makes him incapable of appreciating even the lovely things in *Die Meistersinger*, a listener of today finds him accurately perceptive about the wearisome declamatory style, the absurd philosophical pretensions, the horrible verbal jargon of the other mature works; and what he says about Bruckner's symphonies describes what one has heard in them.

In this country the writings of Philip Hale (issued in a collection, ostensibly of his program notes for the Boston Symphony's concerts, that in fact included some of his newspaper criticism as well) and H. T. Parker in the first part of the twentieth century are worth investigating in the library. Of more recent criticism the collections of reviews and articles by Robert Craft from the 1970s to the 1980s—*Prejudices in Disguise, Current Convictions* and *Present Perspectives*—are made notable for me by Craft's possession of a critic's essential equipment of perception and judgment; which is to say that I have found in the writing a great deal that was confirmed by my experience as a listener, enough to outweigh the statements—for example, about Schönberg's *Moses and Aaron* being "one of the handful of twentieth-century operas with contemporary musical and dramatic power" and deserving "precedence over the Delius and Britten, Henze and Ginastera operas . . ."—that my experience contradicted. And although Craft has limited his conducting almost entirely to the works of Stravinsky, Schönberg and Webern, one is surprised as well as pleased by the large number of articles on music which the majority of the public is interested in—Bach's cantatas, Mozart's piano concertos, the music of Schubert, Chopin, Brahms, Mahler, Berlioz's *Benvenuto Cellini*, Glinka's operas, Wagner's *Ring* music-dramas.

The only newspaper music criticism of recent years worth reading is Virgil Thomson's of the 1940s and 1950s; the collections of his reviews and articles* contain numerous examples of the operation of a critical apparatus of perception and intellect that would make the writing a pleasure to read even without its additional delights of felicitous and witty statement. But I must add that with those pieces of distinguished criticism there are many pieces of irresponsible nonsense.

The difference between sense and nonsense with Thomson is most often the difference between the writing in which his mind is

---

* *The Musical Scene, The Art of Judging Music* and *Music Right and Left;* a fourth volume compiled by Thomson—*Music Reviewed 1940–1954*—combined selected articles from the previous volumes with ones written subsequently; *The Virgil Thomson Reader*, edited by John Rockwell, combined selections from all four volumes with autobiographical and other material; and further posthumous collections may have appeared by the time you read this. —*Ed.*

CRITICISM

in contact with the real facts that are before him—the facts that one recognizes in the music or performance he is discussing; and on the other hand the writing which deals with things one cannot discover in the music or performance—things which exist only in his head, and to which he applies ideas with no more basis in reality. When, in explanation of his opinion that pianist Vladimir "Horowitz's playing is monotonous and, more often than not, musically false," Thomson writes that Horowitz "never states a simple melody frankly. He teases it by accenting unimportant notes and diminishing his tonal volume on all the climactic ones. The only contrast to brio that he knows is the affettuoso style"— he describes what anyone can hear in the playing. So when he writes that Dmitri "Mitropoulos has taken over the Philharmonic-Symphony concerts like an occupying army," refers to Mitropoulos's "Panzer division tactics," and amplifies this with the observations that "all is discipline, machine finish, tension and power" and "he makes every piece . . . sound nervous and violent." But I don't recognize in Yvonne Lefebure's piano-playing what Thomson describes in his statement that "her differentiations between time and accent also aid orchestral evocation, because melodic passages, as on the *bel canto* instruments, are played without downbeat stresses, the accentual pattern being rendered, as in real orchestral playing, by sharp pings, deep bell strokes, and articulations recalling those of harp, bow-heel, and the orchestra's percussion group." Nor do I recognize Toscanini's performances in Thomson's contention that they have meter but not rhythm, and still less in his mumbo-jumbo about the marriage of historical and literary with musical culture in the Great Tradition of Wagner, Hans von Bülow, Artur Nikisch and Sir Thomas Beecham that is lacking in Toscanini's conducting.

Much of Thomson's writing is a spinning out of such fancy schematizing ideas about facts imagined or altered to fit; and much of this schematization is concerned with tradition. An article *Tradition Today,* for example, is about the conductors, dominantly exemplified for Thomson by Fritz Reiner and Pierre Monteux, who operate as the preservers of "the traditions of interpretation as these have been handed down," as against men like Leopold Stokowski and Serge Koussevitzky who operate rather with "a highly personalized ability to hold attention";

about American conductors of the second type who "have the excuse of having passed their youth out of contact with a major musical tradition, of not having known the classics early enough to feel at home with them"; and about one of them, Leonard Bernstein, who "knows what American music is all about, but the western European repertory he is obliged to improvise. . . . That is why, I think, he goes into such chorybantic ecstasies in front of it. He needs to mime, for himself and others, a conviction that he does not have. He does no such act before American works of his own time. He takes them naturally, reads them with authority." And I might add that in conversation Thomson once ascribed a similar ignorance to Toscanini, contending that whereas Toscanini had learned the operatic traditions in the opera house, he had found himself, at fifty, having to deal with the symphonic repertory without knowledge of *its* traditions, and had solved the problem by doing a complete streamlining job on the music.

Actually Bernstein and Toscanini learned the classics as early, and in the same way, as Reiner and Monteux. If Toscanini began his career in the opera house it was because that is where a conductor usually begins in Europe: Karl Muck, Gustav Mahler, Bruno Walter, Fritz Reiner all conducted opera before they conducted the symphonic repertory. And when Toscanini began to conduct this repertory—at thirty, not at fifty—it was with the knowledge of the music and of the traditions of its performance that he had acquired in his youth in the same way as those other conductors: from hearing it performed and studying the scores. The striking differences in Toscanini's performances of symphonic music, like those in his performances of opera, represented not his ignorance of tradition but the modification of it by his personal musical taste: what Thomson called streamlining was actually a personal performing style which, in opera no less than in symphonic music, tended toward plastic simplicity, economy and subtlety—which, for example, tended to set a single subtly modified tempo for the several sections of a movement. Toscanini would have been open to criticism for this only if the tradition had had the authority Thomson mistakenly endows it with: if, that is, it had gone back in a straight line to an authoritative first performance. But actually the line had begun with first performances that had represented nothing more authoritative than the judgment and taste each conductor had applied to what he had found in the score; it had continued with successive modifications of those performances by later conductors in accordance with *their* judgments and tastes; and there was nothing in all this that forbade further modifications by Toscanini in accordance with *his* judgment and taste.

The successive European performances were transferred to this country by the succession of European conductors who came here; and it was from them that American conductors, including Bernstein, learned in their youth the symphonic repertory and the traditions of its performance. It was, then, not for lack of knowledge of these traditions that Bernstein played Beethoven's *Eroica* badly; nor was it possession of this knowledge that caused him to play a Mozart symphony beautifully. And he went into the same chorybantic ecstasies before a Copland piece as before the Mozart.

But such failures of Thomson and the defects responsible for them are those of a man who also has produced some of the finest music criticism written anywhere. And Tovey's observation about Schubert can be applied to Thomson: his occasional weaknesses and inequalities do not make him a critic of less than the highest rank.

Tovey's observation can also be applied to the occasional weaknesses and inequalities of his own writing. These begin with his limitations of sympathy and understanding, which represent the ideas on the history of music that he absorbed from his teacher Parry. But it was also from Parry that he learned his procedure of point-to-point analysis of music; and this procedure, applied to works of composers for whom he does have sympathy and understanding, gives us those excitingly illuminating descriptions of the courses of events in Haydn's symphonies and Mozart's concertos in *Essays in Musical Analysis*—each of which achieves the primary purpose of criticism as it is defined by E. M. Forster: "It considers the [individual work of art] in itself, as an entity, and tells us what it can about its life." Moreover, this examination and description of the life in particular works underlies Tovey's generalizations of a composer's practice, such as are found in the monumental essays on Schubert and Haydn in *The Main Stream of Music.*

With the extraordinary musical perception there is the understanding and knowledge of a mind that has ranged widely in territory outside of music; and there is also formulation of this perception and understanding in statements that are often epigrammatic in their concentration and clarification of sense and their impact and brilliance. But sometimes the mind ranges so far afield, or the formulation becomes so epigrammatic, that the thought is obscure and difficult to follow. It is mostly in the articles and lectures on general matters—*Normality and Freedom in Music, The Main Stream of Music, Stimulus and the Classics of Music,* and others—that one finds the elliptically allusive or epigrammatic obscurities, the embarrassing professorial humor that are additional weaknesses and inequalities in Tovey's writing. And these don't in the slightest degree lessen the magnitude of the powers and achievements he exhibits elsewhere—the powers and achievements of the great critic who is able to describe in such illuminating fashion the courses of events in particular works of Schubert and Haydn, and to derive from these observations of particular behavior the illuminating general statements about each composer like this one about Schubert: "We are right in thinking that his maturest works in large instrumental forms are diffuse and inconsistent. . . . But when we find (as, for instance, in the first movement of the great C major Symphony) that some of the most obviously wrong digressions contain the profoundest, most beautiful, and most inevitable passages, then it is time to suspect that Schubert, like other great classics, is pressing his way toward new forms." Or this one about Haydn: "He is rightly believed to be on a level with Mozart as a master of form; but his form is described as 'regular and symmetrical.' And when you come to look at it, you find not only that all the rules of form as observed by both Mozart and Beethoven are frequently violated by Haydn, but that they are so seldom observed that it would be quite impossible to infer them from his mature practice at all. More recent writers have tried to show some recognition of this by saying that in Haydn's works we see the sonata forms 'in the making.' This only increases the confusion; for Haydn's most nearly regular works are his earlier ones, when he wrote on the lines of J. C. and C. P. E. Bach; whereas his freedom of form becomes manifest just about the time when he came to know Mozart. The mutual influence of Haydn and Mozart is one of the best-known wonders of musical history; and the paradox of it is that while its effect on Mozart was to concentrate his style and strengthen his symmetry, the effect on Haydn was to set him free, so that his large movements became as capricious in their extended course of events as his minuets had always been in the cast of their phrases."

Of the several other excellent books mentioned in earlier chapters Copland's *Music and Imagination,* containing his Charles Eliot Norton lectures at Harvard in 1951–52, includes a little of the fallacious ad hoc reasoning of the propagandist for contemporary music; but for the most part, in these lectures concerned with "the relation of the imaginative mind to the different aspects of the art of music," Copland is the critic—a critic operating with the special insight of the composer and a gift for felicitous statement. Concerning the enormous wealth of color combinations offered by the modern orchestra, for example, Copland remarks that it has been the undoing of the radio or movie orchestrator: "Where there is no true expressive purpose anything goes; in fact, everything goes, and it all goes into the same piece."

Dent's *Mozart's Operas* is a product of the unusual combination of scholarship which provides interesting information about Mozart's materials, problems and methods with each opera; esthetic perception which illuminates the final work of art; and a clear and graceful style which makes the writing a pleasure to read. And equally good is Dent's little book *Opera.*

[Another useful type of book for listeners—given the deficient texts and translations accompanying most recordings of *Lieder* and songs—is one that gives song texts three ways: in the original language, in a free translation for poetic sense, and in a word-for-word transliteration that permits one to see the precise relation between the words and the notes at each point. There are several such books, and Lois Phillips's *Lieder Line by Line* is as good as any.]

Of books about individual composers and their works some of

the best are J. W. N. Sullivan's *Beethoven: His Spiritual Development*, Emily Anderson's translations of Beethoven's letters, Tom Wotton's *Hector Berlioz*, [Hans Gal's books on Brahms, Schubert and Wagner], Cuthbert Girdlestone's *Mozart and His Piano Concertos*, the three volumes of Julian Budden's *The Operas of Verdi*, Frank Walker's *The Man Verdi* [superb in spite of the wish expressed by the author of the new introduction for a different book that would analyze Verdi's psyche in the recklessly speculative way that Maynard Solomon analyzed poor, dead Beethoven's], Arthur Berger's *Aaron Copland*, [and Robert Craft's various books about Stravinsky—of which the first three are *Stravinsky: Chronicle of a Friendship*, *Stravinsky in Pictures and Documents* (written with the composer's widow) and the three volumes of *Selected Correspondence*].

Biographies you might begin with include Alexander W. Thayer's of Beethoven (revised and edited by Elliot Forbes), although you might wish to begin with Turner's shorter one; [David Cairns's multi-volume biography of Berlioz] and Turner's older and shorter one; Edward M. Maisel's biography of Charles Tomlinson Griffes, Karl Geiringer's of Haydn, Turner's of Mozart, Francis Toye's of Rossini, Ralph Kirkpatrick's of Domenico Scarlatti; Toye's biography of Verdi [a good one in spite of its not being up to date in some matters—particularly in its accounts of those early operas that Toye never heard performed]; Frank Walker's *Hugo Wolf;* Robert W. Gutman's *Richard Wagner: The Man, His Mind, and His Music;* [*Schubert: Memoirs by His Friends*, edited by Otto Erich Deutsch; and *Piotr Il'ych Tchaikovsky: Letters to His Family: An Autobiography*, edited by Galina Von Meck].

Good books about performers and other figures include Harvey Sachs's biography of Toscanini and Samuel Antek's *This Was Toscanini*, which is valuable for its insider's account (Antek was an N.B.C. violinist) of Toscanini's working with an orchestra and for Robert Hupka's marvelous photographs of him in rehearsal.* [Charles Reid's biography of Beecham is more percep-

---

*Haggin's *Arturo Toscanini* combines the two books published originally as *Conversations with Toscanini* (Haggin's own recollections and observations) and *The Toscanini Musicians Knew* (interviews with musicians who played or sang under the conductor). —Ed.

tive, better written, and in some instances more accurate than the later one by Alan Jefferson]; and Beecham's own autobiography of the years up to the mid-1940s, *A Mingled Chime*, is delightfully written though historically unreliable. Worth reading as well are Moses Smith's *Koussevitzky*, Flagstad's memoirs (*The Flagstad Manuscript*, edited by Louis Biancolli), and the memoir of Caruso by his wife Dorothy (*Enrico Caruso: His Life and Death*) for the large number of Caruso's letters that it contains—moving human documents that offer fascinating revelations of the behind-the-façade operations of a musician's career.

To those who value the operas Strauss composed to the librettos of Hofmannsthal, their correspondence—*A Working Friendship: The Correspondence between Richard Strauss and Hugo von Hofmannsthal*, translated by Hammelmann and Osers—may be interesting mostly for what it reveals of the joint operation that produced those works. But to those who care nothing about the operas, the correspondence is fascinating for what it reveals about the two men, for what they say about the greats of their time—e.g. Bruno Walter, Max Reinhardt, Diaghilev, Nijinsky—with whom their activities involved them, and for what they report of the private operations in their world of artistic creation—the maneuvering with and about royal ministers, directors of the royal opera companies, conductors, singers, designers—that led up to what in the end was presented to the public in the opera house.

Fascinating in some of the same ways is much of what Stravinsky, talking ostensibly in answer to questions of Craft, has to say in the volumes of their conversations—about himself as a composer, what he recalled of his life, his musical education, his composing of particular works, the now historic events he had observed or had himself been involved in, the famous persons who had been involved in them with him, what he thought about the music of other composers, about jazz, about singing music in translation, and about other matters that interested him—for it reveals him as one of the artists who are perceptive and articulate about their art, and as the possessor of a powerful mind that tends to go in unexpected directions, a sharp eye for human character and behavior, a grim sense of humor, a gift of pungent statement. And the value of Stravinsky's perceptions and testimony is not lessened by those occasions when his attitudes and interests as a composer and his own practice cause him to see what others cannot see. Thus the listener is not likely to be troubled by what makes the first movement of Beethoven's Ninth, for Stravinsky, "a late and terrible example" of Beethoven's frequent lapses into banality: "such quadrilateral phrase-building and pedantic development (of Bars 387–400), such poor rhythmic invention . . . , and such patently false pathos."

The diary in *Dialogues and a Diary*, the fourth volume of Stravinsky-Craft conversations, is Craft's own, concerned with his travels with Stravinsky. Its ironically, irreverently and amusingly perceptive writing, light and deft in style, is in striking contrast to the grim and sardonic statements attributed to Stravinsky in the conversations, and provides conclusive proof that those statements were made by Stravinsky and were not, as some have contended, written by Craft under Stravinsky's name.

Finally, the two volumes of *Letters of Mozart and His Family*. They are interesting for the comments of Mozart and his father on the music of their contemporaries, and for the information they give us about the musical life of the period, which should correct some mistaken ideas about it that are still current. But their chief interest is in what they tell us about the personality and life of the most extraordinary musical genius we know of; and Mozart's own letters are fascinating and moving personal documents.

I should add that what the letters tell us about Mozart does not—as some would leap to conclude—reveal any additional meaning in the music that we wouldn't perceive without them: on the contrary, it is from the music that we learn of emotional and spiritual resources that we wouldn't know of from anything he said—resources which apparently only the artist was able to draw on, and which achieved explicit formulation only in his works of art. That is, Mozart's vivacity and love of fun are delightfully evident in the rush of absurdly mingled German, Italian, French and English in which, at the age of fourteen, he describes a performance of opera in Verona to his sister:

> . . . *Oronte*, il padre di *bradamento*, è unprencipe, (fà il sig: *afferi*) un bravo cantante, un paritono, ma (gezwungen wen er in falset hinauf gügezt, aber doch nicht so sehr, wie der Tibaldi zu Wienn.)

Bradamenta, figlia d'oronte, inamorata di Ruggiero, ma, (sie soll den leone heyrahten, sie will ihn aber nicht.) fà, una povera baroneßa, che hà avuto una gran disgratia, mà non sò chè? Recità (unter einem fremden nam, ich weis aber den namen nicht) hà una voce paßabile, e la Statura non sarebbe male, ma distona come il Diabolo. *Ruggiero* un Ricco principe, inamorato della bradamenta, un Musico, canta un poco manzolisch, ed à una bellißima voce forte, ed è gia Vecchio, hà cinquanta cinque anni, ed à una leiffige gurgel. Leone, soll die bradamenta heyrathen, reichischime est, ob er aber ausser dem Theatro reichist, das weis ich nicht, fà una Donna, la moglie di *afferi*, à una bellißima voce, ma c'è tanto sußurro nell theatro, che non si sente niente. *Irene*, fà una sorella di Lolli, del gran violinisto, che abbiamo sentito à Vienna. à una schnoffelte voce, e canta sempre um ein vierteil zu tardi, ò troppo à buon ora. . . .*

But the letter tells us nothing that we can't hear—and nothing more than we do hear—when we listen to a musical embodiment of the vivacity and love of fun like the final rush of the Piano Concerto K.453. And from the letters we would know nothing of the sublimities we hear in the *Contessa, perdono* passage at the end of *Figaro*.

*Haggin's intention was to give this extract exactly as Mozart wrote it, misspellings, inconsistencies, errors of grammar and all. For this purpose he used the best source at the time (1956): *Die Briefe W. A. Mozarts,* edited by Schiedermair, Munich, 1914. For this revision I have used the later Bärenreiter edition: *Mozart. Briefe und Aufzeichnungen—Gesamtausgabe,* edited by Bauer and Deutsch, Kassel, 1962. I make the point because there are inaccuracies in Schiedermair, and W. J. Turner, who reproduces the entire letter in his biography of Mozart, transcribes it from Schiedermair with mistakes of his own (misreading *ausser* as *asser,* for example, and *schnoffelte* as *schnosselte*). And because Emily Anderson, in her celebrated English-language edition (*The Letters of Mozart and His Family,* London, 1966), translates the German and French portions of this one into English— obscuring the passages in which Mozart himself writes in English—and pedantically corrects Mozart's mistakes in the Italian portions, which she leaves in the original language (she does not acknowledge making any corrections—an incidental act of impropriety that one hopes is unique in her book). Moreover, since Anderson does not append the original letter, its principal value to her readers of today—as an illustration of how Mozart entertained his sister by writing to her in a mixture of four languages—is largely lost. —*Ed.*

24

Musical Procedures and the Forms They Produce

For several centuries the art-music of Europe—that is, the music written by learned and technically skilled composers—was vocal; and it had reached a high degree of complexity and subtlety (with Palestrina, Victoria, Byrd, and others), before, in the sixteenth century, composers began to write for instruments. When they did begin they had to fashion musical styles and forms that were suitable for the instruments. Thus, it had been natural for the voice to sing sustained tones that flowed one into the other. But this style was not natural for an instrument like the harpsichord, in which tone was produced by the plucking of a string and died out almost immediately. Here time had to be filled out by notes in quicker succession; and advantage could be taken of the agility of the fingers on the keyboard—their capacity for speed, leaps, and so on. And a totally different set of conditions, constituting the basis for a different style of music, was imposed by the violin, or by the trumpet, and changed as these instruments were improved. Also, in vocal music the words had constituted a bony structure for the musical substance; now the substance had to produce out of itself, by its own progression and elaboration, a structure or form held together only by internal coherence.

There began, then, a long period of experiment and change—in construction of instruments, in combination of instruments for concerted performance, in technique of performance, in styles of writing, in forms. In time, however, certain structural patterns, procedures and forms achieved both definition and names; and this chapter will consider some of the most common ones by means of examples.

Composers convey to us certain responses to life and experience, certain attitudes, certain states of feeling—as all artists do. "What she wants other people to know," Edmund Wilson once wrote about a novelist, "she imparts to them by creating an object, the self-developing organism of a work of prose." What composers want other people to know they too impart by creating an object, this one the self-developing organism of a work of musical sound. That is, what they want to convey is expressed by their organization of the sounds that constitute the medium of their art. For the fact is that what is usually called classical music has its own medium—a special class of sounds in which its ideas are expressed; and its thought has a logic, and proceeds by operations, which are those of this medium and of no other. What kind of object and organism is created in this way, and out of what substance and by what procedures, you can discover by listening to examples; and two good ones to begin with are Bach's *Passacaglia* for organ in C minor, BWV 582, and the Prelude to Wagner's music-drama *Tristan und Isolde*.

You can, if you wish, merely listen to them in the ways I described in Chapter 2—all the way through repeatedly, or a little at a time—and become increasingly aware of what happens in the course of each piece. Or you may want me to point out what happens—in which case you will have to do a little more than just listen: you will have to gear your listening with my statements, and for this purpose have your eye follow musical notation as your ear follows the sound, the more easily to grasp the musical detail and fix it in your mind.

Even if you intend to follow the second course of action it is a good thing to begin by listening straight through the two pieces to get an idea of certain general characteristics. For one thing, that the object is made of sound which progresses in time (hence the term *movement* of a symphony), and which conveys meaning of the indefinable kind I discussed earlier. Hence that the progression in time reveals gradually not only a developing form in sound but a developing meaning—a train of musical thought.

And that the object in the end has a size and weight commensurate with the magnitude of the thought it embodies.

The next step is to listen to detail and observe by what operations the object is produced and the thought proceeds. Listening again to Bach's *Passacaglia* you can this time hear that the grave opening statement

is repeated—and not just once but a second time, a third, a fourth (stop here for the moment). And you discover from this that musical thought, unlike the thought of prose, proceeds by repeating itself—in some instances by repeating itself exactly.

Having said this I must add a qualification. The opening statement of the *Passacaglia* is repeated without change; but each time you hear something new with it, which makes the repetition a *variation*—the same thing said in a different way. Here are the repeated statement and different accompanying material of the first four variations:

Variation 1

theme marked by asterisks

This progression in terms of a melodic fugure is *figuration.*

Variation 2: Continuation of the figuration of Variation 1.

Variation 3

Variation 4

The *Passacaglia*, then, is produced by the operation of the variation procedure, and is one of the *variation forms*—the one with a continuous succession of variations on a brief repeated theme called the *ground-bass* (though it doesn't stay in the bass).

Another thing you discover from these first variations is that music, unlike prose, can say more than one thing at a time, and that what you hear most often is not a line of sound but a texture. When there are several clearly defined lines or *voices* moving at the same time, as in these variations, you have *counterpoint,* and the texture is *contrapuntal.* And at any point in the progression if you read vertically instead of horizontally the combination of sounds at that point is a *chord,* and the succession of chords is *harmony.*

Still another thing to observe in these first variations is that while the theme maintains its unvarying form and pace, the varying accompanying material becomes increasingly animated, and its texture increasingly dense and complex, with a resulting effect of increasing momentum and intensity. The cumulative impact of the repeated ground-bass, the crescendo of intensity in the accompanying material—these together produce the effect of the passacaglia form.

When now you listen further in Bach's *Passacaglia* you discover that the intensity doesn't increase in one single unbroken crescendo—that it is alternately built up and lessened, until it is eventually carried to a concluding maximum.

In Variation 5 it is lessened:

(simplified)

theme itself varied

Also the figuration is carried into the ground-bass itself; and thus you discover that the theme itself can be varied.

But in Variation 6 the ground-bass is unvaried again, and the flowing accompanying material begins to build up the intensity that is further increased by the denser textures of Variations 7 and 8.

In Variation 9:

theme itself varied

the figuration is again carried into the ground-bass itself; and the momentarily lessened intensity builds up to the force of Variation 10.

In Variation 11 you hear the ground-bass transferred for the first time to an upper voice, with a single line of flowing accompanying material down below. Additional voices create a denser texture and greater urgency in Variation 12; but there is sudden quiet in Variation 13:

in which the intricate texture varies, envelopes, and obscures the ground-bass.

In Variation 14:

the quiet continues, the figuration in which the ground-bass is involved is simpler.

In Variation 15:

the quiet becomes hushed, the figuration even simpler.

The hush is broken by Variation 16:

in which the ground-bass is unvaried and forceful below the explosive figuration. The intensity is maintained in Variation 17, with its brilliant accompanying figuration, and further in Variation 18:

Then, in Variation 19:

the intensity begins to increase; and in Variation 20, with its denser textures, the crescendo of intensity builds up to its maximum point in the powerful conclusion.

When the thunderous final chord of the *Passacaglia* breaks off you hear the first half of the ground-bass once more. Over it Bach has written in the score *Thema fugatum,* which tells you that the theme, after having been subjected to the procedure of a variation in a passacaglia, is now to be subjected to the procedure of *fugue* in a fugue. That procedure is to discuss a theme in several lines of thought that proceed simultaneously—which means that fugue is a contrapuntal procedure, and the fugue a contrapuntal form. The theme discussed is the *subject;* the lines of thought are *voices;* and a fugue is in two or three or four or more voices.

The fugue which follows Bach's *Passacaglia* is in four voices; and the discussion begins with an *exposition* in which one by one the voices enter with a statement of the subject. Usually the first voice enters alone; then, when the second enters with the subject, the first continues with the *countersubject;* then, when the third enters with the subject, the second continues with the countersubject, and the first with material that fits in with both; and so on. In the present example the subject is stated even the first time with the countersubject; and each time the voice that had the subject continues with the countersubject, while the voice that had the countersubject continues with a second countersubject.

Here is the sequence of entries in the exposition of this fugue of Bach:

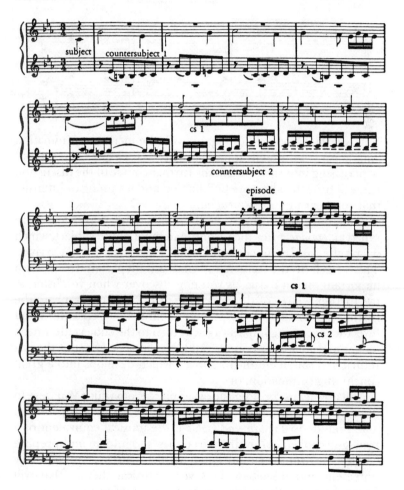

You will have noticed how again, with the increasing animation and density of the contrapuntal texture as the voices enter, there is increasing intensity. And in the further course of the discussion you will hear the alternate building up and lessening of intensity that you hear in the *Passacaglia*.

Something else to notice is the momentary digression, here called an *episode*, after the second statement of the subject, which delays the third statement and adds to its effect when it arrives. This effect of the return to what was departed from is an important one in music, as you now discover when you listen to the further course of the discussion in Bach's fugue—i.e. to the further statements of the subject separated by episodes—and hear the increasing impact of the return to the subject after each longer and weightier episode, and the climactic effect of the last return to a statement of the subject which develops into a great concluding summation, or *coda*.

And now let us consider the other piece from which you were to discover how music operates and what the operations produce. The Prelude to *Tristan und Isolde* is the musical equivalent of a prologue spoken before the curtain rises to inform and prepare you for the drama that is to come—which is to say, a preliminary statement and discussion of several musical themes that will figure prominently in the course of the music-drama. Two of these themes are heard in the opening statement of the Prelude:

There is a pause; then the statement is repeated—not exactly, like the theme of Bach's *Passacaglia,* but with a change—at a higher level of pitch:

The effect of this change is to qualify the original meaning of the statement, to develop it, to carry the musical thought further—as against the variation's saying the same thing in a different way.

Again there is a pause; then another, distended, more forceful repetition at a still higher level of pitch, developing the thought further:

Another pause; then [2] of the last statement is repeated:

then only its concluding two notes—first by the violins:

then by the flutes:

and finally, very emphatically, by the entire orchestra, which carries the line of thought to a momentary conclusion:

Out of the opening statement, then, there has been elaborated, by the procedure of repetition with modification, a musical paragraph—the beginning of an organism which now extends itself by the same procedure as new ideas enter and are developed.

Thus, with the conclusion of the first paragraph this idea:

is developed:

and then is qualified by a new idea and its development:

to the point where another idea enters and is developed:

and continues with this:

And now [3] returns (oboe, clarinets, horn) with increasing sonority and intensity, to bring this second line of thought to its momentary conclusion.

There is a pause in which [3] is reflected on:

These reflections increase in urgency and are carried to an emphatic conclusion; at which point [4] re-enters (oboe, English horn) to set the progression of thought in motion again.

As before, [4] continues with [5] (flute, oboe, English horn, clarinet), whose developments, increasing in intensity, again lead to the re-entrance of [3] (violins, cellos), which also increases in intensity, to the point where the intensity lessens as a new idea enters:

Its developments bring references to [2] (horn, English horn), and work up to the impassioned re-entrance once more of [3] (strings), which now in turn works up to increasingly powerful proclamations of [1] (horns) and [2] (trumpets). This is the climax of the discussion; and from the point of maximum intensity it subsides into quiet recollections of the opening statements, which eventually lead to a hushed transitional passage (cellos and basses) and a pause for the rise of the curtain.

In this piece you have heard one idea stated and repeated with modification to the point where another idea was stated and repeated with modification to the point where still another was so stated and repeated, and so on in the progression of the self-developing organism. Also, you have heard again, as in the Bach fugue, ideas returned to after being departed from, and the end, after the climax, return full circle to the quiet statements of the beginning. These are things you will hear in most of the music you will encounter. But usually with this difference: that the circular deployment of the material of the organism will have a more clearly defined schematic pattern—the pattern of one or another of the forms we shall examine in the next chapter, which may be called *cyclical* forms (in accordance with the dictionary definition of *cycle*).

The Prelude to *Tristan* has demonstrated that there is form in music that is purely organic, like the form of prose. But the pieces you will hear in the next chapter will demonstrate that there are also the forms of music that are schematic, like the forms of poetry.

The schematic patterns are something for you to be aware of, as you are aware of the pattern of a sonnet. But there is a danger of thinking of form in music as being only schematic pattern. And I had you listen to the Prelude to *Tristan* to make you aware of form as something organic, and to impress upon you the necessity—when you are listening to a piece that is in a schematic form—of taking in all the organically related substance that deploys itself within the schematic pattern, as you take in all the organically related substance that deploys itself within the pattern of the sonnet.

And there is one other thing to impress upon you. Someone told me once how at college he had found the first quarter-inch of a number of records almost destroyed by all the students who had played that much and no more in preparation for theme identification in their music appreciation courses. A few themes were all that these students got to know of those pieces of music, and all they thought there was to know about any piece of music; and other people have got the same idea from books like the one that offered the themes of a number of symphonies as "just what the listener wants to know, and all that he, lay or expert, *needs* to know: the stuff of which symphonies are made." What your guided tour through the Bach *Passacaglia* and the Prelude to *Tristan* should have made clear is that you must hear not only the themes but what is elaborated out of them and what happens between them.

25

Musical Forms   II

The simplest cyclical form is one with only one cycle—one departure and return. It can be expressed as *A B A;* and it is called *ternary form* or *three-part song form.* If you listen straight through the second movement of Schubert's String Quintet Op. 163 you will hear a succession of three large sections: the first slow and quietly sustained, the second agitated and vehement, but quieting down at the end for the repetition of—which is to say, the return to—the first.

Something else to notice is that there is also a cycle of keys: the first section is in E major;* the second in F minor; and when it quiets down it maneuvers a return to E major in the third section. Because there is this organization of—and by—keys in the cyclical forms, they are also *harmonic forms.*

And now when you listen the second time give your attention entirely to the substance that deploys itself within the cyclical pattern—the substance that makes the movement one of the most

* C major:

C minor:

The two series of sounds thus related in the major and minor scales can begin with D or E or any other note.

sublime and most affecting utterances in all music. As the movement begins:

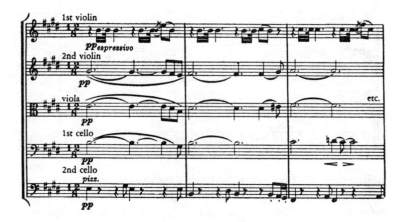

notice the dense and rich texture, which is extraordinary and possibly unique (I can't at the moment recall anything like it); and notice also how this texture works—how, as the sustained melody and harmony of the second violin, viola and first cello progress, their meaning is amplified and intensified by the brief expressive figures of the first violin, the plucked notes of the second cello. And when, after the vehement middle section, there is the return to the opening section:

notice that the first violin and the second cello now play intensifying variations of their original parts, which transform the
brief figures of the one into passages of the utmost poignancy,
and the plucked notes of the other into passages of great dramatic force. Eventually the variations subside into the original figures and plucked notes for the conclusion of the movement.

And so from this piece you learn that the variation procedure is
sometimes applied to the repetitions in cyclical forms.

Our next piece of music, the third movement of Mozart's *Eine
kleine Nachtmusik,* illustrates one of the ways the cyclical pattern
we have just considered can be less simple: each section of the
large cycle *A B A* is itself a smaller cycle; and the pattern of the
movement can be expressed as

A   *B*   *A*

a b a   *c d c*   *a b a*

More exactly, the movement is a *minuet with trio* (accept the term
trio without the historical reason for it); and with the cycle of keys,
and the traditional repetitions of the smaller sections in the
performances you will hear, the pattern becomes

minuet (G major)	trio (D major)	minuet (G major)
a a b a b a	*c c d c d c*	*a b a*

As you listen, then, you hear first *a:*

which is repeated; then *b:*

leads back to *a;* after which *b* is repeated, and again leads back to *a.*

Now the trio, in which *c:*

is repeated; then *d:*

leads back to *c;* after which *d* is repeated, and again leads back to *c.*

And now the minuet again, without repetitions.

I have used this simple, small-scale example because it exhibits the pattern so clearly and can be given in full detail. Now listen to the third movement of Schubert's String Quartet Op. 29, a more expansive and elaborate example—elaborate, among other things, in the wonderful shifts, or *modulations,* of key that are

255

characteristic of Schubert. Because it is more elaborate I can give you only the beginning of each section and let your ear go on from there to complete it.

This is how *a* of the minuet begins, in A minor:

a is repeated; then *b:*

builds up to a climax and pause for the return to *a*. But when [1] is heard from the cello this time, it is with the D changed to D sharp, which brings the breathtaking surprise of C sharp minor instead of the original A minor for [2], after which there is a shift back to A minor. *b* is repeated, and again returns to *a*.

Now *c* of the trio, beginning in A major:

c is repeated; then *d:*

1st violin   etc.

which after several shifts of key returns to the A major of *c*,
though not to its opening statement. *d* is repeated, and again
returns to the A major of *c*.

And now the minuet again, completing the large cycle.

Our next piece of music, Mozart's Rondo K.511 for piano,
illustrates another way in which the cyclical pattern can be less
simple: the piece comprises not one cycle but two; and the pattern
can be expressed as *A B A C A*, with *A* each time in the key of A
minor, *B* in the key of F major, and *C* in the key of A major. Each
of these sections, moreover, is itself a smaller cycle; and a coda
sums up at the end. The complete scheme, then, is

A	*B*	*A*	*C*	*A*	Coda
a b a	*c d c*	only *a*	*e f e*	*a b a*	

And you hear first *a* stating the exquisitely contoured and
poignant melody which the piece keeps departing from and
coming around back to (hence the term *rondo*):

p   cresc.   etc.

Then *b* develops the thought in C major:

mf   etc.

returning to *a* and A minor—but to an *a* with its contours elaborated and its poignancy intensified by the variation procedure:

and this is the point at which to mention that the return is made each time to a new variation of the original *a*.

Now *B:*

which ranges extensively through its cycle of substance and keys before returning to another variation of *a*.

And now *C:*

which ranges even more extensively through its cycle of substance and keys before returning to still another variation of *a*. And the successive variations of *a* that you hear in this last cycle of *A* reach a maximum of impassioned intensity in this final one:

After which you hear last references to *a* in the coda's concluding summation.

Our next piece of music is the first movement of Mozart's *Eine kleine Nachtmusik*, to illustrate another way in which the single large cycle may be less simple than the one we began with.

In the first section of the cycle you hear a sequence of ideas and their developments. First an opening fanfare:

which claims attention for

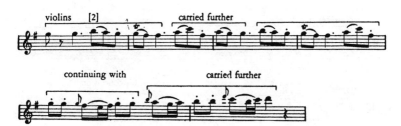

which pauses expectantly for

which is broken into by this transition:

to the following:

which leads to

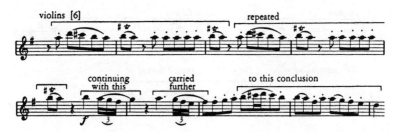

which is repeated and extended:

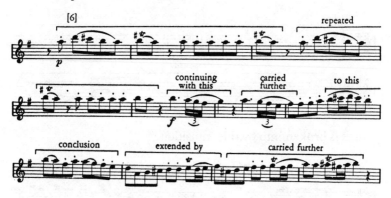

after which this:

concludes the sequence, which may be repeated in its entirety, but often is not.

In the second section of the cycle some of the ideas of the first, taken out of their original context, yield new developments which combine with new ideas to form a new sequence of organically related substance. Thus the opening fanfare:

now claims attention for

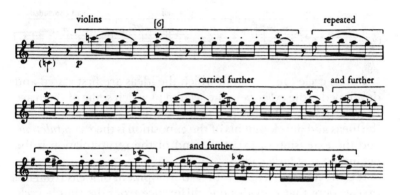

and then

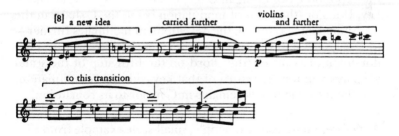

prepares you for the return to

which begins the restatement, with slight modifications, of the sequence of ideas and their developments in the first section.

At the end of this restatement [7] is changed and extended:

and leads to a little concluding flourish:

In this cycle the section in which the ideas are first stated and developed is the *exposition;* the section in which some of them are further developed is the *development;* the section which restates the ideas and developments of the exposition is the *recapitulation;* and the extension of [7] at the end of the recapitulation is the beginning of a little coda.

It is the middle section, with its development of ideas from the first section, that provides one difference from the simple cycle we considered first. And another difference is the cycle of keys: the exposition, beginning in G major, modulates to the *dominant* key, D major (the point of modulation being the C sharp in the transition from [4] to [5]); the development modulates further— to C major, A minor, G minor—until in its last two measures the dominant of G major (the chord on the fifth step of the scale) prepares you for the return of that key with the recapitulation; and the movement now remains in G major to its conclusion.

As before, I have used the simple, small-scale example from *Eine kleine Nachtmusik* because it exhibits the pattern so clearly and can be given in full detail. Now listen to the first movement of Schubert's Piano Sonata Op. 78, in which the cycle, by virtue of its scale and expressive content, is in effect a dramatic narrative, with the exposition presenting the elements of the drama, the development presenting their dramatic involvements, the recapitulation of the original substance of the exposition having the effect of a resolution of those involvements, and the coda providing final conclusions.

The implications of the tranquilly, spaciously meditative opening statement, in G major:

are developed for some time; then a more animated statement, in D major:

is developed with increasing liveliness to moments of force, which break off for quiet statements again:

and the meditative tranquility of the exposition is established with seeming finality by the references to [1]:

which bring it to a close.

We are, therefore, entirely unprepared for what we hear now in the development: the meditative opening statement with the iron-like power it acquires from being hammered out fortissimo in G minor, the tensions this creates in its rhythm, the tensions in the imitations of this rhythm by bare octaves in the bass, the eruptions of these octaves that carry the passage up to a proclamation tremendous in its sonority and distentions. The tension is relaxed momentarily in a quiet development of [2], only to be built up as before to a similar climax, and to be relaxed again in a similar quiet interlude. Then treble and bass octaves in imitation hammer out that development of [2] with increasing intensity, which suddenly relaxes in another quiet and poignant development of [2]; and this eventually brings the return to [1] for the recapitulation of the original substance of the exposition, now entirely in G major, and the more affecting for the dramatic involvements that have intervened. The sequence ends, as before, with [4]; after which the brief coda builds up last references to [1] into a powerful concluding summation.

This three-part cycle is the distinguishing feature of the grouping of movements which achieved definition at the hands of Haydn and Mozart, and which was given different names in accordance with the instruments it was written for: *sonata,* when it was written for one instrument or two; *trio,* when it was written for three; *quartet,* when it was written for four; *symphony,* for the then newly standardized symphonic orchestra that we know; *concerto,* for a solo instrument and orchestra. The cycle is therefore referred to as *sonata form;* but since it is the normally prescribed form for the first movement, it is also referred to as *first-movement form;* and since the first movement is normally in quick tempo, for which the Italian direction *allegro* is used, it is also referred to as *sonata-allegro form.* The terminology is inaccurate and confusing, since sonata form is not the form of the entire sonata or symphony but only the normal form of its first movement; since it may also occur in other movements; and since one of these may be the slow movement of the work. And there is further confusion in the fact that the sonata, symphony, trio, quartet and the rest constitute *the sonata forms.*

In one of *the sonata forms* of Mozart or Haydn we find three or four movements—that is, separate and complete organisms, unrelated in substance (the carrying over of themes from one movement to another is begun by Beethoven), diverse in character, yet bound together in one way that we shall see in a moment, and intended to complement each other and produce the effect of a single artistic experience. The diversity is in part one of tempo: normally the first movement is fast, though sometimes preceded by a slow introduction; the second is slow; the last is again fast; and when there are four movements a minuet with trio—later a faster *scherzo with trio*—precedes the last movement, though sometimes it precedes the slow movement. What binds the movements together is key: in addition to the unifying cycle of keys in each movement there is a unifying cycle of keys in the group of movements. Thus, the first movement of *Eine kleine Nachtmusik* is a cycle which begins and ends in G major; the second movement is in the same way in C major; the minuet movement is again in G major; and so is the finale. In Schubert's Piano Sonata Op. 78 the cycle of keys is G major, D major, B minor and G major; in his Quartet Op. 29 it is A minor, C major, A minor and A major (a work in a minor key sometimes ends in major).

The forms used in the movements are for the most part the cyclical forms we have been examining in this chapter. The distinguishing feature of the sonata forms is the cyclical first-movement form, or sonata form, or sonata-allegro form normally prescribed for the first movement; and prescribed for the minuet or scherzo movement is the cyclical minuet or scherzo with trio. The other movements have more latitude: in the slow movement we find sometimes simple ternary form, sometimes first-movement form; in the finale sometimes a rondo, sometimes first-movement form. Moreover, cyclical forms are not the only ones that are used: sometimes we find a slow movement or finale in variation form.

The only variation form we have examined is the passacaglia; and of this one there is only one example in the literature of the sonata forms: the finale of Brahms's Symphony No. 4. It has one interesting feature: the return of the theme after Variation 15; the return of Variations 1, 2, and 3 after Variation 23; and the return of the theme a second time at the beginning of the coda—all of which introduce a cyclical element into the variation form.

The variation form that you will encounter more frequently in the sonata forms is the one called *theme and variations,* in which the theme that is varied is not a single brief statement but a longer sequence of statements. The third movement of Beethoven's *Archduke* Trio provides an example:

The theme, as usual, is in two parts, the second of which answers and completes the first. The first is played by the piano:

and repeated by the violin and cello. Then the second is played by the piano:

with only its conclusion repeated by the strings. And there are similar repetitions of the two parts in each of the variations which elaborate the theme in different figurations.

Here is the beginning of Variation 1:

Then Variation 2:

Then Variation 3:

Then Variation 4:

And now there is a return to the theme, with the effect such a return has after intervening involvements. But as the theme proceeds this time it is altered by the change of the original F sharp to F natural:

and by further changes in the second part, which expands into an extensive, wide-ranging coda with implications of summation that reach sublime conclusions.

This is an example of the introduction of the cyclical element into a variation form by the return to the theme at the end. And another example of this that you might listen to is the concluding variation movement of Beethoven's Piano Sonata Op. 109, in which the last variation—extraordinary in the increasing momentum of its increasingly rapid figuration that finally effloresces into trills—subsides into a simple restatement of the sublime theme.

Beethoven also provides impressive examples of the combination of variation and cyclical form in which the theme and its variations alternate with a recurring statement or section that remains unvaried. One of these examples is the exalted third movement of the Ninth Symphony.

After a couple of introductory measures you hear

which is the first in a sequence of statements that constitute the theme. Its conclusion leads to

which in turn leads back to a variation of the theme:

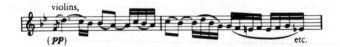

Again [2], unchanged except that it is in G major instead of D major. When it ends you expect the second variation of the theme; what comes instead is a fugal discussion of [1a], which ranges widely before it finally leads to the variation you expected:

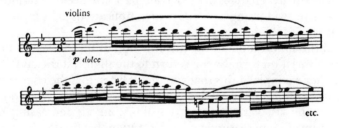

And this time the conclusion of the variation leads to this solemn call:

which introduces the extensive final summation of the coda.

You have just had an example of a fugal episode occurring in a movement of one of the sonata forms; and you will find other such episodes in the second movement of Beethoven's Seventh Symphony, the second and last movements of his *Eroica* Symphony. And not only episodes but entire movements: his Piano Sonatas Op. 106 (*Hammerklavier*) and Op. 110 end with fugues; his Quartet Op. 131 begins with one.

In addition, the second and last movements of the *Eroica* provide extraordinarily impressive demonstrations of something that has been evident in the other pieces of music I have presented—in the occurrence of the cyclical element in the fugue, of the variation procedure in cyclical forms. That something is the freedom with which the organism operates within the schematic pattern.

Strictly speaking, the second movement of the *Eroica* is in ternary form; but it is ternary form that is considerably more than *A B A*—the more being what happens after *B*. You hear, then, a gigantic opening section (*A*), beginning, in C minor, with

continuing with

and ending with

then the middle section (*B*), in C major:

and a return to [1], which leads not to [2] and [3] but to this powerful fugal episode:

which builds up a tremendous climax that breaks off for a momentary reference to [1]. This too is broken into by another forceful outburst, which eventually quiets down into a poignant accompanying figure for [1]:

which this time does continue with [2] and [3]—the ternary pattern being completed at last. And the end of [3] brings

the beginning of a sequence of affecting details in an unusually extensive coda.

And so with the last movement. After a boisterous introductory passage you hear a two-part theme:

followed by several variations. Then the theme is combined with a new two-part melody:

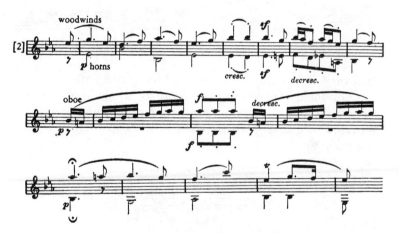

which leads to a fugal discussion of a subject derived from the theme:

This reaches a climax which breaks off for the return of [2], which then is varied. The variation builds up to a vigorous statement of [1] in combination with a new tune:

This is developed and brought to a conclusion; then you hear [2] again, leading to another fugal discussion—this time of [1] inverted:

It is carried to a climax and a conclusion; then, after a pause, comes a melody which you recognize as [2] made solemn and sublime by the slow tempo and poignant harmonization. It is repeated in grandly proclamatory style; then there is a quiet transition to

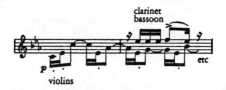

another variation of [2], which builds up to a climax that breaks off for the hush before the joyous outburst that brings this extraordinary movement to an end.

To these two examples I add one more: the great concluding variation movement of Beethoven's Piano Sonata Op. 111. After the wonderful theme:

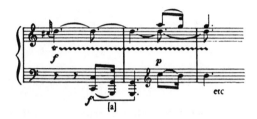

you hear a series of variations which eventually build up to a halt on a sustained trill with references to [a]:

This is the beginning of a wide-ranging digression—concerned with [a], then with [b]—which eventually ends in a return to the theme, heard now over fast-moving figuration, and gradually building up in intensity to a joyous and exalted climax that breaks off for another sustained trill—this one creating a dazzling ethereal radiance for a last superearthly statement of the theme.

These last three examples should impress on you the necessity I spoke of at the end of Chapter 24—of following attentively the detail of the organically related substance that deploys itself within the schematic pattern. It is this that makes each rondo or first movement *that* rondo or first movement and no other—or, to put it more generally, makes each piece of music unique. And your concern, in listening to music, is with the unique series of events in each particular piece of music.

26

Musical Forms   III

TWO MOZART ANDANTES

This chapter is concerned with the element of drama we encountered incidentally in the previous two chapters—the musical drama that manifests itself through a composer's particular use of the traditional forms he inherits—and specifically the drama that manifests itself in Mozart's enlargement and elaboration of traditional concerto form. Mozart wrote piano concertos as an actor might write plays for himself to act in; and he produced a musical equivalent of a play, in which the orchestra, which we hear first, creates suspense in anticipation of the piano's first entrance; the piano then holds attention for a time, alone and in exchanges with the orchestra, before working up to a brilliant exit; at which point the orchestra prepares for the piano's next entrance—and so on. The dramatic alternation of orchestra and piano occurs within what Mozart makes of classical sonata-allegro structure. The first movement is an adaptation of the procedure of the earlier ritornello concerto originated by Italian composers and taken over by Bach. In the first movement of Bach's *Brandenburg Concerto No. 2* or his D-minor Concerto for clavier or violin, we hear an opening statement by the orchestra that keeps returning after alternating passages for the solo instruments—this constantly returning statement of the orchestra being the *ritornello*. What Mozart does is to have the alternation of ritornello and solo passages take place within the succession of exposition, development, recapitulation and coda in the first movement of the symphony: the exposition begins with the orchestra's opening ritornello and is completed by the first solo section; the recurrence of the ritornello brings the second entrance of the piano for the development and the recapitulation; the next recurrence of the ritornello, interrupted by the solo *cadenza*, provides the coda. You will note that in this scheme of Mozart's there are fewer alternations of ritornello and solo passages that are more extensive and elaborate than in the Bach concerto; and another thing to note is that this heightens the dramatic effect of the course of events in the symphony movement, makes it more externally explicit. That is, the more extensive and elaborate opening ritornello delays the entrance of the solo instrument, and in so doing builds up suspense in anticipation of this entrance—very much as the minor characters in a play may create suspense in anticipation of the first entrance of the principal character. And so with the later recurrences of the ritornello. Interesting in addition is the distribution of substance between orchestra and piano, the changes in distribution in the recapitulation as against the exposition. In the exposition some, but not all, of the ideas stated in the ritornello are repeated by the piano, which introduces additional ideas that were not stated in the ritornello. In the abbreviated recapitulation some of the ideas of the exposition are restated and some are not; and an idea originally stated by the orchestra may now be restated by the piano, possibly in a different order and context, and with modifications of the idea itself. All this was contrived by Mozart for sharp-eared listeners who were expected to remember the original progression of material in the exposition and to appreciate the changes and surprises in the recapitulation.

But similar alternation complicates and elaborates whatever structure Mozart uses in the meditative slow movement, the high-spirited finale. And I will be concerned here with two of the slow movements—the tremendous Andantes of the Concertos K.482 and K.453.

The fascination of a particular concerto is in what Mozart contrives for the purpose of impressing the listener. But in the succession of the concertos there is additional fascination in the endlessly new contrivance with which Mozart, in one work after another, fills out his established scheme in the achievement of his purpose.

Cuthbert Girdlestone, in his monumental book *Mozart and His Piano Concertos*, leaves undiscussed the dramatic aspect of the musical progressions he writes about with such love, perception and exhaustive knowledge. Actually, one doesn't always get a clear idea of the course of events in a movement as one pushes through the luxuriant thicket of his emotionally warm but diffuse, involved and unclear writing on the detail of the movement. And one is astonished—in view of this concentration of attention on detail—to find him missing the significance and effect of two enormously important details: the concluding master-strokes of the Andantes of K.482 and K.453.

The effect of those two concluding details—as of the sublime *Contessa, perdono* passage near the end of *The Marriage of Figaro*—comes from where they are placed, what they follow, refer to, derive their expressive meaning from. We must, then, consider the course of events in each movement.

In the Andante of the Concerto K.482 the dramatic alternation of orchestra and solo piano takes place within a structure of theme and variations, with the variations separated by episodes of contrasting material. The orchestra plays first, in preparation for the piano's entrance—the muted violins beginning what develops into an unusually long, eventful and poignant statement in the key of C minor:

This is the theme; and when the piano enters it is to play the first variation on that theme—i.e. to elaborate on the notes of the statement and in this way to intensify its poignant expressive effect:

At the end of this variation the orchestra takes over with the first episode, which presents the contrasts of its key of E-flat major, its instrumental colors of wind instruments, its light-hearted expressive character. It is in two parts, the first of which ends with

in the dominant of E-flat, and the second with a similar statement in the tonic.

After this episode the piano enters again, to play the second variation, again in C minor, with the original melody in the right hand over left-hand passage-work creating a context of agitation and urgency:

At the end of this variation the orchestra again takes over with the second episode, an animated and gay dialogue of flute and bassoon in C major. Then the piano enters again for the third variation—this one a powerful dialogue of orchestra and piano, again in C minor:

The end of this variation brings the coda—the section of concluding summation. Concerning this, Girdlestone does remark on the feeling we have that the supreme moment is at hand; he does characterize what begins here as one of the most magical passages in all Mozart, in which the passion rises to tragic intensity; and he does direct attention to the desolate statement by clarinet and bassoon:

with which the coda begins. But then, having described the repetition of [6] by the piano, he speaks of the closing statement that follows as unfolding wearily, with all feeling of tragedy gone and only saddened resignation remaining. And this, for me, is an astonishing failure of perception; for actually that closing statement brings back [3], originally part of a light-hearted episode, but now—restated, after all that has intervened, in C minor—overwhelming in its poignancy:

It is the climax of the movement, achieved by a concluding master-stroke.

As with the Andante of K.482, so with the Andante of K.453: the substance, the organization of substance in structure, the scale of the operation, of the resulting musical object, of its expressive effect—all these make it one of the greatest of Mozart's utterances. The substance is of course different; and its organization—which builds up tremendous expressive force to another overwhelming concluding master-stroke—is unique.

The movement is organized by the several appearances of what is heard at the very start—a wistfully pensive statement which comes to a stop without attaining a conclusion:

Each time it is heard [1] is followed, after a pause, by a different sequence of ideas, which eventually leads to its next occurrence. Complicating this essential arrangement is the fact that [1] is heard alternately from the orchestra and from the piano; the further fact that of the sequences of ideas which take off from [1] the first comes from the orchestra, but all thereafter from the piano; and the further fact that although each of the piano's sequences begins with a new idea, as it continues it brings in ideas from the orchestra's first sequence.

We get, then, this course of events. It is the orchestra again that plays first, and at length, in preparation for the entrance of the solo piano—the violins beginning with the inconclusive statement [1], followed by a pause, after which the first sequence of ideas begins with this passage:

It leads eventually to this forceful statement:

and this eventually to a poignant conclusion:

Now the piano enters, first to play [1], then, after the pause, to take off in a sequence of ideas that begins with this impassioned statement:

The sequence becomes calmer with [2a] from the orchestra's first sequence, which the piano carries further in an ornate style with great expressive intensity. Eventually it leads to the conclusion [4] of the orchestra's first sequence, which this time continues on and builds up to the next appearance of [1], this one coming from the orchestra's flute.

Again, after the pause, the piano takes off, beginning with this quiet statement:

and then answering the woodwinds' phrases in an increasingly florid style with great expressive intensity. Eventually the orchestra takes over, building up to the next appearance of [1]—this one, more forceful, from the piano.

And again, after the pause, the piano takes off, beginning with this powerful statement:

The sequence becomes calmer, once more bringing in [2a] from the orchestra's first sequence, but then continuing with forceful [3], which the piano carries to a conclusion—at which point the orchestra builds up to the pause on the anticipatory six-four chord that is the signal for the piano's entrance alone to reflect in a cadenza on the happenings of the movement.

The end of the cadenza brings the orchestra in with the last appearance of [1], beginning what Girdlestone recognizes as the "finest [bars] in the movement." But then, quoting this final appearance as follows:

he says that it is no longer a question, but finds its answer in [4] of the orchestra's first sequence. And this is an astonishing misreading of the passage and missing of its point. For the initial statement that has attained no conclusion each time it has been heard is what is played by the flute and oboe in [8], with the affecting changes in the melody (marked by asterisks) and underlying harmony; and the tremendous thing that happens now is that this time, at last, the statement does attain a conclusion—the few measures added in [8] by the piano, which, after all that has happened in the movement, constitute an overwhelming conclusion of summation, resignation, sublimity. Those few measures of the piano are the climax of the movement, achieved by another master-stroke.

PART THREE

27

Performance

One can begin with the twenty-year-old Bernard Shaw's perception of the "highest faculty of a conductor" as the "establishment of a magnetic influence under which an orchestra becomes as amenable to the *batôn* as a pianoforte to the fingers." The "pianoforte" that he referred to presents built-in tonal capacities to the fingers that produce the sounds the pianist puts together in his performance. But the sounds the conductor puts together are those produced by the capacities and efforts of the hundred or so members of his orchestra; and facing the orchestra at a rehearsal or a concert, with an idea in his mind of the sound he wants, he can get those hundred musicians to produce them only if the wishes that he communicates with the movements of his baton are enforced by the magnetic compulsion Shaw spoke of. The famous conductors of the past—Artur Nikisch, Arturo Toscanini, Karl Muck, Gustav Mahler, Felix Weingartner, Richard Strauss, Wilhelm Furtwängler, Leopold Stokowski, Serge Koussevitzky, Guido Cantelli—exercised that extraordinary magnetic power; Toscanini's, according to musicians who played under him, was uncanny. And in recent years that power has been evident in the operation of Pierre Boulez and Michael Tilson Thomas, which sets their performances apart even from those of conductors as gifted and dedicated as Colin Davis and Carlo Maria Giulini.

But there is also the matter of how such powers are employed.

Concerning a performance by Furtwängler and his Berlin Philharmonic in London W. J. Turner wrote: "These extraordinary pianissimos, these marvelously manipulated accelerandos, ritardandos and crescendos can absolutely get in the way of the music when they are all produced for the sake of effect, as a piece of showmanship. . . . On this occasion [Furtwängler and his orchestra] were quite obviously displaying their virtuosity to the disadvantage of the music."* But after a concert of Toscanini with the New York Philharmonic a few months later Turner wrote: "No conductor I have heard has succeeded in achieving such virtuosity and in keeping it always subservient to a purely musical intention."**

Concerning this musical intention Turner—after a Beethoven series a few years later in which Toscanini conducted the BBC Symphony—observed that Toscanini's "grasp of the musical structure of the work he is conducting is unique," and that "one of his greatest virtues is his subtle variation of tempo, but always in the service of shape, and the shape is derived from the rightful expression of the music."*** To this I would add something else that was unique in those days: the seeming control of the operation of Toscanini's powers by a mental governor that held them to the achievement of the unfailing rightness of shape and expression from the first note of a work to the last. And Turner summed up the difference between a Toscanini performance and one that did not exhibit such a grasp of shape and structure by asking his readers to imagine "having only been able to procure Keats's *Ode to a Nightingale* printed in smudged ink on a piece of blotting paper with the stanzas scattered haphazard all over the sheet and either no punctuation or all the punctuation wrong." This, he continued, was how music was very often performed, "and the first distinction between a good reproducing artist and an inferior one is that from the good artist we get an orderly, correct, audible impression."****

---

*W. J. Turner, "Furtwängler," in *The New Statesman*, December 14, 1929.
**W. J. Turner, "Toscanini," in *The New Statesman*, June 17, 1930.
***I have not discovered the source of this comment by Turner. —*Ed.*
****W. J. Turner, *Music—An Introduction to Its Nature and Appreciation* (London, 1936).

There also have been pianists with powers of virtuoso magnitude in the manipulation of their instrument. Some of those pianists—Josef Hofmann, Josef Lhévinne, Moriz Rosenthal, Vladimir Horowitz—have misused the music they have played to excite audiences with displays of their virtuosity and with distortions of musical shape that falsified expressive meaning; others—Artur Schnabel, Vladimir Ashkenazy, Van Cliburn, Maurizio Pollini, Murray Perahia—have used their mastery of the instrument in the service of their shaping of the music with their distinguished insight. This is true of other instrumentalists as well—Jascha Heifetz, with the fussy, wailing inflection of his dazzlingly beautiful violin tone that often produced a sentimentalizing and cheapening performance of the music, as against Fritz Kreisler, Joseph Szigeti, Isaac Stern, Nathan Milstein, Itzhak Perlman, and Anne-Sophie Mutter, who have used their distinguished gifts in distinguished performances of the music. And it is true of singers: in his recorded performance of *O Paradiso!* Enrico Caruso, arriving at a high B flat, holds and expands it from *pp* to an overwhelming *ff*, then breaks off to take breath before completing the phrase; whereas Jussi Bjoerling, in his recorded performance, connects the expanded B flat with the next note as part of the continuous and beautifully shaped phrase. In the Caruso performance one hears an exceptionally beautiful voice and a mastery in its use; in the Bjoerling not only these but the art in musical phrasing that Caruso did not have.

There is, then, a distinction to be made between a performer's playing of an instrument or use of a voice and his or her playing of music. It is a distinction which doesn't occur to most of the people hearing the beautiful and exciting sounds produced by a virtuoso, and which is difficult for them to understand when someone else makes it: to perform music is, after all, to produce the sounds; to produce beautiful sounds would seem to be to perform it well; and the performances by great virtuosos would seem to be not good and bad but only different. But what is bad in a performance in which the virtuoso makes over-emphatic changes in tempo and sonority is that they distort the shape and expressive effect of the music. Bad too, on the other hand, are performances with no enlivening inflection at all. And a good performance is one in which subtle changes in tempo and sonority stay within the limits set by the composer's directions and make precisely detailed the forms in sound which those directions outline roughly.*

The good in art becomes the criterion by which one recognizes the bad; and that is true of performance, but with at least one qualification. The good performance is the one which realizes in living sound the form indicated by the composer's directions about tempo and sonority; but the performance that changes this shape with tempos and sonorities different from those the composer asks for is not necessarily bad. We accept it as valid if it is consistent with what we think is the expressive character of the work, and if in addition it is coherent in tempo and sonority, continuous in impetus, tension, and shape.

A word finally about performances using period instruments. The writings of the authentic-instrument cultists have persuaded people to attend the concerts and buy the recordings of certain untalented performers by putting forward the idea that—as one writer asserted—the experience of hearing Beethoven's symphonies performed on the instruments he wrote them for—the valveless brass instruments, the woodwinds "more sharply differentiated from one another in their tone quality than their modern counterparts," and the "members of the violin family . . . strung with gut" and therefore giving a "clearer articulation and brighter sound than those today"—is like the experience of seeing an old painting after the removal of "successive layers of restoration and dirt." But for me it has been the performances by gifted musicians on modern instruments that have had the

---

*Musical notation is a series of directions for performance which tell players what notes to produce, how loud to make them, how long to hold them, and other things of that kind. Ever since Mozart's and Haydn's time the directions have been increasingly numerous and detailed; but the most detailed directions have to leave something to the player—certain subtle differentiations of loudness, certain time-values a little longer or shorter than written, which cannot be specified in notation, and which the player supplies in accordance with the tradition of performance that he has learned, and with his own judgment and taste. On the other hand the further back we go from Mozart and Haydn the less numerous and detailed are the directions for the player; and even the directions concerning the notes to play are summed up in a form of notational shorthand—the melodic ornaments and figured bass which the player was expected to translate into melody, harmony, rhythm and figuration in the language and style of his period. —B. H. H.

"brighter, clearer sound" and have provided the experience like that of seeing an old painting after the removal of "layers of restoration and dirt."

Likewise, when one fortepiano player contended in his notes for his recording of Haydn trios that the works achieve their effects only when realized in the sounds of the instruments for which they were written, with their "sweetness, delicacy, subtlety, and timbral individuality," not in the "sustained sounds with much body" of the instruments of today—in particular the "bright, pure sound" of the Viennese fortepiano, not the "powerful but wooly treble of the modern piano"—his statements misrepresented, on the one hand, the actual drab, wheezy, asthmatic sounds of the eighteenth-century strings, the weak, short-lived sound of the fortepiano, on that recording, and on the other hand the actual "sweetness, delicacy, subtlety, and timbral individuality" of the sounds a skilled player can produce from a Bechstein, a Hamburg Steinway, or a Bösendorfer piano of today.

Haydn, Mozart, Beethoven and Schubert wrote for the instruments that were available in their time; but I find it impossible to believe they would not have welcomed and preferred the stronger and sustained treble sound of the modern piano, which makes possible legato playing of melody—similar to what is done by the human voice and string and wind instruments—that cannot be achieved on the fortepiano, or that they would not have preferred the modern piano's ample and mellow bass to the metallic clatter of the fortepiano's bass chords, and the luminous, blended sound of today's orchestral instruments to the dullsounding authentic strings, the obtrusively raucous authentic valveless horns and all the rest. And I continue to believe that the sensitive playing of the few gifted performers in this field—the pianist Malcolm Bilson, the conductor John Eliot Gardiner—would be equally impressive, and that the music would achieve its effect equally well, in performances on good modern instruments.

One further contention about authentic performance practice requires comment—the contention that repetitions must be embellished by the performer today as they were by the performer in Haydn's and Mozart's time, and that without such embellishments the repeated sections are tedious. While I am interested in hearing the embellishments Haydn and Mozart saw fit to write into some of the repetitions in their works, I don't find it tedious to listen to the repetitions they left unembellished. What I do find tedious are the embellishments performers began a few years ago not only to insert where none were written but to substitute for some of Haydn's and Mozart's own. Rossini expressly objected to this practise—in his case to singers interpolating embellishments and variations of their own in place of, or in addition to, those he had written out in his operas; yet there are singers and musicologists today who insist that authentic performance requires musicians to take the liberties Rossini objected to.

28

Great Performers
(c. 1900–1986)

Replying to Arturo Toscanini's letter of resignation as conductor
of the NBC Symphony in 1954, RCA Chairman David Sarnoff
wrote that Toscanini's "incomparable re-creations of the great
music of the past and present" had, happily, been "recorded and
preserved for us, and for posterity." What he failed to add was
that the recordings would be available to us and to posterity only
if they continued to be bought in quantities that RCA Victor
considered sufficient to justify continuing production. And actually, within a few years Victor had stopped producing some of
Toscanini's recordings. One reason for the drop in sales of
Toscanini's recordings was the fact that the public buys the
recordings of the currently active performers it reads about, not
of the inactive performers it no longer reads about, not even
inactive performers as famous as Toscanini. Another reason was
the advent of stereophonic recording, which made Toscanini's
recordings uninteresting to those who care more about the latest
in sound than about the greatest in performance.

What happened in Toscanini's case has been happening ever
since the beginning of commercial recording. Always the companies have talked about the phonograph's preserving performers' art for posterity; but always the recorded performances
of yesterday have disappeared from the catalogues, to be replaced by those of today; and with each major change in recording technique—from acoustical to electrical 78-rpm recording,

from 78-rpm to long-playing microgroove, from monophonic LP to stereo, and most recently from analog LP to digital Compact Disc—the recordings made with the old technique have been replaced with recordings made with the new.* And this chapter is concerned with some of the great recorded performances that are worth obtaining while they are still available or watching for among the occasional reissues and in stores that sell old records.

Singers Through the 1920s

What acoustic 78-rpm recording reproduced accurately was singing; and the records preserved some of the achievements in what has been called the golden age of singing—the age of Enrico Caruso, Nellie Melba, Luisa Tetrazzini, John McCormack and their contemporaries. It must be noted that most of the singers in this period misused the music to show off their voices, instead of employing their voices in an effective presentation of the music; and what were recorded were performances like Caruso's of *Una furtiva lagrima* from Donizetti's *L'Elisir d'amore*, in which the outpouring of vocal splendor burst the shape of the musical

---

*The advent of digital Compact Discs—to which 78-rpm records and taped performances could be copied in better sound than to LPs—occurred at a time when the expiration of copyright had already placed a number of historical recorded performances in the public domain. As a result, a great many old recordings, and a number of broadcasts formerly available only privately on underground tapes and records, suddenly appeared in stores on CDs both from the large record companies and from a number of small ones established expressly for the purpose of issuing historical material.

But while the number of historical releases was unprecedented, in other ways the situation had not changed. The large companies still kept their historical issues in the catalogue only for as long as the public bought them in sufficient quantities to make them profitable; and the small companies did the same, or else pressed their records in limited editions.

Moreover, the sound of the CD transfers was not always as good as it might have been. Small companies taking advantage of expired copyrights to release other companies' records seldom were given access to the master discs; instead they copied privately owned shellac discs that in some instances were worn or inferior-sounding to begin with; and in the case of broadcasts, they resorted to home recordings or illicit copies. And some of this material was made to sound even worse by the way it was filtered or otherwise tampered with by the engineers making the transfer—as happened occasionally even when the larger companies worked from their original master discs or tapes. —*Ed.*

phrase, more often than performances like McCormack's of this aria, in which the beautiful voice was employed in a plastically coherent shaping of phase.

McCormack wasn't the only exception: the soprano Frieda Hempel, too, not only had as lovely a voice and spectacular technique as Melba and Tetrazzini but was the great musician they were not: no one in my experience has equalled her sustained phrasing in the closing section of *Dite alla giovine* from Verdi's *La Traviata* in the performance she recorded with Pasquale Amato—certainly not Melba, whose obtrusively self-indulgent slowing down of the phrase *unico ragio di bene* I have never heard from any other singer. And many others who were recorded were worth hearing much of the time only for their manipulation of their voices, as one could discover by listening to Mozart mangled by soprano Adelina Patti, Mozart and Rossini sung ludicrously—but Bellini, Donizetti and Verdi more impressively—by baritone Mattia Battistini, and to the characterless flow of pretty sounds produced by soprano Amelita Galli-Curci in everything. As for Tetrazzini, the extraordinary beauty and spectacular agility of her voice made some of her performances enjoyably straightforward, but in others the total absence of musical phrasing and style and mere exactness of time were painful.

Singing at the Metropolitan at the same time as Hempel and McCormack were the distinguished sopranos Johanna Gadski, Geraldine Farrar (who had an extraordinarily beautiful voice), Olive Fremstad, Alma Gluck, Florence Easton, Mabel Garrison, Celestina Boninsegna and Emmy Destinn (one of whose records provides a glimpse of Toscanini's 1915 revival of Verdi's *Il Trovatore* at the Metropolitan—the accurately and beautifully sung *Miserere* that she and Giovanni Martinelli recorded at the time); also the contraltos Margarete Matzenauer (an unforgettably great artist, both in voice and musicianship), Louise Homer, Margarete Ober, and Ernestine Schumann-Heink (whose later electrical recordings were made when her voice had lost its beauty but retained its steadiness and power, and who recorded impressive performances of *Lieder* as well as of opera).

And with these one heard the tenors Leo Slezak, Jacques Urlus and Carl Jörn—all with remarkable voices which they used as superb musicians in an amazing variety of styles (Slezak's *Ora e per sempre addio* from Verdi's *Otello*, for example, was, when I heard it, the most impressive performance of this excerpt I could recall, exhibiting a heroic tenor voice of great power and beauty which then astounded one with its capacity for the delicate lyricism of his performance of an aria from Flotow's *Stradella*, for his sensitive phrasing in Schubert's *Wohin*, Wolf's *Verschwiegene Liebe*, Richard Strauss's *Cäcilie* and *Ich trage meine Minne*, and art-songs by Reynaldo Hahn); the tenor Hermann Jadlowker, who sang well in the duets he recorded with Hempel; the baritones Mario Ancona (very fine), Titta Ruffo (who sometimes bellowed), Antonio Scotti, Emilio De Gogorza (in whose early recordings an agreeable voice is used with musical taste and achieves delightful subtleties of phrasing in the *Serenade* from *Don Giovanni* that I don't remember hearing from anyone else), and Giuseppe De Luca (whose recording of Rigoletto's *Povero Rigoletto* and *Cortigiani, vil razza dannata* is made notable—for listeners accustomed to the usual bellowing in this scene—by the fact that every note is sung with a style and art that achieve the most intense expressiveness and dramatic force); and the basses Marcel Journet and, somewhat earlier, Pol Plançon.

In Russia there was the lyric tenor Leonid Sobinov, whose recordings gave us his incomparably beautiful and affecting performances of Lensky's arias from Tchaikovsky's *Eugene Onegin* and similar performances—sung in Russian—of arias by Donizetti, Wagner, Bizet, Thomas, Flotow and various Russian composers. And in Austria there was the soprano Selma Kurz, in whose sustained singing one heard a lyric voice with a lovely and touching timbre astonishingly like Hempel's, a feeling for articulation and shaping of phrase also like Hempel's, but enormous liberties of tempo that Hempel didn't take; moreover, in her sensational florid singing Kurz permitted herself interpolations of cadenzas, or minute-long exhibitions of her spectacular trill, or an astronomically high concluding squeak (which Hempel did indulge in). Margarethe Siems, the Marschallin of the first production of Richard Strauss's *Der Rosenkavalier*, recorded an outstanding performance of the first-act monologue. And the Polish soprano Claire Dux, who sang mostly in Europe and England, made records between 1917 and 1921 which preserved her attractive singing in music of Handel, Mozart, Weber, Verdi and others.

Captured in live performance in 1902–03—by Lionel Mapleson, the Metropolitan's librarian, on cylinders on which enough can be heard, in spite of wear and noise and limitations of volume and range, to make the recordings valuable—were a number of voices I had never expected to hear: Lillian Nordica's superbly clear and sustained soprano; the freedom, power and superb fullness of Jean de Reszke's tenor all the way to B flat and B natural; Lucienne Bréval's superb, sustained singing, likewise to B flat and B; a pale image of Marcella Sembrich's voice but a surprisingly vivid impression of the impressive freedom, authority and style of her singing (in contrast to the records she made for Columbia at the same time, which were as tasteless in their distortions as those of many others); Emma Calvé's uncharacteristically superb singing in the "Jewel Song" from Gounod's *Faust;* and the breathtaking verve—in those days—of Melba's *Un di felice* in *La Traviata,* her sustained singing with its succession of high Bs in the *Faust* trio, and her florid singing in parts of Meyerbeer's *Les Huguenots* that is sensational in its accuracy, its tossed-off ornamental high Ds.*

The later studio recordings by the French tenor Edmond Clément, who sang in America before the First World War, reproduced the beautiful voice and lyric style of his maturity. His earlier ones reproduced a different and less beautiful voice, and—in *Ecco ridente* from Rossini's *The Barber of Seville*—his astonishing liberties in phrasing, tempo and interpolation of high notes and trills (though the vocal execution of all this was equally astonishing). The famous baritone Victor Maurel, whose singing in Mozart's *Don Giovanni* and Verdi's *Otello* Shaw wrote about in the 1890s, had little voice left when he recorded the few numbers he did, but he could still use it with impressive vocal art in *Era la notte* from *Otello.* The musical art was less admirable than the

---

*On the records Melba made in the studio between 1904 and 1906—of arias from Donizetti's *Lucia,* Thomas's *Hamlet,* Gounod's *Faust* and Verdi's *La Traviata*—one still heard the steadiness and purity of the sounds she produced, the smoothness of her legato, her effortless execution of florid passages and trills; and one from 1926 had an effective performance of the *Ave Maria* from Verdi's *Otello.* But the records did not reproduce the luster that gave her voice the extraordinary beauty referred to by contemporaries. —B.H.H.

vocal, and Shaw didn't prepare one for Maurel's shockingly mannered delivery of the Serenade from *Don Giovanni;* but his performance of *Quand'ero paggio* from Verdi's *Falstaff* was delightful. Another famous and excellent baritone, Maurice Renaud, sang selections by Berlioz, Bizet, Donizetti and others in a style more acceptable to ears of today, as did the soprano Jeanne Gerville-Réache.

  The impressive baritone Riccardo Stracciari left a few records, one of them a duet with Maria Barrientos, who was at the Metropolitan for a few years from about 1917, and whose own recordings exhibited her lovely small voice, her agility and security in florid passages, and *her* liberties. Another beautiful soprano voice was that of Olimpia Boronat, who sang mostly in Imperial Russia, and who recorded arias by Bellini, Donizetti, Verdi and others between 1904 and 1908. Lilli Lehmann was sixty or thereabouts when she recorded her performances of Verdi, Mozart, Bellini, Handel and Meyerbeer; but the voice, if it had no luster and warmth such as the sixty-year-old Kirsten Flagstad's retained, was extraordinary and amazing in its clarity and power, the absolute security and accuracy of its execution, its musical style (age may have been responsible for the questionable phrasing—the rush, pause for breath, and slow descent—at the climax of *Casta diva*).

Conductors 1900–1940s

Though acoustic recording didn't reproduce the symphony orchestra well, Victor did achieve a remarkable approximation of what I retain in my memory as the sound of the Boston Symphony conducted by Karl Muck—in its recordings of the *Marche miniature* from Tchaikovsky's Suite No. 1, the finale of his Symphony No. 4, and the Prelude to Act Three of Wagner's *Lohengrin*. [The acoustic recordings Toscanini made during his tour of the United States in 1920–21 with the orchestra of La Scala—of the last movements of Beethoven's First and Fifth Symphonies, the minuet and finale of Mozart's Symphony K.543, and short pieces—while dim-sounding next to his later electrical recordings, are valuable for their documentation of an already coherent, steady performance style that was similar in this respect to Muck's but very different from that of many other conductors of his time.] The advent of electrical recording in the mid-1920s brought the beginning of realistic reproduction of the orchestra. [Early electrical recordings gave very good reproduction of Muck's fine performances in Germany of Wagner's *Siegfried Idyll*, the Prelude to Act One of *Die Meistersinger*, extended excerpts from Acts One and Three of *Parsifal* (in which, unfortunately, the singers obscured the orchestra to a degree), *Siegfried's Rhine Journey* from *Götterdämmerung*, and the Overture to *The Flying Dutchman;* less good were Muck's performances of the Prelude to *Tristan* and *Siegfried's Funeral Music* from *Götterdämmerung* made at the same time.]

In the years that followed, Victor recordings preserved the achievements of what might be called a golden age of orchestral performance in this country, in which the Philadelphia Orchestra playing under Leopold Stokowski (through 1940), the Boston Symphony under Serge Koussevitzky (through 1949), the New York Philharmonic under Toscanini (1926–36)—each a group of exceptionally competent performers sensitized to the direction of a conductor extraordinarily equipped with the ear for orchestral precision and sonority and with the personal force and technical mastery to achieve them—produced their marvels of virtuoso execution and, in accordance with the particular conductor's taste, the Philadelphia Orchestra's tonal sumptuousness and splendor, the Boston Symphony's refinement and subtlety of orchestral color, the New York Philharmonic's radiance, transparency and sharpness of definition. And again it must be noted that the Toscanini performances offered orchestral virtuosity in the service of his unfailing sense for plastic proportion and coherence in the shaping of phrase and larger structure, whereas those of Koussevitzky and Stokowski offered orchestral sonorities that were among the wonders of the age, but with Koussevitzky's italicizing plastic distortions of nineteenth-century music, his playing of eighteenth-century music with no enlivening inflection at all, and Stokowski's playing of almost everything with the fever and luxuriance suitable for the Bacchanale from *Tannhäuser* or the second-act duet from *Tristan und Isolde.*

Two Koussevitzky-Boston Symphony performances that were not only examples of dazzling orchestral virtuosity but admirable statements of the music were those of Mendelssohn's *Italian* Symphony and Prokofiev's *Classical* Symphony [of which the first versions made in the 1930s had even better playing by the orchestra than the re-makes of the 1940s]; worth hearing as well—if only for the subtle sonorities Koussevitzky obtained from the orchestra—were his performances of *La Mer* (in spite of his damaging disregard for Debussy's directions in matters of pacing, and even at times for the composer's notes), Ravel's *Daphnis and Chloé* Suite No. 2 [which also existed in early and late recordings], and the Prelude to Musorgsky's *Khovanshchina*.

Four of the best Stokowski-Philadelphia Orchestra performances were the early electrical Victor records of the *Polovtsian Dances* from Borodin's *Prince Igor*, Debussy's *Fêtes*, Rimsky-Korsakov's *Russian Easter Overture* and Stokowski's early and comparatively continent transcription of Bach's *Passacaglia* in C minor.

As for Toscanini, the incandescent operation with the New York Philharmonic that he never duplicated with another orchestra was reproduced most realistically by the 1936 recordings they made at the end of his last Philharmonic season—of Beethoven's Seventh, Brahms's *Variations on a Theme of Haydn*, Rossini's Overtures to *Semiramide* and *L'Italiana in Algeri*, and Wagner's Prelude to *Lohengrin, Dawn and Siegfried's Rhine Journey* from *Götterdämmerung*, and *Siegfried Idyll*. But it could be heard even in the less realistically reproduced performances they recorded in 1929—of Haydn's Symphony No. 101 (*Clock*), Mozart's Symphony K.385 (*Haffner*), Mendelssohn's Scherzo from the music for *A Midsummer Night's Dream*, Rossini's Overture to *The Barber of Seville*, and Verdi's Preludes to Acts One and Three of *La Traviata*.

In addition to documenting the incandescent operation of conductor and orchestra these recordings documented the Toscanini performing style of that period—relaxed, expansive, articulating and organizing and shaping the substance of a piece with much elasticity of tempo, and molding the phrase with a great deal of sharp inflection—as against the style of the later NBC Symphony years that was simpler, tauter, swifter, setting a tempo that was maintained with only slight modification, and giving the phrase only subtle inflection. Further examples of the more effective and impressive earlier style were the performances Toscanini recorded with the BBC Symphony between 1937 and 1939—of Beethoven's Symphonies Nos. 1, 4, 6 (*Pastoral*) and 7, his Overtures *Leonore* No. 1 and *Prometheus*, Mozart's Symphony K.385 (*Haffner*) and Overture to *The Magic Flute*, Debussy's *La Mer*, Rossini's Overture to *La Scala di Seta*, Wagner's *Siegfried's Funeral Music*, the Weber-Berlioz *Invitation to the Dance*, and works by Brahms (including an uncharacteristically unsteady Fourth Symphony), Elgar and others. To these were added the performances he recorded with the newly formed NBC Symphony in 1938 and 1939—of Haydn's Symphony No. 88, Mozart's Symphony K.550 (the great G-minor), Beethoven's Symphonies Nos. 3 (*Eroica*), 5 and 8, his Overtures *Leonore* Nos. 2 and 3 and *Egmont*, the Lento and Vivace from his Quartet Op. 135, Rossini's Overture to *William Tell*—which documented another characteristic of the early NBC Symphony performances: their extraordinary energy and fire, the result of the conductor's being stimulated by the unusual capacities and responsiveness of the many young virtuosos in the orchestra, and their being stimulated by his powers and dedication.

And a towering example of Toscanini's earlier style was the Schubert Symphony No. 9 that he recorded with the Philadelphia Orchestra in 1941, which Victor did not issue until 1963. Toscanini's untraditional performance gave this work a sustained tension, momentum and grandeur that it had in no other; and he achieved with the Philadelphia Orchestra the greatest of his realizations of it—one that was more effective than the great performance he recorded in 1953 with the NBC Symphony. The other performances Toscanini recorded with the Philadelphia Orchestra in 1941–42—of Tchaikovsky's *Pathétique*, Debussy's *La Mer* and *Ibéria*, Berlioz's *Queen Mab* Scherzo, Mendelssohn's *Midsummer Night's Dream* music, Richard Strauss's *Death and Transfiguration*—also were superior to those he recorded at other times.

Most of the Toscanini performances that were available on LPs during the roughly thirty years from the 1950s to the mid-1980s were the ones he recorded with the NBC Symphony from 1944 on. Most of these were in his later, simpler, subtler, tauter and swifter style, [which meant that this style was by and large what most listeners in those years knew, though a few of the later performances were exceptions to the rule: The *Tristan* Prelude that was broader and slower in 1952 than in 1941, the Beethoven *Pastoral* Symphony whose first movement was more leisurely in 1952 than in 1937, the Schubert Ninth Symphony that was more relaxed in 1953 than in 1947, if not as relaxed and expansive as in 1941. But the performances transferred to Compact Discs have been from every period of Toscanini's recording career, and from live concerts as well as from the recording sessions at which he was sometimes tense; consequently the CDs have given the general public a more comprehensive idea of his achievements than before.] The greatest of these performances have not been surpassed; and their greatness is evident even when they are defectively reproduced.

The performances on Victor records included the operas Toscanini broadcast with the NBC Symphony, concerning which the opera specialists among the record-reviewers, and Virgil Thomson among the music critics, created the myth that Toscanini used in these performances only the inexperienced and inferior singers who would submit to the tyranny of his "fast and rigid tempos" that "thwarted" singers' attempts to sing "expressively." Actually the singers he used were not inexperienced and inferior but some of the best available—Zinka Milanov, Licia Albanese, Helen Traubel, Herva Nelli, Nan Merriman, Cloë Elmo, Lauritz Melchior, Jan Peerce, Ramón Vinay, Leonard Warren, Giuseppe Valdengo—who sang as expressively with him in these concert performances as Hempel, Destinn, Homer, Matzenauer, Urlus, Rethberg, Lotte Lehmann and other famous singers of the past had done with him in the opera house. And one heard in the performances a coherent and beautiful plastic flow created by a beat that was never anything but flexible in relation to the music, and was unyielding in relation to the singers only in compelling them to operate within that flow. As against the usual performances in which the orchestra played perfunctorily in tempos that deferred to the singers' every exhibitionistic extravagance, and which had no continuity, no coherence, no clarity of outline or texture, Toscanini's performances offered accurately and beautifully shaped vocal phrases that fitted precisely into the accurate and beautiful orchestral contexts whose every detail was in active expressive relation to what was being sung—all this in a progression that was clear, continuous and coherent. They constituted striking illustrations of W. J. Turner's analogy in explanation of the superiority of a Toscanini performance—the analogy of a poem printed clearly and correctly on good paper, as against the poem printed in smudged ink on blotting paper with the punctuation all wrong. And all of them—the *La Traviata* with Licia Albanese and Jan Peerce, the *Otello* with Herva Nelli, Ramón Vinay and Giuseppe Valdengo, the Verdi *Aida* with Nelli and Valdengo, the *Falstaff* with Valdengo, Nelli, Cloë Elmo, Nan Merriman and Teresa Stich-Randall, the *Un Ballo in maschera* with Nelli and Peerce, the Act Four of *Rigoletto* with Zinka Milanov, Peerce and Leonard Warren, [the Puccini *La Bohème* with Albanese, Peerce and Frank Valentino], and even the Beethoven *Fidelio* with the title role sung inadequately by Rose Bampton—produced the effect of revelation.

An additional fact to mention is that the performances his players recalled as having surpassed any others in their experience were not only his Schubert Ninth, his Mozart G-minor, his Verdi *Otello*, his Debussy *La Mer*, but also the performances of pieces like the *Skaters Waltz* and Overture to *Zampa*. One heard in these the same exquisite molding of melodic phrase, the same plastically coherent shaping, the same clarifying of texture and structure, which produced the same effect of revelation. It was not just that Toscanini's feeling for music was a feeling for any music he performed—for the least as well as the greatest: it was also that he performed the least as if it *was* the greatest—with the same total commitment of his powers. He recorded a few of these light or "pop" numbers in his first years with the NBC Symphony: Paganini's *Moto perpetuo*, Strauss's *Tritsch-Tratsch Polka* and *Blue Danube Waltz*, Waldteufel's *Skaters Waltz*, Sousa's *The Stars and Stripes Forever*, the Overture to Thomas's *Mignon*. Later Toscanini recorded a performance of Gershwin's *An American in Paris* in which it was amazing to hear what—with his feeling for shape of phrase, his grace and rubato, in the playing of melody— he made of the piece and its blues. And in 1952 he recorded the

Overture to Hérold's *Zampa*, the Dance of the Hours from Ponchielli's *La Gioconda*, his own Suite from Bizet's *Carmen*, [several of Brahms's Hungarian Dances], the Prelude to Humperdinck's *Hänsel und Gretel*, and the Overture to Thomas's *Mignon*.

[In addition to the performances originally issued with Toscanini's approval on Victor records, there were many others with the New York Philharmonic, BBC and NBC Symphony Orchestras, the Vienna State Opera (at Salzburg), and other orchestras that he guest-conducted in the 1940s and '50s, that may now be heard on CDs from a number of companies in (for the most part) astonishingly good-sounding transfers.]

Of Toscanini's contemporaries, Sir Thomas Beecham, in the late thirties, recorded with his London Philharmonic dynamically phrased and in other ways excellent performances of Mozart's Symphonies K.297 (*Paris*), 338, 385 (*Haffner*), 425 (*Linz*), 543 and 551 (*Jupiter*), the overtures to Mozart's *Don Giovanni, The Marriage of Figaro* and *The Abduction from the Seraglio;* Haydn's Symphonies Nos. 93, 99 and 104; Schubert's Symphonies Nos. 5 and 8 (*Unfinished*), Franck's Symphony, Tchaikovsky's Fifth and *Francesca da Rimini*, and shorter pieces—Mendelssohn's *Fingal's Cave* (*Hebrides*) Overture, Sibelius's *Festivo*, Weber's *Oberon* Overture, Chabrier's *España* Rhapsody, three excerpts from Berlioz's *The Damnation of Faust* (the Dance of the Sylphs, Minuet of the Will o' the Wisps, and Hungarian March), the Suite from Bizet's *Carmen*, the First Suite and part of the Second from *L'Arlésienne*, several of the better works of Delius (and some of the poorer ones), and the Rossini-Respighi ballet suite *Rossiniana*.

Beecham also provided superb accompaniments in those years for Joseph Szigeti's recordings of three violin concertos— Mozart's K.218, Mendelssohn's in E minor and Prokofiev's First. And two of Beecham's superb opera performances of the 1930s were recorded as well: Mozart's *The Magic Flute*—made in the studio in 1937 with a group of outstanding singers and the Berlin Philharmonic and released at the time—was enlivened overall by Beecham's forceful shaping of the orchestral part around the singing, though it was damaged in a few places (notably in the overture) by over-deliberate tempos. And Wagner's *Tristan und*

Isolde, of which a set was compiled many years later from two
1937 Covent Garden broadcasts of staged performances, had
Kirsten Flagstad in her prime, Lauritz Melchior singing less
satisfactorily, two impressive Brangänes (Margarete Klose and
Karin Branzell), and the superb expressive effect throughout of
Beecham's enlivening pacing and shaping of the work, even with
recorded sound that did not reproduce the orchestra as well as it
did the voices.

On the other hand, Beecham's London Philharmonic recording in the thirties of Mozart's Symphony K.550 in G minor was
made unacceptable by an unsuitably jaunty treatment of the
opening movement, K.504 (*Prague*) by the shocking, arch inflection of bar 34 of the Andante, and K.201 by the ponderously slow
tempos that destroyed the work's animation and grace. And
many of the performances he recorded with his Royal Philharmonic in his last years—notably the ones of Haydn's last twelve
symphonies and his remakes of several of Mozart's—suffered
from tempos that made the music ponderous or static, and from
over-elaborated inflection of phrase and exaggerated accentuation. The exceptions in those years were Mozart's *Haffner* Symphony, his Clarinet and Bassoon Concertos, the complete *Abduction from the Seraglio* (which had Léopold Simoneau's ear-
ravishing singing as Belmonte but as Constanza the unlovely and
quavering voice—on this occasion—of Lois Marshall), Beethoven's Mass in C and Symphonies Nos. 2 and 7, Brahms's
Symphony No. 2, Schubert's Symphonies Nos. 3 and 5, Dvořák's
Symphonic Variations, Berlioz's *Te Deum* and *Symphonie fantastique*
and Bizet's complete *Carmen*.

I was a witness, at Willem Mengelberg's daily rehearsals, of the
training he gave the New York Philharmonic from 1921 to 1926,
and can testify to the discipline and finish of its playing under his
direction; but although I did not witness Toscanini's work at
rehearsals of the Philharmonic, I did hear that it was only when
the orchestra began to play under him in 1926 that it began to
exhibit the dazzling virtuosity and tonal beauty comparable with
those of the Philadelphia Orchestra and Boston Symphony. As
for Mengelberg's musicianship in those years, and later with his
Concertgebouw Orchestra in Amsterdam, it is unquestionably I

who have changed; and I blush to think that his inability to let a phrase or section of a symphonic movement, or even a simple chorale in one of Bach's Passions, take its course without a distention of tempo and sonority once seemed to me the highest musicianship. Now it seems to me to achieve sheer absurdity.

In much the same way, re-issues on LP in the 1950s and later of Felix Weingartner's recordings with the Vienna Philharmonic and various London orchestras made it possible not only to hear again the works of Beethoven and Brahms as they were performed by one of the other legendary greats of the century, but also to perceive the operation of a process of art history in the fact that these performances, which in the 1930s were considered wholly admirable, revealed inadequacies and defects when listened to later. That is, having heard subsequently the perfections produced by Toscanini and a few others after him—perfections in orchestral execution, in inflection of phrase, in shaping of structure with modifications in tempo and dynamics—caused one to hear imperfections in the Weingartner performances that had seemed perfect in the thirties—above all the characteristic lack of energy and cohesive tension that made many of them seem sluggish, the often slow tempos, the occasional pauses and changes of pace. Of Weingartner's series of recordings of the nine Beethoven symphonies, the one of the First was the most satisfying, the work being one that suffered least from this lack of energy. I feel a need for more intensity in the *Eroica*, but in its unemphatic way this performance of Weingartner's was a good one, too. And his early recording of Mendelssohn's *Scotch* Symphony with the old Royal Philharmonic was an enlivening one that realized the music's charm and grace.

Bruno Walter recorded in the 1930s superb performances with the Vienna Philharmonic of Act One of Wagner's *Die Walküre* (with Lotte Lehmann and Melchior), Mahler's *Das Lied von der Erde* (in concert with Kerstin Thorborg and the fine tenor Charles Kullman); also Haydn's Symphonies Nos. 86 with the London Symphony, 92 (*Oxford*) with the Paris Conservatory Concerts Orchestra and 100 (*Military*) with the Vienna Philharmonic. After the war he recorded excellent performances of *Das Lied von der Erde* (with Kathleen Ferrier, Julius Patzak—struggling with an old voice—and the Vienna Philharmonic), Mahler's Symphony No. 1 (first with the New York Philharmonic and later with the Columbia Symphony) and the Symphony No. 2 (*Resurrection*), Mozart's *Requiem*, Dvořák's Symphony No. 8 and Bruckner's *Te Deum*—all with the New York Philharmonic. His superb performances of *The Marriage of Figaro* and *Don Giovanni* at the Metropolitan in the early 1940s have been preserved in recordings of the broadcasts. But his post-war performances of Mozart (except for the *Requiem*), Haydn, Beethoven and Schubert were increasingly nerveless and flabby, illustrating the observation by Toscanini that someone reported to me in Salzburg in 1937: "When Walter comes to something beautiful he melts."*

As for Wilhelm Furtwängler, who clearly had to an impressive degree what the twenty-year-old Bernard Shaw described so well as "that highest faculty of a conductor, which consists in the establishing of a magnetic influence under which an orchestra becomes as amenable to the *batôn* as a pianoforte to the fingers," I found it impossible to accept what Beethoven and Schubert were made to mean by the self-indulgent vagaries and excesses in tempo which distorted shape and destroyed continuity in the works. In the amorphous music of Wagner, however, Furtwängler operated with a feeling for continuity; and the superb *Tristan und Isolde* he recorded with Flagstad and Ludwig Suthaus is for me the monument to his capacities as conductor and musician—even though at times it moves more slowly than I can believe Wagner intended with his directions *Langsam, Mässig langsam* and *Immer sehr ruhig*, and as a result with less expressive effect than Beecham achieved with tempos that seem to me exactly what Wagner's written directions call for. Good too was Furtwängler's record in the 1930s of the Prelude and Good Friday music from *Parsifal*. The possibility that he might have exhibited the same feeling for continuity in Mahler's symphonies is suggested by the orchestral context he provided for Dietrich Fischer-Dieskau's singing in the *Lieder eines fahrenden Gesellen* (*Songs of a Wayfarer*).

---

*The one flaw in Walter's Haydn symphony recordings of the thirties is his melting over the second subject of the opening movement of No. 86. —*B. H. H.*

One extraordinary performance of an orchestral work was recorded in the thirties by someone who was not primarily a conductor—the pianist Edwin Fischer, whose performance of Haydn's Symphony No. 104 (*London*) with his chamber orchestra not only was admirably paced and shaped but offered the additional delights of brilliant small-group ensemble operation.

Keyboard Players 1900–1940s

The pianist in whose performance of a Beethoven sonata one heard—as in Toscanini's performance of a Beethoven symphony—a clarifying articulation which seemed to reveal the structure of the work for the first time, was Artur Schnabel. And the force and authority of this new image of the work were such as to establish Schnabel's performances of the sonatas and concertos, like Toscanini's of the symphonies, as definitive—the ones by which others were judged and, to this day, found less satisfying. There were listeners for whom Schnabel's playing was an operation of intellect without emotion; but actually, though the operation of a powerful mind was evident, it was excess of emotion, not of intellect, that produced the flaws in the performances—the occasional distention of phrase to the point of distortion, the occasional tempo too fast for clarity or accuracy, the occasional fortissimo beyond the limit of agreeable sound—these in addition to the occasional inaccurate execution of some of Beethoven's awkward passage-work that Schnabel's fingers couldn't manage, though he was a superb pianist with a technique equal to the demands of most of the music he played.

Inevitably one thinks first of his performances of the last and greatest of Beethoven's piano music, in which the concluding variation movements of the Sonatas Opp. 109 and 111, the concluding Arioso dolente and fugue of Op. 110, the slow movement of Op. 106 (*Hammerklavier*) and No. 20 of the *Diabelli* Variations communicated their special expressive content as they did in no one else's performances. But what operated in these operated with similar effect in the earlier music: what made the slow movement of Op. 106 overwhelming was the Schnabel way of prolonging time values which, enlarging the physical shape of the music, enlarged its expressive dimensions; and the same prolonging of time values made the Adagio of the Sonata Op. 53 (*Waldstein*) the spaciously, profoundly meditative and powerfully dramatic utterance that it was in no other performance. Similarly, what caused the *Eroica* Variations Op. 34 to hold one's attention was the same lyrical grace that he imparted to the opening movement of the Sonata Op. 101. And these achievments were not lessened by the first movement of Op. 106 that Schnabel—in an obedience to Beethoven's metronome marking which Tovey rightly called a "mistaken form of piety"—made into a frenetic rush which he couldn't even execute clearly; or by the similar frenetic rush he made of the finale of the Sonata Op. 57 (*Appassionata*); or by the first movement of the Sonata Op. 26 which should flow gracefully, but which—in his attempt to give it greater expressive weight with slow tempo and intensifying inflection—he made unattractively pretentious.

Of the concertos, Schnabel's performances of the thirties with English orchestras under Sir Malcolm Sargent were his best, though the performances of Nos. 4 and 5 (*Emperor*) that he recorded with the Chicago Symphony under Frederick Stock in 1942 were very close to the early performances, and the better orchestral playing was reproduced with more spacious and lustrous sound. The post-war Nos. 2, 3, 4 and 5 with the Philharmonia under Issay Dobrowen and Alceo Galliera were excellent and satisfying when heard by themselves, but revealed losses in suppleness, grace, and continuity of tension and outline when compared with the earlier performances. So with the 1942 remakes of the Sonatas Opp. 109 and 111 that were issued for the first time in 1976: comparison with those of the thirties revealed how much the performances had lost of their earlier continuity and perfection of proportion in the shaping of phrase, the relating of one phrase to the next, the building of the whole structure of a movement—to say nothing of the lessened accuracy in execution of fast passage work; but listened to by themselves they were, even with those losses, effective statements of the works (and better recorded than the earlier versions).

However, with Pierre Fournier Schnabel recorded superb performances after the war of all of Beethoven's cello sonatas; and before the war he recorded the Cello Sonata Op. 5 No. 2 with

Gregor Piatigorsky, and excellent performances of all the Bagatelles for piano.

As with late Beethoven so with late Schubert: with his enlarging of its physical shape and expressive dimensions Schnabel made the exalted slow movement of the posthumous Sonata in B flat an overwhelming utterance that no other performance in my experience achieved. Nor did any other performance give the Scherzo the enchanting grace that Schnabel gave it. This grace also produced incomparable performances of Schubert's smaller pieces—the *Moments musicaux, Impromptus* and others. And again the great achievements were not lessened by the Impromptu Op. 90 No. 1 performed with unsuitable turbulence, the lyrical opening section of the second movement of the Sonata Op. 53 distorted in shape by the pauses at the ends of phrases, or the excited, hurried portions of the first movement of the Sonata in B flat which failed to maintain the tone of calm elevation established by the opening reflective statements.

The grace was prominent also in Schnabel's playing of Mozart, unique in its subtle articulation of clearly outlined melodic phrase, its delicacy and suppleness and at the same time its cohesive tension and strength. His delivery of the long progression of melody in the extraordinary Andante of the Concerto K.467 and the effect it imparted to the music have rarely been equalled. And again an achievement like that, or like the powerfully phrased performance of Mozart's extraordinary Rondo K.511, was not lessened by things like the overly slow pace of the second movement of the Concerto K.595, or the excessive turbulence and rhythmic unsteadiness of the first movement of the Sonata K.310.

Off-the-air recordings of broadcasts preserve Schnabel's performances of a few works he did not record in the studio: his incomparable performances with Szigeti of Mozart's Violin Sonata K.481 and Beethoven's Violin Sonatas Opp. 24 (*Spring*) and 96; Mozart's Piano Concertos K.482 (with Walter) and K.488 (with Artur Rodzinski—superb in spite of Schnabel's momentary memory lapse in the last movement); Mozart's Piano Sonatas K.333 and 533 and Rondo K.494; and Schubert's Trio Op. 99 with Szigeti and Fournier. Schnabel did record Mozart's Concertos K.466 and 491 (with Walter Susskind) at the end of his life, but recordings exist also of his even better live performances of the mid-1940s (with Alfred Wallenstein and George Szell, respectively).

Outstanding performances recorded by contemporaries of Schnabel included, in the twenties, two by Wilhelm Backhaus—a straightforward and effective one of Brahms's *Variations on a Theme by Paganini*, and one of Chopin's *Études* Opp. 10 and 25 that confirms my recollection of a pianist with prodigious technical powers that produced the figurations of the ones in fast tempo in completely unaffected fashion with astounding speed, ease and perfection, but an uninteresting musician who inflicted appalling distortion of phrase on the slower ones.

Walter Gieseking, in the 1930s, recorded sparkling performances of Mozart's Concerto K.271 and Beethoven's No. 1, and an excellent one of Beethoven's Sonata Op. 31 No. 2; in the 1950s he made a superb record of Franck's *Variations symphoniques* with Herbert von Karajan. These performances were quite different from Gieseking's usual finely chiseled small-scale playing, which was effective in Debussy's music (except for passages requiring greater power, like the climax of *La Cathédrale engloutie*), and in some of Mozart's, but not in Beethoven's Concertos Nos. 4 and 5 (*Emperor*) and *Waldstein* and *Appassionata* Sonatas. And in the 1950s he broadcast a performance (which has been preserved) of Mozart's Concerto K.467 with Guido Cantelli, in which he played, presumably under the magnetic compulsion of Cantelli, with an unprecedented power of tone and style that must have surprised him as much as it did the audience, and that made his performance of the Andante the only one in my experience that equalled Schnabel's in musical and expressive effect; and unlike Schnabel's it was supported by a superb orchestral context.

Edwin Fischer made excellent recordings, except for a few questionable details, of Mozart's Concertos K.482 and K.491 in the thirties, and of K.466 in the fifties. And one heard in his studio recordings of Beethoven's Sonatas Opp. 110 and 111 in those last years outstanding realizations which accounted for Fischer's having been regarded as equal in stature to Schnabel.

Outstanding, too, was the recording the composer Sergei Prokofiev made in the 1930s of his own Piano Concerto No. 3.

As for the celebrated harpsichordist Wanda Landowska, it was some of the performances she recorded in Europe in the thirties—of Bach's *Chromatic Fantasy and Fugue, Goldberg Variations,* Concerto in D minor and Toccata in D major, Haydn's Concerto in D, Scarlatti sonatas, Handel suites and music of Rameau (though not her exaggeratedly dynamic performance of Bach's *Italian Concerto,* with its distorted second movement)— that deserved the adulation she demanded and received. Her post-war gigantesque pounding and distortion—offered by her, and accepted by awed listeners, as divine revelation—I heard as unmitigated murder.

Of the performances by pianists of an earlier generation, those that Sergei Rachmaninoff recorded in this country from 1919 to the end of his concert career revealed that he played a comparatively small amount of music of high quality, and that he played this music in the same idiosyncratic way that excited audiences in his playing of music of low quality, largely his own.* What audiences were excited by was the manifestation of power of two kinds: the technical brilliance that was the manifestation of the power his fingers exercised over his instrument; and the sudden willful distention of tempo and the cohesive tension maintained in the distorted phrase that were the manifestation of the power his mind exercised over the music. Consequently, after the shocking distortions inflicted on a Scarlatti sonata, the opening movement of Mozart's Sonata K.331, Beethoven's Thirty-two Variations in C minor, Chopin's Second Sonata Op. 35 and Schumann's *Carnaval,* one was surprised by the simple and beautiful phrasing of the first part of Chopin's *Nocturne* Op. 15 No. 2 (and its repetition after the distorted middle part), and the enchanting grace and incisive pointing up of details in his performances of some (not all) of the Chopin Waltzes he recorded. Such exceptions were few, however, and the most considerable of them were his superb performances of Beethoven's Violin Sonata Op. 30 No. 3 and Schubert's Sonata Op. 162 with the beautiful playing of Fritz Kreisler.

*Rachmaninoff recorded performances of his four piano concertos, his Rhapsody on a Theme of Paganini, some of his solo piano pieces, and, as conductor, his Third Symphony and *The Isle of the Dead.* —*Ed.*

Josef Hofmann's recordings have been offered as incomparably great examples of what some have contended is the correct way of playing Chopin (and other Romantic composers) that pianists of today are ignorant of. But I consider his willfully mannered and distorted performances to have been demonstrations of how the music should *not* be played, which is all they can teach pianists of today. And the same may be said of other legendary pianists of that era—Moriz Rosenthal, Vladimir de Pachmann, Percy Grainger, Ignaz Friedman and the rest. But Josef Lhévinne, whose usual playing was as mannered as that of the others, did make a recording of Chopin's Polonaise in A flat in which he played with simplicity and continuity of phrase outline to produce what I consider an effective performance.

String Players and Chamber Groups
1900–1940s

What I remember as the greatest playing of music on the violin was Joseph Szigeti's in the thirties and forties—its excitingly enlivening inflection of phrase with continuity of tension and outline from note to note, its further continuity of tension and shape from phrase to phrase in the larger structure. I have heard nothing like the tremendous performance this produced of Bach's *Chaconne;* nothing like the incandescent performance of Bach's Concerto in D minor that Szigeti recorded with the New Friends of Music Orchestra under Fritz Stiedry (in his post-war performance with the Prades Festival Orchestra under Pablo Casals Szigeti's tone was wiry and granular, his phrasing unimpressive). No other violinist has made of the violin's first entrance in Beethoven's Violin Concerto what Szigeti made of it, in the first (1932) performance he recorded with the British Symphony under Bruno Walter, with his dynamic inflection of the very first phrases, his breathtaking crescendo of energy in the ascending rush of two-note figures to the conclusion of the passage; and no one has achieved anything like his similarly dynamic playing in the rest of the work. (Szigeti himself didn't achieve its equal in the excellent performance he recorded some years later with the New York Philharmonic under Walter.) Nor has anyone else achieved the impassioned elegance of Szigeti's performance of the first movement of Mendelssohn's Concerto with the London Philharmonic under Beecham, with whom he recorded also superb performances of Prokofiev's Concerto No. 1 and Mozart's K.218. And to these he added similar performances of Handel's Sonata Op. 1 No. 13, Mozart's Sonata K.304 and Divertimento K.287 for strings and horns, Brahms's Violin Concerto (with Sir Hamilton Harty—a better performance than the later one with Eugene Ormandy), Bach's Concerto in D minor for two violins (with Carl Flesch as the impressive second soloist), an astounding performance of the fine Prelude to Bach's E-major Sonata for unaccompanied violin that he recorded at the age of fifteen, Tartini's Concerto in D minor, and recordings of works of Bloch, Bartók and others.

All the Beethoven violin sonatas were recorded in recitals at the Library of Congress in the early forties, in which Claudio Arrau's wooden piano playing had a dampening effect on Szigeti much of the time, but not in the *Kreutzer* Sonata, where Szigeti's own feeling was enough to produce fine playing; in another Library of Congress recital he was stimulated by the piano playing of Béla Bartók to superb performances of the *Kreutzer* Sonata, Debussy's Sonata, and two Bartók works. A recording of a recital at the Frick Collection in the late forties reproduced Szigeti's and Schnabel's incomparable performances of Beethoven's Sonatas Opp. 24 (*Spring*) and 96 and Mozart's K.481. Another recital recording had his performance with Schnabel and Fournier of Schubert's Trio Op. 99. And there was a further one with his performances in 1943, with Andor Foldes, of several Mozart Sonatas—K.301, 305, 377, 380 and 526—that exhibited the strong bright tone, and the intensity contained within distinguished style, of Szigeti at the height of his technical and musical powers. Regrettably, his later studio recordings of Mozart sonatas, with Szell and Mieczyslaw Horszowski at the piano, were made when he could no longer produce beautiful sounds with his instrument.

It was Szigeti's performances that made me aware of the distinction in Jascha Heifetz's between his playing of the violin, with its dazzling tone and technique, and his playing of the music, with its mincing, wailing little swells on every two or three notes which kept breaking the line of the phrase, and its alternation, in a passage that should flow evenly, of holding back and hurrying forward in a mannered and exaggerated style that was as sentimental and vulgar in Beethoven as it would have been in Liszt's *Liebestraum*. However, in his recordings of chamber music—of Beethoven's *Archduke* Trio and Schubert's Trio in B flat with the pianist Artur Rubinstein and cellist Emanuel Feuermann, Mozart's Divertimento K.563 with Feuermann and the violist William Primrose, some of Beethoven's violin sonatas with Emanuel Bay, Tchaikovsky's Trio and some of the other recordings he made with Primrose, Piatigorsky and various colleagues— Heifetz played with surprising and admirable simplicity and respect for the rights of the other parts.

Some of Fritz Kreisler's finest playing in his prime was to be heard in his performances of Beethoven's Sonata Op. 30 No. 3 and Schubert's Op. 162 with Rachmaninoff, and in his recordings in the late 1920s of the Beethoven, Brahms and Mendelssohn concertos with the Berlin State Opera Orchestra under Leo Blech. His later recordings of these concertos with Sir John Barbirolli were no better coming from him than they would have been coming from a less celebrated artist. And in the second of his two recordings of Mozart's Concerto K.218 (with Sargent) his playing, though beautiful, was without the vitality and sparkle and style heard in Szigeti's performance with Beecham.*

Other great violinists of the twenties and thirties were Jacques Thibaud, who contributed his elegance of style to the famous performances of Haydn, Beethoven and Schubert trios with Casals and the pianist Alfred Cortot; Carl Flesch, with whom Szigeti recorded Bach's Concerto in D minor for two violins; and Bronislaw Huberman, who recorded highly individual perfor-

---

*In Kreisler's first recording of K.218 in 1924 the orchestra's part had been rescored for a tiny band to satisfy the exigencies of acoustical recording, and Landon Ronald's conducting was slovenly.

In addition to the works mentioned in the text Kreisler recorded all of Beethoven's violin sonatas in 1935 with Franz Rupp. Haggin's recollection was that the deterioration in Kreisler's intonation and technique by then had spoiled the performances. However, listening to recent digital transfers, which Haggin did not live to hear, my own impression now has been that Kreisler's difficulties in a few of the fast passages are insignificant measured against the musical distinction and tonal beauty of his playing the greater part of the time, and against the integration of that playing with Rupp's equally distinguished performance of the piano part. —*Ed.*

mances of the Beethoven and Tchaikovsky concertos and Mozart's K.216. The considerably younger Szymon Goldberg, in the thirties, recorded radiant performances of Mozart sonatas with the pianist Lili Kraus,* Haydn trios with Kraus and the cellist Anthony Pini, fine performances with Kraus of Beethoven sonatas, and Beethoven's Serenade Op. 8 for string trio with the composer Paul Hindemith playing viola and Feuermann playing cello. Goldberg also recorded several distinguished performances after the war—of Bach's Concerto No. 2, Mozart's Concertos K.216 and 218, Handel's Sonata Op. 1 No. 13, and Mozart's Trios K.502 and 548 with Joanna and Nicolai Graudan; and he conducted excellent performances of Bach's *Brandenburg* Concertos and other works with his Netherlands Chamber Orchestra. By the 1970s he no longer produced the beautiful violin tone of his earlier years, but he exhibited his undiminished musical sensitivity in the complete set of Mozart sonatas he recorded with admirable ensemble rapport with the pianist Radu Lupu.

As a solo performer the violinist Adolf Busch produced an unattractive tone and was musically uninteresting much of the time; but he worked more effectively in the Busch-Serkin Trio, whose performance of Schubert's Trio Op. 100 had the sensitive and beautiful-sounding playing that Rudolf Serkin did in ensemble performances with Busch in those early pre-American years; good too was the Busch-Serkin recording of the *Kreutzer* Sonata.** And Busch led his Chamber Players in performances of Bach's *Brandenburg* Concertos and Orchestra Suites in the thirties that set new standards for these works.

As for cellists, one of the high points of the performer's art in my experience occurred in Pablo Casals's pre-war performance of Beethoven's Sonata Op. 102 No. 2 with Horszowski, at the return

---

*Except for an excellent pre-war performance of Mozart's Piano Concerto K.456, Kraus's playing without Goldberg was poor. —B.H.H.

**I advise against Serkin's playing in the years after the war: his violent belaboring of instrument and music that generally held opinion regarded as impressive performance of Beethoven; his nerveless playing—with its tone that changed from a pallid *piano* to an unpleasantly percussive *forte,* its melodic legato that was without continuity of dynamics, cohesive tension and outline—that generally held opinion regarded as a model of Mozart style. —B.H.H.

of the opening section after the middle section of the slow movement: Casals's inflection and timing of the cello's comments on the piano's statements, and at the end of the section his sustained delivery of the raptly meditative passage leading to the concluding fugue. And the unique powerfully sustained tone and phrasing produced comparable performances of the Sonatas Op. 102 No. 1 [and the two of Op. 5] with Horszowski, and of Op. 69 with Otto Schulhof.

The life which Bach's Suites for unaccompanied cello had in the recordings Casals made before the war was the life created by the coloring, the movement, the tensions of his phrasing—not only the bold, powerful distention of the phrases in the vigorous movements, but the subtle inflection of quiet movements like the Sarabandes of Nos. 1 and 2 or the ornate Allemande of No. 6. This was something you would almost have believed you had not heard in a performance, after it was over; but you could start the record back at the beginning of the Sarabande of No. 2 and find that it had happened, that it was there on the record for all time, as other such achievements are on canvas or in print.

In addition there were the famous performances of Beethoven's Trio Op. 97 (*Archduke*), Schubert's Op. 99 and Haydn's Op. 73 No. 2 that Casals recorded in the twenties with Thibaud and Cortot, after the three had been playing together for their own pleasure almost twenty years. They were fascinating as the complementary working together of three strikingly dissimilar players—Casals with his power of tone and phrasing, Thibaud with his grace and elegance, Cortot with his warmth and intimacy (and without the excessive mannerisms of his Chopin-playing).

In the post-war Perpignan Festival performance of Beethoven's Trio Op. 97 and Prades Festival performance of Schubert's Op. 99 one heard the pianist Eugene Istomin and violinist Alexander Schneider playing with less grace and more force than Cortot and Thibaud, but Casals dominating again with the power of his tone and phrasing. And this was true also of the Prades Festival performance of Schubert's Op. 100 by Horszowski, Schneider and Casals. However, the Prades performance of Schubert's String Quintet Op. 163 had beautifully integrated ensemble playing by Isaac Stern, Schneider, violist Milton Katims, Casals and cellist Paul Tortelier. Casals's playing in Beethoven's Sonatas Opp. 69 and 102 No. 2 didn't equal his pre-war playing in those works; but it was powerful and moving for someone who didn't know that pre-war playing. (Rudolf Serkin, striving for comparable power in his playing of the piano parts, achieved mere loudness and crudeness.)

The one cellist of the same towering stature as Casals was Emanuel Feuermann, whose early death resulted in his leaving a comparatively small number of recorded performances—the major ones being Beethoven's Trio Op. 97 (*Archduke*) with Heifetz and Rubinstein, Sonata Op. 69 with Dame Myra Hess, Variations on *Ein Mädchen oder Weibchen* from *The Magic Flute* with the incomparable Franz Rupp, Serenade Op. 8 with Goldberg and Hindemith, and his Duo in E flat with Primrose; Chopin's *Introduction and Polonaise Brillante* Op. 3 with Rupp; Mozart's Divertimento K.563 for string trio with Heifetz and Primrose; Schubert's Trio Op. 99 with Heifetz and Rubinstein and *Arpeggione* Sonata with Gerald Moore; Weber's *Andantino* with Moore; Richard Strauss's *Don Quixote* with the Philadelphia Orchestra under Ormandy; Bloch's *Schelomo* with the same orchestra under Stokowski; and, earlier, Dvořák's Cello Concerto with the Berlin State Opera Orchestra under Michael Taube. Feuermann was the cellist also in Toscanini's marvelous 1938 NBC Symphony performance of *Don Quixote*, which exists on records of the broadcast.

In the thirties the Budapest Quartet's first European recordings, issued here by Victor—of Mozart's String Quartets K.465, 499, 590 and Clarinet Quintet K.581 (with the lifeless playing of Benny Goodman), Beethoven's Op. 18 Nos. 2 and 3, Op. 59 No. 2, Op. 74 (*Harp*) and Op. 130, Schubert's Op. 29 and his *Quartettsatz*, Wolf's *Italian Serenade*, and works by Brahms, Dvořák, Grieg, Mendelssohn, Bartók and Sibelius—acquainted American listeners with a tonal, musical and ensemble excellence beyond any previously experienced here in quartet performance.*

*Earlier a somewhat differently constituted Budapest Quartet had recorded several performances—of Beethoven's Op. 59 No. 1, Op. 130 and the *Grosse Fuge*, Dvořák's Op. 96, Haydn's Op. 76 No. 1, Mozart's K.458, Schubert's *Death and the*

After recording for Victor in this country Haydn's Op. 54 No. 1 and Mozart's K.458 (*Hunt*), the group began its association with Columbia, for which it recorded in the forties Mozart's K.387 and 421, his Quintets K.406, 515, 516, 593 and 614 (all with Katims, second viola), and his Quartets for piano and strings K.478 and 493 (with George Szell's cold, brittle rattling-off of the piano part of K.478, his better playing in K.493), Haydn's Op. 64 No. 5, Op. 74 No. 3 and Op. 76 No. 4 (*Sunrise*), Beethoven's Op. 18 Nos. 1, 4 and 6, Op. 59 No. 3, Opp. 95, 127, 131, 132 and 135, his Quintet Op. 29 (with Katims), and Schubert's Quintets Opp. 114 (*Trout*, with Horszowski) and 163 (with the cellist Benar Heifetz), and works by Debussy, Dvořák, Hindemith and Ravel.

In the fifties it recorded for the new long-playing records all of Beethoven's quartets, all of Mozart's quartets and quintets (with Walter Trampler this time), Schubert's Quartets *Death and the Maiden* and Opp. 29 and 161 (almost the only performance on records with tempos sufficiently animated to give the music, and particularly the finale, its proper effect), all six of Haydn's Op. 76, and Schumann's Piano Quintet in E flat (with Clifford Curzon), as well as works by Brahms, Debussy, Dvořák, Franck, Grieg, Milhaud, Ravel and Sibelius. If one listened to these performances by themselves one found them completely satisfying; only if one listened to them after the ones of the thirties and forties—to the 1955 Mozart K.499, for example, after the 1933 78-rpm version, or to the Mozart quintets of the fifties with Trampler after those of the forties with Katims—did one discover the loss in the later ones of some of the earlier sensitiveness, grace and life.*

But it was in the performances recorded in the sixties for

Maiden and *Quartettsatz*, Tchaikovsky's Quartet No. 2, and single movements of other works—which were not as remarkable as the Budapest's later ones. The members of the later quartet in the recordings it made in Europe between 1932 and 1936 were Joseph Roisman, Alexander Schneider, Istvan Ipolyi and Mischa Schneider. From 1936 on Boris Kroyt was the violist; from 1945–48 Alexander Schneider was replaced as second violin by Edgar Ortenberg, and from 1949–55 by Jac Gorodetzky, after which he returned and remained until the end. —*Ed.*

*One exception was Beethoven's Op. 130, which was realized with more grace and poise in better tempos in the recording of the 1950s—revealing, as Haggin observed, that with the losses in the playing, there had been in some instances gains "in musical understanding and taste." —*Ed.*

stereo—of all the Beethoven Quartets, Mozart's Clarinet Quintet (with David Oppenheim), his two piano quartets (with Horszowski), Schubert's Quintets Opp. 114 (*Trout*—with Horszowski) and 163 (with Benar Heifetz), Schumann's E-flat Piano Quintet (with Rudolf Serkin), Smetana's Quartet in E minor (*From My Life*) and Wolf's *Italian Serenade,* as well as works by Brahms and Dvořák—that the deterioration in tone and intonation and even in the treatment of the music reached the point where the playing was not only musically unsatisfying but unpleasant to listen to.

One other quartet in the thirties made a recording that could stand beside the Budapest's—the Kolisch Quartet, with its set of Schubert's Quartet Op. 161.

Singers 1920s–1940s

Caruso's death at the beginning of the twenties may have marked the end of the particular period referred to as the golden age (though a few of the greats of that period—McCormack, Homer, Matzenauer and De Luca—continued to sing); but it didn't mark the end of extraordinary voices and great singing. One of these voices, Rosa Ponselle's, was in fact first heard at the Metropolitan with Caruso's in the company's first production of Verdi's *La Forza del destino* in 1918. Her recorded performances revealed insufficient feeling for the shape of the musical phrase; but *Tu che invoco* from Spontini's *La Vestale* and *Vedi?. . .di morte l'angelo* in the final act of Verdi's *Aida* showed her to have been capable in some instances of being taught to sing with better taste than her own—something the tenor Beniamino Gigli was *in*capable of.

Elisabeth Rethberg, on the other hand, had not only an extraordinarily lovely voice but flawless musical taste; and her performance of *Ave Maria* from Verdi's *Otello*—the seemingly effortless emission of ear-ravishing vocal sound in a sustained flow which articulated and shaped the phrases with plastic perfection—was one of the examples of great vocal art on records. The same may be said of Tito Schipa's electrically recorded singing at the beginning of *Parigi, o cara* from Verdi's *La Trav-*

iata, in which he sang with the delicate tonal and rhythmic inflections and accents of an enchantingly elegant musical style (and Galli-Curci answered with a spineless, characterless slithering around of her by now unattractive-timbered voice), and of his *Parmi veder le lagrime* from Verdi's *Rigoletto.* His use in this period of his distinctive light tenor voice left one unprepared for the tasteless accelerations and retardations and distortions of phrase in some of his early performances.

And a soprano of that time who in Mozart and Verdi exhibited similar enchanting style in the use of her exquisite voice was Maria Ivogün (though in arias of Rossini and Donizetti she indulged in shocking exhibitionistic interpolations). Her most sensational feat was her deployment of her voice with grace and seemingly effortless agility in the pyrotechnical *Grossmächtige Prinzessin* from Richard Strauss's *Ariadne auf Naxos.*

As for Lucrezia Bori, her early, acoustical records included a *Traviata* duet with McCormack in which the singing was lovely, but others that suffered from her later excessive archness; and in her electrically recorded performances the voice was thin and edged.

Gigli was one of the tenors whom it was considered possible to discuss as Caruso's successor, but whose voices actually didn't resemble Caruso's at all. However the tenor Alfred Piccaver, whom I don't recall being discussed in that way—possibly because he sang only in Vienna and Berlin—did, by the evidence of his recorded performances of the early twenties, have a voice with something like the unique timbre of Caruso's, its power and its freedom, which he used with a musical taste that Caruso didn't have. Beautiful singing was to be heard from Georges Thill and Giacomo Lauri-Volpi, too; and early in his career Richard Tauber recorded fine performances (in German) of arias and duets by Verdi, Bizet and Richard Strauss, among others—performances without the mannerisms and distortions of his singing later on.

Singing at the same time as Piccaver in Vienna was the superb soprano Helene Wildbrunn, who never sang here, but who recorded excerpts from *Don Giovanni, Fidelio,* Verdi's *Un Ballo in maschera* and the Wagner music-dramas. In Berlin there was the contralto Sigrid Onegin, whom I heard, in the early twenties, flood the Metropolitan with her opulent singing of *Brangäne's Warning* in *Tristan und Isolde*, and whose records of arias by Saint-Saëns, Ponchielli, Mozart, Gluck and Handel exhibited the voice's extraordinary range, power and suppleness, and its amazing agility in works like Mozart's *Exsultate, jubilate* (however, her pulling-about of *Lieder*, on occasion, seemed absurd even by the general standards of the time). There was the fine bass Alexander Kipnis, whom I heard later in Salzburg in the *Fidelio* and *Magic Flute* Toscanini conducted there, in the Beethoven *Missa Solemnis* he conducted here (notably the performance of 1940), and on records in songs by Brahms and Wolf, in which a German would have been aware that the German words were sung by someone born in Russia. Finally, Rosa Raisa, a Polish soprano who was so impressive in *L'Altra notte* from Boito's *Mefistofele* that I was sure the unimpressive other recordings I heard were not representative, and an Argentine soprano, Hina Spani, whom I had never heard of until an LP issued in 1963 of her recordings of the 1920s astonished me with her beautiful singing in arias from *Il Trovatore* and *Un Ballo in maschera,* among other things.

It was in the thirties, in the singing of Jussi Bjoerling, that one heard the tenor whose voice stood out among all others as Caruso's had done, in its unique timbre—a silvery luster as against Caruso's darker splendor—combined with extraordinary range, power and freedom; and who exhibited in his use of that voice an unfailing sense for continuity and shape in the musical phrase that Caruso distorted. The performance of Lensky's second-act aria in Tchaikovsky's *Eugene Onegin,* recorded at Bjoerling's last concert before his sudden death in 1960, was one of only two—Nicolai Gedda's was the other—comparable with Sobinov's in vocal and expressive effect. Bjoerling also contributed marvelous singing to Toscanini's performances in 1940 of Beethoven's *Missa Solemnis* and Verdi's *Requiem.*

As unique a phenomenon among soprano voices as Caruso's among tenors was Kirsten Flagstad's; and as phenomenal as the voice itself, with its voluminous splendor all the way to the top when it was first heard here in the 1930s, was the manner of its production and deployment—the production that made the singing seem as natural and casual as speech, the deployment that had the voice go effortlessly wherever the music required it to go, rising to a squarely attacked and securely held high note, and from this one to another and still another, before descending to complete the phrase—all as though this presented no difficulty and breath were not even involved. And in addition there was the musical rightness of the singing—the unfailing perfection of the simply-shaped phrases of the early years, as in the first recorded finale of *Tristan*, and the subtly inflected ones of the post-war years, as in the complete *Tristan* recorded with Furtwängler in 1952.

Though in this country we heard Flagstad almost exclusively in Wagner, she had achieved her eminence in Europe with her singing also in other music. This singing, impressive in voice and style, we were able to hear on records in acoustically recorded performances (in German) of *Or sai chi l'onore* from Mozart's *Don Giovanni*, *Porgi amor* and *Dove sono* from his *Figaro*, *O don fatale* from Verdi's *Don Carlo*, and Beethoven's concert aria *Ah! Perfido!* among other things. And performances she recorded electrically between 1928 and 1931—the voice still beautiful, the style even more impressive—gave us the same aria from *Don Giovanni* (in Italian) and *Abscheulicher!* and *Komm' Hoffnung* from Beethoven's *Fidelio*, in addition to her singing in some of the passages that she and Melchior recorded of their performances together in *Tristan und Isolde*, and in their broadcasts of the entire opera in 1937 with Beecham. And in the 1950s, in addition to *Tristan*, she recorded songs by Schubert, Brahms, Wagner and Richard Strauss, and a superb performance of Purcell's *Dido and Aeneas*, with Elisabeth Schwarzkopf and Thomas Helmsley, conducted by Geraint Jones.

Someone reported to me the opinion Stokowski had expressed to him that the three greatest musical performers of this century had been Toscanini, Caruso and the Russian bass Feodor Chaliapin. And Chaliapin is one of the two singers—Elena Gerhardt is the other—who stand out in my recollection of the 1920s.

What I recall chiefly, of course, is his Boris Godunov in the Musorgsky opera, one of the greatest operatic impersonations of all time, which I imagine Stokowski had in mind. But what I was shocked to discover from a recent chance hearing of Chaliapin's performance of the Catalogue Aria from *Don Giovanni* and the Serenade from Gounod's *Faust* was his use of his extraordinary powers in a hamming-up of some of his other roles to the point of ludicrous travesty.

As for Elena Gerhardt, by the twenties her mezzo-soprano voice, though still lovely much of the time, was past its prime and a little tremulous; but her subtle use of it—with sensitiveness to the shape as well as to the expressive content of the musical phrase—made her performances of the songs of Schubert, Schumann, Brahms, Wolf and Richard Strauss (with marvelous accompaniments by Coenraad van Bos) some of my most exciting and memorable experiences of those years. In the songs of Schubert, Schumann, Wagner, Wolf and Strauss that she recorded in 1907 and 1911 with the conductor Artur Nikisch playing the piano, one heard not only the loveliness of the younger voice, but, astonishingly, the same wonderful inflection of voice and phrase as in the performances recorded at fifty.

It was not until the 1930s that I began to hear on records the equally exciting performances of these songs by Elisabeth Schumann—the distinguished art in her use of her unique silvery voice, which had a tensile strength in its delicacy that made her spinning out of the sustained phrases of Schubert's *Nacht und Träume, Litanei* and *Nähe des Geliebten* especially effective—the performance of *Nacht und Träume* being, in fact, the definitive one in my experience, which I have heard no other singer equal. Enchanting too were her performances of songs by Wolf and Richard Strauss, of arias from Mozart's operas, and her Sophie in the historic recording of parts of Strauss's *Der Rosenkavalier* conducted by Robert Heger, with Lotte Lehmann's Marschallin, mezzo Maria Olczewska's Octavian and bass Richard Mayr's Baron Ochs.

In Schumann's earliest, acoustical recordings, one heard her voice with the amplitude and bloom it had at the beginning, used with the flawless musical art that was hers already then; her first electrical recordings exhibited the voice in its prime, and the post-war recordings with much of the bloom gone, the voice's characteristic edge sharper.

Chaliapin is the pre-eminent figure among a number of singers who used extraordinary voices in the service of extraordinary dramatic powers. One who is accepted as having been such a singer, Mary Garden, I found—when she appeared in New York with the Chicago Opera Company from 1917 to 1922—to be the possessor by that time of an unattractive voice and a half-dozen dramatic mannerisms. But the tenor Lucien Muratore who appeared with her did have the superb voice and compelling stage presence of the great singing actor she was not. One heard a fine voice in the arias he recorded from *Carmen* and Massenet's *Werther* and *Manon* (and a few details in its deployment that aren't in good musical taste by today's standards); and in one aria from Henri Février's *Monna Vanna* it had an additional luster which made it the wonderful voice I remember hearing in that opera.

Such compelling stage presence and a voice of remarkable dramatic expressiveness made Frida Leider the outstanding Isolde and Brünnhilde of the twenties and thirties; these roles were all she did outside of Germany, but her recorded performances indicate that she was equally impressive as Leonore in *Fidelio*, the Countess in *Figaro*, Donna Anna in *Don Giovanni*, and in other roles in operas by Weber, Verdi and Puccini; and Kerstin Thorborg was her mezzo-soprano counterpart of the thirties and forties—among other things the Fricka of comparable magnitude with Leider's Brünnhilde; she recorded songs by Schubert and Mahler as well, and Mahler's *Das Lied von der Erde* with Bruno Walter.

As against the grandeur achieved by these two, Lotte Lehmann offered warm humanity. The short-breathed singing she did with her distinctively luscious voice even in her prime, in the twenties and thirties, broke the musical phrase too often but was suffused with the personal warmth and magnetism that achieved the miracle one witnessed in the opera house—of dull Elisabeth in Wagner's *Tannhäuser* and pallid Elsa in his *Lohengrin* being transformed into living beings who touched one's heart—and that made her Fidelio and Marschallin historic achievements in operatic impersonation.*

In her *Lieder*-singing of these years Lehmann loaded onto a dramatic song like Schubert's *Der Doppelgänger* the expressive intensity and projection suited to an operatic aria, which burst through the musical shape within which the song's expressive content was contained; but she did well with a quiet song like *An die Musik* or a vivacious one like Schumann's *An den Sonnenschein* and was incomparable in his humorous *Die Kartenlegerin*. By the 1940s the need of care and skill in the use of an aging voice resulted not only in an improved quality of the high notes that had been constricted and shrill, but in a refinement and subtilization of style: expressive effect was no longer achieved directly by bursts of vehemence without regard for the damage to the musical phrase, but was achieved instead by inflection of the voice within the phrase that retained continuity and shape.

Unfortunately there were no studio recordings to document this perfected art; nor, fortunately, were there any to document the deterioration of the last years in which Lehmann titillated her adoring public with vast amounts of archness and cuteness. But one record, of her last New York recital on February 16, 1951, enabled one to hear not only the concluding scene of renunciation and farewell in this public love affair, but that her voice, after warming up in the opening Schumann group, was still amazingly lovely, and that in many—though not all—of the songs she used it with beautiful art.

Another distinguished singing actor of that time was Friedrich Schorr, whose fine baritone voice served his outstanding impersonation of Hans Sachs in Wagner's *Die Meistersinger*—preserved in the excerpts from that opera which he recorded between 1927 and 1931 with Schumann, Rethberg and Melchior.

Also in this period the German baritone Heinrich Rehkemper recorded a superb performance of Mahler's *Kindertotenlieder* with the Berlin Philharmonic under Jascha Horenstein; Karl Erb

---

*Lehmann recorded only her aria from *Fidelio,* but she recorded scenes from *Der Rosenkavalier,* with Schumann, Olczewska and Mayr, and Acts One and Two of *Die Walküre* with Melchior, conducted by Bruno Walter and Bruno Seidler-Winkler. —Ed.

made several recordings that documented the beautiful tenor voice of his youth (used occasionally with almost too much art); Kolomon von Pataky, the Don Ottavio of the pre-war Glyndebourne *Don Giovanni*, recorded excellent performances of tenor arias from Mozart's *Così fan tutte, The Magic Flute, The Abduction from the Seraglio* and the Italian and French repertory; sopranos Aulikki Rautavaara, the superb Countess of the recorded 1934 Glyndebourne *Figaro*, and Jarmila Novotna, Toscanini's Pamina in *The Magic Flute* in Salzburg and Walter's Cherubino in *Figaro* there and at the Metropolitan, both made recordings of operatic excerpts and songs; Lina Pagliughi, who was heard here in the thirties, employed her lovely soprano voice on records in music by Rossini, Bellini, Donizetti, Auber, Rimsky-Korsakov and others; Mariano Stabile, Toscanini's Falstaff at La Scala and in Salzburg, recorded excerpts from that opera (and others) in which he used his good baritone to superb expressive effect. Excerpts from performances at the 1936 Bayreuth Festival documented the magnificent singing of the tenor Franz Völker and the soprano Maria Müller in *Lohengrin* and *Die Walküre,* and the impressive singing of the tenor Max Lorenz in *Siegfried.* And other recordings in those years provided opportunities to hear several additional excellent German singers—the soprano Marta Fuchs, alto Emmy Leisner, and tenors Peter Anders, Walter Ludwig and Lorenz Fehenberger.

The German singers whom Beecham chose for his 1937 recording of *The Magic Flute* included the brilliant coloratura soprano Erna Berger, who sang at the Metropolitan after the war, and three who did not sing here: the soprano Tiana Lemnitz, the tenor Helge Roswaenge and the baritone Gerhard Hüsch. Berger could be heard in the *Rigoletto* with tenor Jan Peerce, conducted by Renato Cellini (and with Roswaenge in an earlier, inferior version in German, conducted by Heger), and in arias by Mozart, Donizetti and Verdi. Lemnitz deployed her extraordinarily lovely delicate voice in exquisitely nuanced phrasing in operas by Mozart, Gluck, Weber, Wagner, Verdi, Tchaikovsky and Richard Strauss—surpassingly in the Countess's arias from *Figaro,* the fourth-act duet with di Luna from *Il Trovatore* (with baritone Karl Schmitt-Walter), the duet and quartet in Philip's study from Verdi's *Don Carlo* (with Margarete Klose and basses Georg Hann and Mathieu Ahlersmeyer), and the Presentation of the Rose from *Der Rosenkavalier* (with the fine soprano Maria Cebotari); she also recorded songs of Brahms and Wolf. Roswaenge, the possessor of a tenor voice of unusual splendor, sang in Toscanini's *Magic Flute* in Salzburg in 1937 and in his performance of Verdi's *Requiem* in London in 1938, and he recorded arias by Mozart, Weber, Verdi, Bizet and Richard Strauss. Hüsch recorded operatic arias and a fine performance of Beethoven's song-cycle *An die ferne Geliebte* (but less good ones of Schubert songs).

A contemporary of theirs who also did not sing here was the lyric tenor Julius Patzak, whom one heard on records as an outstanding singer of Mozart, but who sang other music as effectively—those who know only his quavering old voice in Walter's first post-war recording of Mahler's *Das Lied von der Erde* can hear the fine one of his youth in arias by Mozart, Verdi, Tchaikovsky, Smetana, Thomas and Offenbach.

With Flagstad in her first Metropolitan *Tristan* in 1934 were the excellent contralto Karin Branzell and the tenor Lauritz Melchior—past his prime but enduring; Melchior's best singing was heard in the European performances of the twenties. In the performances he began to record here in 1937—the Wagner excerpts with Flagstad, the songs of Richard Strauss and Wolf that he phrased with admirable sensitiveness—the voice had lost the glow of its best years but was still impressive; however, it had lost a great deal more by 1941, when he sang excerpts from *Götterdämmerung* and *Die Walküre* under Toscanini with Helen Traubel.

Mezzo-soprano Conchita Supervia exhibited an excitingly individual voice and style in recorded excerpts from Rossini's operas and *Carmen*, Cherubini's arias from *Figaro,* and duets from *Der Rosenkavalier* (in Italian), among other things. And Claudia Muzio left recordings of her simply phrased performances of operatic duets, as well as performances of arias which exhibited the constant swelling and contracting of lovely vocal sound that I recall as her way of singing at the Metropolitan.

And finally there was Ezio Pinza, with a magnetic stage presence in *Don Giovanni* and *Figaro,* and a bass voice which in the recorded performances of the late 1920s had an amplitude and richness all the way down to its lowest notes that it gradually lost as his use of it gained the refinement of musical phrasing and style of the performances of the forties, but which retained a dusky magnificence even in those later performances. These changes were demonstrated most clearly in the early and late recordings of Philip's monologue from *Don Carlo*. Pinza also sang in Toscanini's 1935 *Missa Solemnis* with the New York Philharmonic (as did Rethberg) and in his 1938 Carnegie Hall broadcast of Beethoven's Ninth Symphony, both of which have been preserved.

The years that followed brought to the Metropolitan Zinka Milanov, whose dramatic soprano at that time was extraordinarily beautiful when it was under control, as it frequently was not. Her voice in its prime was heard in Toscanini's performance of Act Four of *Rigoletto* and in his 1940 broadcasts of the *Missa Solemnis* and Verdi's *Requiem;* it was still beautiful in the later *Il Trovatore* with Bjoerling and Leonard Warren conducted by Cellini; but its thin, unattractive, tremulous sound in the still later *Aida* under Jonel Perlea made this performance, even with Bjoerling's singing, one to avoid. Just before this *Aida*, however, at a time in the early 1950s when her unpleasant-sounding and wobbly singing at the Metropolitan was pitiful to listen to, she was able to produce in the recording studio excellent performances of arias from *Aida*, *La Forza del destino* and *Un Ballo in maschera,* and an agreeable and well-phrased *Casta diva* from *Norma.*

Also singing at the same period were the sopranos Bidu Sayão, Licia Albanese, Helen Traubel and Jennie Tourel. Sayão had a lovely lyric soprano voice. Albanese's voice was sometimes dry and afflicted with strong vibrato, but her singing was made exciting by its style and intensity; Toscanini chose her for his NBC Symphony performances of *La Traviata* and Puccini's *La Bohème,* and she made excellent 78-rpm records of the Letter Scene from *Eugene Onegin* and arias from *Figaro, Don Giovanni, Carmen* and Donizetti's *Don Pasquale.* Traubel's opulent soprano was at its peak, and deserved Toscanini's delighted exclamation *"Che bella voce!",* in the finale of Wagner's *Götterdämmerung* she recorded with him in 1941. And Tourel made a number of fine recordings, among them ones of songs by Tchaikovsky, Musorgsky, Glinka and others, and of arias and songs by Rossini and Bizet and various other French composers.

There was also the tenor Jan Peerce, whom Toscanini chose for his first NBC performance of Beethoven's Ninth in 1938, and continued to use thereafter. And Maggie Teyte sang here in Debussy's *Pelléas et Mélisande* in the late 1940s, with an exquisitely pure and bright soprano voice that she retained into her sixties, and that could be heard on her recordings of songs by Berlioz, Debussy and others.

But it was soprano Eleanor Steber's performances in those years—above all her Countess in *Figaro*, one of the outstanding operatic characterizations in my experience, her Donna Anna in *Don Giovanni*, her Fiordiligi in *Così fan tutte*—that offered in voice, phrasing and style what added up to the grandest and greatest singing at the Metropolitan after Flagstad's. She recorded arias from operas by Mozart, Verdi, Bizet and Gounod in the 1940s and early '50s; her Countess in *Figaro* is preserved in two complete Metropolitan broadcasts of the mid-forties superbly conducted by Walter (with Pinza in the title role); and she recorded an overwhelming performance of Berlioz's *Les Nuits d'été* with an orchestra under Dmitri Mitropoulos.

The contralto Marian Anderson had her first success in Europe and did not sing in the opera house, though she recorded a few arias in the late 1920s and Ulrica's scene from *Un Ballo in maschera* in the 1950s (the latter following her engagement for the role by the Metropolitan—a tribute that was overdue and came too late). In her first Victor recordings in the 1930s she displayed the extraordinary timbre and richness of her voice in fine performances of songs by Bach, Schubert, Schumann, Brahms and others. By the mid-1940s her voice had begun to lose its beauty in the upper range and to be not always on pitch, but she was still able to give impressive effect to the second part of Schubert's *Der Tod und das Mädchen,* to the differentiation of voices in *Erlkönig,* and to songs like *Ave Maria* that called only for sustained legato singing. Her accompanist in the thirties was Kosti Vehanen, who played sensitively and with good taste. But it was after 1939, when she began to be accompanied by Franz

Rupp, that her singing was heard in the context of wonderfully enlivened piano parts; and in later years the life in many of her performances was created not by her phrasing but by Rupp's playing.

In the thirties the recordings of the Glyndebourne Festival performances of *The Marriage of Figaro, Don Giovanni* and *Così fan tutte* offered not only the first performances of the entire works on records (though all but the orchestrally accompanied recitatives were omitted from *Figaro*), but performances conducted by Fritz Busch with elegance, style, wit and, in the case of *Don Giovanni,* power that made them definitive—the ones by which others later were judged and usually found inferior in spite of better individual voices in some instances.

Busch, who conducted at the Metropolitan during the war, returned to Glyndebourne after it; and recordings were issued of excerpts of the performances of Mozart's *Idomeneo* and *Così fan tutte* he conducted—the first with soprano Sena Jurinac and tenors Richard Lewis and Alexander Young, the second with Jurinac, mezzo Blanche Thebom, Lewis and baritone Erich Kunz. A later recording of the complete *Idomeneo* (but with some cuts) offered a bland performance conducted by John Pritchard, but superb singing by Jurinac, Lewis and tenor Léopold Simoneau. And when Glyndebourne added works of other composers to those of Mozart, the one of Rossini's *La Cenerentola* conducted by Vittorio Gui in 1953, with mezzo Marina de Gabarain, tenor Juan Oncina, bass Sesto Bruscantini and others, provided one of the most extraordinary examples of joint operation in operatic performance heard up to that time. It remained so for many years, until Claudio Abbado recorded a set in the 1970s that astonished one by surpassing what one had never expected to hear equalled. *La Cenerentola* was followed by Gui's impressive performances of Rossini's *Le Comte Ory* (with the bloom and ease gone from Oncina's voice) and of *The Barber of Seville* with Bruscantini, soprano Victoria de los Angeles and tenor Luigi Alva (who sang well but did not achieve the swift and light pointed-up delivery of florid passages he did later in another of Abbado's recordings).

Conductors 1940s–1970s

Whereas recordings show Busch to have been a good conductor of symphonic music as well, Fritz Reiner, whose technical gifts made the Chicago Symphony a superb instrument in the 1950s and early '60s, operated as a musician most effectively as a conductor of opera—a strength which was exemplified by the powerful orchestral contexts he provided for scenes from Richard Strauss's *Salome* and *Elektra* that he recorded—first with Ljuba Welitsch and the Metropolitan Opera Orchestra in 1949, and then with Inge Borkh and Paul Schöffler (and the tremulous Frances Yeend) with the Chicago Symphony in the fifties—and by a recording of a Covent Garden broadcast of Wagner's *Tristan* with Flagstad and Melchior in 1936. His weaknesses as a symphonic conductor, on the other hand, were exemplified by his overemphatic ponderous distentions of tempos in Beethoven's Ninth Symphony, Verdi's *Requiem* and the Beethoven Fourth Piano Concerto he recorded with Van Cliburn, by his tempos and changes of tempo in Mahler's genial Fourth Symphony, which made the first movement nervous, abrupt and discontinuous, and by his poorly chosen tempos in some of Haydn's symphonies and in some sections of Berlioz's *Les Nuits d'été* in the recording of Leontyne Price's great performance. But in 1950 he recorded performances of Bach's *Brandenburg* Concertos with an assembled orchestra that were for the most part well-paced, light, admirably executed and the nearest thing at that time to the Busch Chamber Players' performances of the 1930s.

George Szell's strength, like Reiner's, was technical, revealing itself in the precision and beautiful tone with which he could get an orchestra to play; his weakness, like Reiner's, was musical, revealing itself in defects in the pacing and shaping of the work the orchestra was playing. The strength made the Cleveland orchestra into another superb instrument by the 1950s and '60s; the weakness produced pedestrian, insensitive and at times hard-driven performances of the German repertory—exemplified on the one hand by the overall stolidity of *his* recording of Beethoven's Ninth Symphony, and by his slowing down ponderously at the end of the first movement and in the latter part of the third; and on the other by *his* way of dealing with Mahler's Fourth, which was to point up its relaxed character and style enormously to the point of unrelaxed excessiveness. But Szell produced well-integrated contexts for the solo parts in concertos, as his recordings with pianist Leon Fleisher testified; he conducted the music of Dvořák well, producing an excellent performance of the Symphony No. 8 and superb ones of the *Slavonic Dances* and *Carnival* Overture; and he did well with modern works from Richard Strauss onward—one example being his excellent recording of *Don Quixote* with Pierre Fournier.

Victor de Sabata recorded a performance of Mozart's *Requiem* in the late 1940s with a sustained impetus and control, a continuity of inner tensions, that built up tremendous intensity, passion and dramatic power and made it one of the greatest things ever put on records. But his recording of Verdi's *Requiem* a few years later disappointed the expectations aroused by the Mozart: the *Dies Irae*, the *Sanctus* and the concluding fugue of the *Libera me* (after a slow beginning) were the only parts that moved in correct and effective tempo; everything else—in disregard of the metronome markings with which Verdi tries to enforce directions like *Andante* and *Allegro*—was stretched and dragged out ponderously and lugubriously by excessively slow tempos, and with a lot of fussing in addition (e.g. in the trumpet passage at the beginning of the *Tuba mirum*). And he further revealed his poor sense for tempo later in his excessively fast pacing, in the 1952 La Scala broadcast of Verdi's *Macbeth* with Maria Callas, of not only the prelude but also the great Sleepwalking Scene; and he revealed it again in Beethoven's *Eroica* with the London Philharmonic, where this time his slow tempos made the first movement and the beginning of the finale ineffective. However, his performance of Berlioz's *Roman Carnival* Overture with the same orchestra was excellent.

Guido Cantelli's death in a plane crash in 1956 deprived us of the one young conductor with technical and musical powers of the magnitude of Toscanini's, a fanatical integrity and dedication like Toscanini's, a similar way of operating in relation to music that produced a similar result: a similar shaping of the work strictly on the lines laid out by the composer's directions about tempo and dynamics; a shaped progression with a similar steadiness, continuity and organic coherence, a similar clarity of outline, texture and structure, achieved with a similar precision of execution and sonority. But there were also important differences: as against the powerful tension in a Toscanini performance, one heard in Cantelli's performances serenity and youthful lyricism and grace; and in addition to this difference in general character and style there were differences in tempo, inflection of phrase, shaping of larger structure, which revealed Cantelli as someone with a mind and taste of his own. And though they were the performances of a young man, they didn't exhibit a trace of the immaturity which, inevitably, some critics claimed was detected by their discerning ears: the performances undoubtedly would have changed in time, but each as it was produced then emerged as something completely achieved and completely satisfying.

His early death resulted in his leaving only a small number of studio recordings—with the orchestra of La Scala Tchaikovsky's Fifth; with the NBC Symphony Haydn's Symphony No. 93, the Musorgsky-Ravel *Pictures at an Exhibition,* Franck's Symphony and Hindemith's symphony *Mathis der Maler;* with the New York Philharmonic Vivaldi's *The Four Seasons;* and with the Philharmonia Orchestra Mozart's Symphony K.201 and *A Musical Joke,* Beethoven's Seventh (and an uncompleted recording of the Fifth), Schubert's *Unfinished,* Mendelssohn's *Italian,* Tchaikovsky's *Pathétique* and *Romeo and Juliet,* Wagner's *Siegfried Idyll,* Brahms's Symphonies Nos. 1 and 3, Schumann's Symphony No. 4, Dukas's *The Sorcerer's Apprentice,* three dances from de Falla's *The Three-Cornered Hat,* Ravel's *Daphnis and Chloé* Suite No. 2, and Debussy's *La Mer, Prélude à l'après-midi d'un faune, Nuages* and *Fêtes.*

Some of Cantelli's live performances were preserved on tapes of his broadcasts—notably the complete Mozart *Così fan tutte* and his *Requiem* with the La Scala company; with the Boston Symphony Tchaikovsky's Fifth, Verdi's *Requiem* and Stravinsky's *Jeu de cartes;* with the NBC Symphony Beethoven's Fifth, Schubert's Ninth, Tchaikovsky's Fourth, Fifth and *Pathétique,* and Bartók's Concerto for Orchestra; and with the New York Philharmonic Verdi's *Te Deum,* Mozart's Divertimento K.287 and Piano Concerto K.467 (with Gieseking), and Beethoven concertos (with

Gieseking and Backhaus) and the Mendelssohn Violin Concerto (with Heifetz).

One other conductor after Cantelli produced a performance that one could have thought was Toscanini's—Carlo Maria Giulini, of Verdi's *Te Deum*. And in fact, the taste and the beautiful playing that characterized Giulini's other superb first recordings—of Rossini's *L'Italiana in Algeri*, Verdi's *Don Carlo, Rigoletto, Requiem* and the other works that make up his *Four Sacred Pieces*, Mozart's *Don Giovanni* and *Figaro* (the latter, unfortunately, with uneven singing), and a number of symphonic works recorded with the Philharmonia Orchestra—established him as one of the most distinguished conductors of the time.

Later, with the Chicago Symphony, he made excellent recordings of Dvořák's Eighth and Prokofiev's *Classical* Symphonies, Schumann's Piano Concerto (with Artur Rubinstein) and Musorgsky's *Pictures at an Exhibition,* but also a mistakenly over-emphatic performance of Brahms's Symphony No. 4, one of Schubert's Ninth Symphony whose first and second movements were made ineffective by excessively slow tempos, and a performance of Dvořák's Ninth of which parts were also extremely slow. And while one had no reservations about his beautiful performances of Chopin's two piano concertos with Krystian Zimerman and the Los Angeles Philharmonic a few years after that, this new tendency to distention and over-emphasis affected a number of his other later performances: his Beethoven's Fifth Symphony with the Los Angeles Philharmonic began well, with an enliveningly paced first movement, but his slow tempos made the rest stodgy; and he paced much of Tchaikovsky's *Pathétique* well in his recording with the same orchestra, but in several passages of lament he attempted to achieve heightened expressiveness with tempos enormously slower than Tchaikovsky's which distorted shape and achieved ponderous expressive excess.

However, the *Falstaff* he conducted near the end of his time in Los Angeles was merely relaxedly ruminative, and thus only less effective than it would have been if it had been more animated; and it was heard with pleasure not only from Verdi's writing, but from the singing in the major roles and from the Los Angeles

Philharmonic's playing. And the same was true of his relaxed, spacious and powerful shaping of *Il Trovatore* a year or so afterward with the Orchestra and Chorus of the Academy of Saint Cecilia in Rome.

The premature death in the 1960s of the remarkably gifted Ataulfo Argenta resulted in his leaving even fewer recordings than Cantelli had—of Berlioz's *Symphonie fantastique* with the Paris Conservatory Concerts Orchestra, Rimsky-Korsakov's *Capriccio espagnol* with the London Symphony, Tchaikovsky's Fourth Symphony and Debussy's *Images* with L'Orchestre de la Suisse Romande, as well as a surprisingly phlegmatic Schubert Ninth Symphony with the Orchestra di Centi Soli.

Two other young conductors with impressive capacities who died early were the American Thomas Schippers and the Hungarian Istvan Kertész. Schippers had a feeling for the style of nineteenth-century Italian opera that one hadn't expected from someone born in Kalamazoo, Michigan; and he demonstrated discerning taste in orchestral music in his selection of the pieces by Durante, Vivaldi and Salieri that he paced and shaped well with the Scarlatti Orchestra of Naples in one of his first recordings, and in his excellent performance with the Philharmonia Orchestra of Prokofiev's Symphony No. 5. [However, his recording of Schubert's Ninth with his Cincinati Symphony the year he died was grotesque in its pointless distortions.] For his part, Kertész left fine recordings of symphonic music by Mozart, Schubert, Brahms and Dvořák, and of Mozart's *Requiem*, Donizetti's *Don Pasquale* [and Bartók's *Bluebeard's Castle*].

Other good conductors active in the same period included Eugen Jochum, who left beautiful performances of Haydn's *The Creation*, his Symphonies Nos. 93 through 104, Beethoven's *Missa Solemnis*, and (with the Boston Symphony) Mozart's Symphony K.551 (*Jupiter*) and Schubert's *Unfinished;* André Cluytens, who made an exceptional recording of Fauré's *Requiem* with de los Angeles and Fischer-Dieskau and good ones of Beethoven's symphonies; Paul Kletzki, who in addition to Mahler's *Das Lied von der Erde* with Fischer-Dieskau, recorded one of the best performances of his Fourth Symphony with the Philharmonia Orchestra and Emmy Loose; Rafael Kubelik, who recorded all of Mahler's and Dvořák's symphonies, Mendelssohn's music for *A Midsummer Night's Dream* and Janáček's *Slavonic Mass* in the 1960s and '70s; Willem van Otterloo, whose records—of Berlioz's *Symphonie fantastique* and works of Mahler, Beethoven, Mozart and Schubert—were major events in the 1950s and '60s; and Rudolf Kempe, who recorded as yet unsurpassed versions of *Die Meistersinger* and Smetana's *The Bartered Bride* and good ones of Mozart's Symphony K.338, Haydn's No. 104 (*London*) and works of Richard Strauss.

Igor Markevitch left superb performances of Haydn's *The Creation*, Cherubini's *Requiem* in D minor, Mozart's *Coronation Mass* and Concertos K.466 and 491 (with pianist Clara Haskil playing on this occasion with the correct combination of sensitivity and strength), Berlioz's *The Damnation of Faust*, Prokofiev's *Scythian Suite*, and one of Stravinsky's *Le Sacre de printemps* that was similar in its animation and tension to Stravinsky's own. Ernest Ansermet left outstanding recordings of Fauré's *Requiem* and Debussy's *Pelléas et Mélisande*,* Delibes's *Coppélia* ballet and Tchaikovsky's *Sleeping Beauty* and *Swan Lake* (the latter badly cut), and of certain works of Stravinsky in which his performances had something near the energy of Stravinsky's performances. But his coolness as a musician, and his more than occasional lack of a sense for continuity, made him not a great interpreter of most other music.

Antonio Janigro was known to the musical public not only as a first-rank cellist but as conductor of the superb little string group I Solisti di Zagreb. However, it was in his performances of six of the so-called *Sturm und Drang* symphonies of Haydn, Nos. 44-49, with the Symphony Orchestra of Radio Zagreb, that one heard remarkable conducting powers being exercised on a larger scale as he literally conducted his players from one note to the next in a marvelously sensitive shaping and articulating of the music in a flow with unfailing cohesive tension, continuity and structural

---

*Ansermet recorded *Pelléas et Mélisande* twice. Haggin is referring to the earlier monophonic version; the later stereophonic set also had an excellent cast, but Haggin never heard it. —*Ed.*

coherence. And one regrets that this playing was done only in these vastly over-rated early Haydn symphonies instead of in some of the great last ones.

Igor Stravinsky's conducting had a characteristic and appropriate hard clarity, exciting tension and force that made his performances of his own music the best. However, some of the works he recorded more than once were better played in the earlier versions—by the New York Philharmonic (*Le Sacre de printemps*, Symphony in Three Movements), the Cleveland Orchestra (*Pulcinella, Le Baiser de la fée,* Symphony in C), the Cologne Radio Orchestra and Chorus (*Oedipus Rex*), the Metropolitan Opera Company (*The Rake's Progress*—in a performance which also had the enormous superiority of Mack Harrell's singing as Shadow). And Stravinsky's conducting itself had more power and tension in the first and last movements of the Symphony of Psalms in his recording in the 1950s with the Columbia Broadcasting Symphony and mixed chorus than in his excellent later one with the CBC Symphony and Festival Singers of Toronto.

Whereas Stravinsky performed very little music by anyone but himself (he liked to conduct Tchaikovsky's Second Symphony), Benjamin Britten performed, in addition to his own works, the music of Bach, Mozart and Schubert at his Aldeburgh Festival in England. The spaciously grand *Adagio* introduction to Mozart's Symphony K.504 (*Prague*), as Britten performed it with the English Chamber Orchestra, was overwhelming, and one continued to be overwhelmed by his treatment of what followed. He also left animated performances of Mozart's Symphonies K.183, 201 and 550, Schubert's *Unfinished* and Bach's *Brandenburg* Concertos. And he created wonderfully enlivened orchestral contexts in recordings of three of Mozart's piano concertos—whether it was for his own excellent piano playing in K.414 or for Clifford Curzon's strange and lifeless playing in K.466 and 595. The close working together of Britten's perceptive piano-playing and the tenor Peter Pears's agreeable-sounding and expressive singing made their recorded performances of Schubert's song-cycles *Die schöne Müllerin* [and *Winterreise* and Schumann's *Dichterliebe*] especially effective, too. And the same can be said of the recording Britten made of Tchaikovsky's songs with the soprano Galina Vishnevskaya.

About Otto Klemperer there was the same excitement in England in the 1960s, and specifically about his performances of Beethoven, as there had been earlier about Toscanini, with talk of the similarity of Klemperer's operation to Toscanini's in its strict obedience to the letter of the score, and the consequent similarity of Klemperer's performances to Toscanini's in authenticity and effectiveness. And it was true that Klemperer, like Toscanini, had the orchestra play with strict obedience to Beethoven's every direction for loud and soft, for crescendo and decrescendo, for legato and staccato. But Klemperer's disregard of Beethoven's directions for tempo, and for the expressive character of the music that dictated those directions, produced strange slow-motion performances that made most of his Beethoven recordings something to avoid. However, in *Fidelio* his tempos most of the time conformed to the meaning of words like *Allegro* and *Andante con moto* sufficiently for the music to have its right expressive character and effect.

Many of Klemperer's performances of music by other composers were also unusually slow, though—as in the case of Schubert's Symphony No. 9—not always so slow as to make the performances ineffective. And Klemperer produced wholly satisfying performances of Bach's *St. Matthew Passion, B-minor Mass, Brandenburg* Concertos and suites for orchestra, Mozart's Symphonies K.201 and 551 (*Jupiter*), Haydn's Symphonies Nos. 88, 98 and 104 (*London*), Mahler's Symphony No. 2 (*Resurrection*) and *Das Lied von der Erde* (with mezzo Christa Ludwig and tenor Fritz Wunderlich), Tchaikovsky's Fifth Symphony, and Brahms's Second, Third and Fourth Symphonies. Moreover his performances of the Prelude and *Liebestod* from *Tristan und Isolde* and of the Funeral Music from *Götterdämmerung* did approximate Toscanini's in tension and power, and the one of the Prelude to Act One of *Lohengrin* was more effective than Toscanini's for being more relaxed. And in his collaboration with the outstanding players of the London Wind Quintet and Ensemble in Mozart's Serenade for Winds K.361 the tempos, which were well chosen, the phrasing, which was marvelous, and the relationships of balance and phrasing that Klemperer achieved between the individual lines, produced not only an unbelievably wonderful performance of this piece but one of the most remarkable performances I had ever heard of anything.

As for Herbert von Karajan, from the start his performances on records and in concerts with the Philharmonia and the Berlin and Vienna Philharmonic Orchestras showed him to be the possessor of powers of virtuoso caliber and magnitude that he used erratically and capriciously. In Carnegie Hall in 1956 I heard him use his technical powers to get the Berlin Philharmonic to play with remarkable delicacy in performances that he kept low-keyed not only when the music was a Mozart violin concerto but, perversely, when it was Richard Strauss's *Don Juan* and even the first movement of Beethoven's *Eroica*. And though the recorded performance of the *Eroica* with the Philharmonia at about that time didn't exhibit this playing around with orchestra and music, it did exhibit an occasional error in musical judgment—e.g. the disruptive slowing down of the first movement after the dissonant climax in the development. In his second set of all nine of Beethoven's symphonies, which he recorded in 1961–62 with the Berlin Philharmonic, the virtuoso who obtained balanced and clear textures of ear-ravishing sounds from an orchestra now marvelously sensitized to his direction* operated as a serious musician applying impressive skill to a pacing and shaping of the works that much of the time was highly effective and satisfying— though not, for me, as effective and satisfying as Toscanini's, and still not without occasional errors in musical judgment. But both of the Beethoven symphony-cycles he remade with the Berlin Philharmonic afterwards—the badly recorded one of 1976 and the one of 1985—had new oddities that made the 1961–62 set preferable.

This erraticism continued to operate in everything he conducted—producing on the one hand a Tchaikovsky *Pathétique*

---

*Interestingly, the sound of this orchestra did not—unlike that of Stokowski's Philadelphia Orchestra or Koussevitzky's Boston Symphony—have a distinctive character analogous to the various timbres of one singer as against another. —B.H.H.

that suffered from an excessively slow first movement, a *Magic Flute* flawed by the eccentricity of having some ensembles sung by one singer or group in full voice while another sang in half-voice, a *Boris* flawed by the decision to use the Rimsky-Korsakov version in place of Musorgsky's own, a *Don Carlo* flawed by the decision to record the four-act instead of the five-act version and damaged further by the occasional peculiarities of von Karajan's conducting—specifically, his drawing out, lingering over, and pausing after phrases, as in the second-act Carlo-Elisabeth and Philip-Rodrigo duets. And on the other hand producing superb recordings of *Così fan tutte*, *Falstaff* and *Il Trovatore*, Mozart's Symphony K.543 and Divertimento K.287 for strings and horns (with the Philharmonia), his horn concertos (also with the Philharmonia and with the unequalled horn-playing of Dennis Brain), his Symphony K.550 (with the Vienna Philharmonic), Haydn's *The Creation*, Beethoven's First, Second and Fourth Symphonies (in the 1961–62 Berlin Philharmonic versions), the last three of Brahms's symphonies (also in the Berlin Philharmonic versions of the 1960s), Dvořák's Eighth Symphony, Tchaikovsky's Fourth, Serenade in C and *Nutcracker* Suite, Berlioz's *Symphonie fantastique*, and Debussy's *La Mer* and *Prélude à l'après-midi d'un faune*— to list only some of the pieces in which von Karajan operated with unfailing responsibility to his task and achieved performances that were unforgettable demonstrations of technical and musical mastery.

Keyboard Players 1940s–1970s

Reviewing a recital of Vladimir Horowitz once, Virgil Thomson regretted that a man who could play his own pyrotechnical elaborations of things like Sousa's *Stars and Stripes Forever* so satisfyingly "should spend so much of the evening worrying standard repertory." I cite this to establish the fact that I am not alone in my low estimate of the musical value of the Horowitz manner of exciting an audience. His infinite gradations of tone and bursts of supercharged virtuosity represented masterly playing of the piano, but his *affettuoso* teasing of melody, in alternation with the Horowitz fireworks, represented his one way of dealing with every composer—whether Chopin, Schubert, Mozart, Scarlatti, Beethoven, Brahms or Schumann—and a way that was good for none.

Artur Rubinstein, on the other hand, began with a flamboyance that produced performances of Mozart and Beethoven with the unsuitable, elegant melodic inflections of his mannered Chopin playing. But in his seventies he amazed one not only with the tempering of his flamboyant style that gave his late performances a new continence, repose, and refinement, but with the continuing technical powers that produced the subtle variations of his beautiful tone, the clarity and accuracy of his rapid passage work. His Chopin playing continued to be in the mannered style I don't like (though his recordings of the Impromptus, the Mazurkas, and the First Concerto with Stanislaw Skrowaczewski were played with taste in this style), but these years gave us his relaxed, spacious, and beautiful-sounding playing in Schumann's Piano Concerto with Giulini, his equally fine playing in Dvořák's Quintet Op. 81 with the Guarneri Quartet (his performances of Mozart's piano quartets with three of the same players had insufficient animation, and his good ones of Schubert's two piano trios with Fournier and Henryk Szeryng were marred by Szeryng's violin tone, which wasn't always agreeable), his miraculous performance—in his eighties—of Schumann's *Kreisleriana*, and his set of Beethoven's concertos with Erich Leinsdorf and the Boston Symphony, which had a correctness of style his earlier playing of Beethoven hadn't had. One was surprised, therefore, to hear in his recording of Schubert's B-flat Sonata how much he had failed to perceive in a work he had loved and studied so long before finally playing it in public; and subsequently one was saddened to find that the sensitiveness and grace, the beautiful playing of the piano, that one had heard in the Beethoven concertos with Leinsdorf were not to be heard in the later ones conducted by Daniel Barenboim.

It should be added that there were some satisfying recordings in the thirties and forties, too—notably of Schubert's Trio Op. 99 and Beethoven's *Archduke* Trio (both with equally sensitive playing by Heifetz and Feuermann), Chopin's Mazurkas, some of his Polonaises, the *Andante Spianato and Grande Polonaise*, and some of his Scherzos.

In the playing of Webster Aitken in the 1940s and '50s one heard a powerful musical intelligence operating with carefully thought-out and impressively executed purpose, which led Virgil Thomson, in 1948, to describe him correctly as "the most masterful of all our American pianists." Aitken didn't achieve general recognition of his mastery even after Thomson had proclaimed it; and in the forties, when he produced the clearly and powerfully shaped performance of Beethoven's Sonata Op. 111 that impressed Thomson, and an equally impressive performance of Beethoven's *Diabelli* Variations, he was given the opportunity to record only Mozart's C-minor Fantasy K.475 and Schubert's posthumous Sonata in C minor for a small label (Gamut).

By the early 1950s, when he recorded all the late Schubert sonatas for another small label (EMS), it had become clear that he was a pianist who used his extraordinary powers in whatever music he played for private ends—with results that were sometimes good for the music and sometimes not. Thus, in the later recording of Schubert's posthumous C-minor Sonata the continuity of the playing tightened up the occasional looseness of the music and made of each movement—most remarkably in the case of the rambling finale—a coherent entity. And the performance also realized the duality in Schubert's music—building up the sustained power of the developments in the first and last movements, but also relaxing for the plasticity and grace of the lyrical passages. Aitken's statement of the slow movement of the posthumous A-major—and especially of the extraordinary middle section—was another impressive demonstration of his powers as musician and pianist; but his treatment of the other movements appeared to represent a determination to produce something as different from Schnabel's relaxed, spacious performance as possible; and though Aitken's performance came off in its own way, it inflicted a loss on the work. For the rest, Aitken's stop-and-go manner of playing much of Opp. 53 and 78 was very damaging to these works (though his playing of the opening section of Op. 78—the subtle changes of pace and dynamics within the repetitions of the opening statement, and in the transitions from one repetition to the next—was one of the high-points of the performer's art in my experience). Even more damaging was his iron-fisted treatment of the posthumous B-flat Sonata.

There was, nevertheless, always the mastery that was so striking in his operation—mastery in the treatment of the piano, mastery even in making of the music something that one couldn't accept. But in 1975, after his death, a record was issued of performances of Beethoven's *Hammerklavier* Sonata and *Diabelli* Variations taped at the University of Illinois in 1961, in which fast passages in the rushed first movement of the sonata, as in the fast variations of the *Diabelli,* were without clarity or shape, and the phrases of the slow movement of the sonata were distorted and not allowed their natural flow. And his erratic tempos and changes of tempo on a record of Schubert's Sonata Op. 53 that was issued in 1979 produced another performance of the work that I was unable to hear as a valid statement of it.

In the few years before his death of leukemia in 1952 the young pianist Dinu Lipatti recorded a small number of performances— of Bach's Partita No. 1, a couple of Scarlatti sonatas, Mozart's Sonata K.310, Schumann's Concerto (with von Karajan), Chopin's Sonata No. 3, all the Waltzes, the Barcarolle, the Nocturne Op. 27 No. 2, the Mazurka Op. 50 No. 3, and Ravel's *Alborada del Gracioso*—in which one heard the lyricism, grace, elegance and verve, the unfailing taste and feeling for continuity in phrase and large structure, in addition to the precision of execution and tonal beauty, that made the playing outstandingly distinguished and his death an irreparable loss. Afterwards, recordings of his broadcasts gave us in addition his concert performances of Mozart's Concerto K.467 (with von Karajan), Bach's D-minor Concerto (with Eduard van Beinum), Chopin's Concerto No. 1* (with Otto Ackermann), and another, later performance (with Ansermet) of Schumann's Concerto—a little grander and more meditative than the earlier one with von Karajan but without that one's energy. Another broadcast record gave us his performances of the same Bach partita, Mozart sonata and Chopin waltzes (minus one) that he had recorded in the studio, and of two Schubert Impromptus, made at his last public recital at the 1950

---

* In the 1960s a studio performance of the Chopin concerto by Halina Czerny-Stefanska was mistakenly issued, and was accepted by all for some fifteen years, as Lipatti's. Lipatti's actual performance was discovered and issued in the 1980s. —*Ed.*

Besançon Festival, where he was so ill and weak that he could barely climb the stairs to the auditorium, but where, by an almost unimaginable effort of will, he not only managed to play the works with his precision, lyricism, elegance and verve, but—under the stimulation of the occasion—raised the performances to sheer incandescence.

Though reviewers persisted in hearing Van Cliburn as a pianist who had mastered the flamboyantly romantic style of Tchaikovsky and Rachmaninoff but needed to learn how to play other music, the complete naturalness and rightness of his performance of that other music—the unfailing sense for proportion, for note-to-note continuity of tone, tension and outline, the absolute accuracy of tonal values and timing, the characteristic simply, subtly achieved grandeur—revealed him as one of the most distinguished of musicians and pianists.

In Cliburn's performance of Beethoven's Piano Sonata Op. 81a (*Les Adieux*) each note went on to the next in what emerged as a completely imagined and completely realized, integrated progression. His performance of the Sonata Op. 57 (*Appassionata*) was like no other in the spacious grandeur of its impassioned character. And it was overwhelming to hear Chopin's Sonatas Nos. 2 and 3 performed with a sustained grandeur that was unprecedented in my experience and with the new expressive dimension this gave them.

And so with the other works in the limited repertory he played—the *Handel Variations,* smaller solo pieces, and Concerto No. 2 of Brahms, the solo pieces and Concerto No. 1 of Chopin, the Sonata K.330 (and the unrecorded Concerto K.503) of Mozart, the *Pathétique* and *Moonlight* Sonatas, the Concertos Nos. 3, 4 and 5 (*Emperor*) of Beethoven, the solo pieces of Debussy, Schumann, Granados, Liszt, Rachmaninoff and Ravel, the concertos of Schumann, Grieg, Tchaikovsky (No. 1), Prokofiev (No. 3), MacDowell and Rachmaninoff (Nos. 2 and 3): one heard in Cliburn's performances the operation of awesome musical powers in some of the greatest making of music on the piano one had heard in this century.

Cliburn's 1958 performances of Tchaikovsky's Concerto No. 1 and Rachmaninoff's Concerto No. 3 should be listened to, in fact, for their demonstration that from the beginning he applied to these works of low musical value the same mastery and matured perception he applied to works of greater value—the mastery and perception that reviewers at the time claimed he had yet to acquire. In the Tchaikovsky concerto, that is, the operation was not that of someone playing a virtuoso display piece, but, like Toscanini's performance of a "pops" number, strictly that of a musician playing a piece of music and employing for the purpose not only a remarkable technical equipment but an equally remarkable and distinguished musical perception and taste. And in the Rachmaninoff concerto—in the cadenza of the first movement, and in the scherzo-like episode in the second movement— Cliburn's perception of what others had not perceived left one astounded: the voices, previously unheard in the texture, that now were clearly audible and brought into relation to each other; in the cadenza the more detailed shaping, and the build-up of tension, by the alternation of gradual acceleration and deceleration, which were carried to an overwhelming high point in the grandly climactic pronouncements of the first movement's principal theme.

The pianist who seemed at the time to be Cliburn's peer was Glenn Gould. But the tragedy of his career, for me, was not the one described in the obituaries—the death in 1982 of so gifted a musician at the very moment that his newly recorded performance of Bach's *Goldberg Variations* revealed the impressive maturity of his gifts. It was instead, for me, the life in which, from first to last, Gould had offered an alternation of what excited one with its marvelous execution and musical rightness, and on the other hand what, however impressively it was executed, one could not hear as a valid statement of the music.

Though Gould recorded several of his finest performances in the early years of his career, even one of the very first of them, the remarkable recording of the *Goldberg Variations* in 1955, offered the alternation I have described—one example being the opening aria that was made excitingly effective by the extraordinary enlivening inflection in an *andante* tempo that seemed exactly right, and that left one unprepared for the excessively fast tempo of the first variation. And the superb performances of Bach's Concerto in D minor in 1957 and Beethoven's Concerto No. 1 in 1958 followed the ones of Beethoven's last three sonatas in 1956, whose eccentricities included Variation Four in the finale of Op. 109, for which Beethoven prescribes, in Italian and German, a tempo slower than the *andante* of the theme, but which Gould played in a tempo faster than the *andante,* giving the variation a light-hearted expressive character instead of the profoundly serious and impassioned character it has in Beethoven's tempo. Mozart's Sonata K.330, which Gould shaped and articulated so effectively in 1958, he ripped through in 1972 at speeds that made it meaningless; and even in 1958 one heard a few instances of two idiosyncratic practices that became increasingly damaging in his performances—the over-emphasizing of left-hand accompaniment as if it were melody, and the arpeggiating of what Mozart writes as solid left-hand chords. In Mozart's Concerto K.491 in 1962 Gould carried these practices to an extreme that was made especially deplorable by the extraordinary nature of the performance—the powerful sculpturing of phrase, the energy of fast runs and figurations, the sustained tension and momentum that were unprecedented in the playing of this music and gave the work new and overwhelming magnitude.

And all this continued to the end in 1982. One heard in the last six of Haydn's sonatas—one of his last recordings—the electrifyingly executed inflection of a *cantabile* phrase in a slow movement that gave it continuity of tension and shape, followed by the unsuitable exaggerated staccato treatment of the next *cantabile* phrase; the over-emphasized accompaniment figuration that predominated over a melodic statement; the disturbingly obtrusive "brrrrups" of arpeggiated accompaniment chords. And in the final new performance of Bach's *Goldberg Variations* the results of Gould's continued thinking about the initial aria and the thirty variations in the years since the performance in 1955 turned out to be only a different alternation of what was wonderfully effective and what was musically unconvincing—the first variation's slower tempo that was not only right in itself but related to the tempos of the next three variations, giving the series a coherence it hadn't had in 1955, but this series preceded by the

extreme slowness, softness, and elimination of expressive inflection in the opening statement of the aria that made his ability to
maintain coherence in the perverse progression a tour de force
but not, for my ears, a convincing statement of the music.

And what was true of the performances mentioned here was
true in some degree of most of the others—notably Bach's *Well-
Tempered Clavier*, Partitas, Toccatas, Inventions, and *Italian Concerto;* Handel's suites; Beethoven's Concertos Nos. 4 and 5, many
of the sonatas, the *Eroica* Varations and Bagatelles. Two exceptions were his records of music by seventeenth-century English
composers, and of Bizet's remarkable *Variations chromatiques*.

For the rest, William Kapell's commercial recording of Beethoven's Second Concerto in the late 1940s, and the recordings
that survive of his broadcast solo and chamber recitals, provide
valuable documentation of this gifted young musician's playing
before his early death in 1953 in a plane crash. Leon Fleisher
recorded with Szell superb performances of Mozart's Concerto in
C K.503 and Beethoven's Fourth, good ones of the other Beethoven concertos, and solo works by Schubert, Brahms, Franck
and others, before a disabling injury compelled him to restrict his
playing to the repertory for piano left-hand.

Claude Frank's performances of all the Beethoven sonatas in
the 1970s were those of an excellent pianist and musician. In the
1960s Jacob Lateiner produced performances of Beethoven's
Bagatelles Op. 126 and Sonata Op. 111 that were similar to
Schnabel's and comparable in effect, but with detailed playing
that was Lateiner's own and very fine; however, his performances
of Opp. 109 and 53 (*Waldstein*) were not good. Dino Ciani, who
died at an early age in 1974, recorded performances of Weber's
Piano Sonatas Nos. 2 and 3 which admirably realized their grace
and elegance. Aldo Ciccolini recorded excellent performances of
Chabrier's *Dix Pièces pittoresques,* Albéniz's *Ibéria* and Chopin's
Sonata for Cello and Piano (with Paul Tortelier). And superb
performances were recorded by Paul Jacobs of Debussy's *Études*
(though his subsequent performances of *Estampes* and the two
sets of *Images* were unexpectedly dull); by Robert Casadesus of
Schumann's *Carnaval, Études symphoniques* and *Papillons* (but not
of Mozart, which he played in a bland style that was inadequate);

by Mieczyslaw Horszowski of Chopin's Piano Concerto No. 1 (with Hans Swarowsky); and by Clifford Curzon of Schumann's Fantasy and *Kinderszenen,* Schubert's *Moments musicaux,* Beethoven's *Eroica* Variations, and Dvořák's Piano Quintet Op. 81 (with the Vienna Philharmonic Quartet).

The English harpsichordist George Malcolm recorded on a lovely-sounding instrument performances of a number of Scarlatti sonatas that were the best I could recall hearing—performances with, among other things, a continuity of impetus and tension that was equally exciting in the brilliant fast pieces and in the powerful slow ones. And his similar playing in his first recording (for Decca-London) of Bach's *Italian Concerto* and *Chromatic Fantasy and Fugue*—at once delicate and strong—gave continuity to the ornamented melody of the wonderful slow movement of the concerto and to the improvisatory flourishes and declamation of the superb Fantasy, energy to the fast movements of the concerto, and power to the climaxes of the Fugue— all without forcing or pounding his instrument (his subsequent recordings of these works were disappointing). Malcolm contributed equally beautiful playing of the harpsichord to recordings of, among other things, the music of Purcell, Handel's *Messiah,* Bach's Concerto in D minor and his *Brandenburg* Concertos (the set conducted by Klemperer—not the one conducted by Yehudi Menuhin, in which Malcolm's playing in No. 5 was fussy).

Another English harpsichordist, Thurston Dart, made several fine records of keyboard works of Handel and various English composers, and conducted good performances of Handel's *Water Music* and Dowland's *Lachrimae.* A performer who was equally fine as an organist and as a harpsichord-player was Anton Heiller. His recordings of Bach's organ music offered fine examples of the performer's art, as did his performances on the harpsichord of Bach's keyboard concertos. And in Canada Greta Kraus recorded marvelous performances on the harpsichord of Bach's *Chromatic Fantasy and Fugue* and other pieces, and on the piano she produced overwhelming ensemble performances with Lois Marshall of Schubert's song-cycle *Die schöne Müllerin* and, in a broadcast, of songs of Hugo Wolf.

String Players, Chamber Groups
and Instrumentalists 1940s–1970s

After the war the violinist Ruggiero Ricci recorded the Beethoven Violin Concerto with mastery of his instrument and youthful, warm and lovely lyricism, the Tchaikovsky Concerto with freedom and exuberance that stayed mostly within the limits of musical good taste, and the Mendelssohn Concerto with taste and warm expressiveness; his subsequent recordings were also very fine. There were good performances as well by Zino Francescatti, Ossy Renardy and Max Rostal. And in the 1950s the thirteen-year-old Gérard Poulet played Mozart's Concertos K.216 and 218 with youthful warmth and purity and extraordinarily sentient inflection (and with outstanding playing also by the Austrian Symphony under his father Gaston Poulet) that made these two of the most remarkable and beautiful performances on records.

Nathan Milstein's luminous tone and unaffected phrasing were heard in recordings of the Beethoven, Brahms, Mendelssohn and Tchaikovsky concertos with various orchestras and conductors over the years (though the early performances were not entirely free of virtuoso mannerisms), in several concertos by Bach, in a performance of Mozart's Concerto K.219 whose excellence was not only in Milstein's playing but in the wonderful orchestral context Harry Blech created around it with his superb Festival Orchestra, and in admirable performances of Bach's Sonatas and Partitas for unaccompanied violin (though Szigeti's were even more impressive) and the sonata for violin from Handel's Op. 1 (with Artur Balsam playing the piano).

What delighted one similarly in David Oistrakh's first recordings in the early 1950s—of sonatas by Beethoven (Op. 24—*Spring*), Prokofiev (Op. 80) and Schubert (Op. 162) with the pianist Lev Oborin, of Beethoven's Violin Concerto with the Russian State Radio Orchestra under Alexander Gauk, Prokofiev's Concerto No. 1 with the London Symphony under Lovro von Matacic, and in particular Mozart's Concerto K.219 with the Russian State Radio Orchestra under Nicolai Golovanov—was the excellent taste evident in the purity and sweetness of Oistrakh's tone and his simple sustained phrasing. Consequently, one was shocked by the momentary deterioration in taste—in his concert performance of the Mozart concerto with the New York Philharmonic in 1956, in the recordings of Mozart's K.218 and the Mendelssohn Concerto that he made at that time with Ormandy—a deterioration that was evident in the excessive vibrato, the swells and portamentos, that made these the fat-toned, high-powered performances, without delicacy, grace or elegance, that one might have gotten from a Western violinist throwing his virtuosic weight around. But subsequently Oistrakh recorded performances—of all of Beethoven's sonatas (with Oborin), his concerto (with André Cluytens), and of Bach's Sonatas for Violin and Harpsichord Nos. 2 and 3 (with Hans Pischner) and various of his concertos—that were very good.

In Isaac Stern's first recordings of Tchaikovsky's and Mendelssohn's violin concertos, made between 1949 and 1951 with the Philadelphia Orchestra under Alexander Hilsberg and Ormandy, the music was exaggerated and distorted by Stern's own excessively impassioned throwing around of his weight. And in a few later recordings—of Bach's Violin Concertos in A minor and E major with Alexander Schneider conducting, of Mozart's Divertimento K.563 with Pinchas Zukerman, viola, and Leonard Rose, cello—Stern's playing had a robustness and occasional vehemence that made the performances less satisfying than those of some other players.* But beautiful playing of music and violin could be heard in Stern's performances of concertos and chamber music at Casals's festivals in the early 1950s; in recordings in 1960 of the Mendelssohn and Tchaikovsky violin concertos again, this time performed well by Stern and with almost unbelievably sensitive execution and ravishing tone by the Philadelphia Orchestra under Ormandy; in the superb recording with Ormandy of Prokofiev's Concerto No. 1 a few years later; in good ones of Mozart concertos conducted by Szell and Schneider; in the Tchaikovsky Concerto again in 1979 with Mstislav Rostropovich conducting; and in the Stern-Rose-Istomin Trio's ex-

---

*Milstein was quoted in the *New York Times* in 1979 as saying: "People now make such accents in Bach: *dee,* dee, *dee,* dee, dee, *dah.* So heavy. Once I was playing with Isaac Stern privately in Geneva—we went to a violin maker there—and he was doing that. I asked him what was the matter and he said Bach was a real man who had twenty children. That's a good thing, I said, but the music is not about that." —*Ed.*

cellent performances of all the Beethoven trios. (The group's records of Schubert's trios were very good, too, but there were others at the time that were even finer.)

The violinist Arthur Grumiaux, in the period from the 1950s through the 1970s, recorded his beautiful performances of the concertos of Mozart, Beethoven, Mendelssohn and Tchaikovsky several times under different conductors (of the Mozart, the versions with Colin Davis had the best realization and integration of the orchestra parts); and he made good recordings with Clara Haskil of Beethoven's and Mozart's violin sonatas (though Haskil's playing did not have the sparkle the Mozart works call for), and superb ones with various associates of Mozart's string quintets, the Divertimento K.563, the Clarinet Quintet K.581, and Schubert's String Quintet Op. 163 and *Trout* Quintet (in which the unusual lightness and grace of the string-playing elicited unusually sensitive piano-playing from the normally bland Ingrid Haebler).

Pierre Fournier's recording with Schnabel, a few years after the war, of all of Beethoven's cello sonatas gave us the cello parts played very beautifully, though with less powerful tone and style than Casals's and consequently less meaning and impact, and the piano parts with a revealing clarity and force that were lacking in Schulhof's and Horszowski's playing with Casals. [A later recording by Fournier and Wilhelm Kempff suffered from Kempff's fussy playing.] Fournier also recorded superb performances of sonatas by Vivaldi, and an excellent one of Richard Strauss's *Don Quixote* with Szell.

In the 1950s the superb cellist János Starker, whose playing had elegance and distinction of style and a dark sumptuous tone, recorded performances of Mozart trios with Victor Aitay and the pianist Agi Jambor that were outstanding in their fluidity and grace, and ones of Beethoven's cello sonatas with Abba Bogin, whose playing did not equal his in power and tension. In the 1970s Starker recorded the Beethoven again, this time with playing by Rudolf Buchbinder that was admirably coordinated with his; he also recorded Chopin's Cello Sonata, Bloch's *Voice in the Wilderness* and *Schelomo*, and concertos by Dvořák, Haydn and others.

Before illness compelled the young Jacqueline Du Pré to retire in 1973, she recorded—in addition to concertos by Boccherini, Haydn, Dvořák and others—superb performances of Beethoven's Cello Sonatas Opp. 69 and 102 No. 2 with the excellent pianist Stephen Bishop-Kovacevich. However, in her recording of the Piano Trios Op. 70 Nos. 1 and 2 and Op. 97 (*Archduke*), her own merits, and those of the violinist Pinchas Zukerman, were outweighed by Daniel Barenboim's deficiencies as pianist and musician.

Already in the 1940s the short-lived New Music Quartet (Broadus Erle, Matthew Raimondi, Walter Trampler and Claus Adam) had been exhibiting an almost unprecedented technical, musical and ensemble incandescence in its performances. After recording Mozart's Quartets K.173 and 499 for Griffon Records, and pieces by Gibbons, Locke, Purcell, Tartini, Scarlatti and Boccherini and Beethoven's Quartet Op. 59 No. 3 for Bartók Records, it recorded for Columbia (with David Soyer replacing Adam) four delightful Boccherini quartets and four early Mozart quartets (K.155–158), among other things, before it disbanded in the early 1950s.

In the 1950s the New York Quartet (Alexander Schneider, Milton Katims, Frank Miller—the NBC Symphony's great first cellist*—and the pianist Horszowski) recorded wonderfully alive performances of Mozart's K.478 and Beethoven's inconsequential Op. 16. The Schneider Quartet (Alexander Schneider, Isidore Cohen, Karen Tuttle and Madeline Foley) made a series of Haydn quartet recordings that were notable for their energy, their enlivening inflection of the four parts, their integrated operation—and for the fascinating differences between the Schneider's energetically detailed inflection and sharper rhythm and the refinement and smoothness of the Budapest Quartet's playing in some of the same works. The Griller Quartet made a few superb recordings of Haydn quartets at this time as well.

---

* Miller was the cello soloist in Toscanini's 1953 recording of *Don Quixote.*—*Ed.*

In the 1960s the Yale Quartet (Broadus Erle with various others), in the few years of its existence, made records of Mozart's K.421 and 575, the like of which in pacing, phrasing and articulation I hadn't heard since the Budapest Quartet's of the thirties. It followed these with superb recordings of Beethoven's Opp. 127, 131 and 132. However, its last recordings, of Beethoven's Opp. 130, 133 and 135, while effective, would have been more so if the performances had been less hurried, more relaxed and expansive, and therefore more sensitively phrased.

In Europe the Quartetto Italiano, which had amazed one in the 1950s with the extraordinary transparency and radiance of the blended tone of its four strings, the refinement of its execution and phrasing, began to astonish music-lovers in the 1960s with an ability it hadn't had earlier to play the music of Beethoven, Haydn and Mozart as superbly as it had always played its instruments. It recorded all of Beethoven's quartets, the six of Mozart's dedicated to Haydn, and several by Boccherini, Haydn and Schubert (as well as ones by Schumann, Brahms and Debussy) before it finally disbanded. And one's pleasure in the playing was not much diminished by the occasional miscalculations that became apparent if one listened to the Italiano's performances after those of the Budapest Quartet: the hurried and unpoised first movement of Mozart's K.387 and second movement of K.421, the slowing down of the minuet of K.458 and of the D-major variation in the finale of K.421, the excessive vehemence in Beethoven's Op. 18 Nos. 1 and 3 where the works call for grace and elegance, and the slow tempos for the first movement of Op. 59 No. 1, for the first movement of Schubert's Op. 29 and for much of the first and second movements and the entire finale of Op. 161.

Another European string quartet of the first rank, the Danish Quartet, provided long-needed modern-day performances, with an assisting violist, of Mozart's string quintets—performances which exhibited, in addition to their excellences of tone and ensemble execution, an extraordinary sensitivity to the music's every point of style, shape and expressiveness. To these the group added the engaging Horn Quintet K.407 (with remarkably fluent playing of the occasional florid passages for horn by Jacky Magnardi), the marvelous Clarinet Quintet K.581 (with playing of the clarinet part by Guy Deplus that would not interest anyone familiar with Gervase de Peyer's), the Adagio and Fugue K.546, and *Eine kleine Nachtmusik.*

Several mixed ensembles in the 1960s recorded a few superb performances each: the Melos Ensemble's of Mozart's Clarinet Quintet K.581 (with de Peyer), Schubert's Octet (with de Peyer and others) and his *Trout* Quintet (with pianist Lamar Crowson); the Koeckert Quartet's of Schubert's *Trout* Quintet (with Christoph Eschenbach); the Trio di Trieste's of Beethoven's *Archduke* Trio and the two trios by Schubert; the Trio Italiano d'Archi's of Mozart's Divertimento K.563; and the Weller Quartet's of Schubert's String Quintet Op. 163 (with an assisting cellist).

Three Italian chamber orchestras that began to be heard here in concerts and on records in the 1950s—the Virtuosi di Roma, I Musici and the Societá Corelli—exhibited not only a beauty and refinement of style equivalent to that of the Quartetto Italiano, but a precision of execution and an expressive warmth and grace that were unique. For many years their performances of Italian Baroque music (as well as Mendelssohn's Octet and the music of Bach and others) set the standard for performances of this kind.* In the years that followed, other groups—I Solisti di Zagreb under the cellist Antonio Janigro, the Chamber Orchestra of the Vienna State Opera under Felix Prohaska and Mario Rossi, the Netherlands Chamber Orchestra under Szymon Goldberg, and the Hewitt Chamber Orchestra under Leslie Hewitt—also gave first-rate performances of music ranging from the works of Vivaldi and his contemporaries to those of Haydn, Mozart and some later composers. And Alfred Deller's Consort in England, and in America Noah Greenberg's vocal group the Pro Musica Antiqua of New York (which included the marvelous countertenor, Russell Oberlin), recorded superb performances of the vocal and instrumental music of earlier centuries.

Still later there was a series of fine recordings of Baroque music conducted by Yehudi Menuhin. As a violinist Menuhin's playing was, in his maturity, rhythmically unsteady and tonally and

---

*Surprisingly, the Societá Corelli's record of Vivaldi's *The Four Seasons* was both musically undistinguished and not as well excuted as its other performances. —B. H. H.

stylistically undistinguished (consistently in his solo performances it was the piano playing of his sister, Hephzibah, that was
exciting to hear); but he operated very impressively as a conductor in excellent performances with his Bath Festival Orchestra of
the instrumental music of Purcell, the suites for orchestra of
Bach, and the *Water Music, Royal Fireworks Music,* Concerti
Grossi Op. 6 and works for organ and orchestra of Handel.

Five instrumentalists stood out as well in this period: Marcel
Tabuteau, the principal oboist of the Philadelphia Orchestra
from the 1930s through the early 1950s, recorded beautiful
performances at the 1951 Perpignan Festival of Mozart's Divertimento K.251 for oboe, horns and strings under Casals, and of
Mozart's Quartet K.370 for oboe and strings, with Stern, Primrose and Tortelier; and with the Philadelphia Orchestra he
performed Handel's Oboe Concerto No. 3 under Ormandy, and
Mozart's less interesting Sinfonia Concertante K.297b with other
first-desk players of the Philadelphia Orchestra under Stokowski.
A record in the 1950s by the Philadelphia Orchestra's great
principal flutist, William Kincaid, provided opportunities to marvel at the unique silvery tone and other perfections of his playing
in Marcello's charming Sonata in F, Debussy's *Syrinx,* a pleasant
Sonatine by Dutilleux, and some less consequential pieces. English clarinetist Gervase de Peyer's performances of concertos
and chamber works by Mozart, Schubert, Weber and others
offered the most beautiful clarinet tone and phrasing I could
recall hearing in those works; this was true especially of the earlier
recordings of the 1950s and 1960s (his tone in his later recording
of Mozart's Quintet K.581 with the Amadeus Quartet, for example, was not as beautiful as it had been in his earlier recording with
the Melos Ensemble).

Dennis Brain, the young English horn-player who was killed in
an automobile accident in 1956, produced an extraordinarily
supple sustained tone with which he achieved in Mozart's four
horn concertos calmly sustained and subtly detailed phrasing that
was astounding—this in a context of beautifully sensitive playing
by the original Philharmonia Orchestra under von Karajan in a
recording that was never equalled by any other. [Brain's other
surviving performances as a soloist and chamber player were of
less consequential pieces by Mozart, Beethoven, Schumann,

Brahms, Richard Strauss, Hindemith and others; but his playing as the first horn of the great Philharmonia Orchestra could be heard in many of its recordings—among them Verdi's *Falstaff* (the last scene) and Mozart's Sinfonia Concertante K.297b, both with von Karajan, the last scene of Richard Strauss's *Capriccio* and his *Four Last Songs,* sung by Elisabeth Schwarzkopf, with Ackermann conducting. Finally, there was Maurice André, the amazing French trumpet player, who from the 1960s on made superlative recordings with numerous chamber orchestras of most of the concertos of the Baroque and classical repertory.]

Singers 1940s–1970s

In those post-war years one also made the acquaintance of a number of fine singers. In addition to those already mentioned in connection with the Glyndebourne Festival recordings there were in England the sopranos Isobel Baillie, Margaret Ritchie (who recorded an unequalled performance of Schubert's *Der Hirt aus dem Felsen* with de Peyer), Elsie Morison, Jennifer Vyvyan, April Cantelo, Sheila Armstrong and Helen Watts. And in Europe Anny Felbermayer (excellent in Mahler and Richard Strauss songs), Martha Mödl, Elisabeth Grümmer, Maria Stader, Hilde Güden, Rita Streich, Anneliese Rothenberger, Erna Spoorenberg, Edith Mathis and, in her early years, Irmgard Seefried.

Over here one heard Mattiwilda Dobbs (who used a comparatively small soprano voice—with its exquisite purity and sweetness, its extraordinary ease, range and security—in a wide repertory), Lisa della Casa (whose voice had a beauty on records one did not always hear in the opera house, and who recorded, in addition to her roles in operas by Mozart and Handel, highly distinguished performances of *Lieder* by Schubert, Wolf and Richard Strauss), Anna Moffo (the Nannetta in von Karajan's *Falstaff,* who in addition delighted one's ear and mind with her luscious voice and plastic phrasing in Mozart); Adele Addison, Inge Borkh, Leonie Rysanek (whose voice became tremulous in the middle years of her career, and miraculously steady again later), Teresa Stich-Randall (whose lyric soprano, though dry later on, was steady and powerful and lent itself to her shaping of phrase with a coherence and force that made her singing impressively eloquent), the sometimes steely-voiced Ljuba Welitsch, Maria Kurenko (who used a lovely voice well in music by Handel, Mozart, Cherubini, Berlioz and Musorgsky), Pierrette Alarie, and Suzanne Danco (Ansermet's Mélisande in his first, monophonic recording of *Pelléas et Mélisande*).

In Italian opera there were Renata Tebaldi (whose use of her beautiful voice was occasionally expansive to the point of self-indulgence), Graziella Sciutti, Herva Nelli (who, under Toscanini, sang with great purity and expressiveness), and later Mirella Freni (a fine Desdemona in *Otello* and Micaela in *Carmen*, among other roles) and Beverly Sills (whose voice, except for an occasional edge and tremulousness, was agreeable to the ear and an instrument for her impressive security and musical style in spectacular and ornamented writing).

The Dutch soprano Elly Ameling sang principally *Lieder*, French songs and sacred music (an album of arias from Mozart's operas had her flawlessly phrased singing, but with a voice which never varied in timbre in all these utterances by different characters in different operas, with the result that they all sounded like the utterances of one character). Elisabeth Søderstrøm was outstanding in the 1970s and '80s in Janáček's operas and in songs by Schubert, Tchaikovsky, Musorgsky and Chopin. But the word sensational is the one to use about Eileen Farrell, whose voice and way of using it placed her among the greats of her time. She could be heard in Wagner's *Wesendonck* songs with Stokowski, excerpts from Cherubini's *Medea*, arias and duets by Gluck, Beethoven, Weber, Verdi and others, Dmitri Mitropoulos's recording of Berg's *Wozzeck*, and Toscanini's 1952 recording of Beethoven's Ninth Symphony.

The outstanding mezzos of the time were Christa Ludwig (a remarkable vocal actress and a fine singer of *Lieder*), Teresa Berganza and Giulietta Simionato (both of whom made recordings of Italian operas in which they exhibited superb style in ornamented cantilena and bravura rapid passages alike). The notable contraltos were Ebe Stignani, Kathleen Ferrier, Cloë Elmo, Nan Merriman, Fedora Barbieri (though her singing was sometimes tempestuous and unfocussed) and Elena Nikolaidi (a superb singing actress, even after her powerful voice had lost its former sensuous richness).

Among the tenors were Richard Lewis (I have heard no performance of *Total Eclipse* from Handel's *Samson* as affecting as his), Ian Partridge, Werner Krenn, Ernst Häfliger, Wolfgang Windgassen, Fritz Wunderlich (who used his beautiful voice simply, but also without expressive subtilties of inflection or rhythm), Alfredo Kraus [before the shocking ham acting of his later career], Jon Vickers (an outstanding Tristan, Radames, Otello and Don José, and the Aeneas of Colin Davis's recording of Berlioz's *The Trojans;* the earlier recordings offered his sensitive use of his lustrous voice, but the later ones had an additional expressive power that was overwhelming), Ramón Vinay, Cesare Valletti (who had something like the voice and style of Schipa), Giuseppe di Stefano (the possessor of a beautiful voice that he used for the most part in an irritatingly mannered style), and Carlo Bergonzi (the great Verdi tenor after Bjoerling, with a luster and ease of flow of voice, a sensitiveness and feeling for shape of phrase, and a grace and lilt of style reminiscent of Schipa's).

The uniquely great performance of Lensky's second-act aria in *Eugene Onegin,* in its vocal beauty and musical phrasing, has been, for me, the one recorded early in this century by Sobinov; and a close approximation of it was the one recorded shortly before his death by Bjoerling; but Nicolai Gedda, at a Metropolitan performance in 1977, when he was in his fifties, manipulated a by then less beautiful voice than theirs with such skill, in phrases so marvelously imagined—in his pianissimo repetition of the piece's opening statement, his dwelling on the little figure whose repetition builds up to the piece's climax—that the performance, in the end, was one of those in which one was aware of having heard a great operation of extraordinary human powers. And this great vocal artist with the remarkable voice—astonishing in its continuing brightness, steadiness and power after thirty years—used it in a range of opera and song (Bach, Mozart, Donizetti, Berlioz, Richard Strauss, operetta) that was itself astonishing.

Also singing at the time were the marvelous counter-tenor Russell Oberlin, and Hugues Cuénod—whose musical intelligence and unusual and affecting tenor voice brought life to Couperin's motets and Tenebrae Services, sixteenth- and seventeenth-century songs and Schubert *Lieder*. And there were the baritones Tito Gobbi, Giuseppe Valdengo, Rolando Panerai, Ettore Bastianini, Eberhard Wächter (the Don in Giulini's *Don Giovanni*), Leonard Warren and the superb Mack Harrell (who could be heard in Berg's *Wozzeck* with Farrell and in Stravinsky's first recording of *The Rake's Progress*); the bass-baritones Paul Schöffler and George London (a distinguished artist with a magnificent voice, whose fine record of Musorgsky's *Songs and Dances of Death* was one of the few in those years to use the original Musorgsky texts); and the basses Jerome Hines (who also had a wonderful voice), Fernando Corena, Cesare Siepi, Giorgio Tozzi, Nicola Zaccaria, Otto Edelmann, Ludwig Weber, Gottlob Frick and, later, Nicolai Ghiaurov, and in Russia Mark Reizen.

Notable among the singers of the post-war period who sang *Lieder* as well as opera was bass-baritone Hans Hotter, who left recordings of Schubert's *Winterreise* and *Schwanengesang* (with Gerald Moore), and of songs by Wolf and Brahms, that were made especially valuable by their vocal beauty, understatement and expressive point. In his later recording of *Winterreise*, Hotter's voice had a little less of its former beauty but remained an adequate medium for the art that achieved even more impressive results in some of the songs this time, with accompaniments by Erik Werba that were more effective than Moore's. (In his first recording, with Michael Raucheisen, Hotter lingered over and made too much of details in the music and in the text, and Raucheisen's playing of the highly significant piano part was subdued to the point of complete lifelessness and meaninglessness).

And the French baritone Gérard Souzay, in his performances of Schubert songs, used a voice that sounded more beautiful on records than the one I heard in the hall, and used it always with intelligence and expressive power (the accompaniments by Dalton Baldwin revealed this pianist to be one of those exceptional players—like van Bos and Rupp—with the special gift for creating continuous life around someone else's singing). And baritone Alfred Poell recorded albums of *Lieder* by Mahler,

Richard Strauss and Wolf in which he sang with vocal magnificence, musical intelligence and expressive projection.

However, when Dietrich Fischer-Dieskau's first recorded performances of German *Lieder* began to be heard in the early 1950s there was immediate recognition that his baritone voice—extraordinary in timbre and sensuous beauty—and his musical use of that voice with sensitivity and continuity in phrasing, placed him among the greats of this special field. Nevertheless, from the beginning there was also difficulty in understanding the occasional excessively vehement crescendo, overemphasizing its expressive point, that now and then broke through the limits of his coherent inflection of vocal line—for example, in his recording, with Moore in the early 1950s, of Schubert's *Winterreise*. What, in time, maturity added to vocal beauty and musical distinction in his performances of *Winterreise* could be heard in the version he recorded afterwards with Jörg Demus. But the one he recorded even later, again with Moore, revealed the beginning of vocal deterioration—the loss of bloom and glow, though not of distinctive and moving timbre; and his performances in the concert hall in the late 1970s revealed further losses: while the voice still retained its distinctive timbre in quiet passages, it lost it in forceful ones, the vehement crescendos now ending in hoarse shouts—and there seemed to be more of these outbursts than before.

The voice was at its best in the 1950s—in the Schubert and Wolf songs he recorded with Moore, Werba and Hertha Klust, in his first recording of Mahler's *Lieder eines fahrenden Gesellen* with Furtwängler, and in his first recording, with Kletzki, of Mahler's *Das Lied von der Erde*, whose songs, usually done by a contralto, he sang in a manner that made them sound as though they were intended to be sung only by him (unfortunately, the recording had the unattractive tenor voice of Murray Dickie in the other songs). Later Fischer-Dieskau recorded marvelous performances of four of Mahler's Rückert songs (and a lugubrious performance of the already excessively lugubrious *Kindertotenlieder*) with Karl Böhm. Fischer-Dieskau was outstanding also in the operas of Mozart and Beethoven—less as an overly vehement Count in *Figaro* than as Don Giovanni, Papageno in *The Magic Flute* and Florestan in *Fidelio* (especially in the early recordings conducted by Ferenc Fricsay) and as Don Alfonso in *Così fan tutte* (conducted by Jochum); he also sang the title role of Berg's *Wozzeck* with distinction. But astonishingly, the voice and art that were so overwhelming in all these did not work convincingly in Verdi.

Elisabeth Schwarzkopf, like Lotte Lehmann, was a very gifted singer, with a beautiful voice and the capacity for exquisite musical phrasing; and hearing her on records or in recital, one was every now and then held spellbound by a piece of flawless sustained singing. She was also a singer with a gift of dramatic projection, and one was often moved or charmed by that. But unfortunately these gifts, like Lehmann's earlier, served an inclination to ham; and in her hamming—her exaggerated pouting and pertness and archness, her gasps and whispers—Schwarzkopf was capable of lapses of taste even worse than Lehmann's—for example her singing and miming of Wolf's *In dem Schatten meiner Locken* at one recital in the style of Marlene Dietrich, or her fussing, pouting, gasping and whispering in her recording of Schubert's *Gretchen am Spinnrade* with Edwin Fischer, and even, so help me, in Verdi's *Requiem* with de Sabata.

In the singing of Maria Callas one heard an even stronger gift for dramatic projection. In her earliest recordings one also heard the extraordinary beauty of the voice Callas began with. But in some of them one heard in addition the reckless forcing whose cost to the voice was audible from the mid-1950s on—in its wobble, and its shrill and tremulous high notes that were sometimes indeterminate in pitch. Nevertheless, up to the end the voice continued to exert unusual compulsion with the strange and beautiful timbre of its lower range, and her singing continued to do so with its sovereign assurance and style, its powerful continuity of subtle inflection of phrase that conveyed a wealth of expressive point—humorous point in the case of Rossini's comic operas, dramatic or tragic point in the case of the serious operas of Verdi, Bellini, Donizetti and Cherubini.*

The singer who was talked of as Callas's successor was Joan Sutherland, though actually the impressive gifts she began with were not of that dramatic kind. Nevertheless, Sutherland's ear-

---

*Of the two versions of Callas's *Lucia* and *Norma*, the earlier monophonic performances are the ones to acquire, in preference to the later stereo versions in which the voice's deterioration is more evident. —B. H. H.

liest records—of arias by Donizetti, Bellini, Verdi, Mozart and others—did exhibit her breathtaking ease, accuracy, tonal brilliance and style in florid passages, and her musical phrasing of melody. However, her subsequent recordings offered her remarkable and at times spectacular control, but of a voice that was now attractively bright only in its upper range; and in place of the sense for shape of phrase and style that now operated only part of the time, there were the mannerisms that she indulged in the rest of the time—the little explosions of tone, the pathetic inflection of low notes in a mournful moaning that got to be monotonous, and which she did sometimes without regard for words that referred to joy and happiness.

In contrast, Montserrat Caballé, who sang much the same repertory, and who also had a high degree of security in florid passages, deployed her more agreeable soprano voice in sustained cantilena with a fine sense for emerging shape of phrase, for style, for dramatic expressiveness—and with results that were impressive and even exciting. And Marilyn Horne used a mezzo voice that was extraordinary in its beauty, range and power, its agility in florid passages, in a way that created a sensation when she first sang in Rossini's *Semiramide,* and that continued to be magnificent most of the time even with the later loss of some of the luster in its upper range.

Another soprano who caused a sensation when she first sang here was Birgit Nilsson, whose appearance in *Tristan und Isolde* at the Metropolitan in the 1959–60 season elicited comparisons with Flagstad. As one who heard Flagstad's first Isolde at the Metropolitan in 1935 I can testify that Nilsson's voice didn't have the unique voluminous luster that Flagstad's did, but that on that occasion it was a remarkably beautiful one, which produced even its highest notes as effortlessly as Flagstad's had, and which like Flagstad's was deployed in admirably shaped musical phrases. The beauty of the voice was reproduced by the recording of the first-act narrative and the *Liebestod* that Nilsson made around that time with Hans Knappertsbusch; and at a Metropolitan performance of *Tristan* in 1972 its cool, bright tone also sounded agreeable to the ear, and in moments of great amplitude acquired a glow and sheen. But in both of her recordings of the complete opera (and in her recordings of other works as well) I found the timbre not pleasant to listen to in spite of the voice's power and steadiness and accuracy.

The extraordinary ease, security and tonal beauty, and the expressiveness and taste, of Leontyne Price's singing at her best could be heard in her first recording of *Aida* (under Georg Solti, with Vickers), in her first two (RCA) recordings of *Il Trovatore* (of which I preferred the second, in spite of Zubin Mehta's too permissive conducting, because it had Placido Domingo's tenor in place of Richard Tucker's, and the lustrous baritone of Sherrill Milnes in addition), in her great performance of Berlioz's *Les Nuits d'été* with Reiner, and in *Porgy and Bess* with Skitch Henderson (an abbreviated version of the work, but one that contained all of its valuable music—which is to say the principals' songs and some of the choral passages—and which was better sung and more animatedly conducted than any other). Later Price's voice could sound strained and worn, as it did in *Così fan tutte* and *Carmen;* and in some of her recordings of arias and excerpts one heard a prolonging of notes with no concern for the resulting distortion of phrase.

The soprano Victoria de los Angeles's luscious voice was used to wonderful effect in operas by Rossini and Bizet and in a wide repertory of French, Italian and Spanish songs—all of which she made now moving, now delightful with her musical taste and her personal warmth and charm. By the time she recorded Purcell's *Dido and Aeneas* in 1965 the voice had deteriorated; but what remained was an agreeable-sounding medium for her subsequent performances of Spanish folksongs and Sephardic songs.

In Janet Baker's performances of German *Lieder,* French and English songs, and operas by Berlioz, Mozart, Gluck, Handel and others, one heard a remarkably beautiful mezzo-soprano voice and an operation of musical intelligence, taste and intensity of involvement that was very moving; her recording of Mahler's *Das Lied von der Erde* (with tenor James King and the Concertgebouw Orchestra under Bernard Haitink) was one of the best I could recall. However, the color of the voice turned out to be obtrusively wrong for Verdi's *Requiem* and Bellini's *I Capuleti e i Montecchi.*

Maureen Forrester's rich contralto could be heard in recordings of arias by Handel, and in Mahler's *Resurrection* Symphony (under Walter), *Des Knaben Wunderhorn* (with bass-baritone Heinz Rehfuss, conducted by Prohaska) and *Das Lied von der Erde* (with tenor Richard Lewis, conducted by Reiner).

Finally, Galina Vishnevskaya and Lois Marshall—two sopranos with voices that were not sensuously beautiful who used them to remarkable effect. Though Vishnevskaya's voice was at times tremulous and hard, it was much of the time an excellent instrument for her dramatically effective, expressive singing—in Tchaikovsky's opera *The Queen of Spades* (but not in her second recording of *Eugene Onegin*, conducted by Mstislav Rostropovich), in Tchaikovsky's songs (in which she was accompanied at the piano on separate recordings by Rostropovich and Benjamin Britten), and in songs by Musorgsky—particularly his *Songs and Dances of Death*, where her singing combined with Rostropovich's vivid playing of the piano part to create a tremendous performance.

Lois Marshall's voice by the 1970s no longer had the clear bright sound one had heard in Toscanini's 1953 *Missa Solemnis* [and in Bach's *St. Matthew Passion* and Handel's *Messiah* (both with Sir Ernest MacMillan), Schumann's *Frauenliebe und -Leben* (on a Melodiya ten-inch disc, with the accompanist Weldon Kilburn), and in arias by Bach, Bellini, Donizetti, Haydn, Purcell and others recorded with English orchestras in the fifties]. But its dark timbre at the end of her career was something one accepted willingly for the way she used it, with extraordinary tension and feeling for shape of phrase, in her recordings of *Winterreise* and *Die schöne Müllerin*, and in a broadcast recital of Wolf songs; moreover, she sang *Die schöne Müllerin* and the Wolf songs with the extraordinary ensemble pianist Greta Kraus, whose playing worked expressively with the music and sensitively not only with Marshall's every inflection but with her very act of singing—even with her breathing—to produce an ensemble operation that was unique and overwhelming.

Conductors Through the 1980s

And so we come to the great performers still active as this is written. After years of Bernstein conducting the New York

Philharmonic, Reiner conducting in Chicago, Szell in Cleveland, Charles Munch, Erich Leinsdorf and Seiji Ozawa in Boston, and Ormandy* in Philadelphia—and with Lorin Maazel's erratic tempos and Barenboim's tasteless italicizing and lack of even a crude feeling for orchestral balance still reverberating in my memory—it has been refreshing and heartening to find in Colin Davis a conductor and musician of outstanding powers operating with complete unself-conscious absorption and impressive efficiency in his task of getting an orchestra to produce effective and convincing realizations of whatever work he performs. So after his fine recordings over the years of Handel, Mozart, Beethoven, Berlioz and Verdi it was all the more surprising recently to hear his lethargically paced performance of *The Magic Flute* with the Dresden State Orchestra, and his ponderously stolid performance of Beethoven's Ninth Symphony with the Bavarian Radio Symphony.

Another refreshing and heartening experience has been Claudio Abbado's conducting of opera with, again, complete unself-conscious concentration on his task. The precision of attack and inflection have demonstrated his control and authority over an orchestra and his ear for orchestral sonority and balance; and the disciplined and impassioned shaping of the music has revealed his feeling for continuity in tension and shape—in particular the feeling for the *espansione* needed to give Verdi's music rhetorical effect, and the discipline that has held it within the limits of proportion and coherence. Consequently, it has been hard to account for Abbado's uneven operation in his performances of symphonic music, for the occasional deficiencies in musical judgment and taste, that have produced on the one hand admirably straightforward and effective recordings of Tchaikovsky's Second and *Pathétique* Symphonies, symphonies of Mahler, and

---

*As readers will have observed, Haggin admired Ormandy's superb accompaniment of concertos. And he once spoke of Ormandy's impressive mastery of the then new Cooke realization of Mahler's Tenth Symphony, which, he said, had merited the ovation Ormandy was given by both the Carnegie Hall audience and the orchestra. Haggin thought Ormandy's performances of the main symphonic repertory, however, were too ordinary to justify his being at the head of a great orchestra; and there was a time, in the late forties and early fifties, when Ormandy seemed to him to be exploiting the music he recorded to show off his orchestra's tone. —*Ed.*

works of Musorgsky that have included the first recorded performance, to my knowledge, of the composer's own version of *A Night on Bald Mountain;* and on the other hand the pulling-about of Tchaikovsky's Fourth and Fifth Symphonies that distorted the music's shape and expressive content.

Carlos Kleiber's recordings of operas (Verdi's *La Traviata,* Weber's *Der Freischütz,* Wagner's *Tristan und Isolde*) have also been extraordinary in execution and impact—in the expressive plasticity of the singing, and the amazing precision with which it has been held and fitted to Kleiber's plastic and expressive shaping of the music. His performances of symphonic music have been, for the most part, highly impressive, too, flawed only by occasional exaggerations of contrasts of loud and soft, and by a few unrelated changes of tempo within movements.

James Levine astonished audiences as a young American with performances of Verdi's operas that, like the older Abbado's, exhibited a feeling for the Verdi *espansione* and a discipline which maintained proportion and coherence. The years since then have brought performances of Mozart, Wagner, Smetana, Tchaikovsky, Stravinsky and Berg that have shown him to be as outstanding a conductor of their operas as of Verdi's. Levine is also an effective symphonic conductor (which not all great conductors of opera are)—or at least he is an effective conductor of Mahler, Dvořák and Stravinsky, for it must be remarked that his recordings of symphonies of Brahms and Tchaikovsky have suffered from some of Levine's misjudgments and changes of tempo.

Many of Georg Solti's operatic recordings—notably of Verdi's *Don Carlo, Un Ballo in maschera, Otello* and his *Four Sacred Pieces* (but not of his *Requiem*), Mozart's *Figaro* and *The Magic Flute* (and to a lesser extent *Don Giovanni*), Beethoven's *Fidelio* and Tchaikovsky's *Eugene Onegin*—have been superb, too; which is to say they have been free of Solti's usual excessive nervous tension and vehemence, and shaped with the sense for right tempo and for modification of tempo that many of his performances of symphonic works have lacked.

However, it was in Pierre Boulez's conducting that I first encountered again an operation on what I regarded as the genius level of Toscanini and Cantelli, as against what I had heard achieved by conductors as gifted as Colin Davis and the others. Boulez's complete grasp of the music and command of the orchestra, the marvelous sound of the wind chords, their precision of attack, shape and release, testified to his possession of an ear in balancing the orchestra and a power of magnetic compulsion as phenomenal as Toscanini's and Cantelli's, which produced a marvelous clarity of orchestral texture like theirs. And the complete adequacy, and never more than adequacy, of his unemphatic gestures for what they got the orchestra to do, made his the most impressive conducting operation since theirs. Moreover, this extraordinary playing was done in a musical progression in which every sound fell into place naturally and inevitably, a statement of the work that resembled Cantelli's in the way it seemed not to be produced by human effort but simply to come into being and assume its emerging shape of itself.

I speak of the unusual, restrained manner of Boulez's conducting in his first years in North America because of the misconceptions it led to—about the "metronomic approach and emotional tightness" of his "cool, literal performances" of nineteenth-century Romantic and eighteenth-century classical music, and the "rigidly controlled style" in which Boulez "put the score [of *Le Sacre*] through its paces like an ace equestrian directing a showhorse," which one read of in the *New York Times*. The reality was the contrary that one heard in his performances—the admirably shaped concert performances of Berlioz's *Romeo and Juliet* and *Les Nuits d'été*, Schubert's Fifth Symphony, Beethoven's Second, and Mozart's Piano Concertos K.453 and 467 with the Cleveland Orchestra, the one of Mozart's Symphony K.201 with the BBC Symphony that was enchanting in its plasticity and grace, the coherent, warmly expressive and beautiful-sounding statements of Brahms's *Haydn* Variations, Mahler's Third Symphony and Berlioz's *Damnation of Faust*, the clarity, continuity and tension of Stravinsky's *Le Sacre*, with the New York Philharmonic, and the similar performances of Handel, Berlioz, Debussy and Stravinsky on records. (What could be complained of was not the supposed rigidity, but the perversity that was the only conceivable explanation of Boulez's unprecedentedly slow tempos for the first and third movements of Beethoven's Symphony No. 5 in his recorded performance with the Philharmonia Orchestra.)

I had my first encounter with another conductor on the genius level when, in 1971, I heard the Boston Symphony with Michael Tilson Thomas, and I was astounded again by what had astounded me in the Boulez performances. I was in fact even more astounded this time, since it was someone so young whose extraordinary gifts produced those marvelous sounds and textures, those perfectly shaped progressions, that absolutely right exactness of statement.

Like Boulez, too, Thomas has made it known that he likes to hear music that he has never heard before—by Mouret, Stamitz, Richter and Filtz of the seventeenth and eighteenth centuries, by Liszt (his *Hexameron* for six pianos) in the nineteenth century, and by Ives, Ruggles, Berio, Cage, Wuorinen and Reich in the twentieth. And these odd musical interests have led him to apply his gifts not only to the great music worthy of them, but to music that is unworthy of them—something that has left one wishing that Thomas would be content to do what he was put on earth to do: produce the performances with which he imparts exciting new life to the great works of our musical heritage.

Fortunately he has done that, too—in superb recordings of Tchaikovsky's orchestral Suites, [the complete *Nutcracker* ballet] and his *Manfred* and First Symphonies, Debussy's *La Mer* and *Nuages* and *Fêtes*, Stravinsky's *Petrushka* and *Le Sacre*, and all of Beethoven's symphonies. (It should be observed that the unfailing rightness of pace and shape of his recording of Beethoven's *Pastoral* Symphony did not extend to the concluding phrases of retrospective summation, which can be slowed down slightly, but not, as in Thomas's performance, lingered over sentimentally; or in Beethoven's Seventh Symphony to Thomas's excessively slow tempos for the first and last movements, whose boring effect was increased by his taking more than the customary repeats.)

One of Thomas's unusual interests that others can share has been the music of George Gershwin. And an astounding experience, for me, was Thomas's recording with the New York Philharmonic of Gershwin's *An American in Paris,* in which he made prominent and significant detail after detail in the texture that until then had passed unnoticed. With the Buffalo Philharmonic he recorded a collection of the overtures to Gershwin's musical comedies—beautifully fashioned performances such as Gershwin and the audiences of his time didn't hear. And his performances of Gershwin's *Rhapsody in Blue* and *Second Rhapsody* with the Los Angeles Philharmonic offered what Thomas had arrived at as authentic texts of the works and realizations of them that, like that of *An American in Paris,* had for me the effect of clarifying revelation. (An earlier recording had Thomas's skillful combination of the original Grofé orchestration of *Rhapsody in Blue* with the passages for piano extracted from Gershwin's own Duo-Art piano roll of his arrangement of the piece for solo piano.)

In a *New York Times Magazine* article about the then twenty-seven-year-old Thomas, Leonard Bernstein was reported to have said to Thomas on one occasion, "You're *me* at that age"—which fortunately was not true. What Bernstein had in mind was the fact that the young Thomas, like the young Bernstein, had the gifts which enabled him, without rehearsal, to substitute effectively for William Steinberg in the second half of a Boston Symphony concert, as Bernstein had substituted for Bruno Walter in 1943. But with this similarity there are dissimilarities which make Thomas's operation and the performances it produces strikingly different from Bernstein's. And this difference provides an occasion to point out again that the mere possession of gifts—even gifts as impressive as Bernstein's—doesn't guarantee value in what they produce (as the even more impressively gifted Stokowski demonstrated before him). Gifts must be used; and value in the results depends on how they are used—more specifically, on whether the use is controlled by the discipline that is the rarest of artistic gifts, and the crucial one.

I recall a Bernstein concert performance of Mahler's Second Symphony years ago in which—at the point in the *Andante moderato* second movement where the lilting opening section returns with a new counter-melody of the cellos—Bernstein, giving all his attention to the counter-melody and visibly demonstrating his intense feeling about it, lingered over it without regard for the fact that the slowing down destroyed the lilt of the section and its forward momentum. This was one of the countless times then and in the years which followed when the lack of discipline evident in the platform exhibitionist's demonstration of his intense emotional involvement with the music showed itself also in details of performance that were not in coherent relation with their context.

The discipline I am talking about is what is usually referred to as taste; and the difference between Thomas and Bernstein is that Thomas's performances have exhibited an unfailing musical taste which the young Bernstein didn't have at the beginning and the older Bernstein didn't acquire.

Bernstein has tended to deal straightforwardly with modern works—though I must add that his recordings include a frenetically whipped-up performance of Stravinsky's *Le Sacre* and one of the *Firebird* Suite in which there is a lingering and melting over details, a fussing with exaggerated nuances of sonority and tempo, that I doubt Stravinsky would have found acceptable. And in the symphonies of Mozart and Haydn he has tended to accept the limits set by their style, and to produce fine performances without his usual distorting italicizing—though again, it must be noted that in his later performance of Mozart's Symphony K.543 with the Vienna Philharmonic the Andante is marred by fussy and sentimentalizing inflections of tempo and dynamics. But most of the standard repertory he has treated with no restraint on what has impelled him to distort the shapes of the works and their expressive effect.

After this, it is a pleasure to note the beautiful performances that have been offered on records by a few others—Andrew Davis's of Respighi's *La Boutique fantasque* and Fauré's *Requiem* and incidental music for *Pelléas et Mélisande;* Neville Marriner's of instrumental music of Bach, Handel, Vivaldi, Haydn, Mozart and others, and operas of Rossini; Sir David Willcocks's of choral music—notably Haydn's *Missa in tempore belli;* Bernard Haitink's of a wide range of the standard symphonic and operatic repertoire from Haydn, Mozart, Beethoven and Schubert through Mahler and Debussy; Klaus Tennstedt's of Mahler's First Symphony (not only one of the few outstanding performances of those I have heard him conduct, but one of the most expressively effective of all the realizations of this work) and of Mahler's Third

Symphony; and Rafael Frühbeck de Burgos's recording of *Carmen* (with Grace Bumbry—doing some of the best singing I have heard from her—and Vickers).

As for Riccardo Muti, his performances have demonstrated a sense for coherent shape and an ability to obtain phenomenal playing from an orchestra, but also a tendency to play what is marked *poco f* or *poco sfz* or *poco cresc.* as *molto f* or *molto sfz* or *molto cresc.*

Pianists Through the 1980s

Of the pianists the already legendary Sviatoslav Richter's performances of early Beethoven sonatas at his first recital in New York in 1961 showed him to be a superbly equipped musician and pianist, but did not justify the hysteria in Carnegie Hall or the extravagant estimates in the press: they offered precisely and beautifully executed realizations of well thought-out conceptions of the works, but not the largeness of expressive communication that one got from Schnabel's performances of Beethoven. Similarly Richter's playing in the Schumann Concerto at the time did not have the tonal beauty, musical distinction and projective force of Cliburn's, or the *affettuoso* warmth of Lipatti's or Fleisher's; and his performance of Bach's D-minor Concerto was a mere playing of the notes without enlivening inflection.

On the other hand he recorded a brilliant performance of Prokofiev's Concerto No. 1, and later an imaginatively vivid and technically outstanding performance of the original piano version of Musorgsky's *Pictures at an Exhibition,* in which the only defect was the strangely fast pacing of the Promenades that conveyed the image of the spectator running from picture to picture instead of sauntering. And similar playing—highly accomplished much of the time, but occasionally flawed by excesses of dynamics and tempo that don't justify themselves by the effect they give to the music—is heard on many of Richter's other records.

Maurizio Pollini, who in 1960, at the age of eighteen, recorded an extraordinarily beautiful performance of Chopin's Concerto No. 1 under Kletzki, disappeared for several years of further study, and reappeared later in performances that were operations on the highest level of instrumental mastery and insight. The special qualities of his performances—of Mozart's concertos, Beethoven's sonatas and concertos, [Schubert's sonatas] and works by Schumann and Chopin—are strikingly demonstrated by the differences in the ways Pollini and Vladimir Ashkenazy treat the *maestoso* opening pronouncements of Beethoven's Sonata Op. 111 and the *adagio espressivo* second subject of the first movement of Op. 109: Ashkenazy, to achieve the utmost in *maestoso*, slows down and distends the opening pronouncements of Op. 111 to the point where the distention distorts their shape and makes them ponderous and bombastic; whereas Pollini is content with their *maestoso* character in strict tempo. And for the utmost in *espressivo* Ashkenazy slows down the second subject in Op. 109 excessively to an *adagio* which is out of proportion to the *allegro* that precedes and follows it, and which makes the passage over-emphatic; whereas Pollini is content with the expressiveness of the passage in an *adagio* tempo in which its shape is related to the shape of what precedes and follows.

The over-intensified expressiveness and resulting distortion of shape, the unevenness, that are heard occasionally in Ashkenazy's otherwise superb performances—particularly in the later playing, which is at times sensitive and imaginative, at other times merely fluent or damaged by finicky inflection, oddities and excesses—are never heard in Pollini's: his playing, like Toscanini's conducting, is contained within perfect shape by an unfailing plastic sense. However, I must add that although Pollini plays the fugues of Beethoven's Sonatas Opp. 106 (*Hammerklavier*) and 110 effectively, Ashkenazy achieves an extraordinary clarification of their texture and structure in his recordings that I cannot recall hearing from anyone else. (As a conductor Ashkenazy is less impressive.) Furthermore, after Pollini's beautifully conceived and executed Beethoven concertos with Böhm and Jochum it was astounding to hear the even greater expressive force of Cliburn's grander statements in No. 3 that revealed so much more in what they stated.

Another outstandingly gifted pianist is Murray Perahia, who has recorded admirable performances of some of Beethoven's sonatas, Schumann's *Études symphoniques* and *Davidsbündlertänze*, Chopin's *Berceuse*, Preludes, Concerto No. 1 and Sonatas Nos. 2 and 3 (though again these last don't exhibit the power and tension of Cliburn's, nor the awareness of all that Cliburn's show his awareness of in the music—as, for example, in what Cliburn has his left hand do in the middle section of the Scherzo of No. 3).

But Perahia has also recorded performances in which at times he carries his sensitiveness to extremes of delicacy—as in the otherwise fine recording of Schubert's Impromptus, in which pianissimos fade into inaudibility, the one of Beethoven's *Appassionata* and Op. 10 No. 3 sonatas that is flawed by such occasional excessive delicacy, and the recordings of Mozart's concertos, many of which are made ineffective by the pallid sound and excessive understatement of the piano part, by the phrases that begin with a force that diminishes to barely audible whispered conclusions, and by Perahia's insufficiently animated tempos (e.g. for the last movement of K.488). In his recording with Radu Lupu of Schubert's Fantasia Op. 103 for piano four-hands and Mozart's Sonata K.448 for two pianos the Schubert is made ineffective by the moderating of its prescribed *Allegro molto moderato* tempo to the point where it is not *allegro* at all, [and the Mozart by their dainty playing of the piano]. (As for Lupu himself, he played admirably with Szymon Goldberg in their set of Mozart's violin sonatas, but apart from that recording Beethoven's music has elicited his best playing, with the vital energy that is lacking in his sensitive performances of other music; and even in Beethoven Pollini's and Perahia's performances reveal greater musical awareness: they hear more in the music and let us hear it.)

However, in contrast to Perahia's rarified playing in these pieces, one hears in his recordings of Beethoven's five piano concertos an operation of unfailing musical insight in the shaping of phrases with coherence and projective force—an operation sustained from first note to last, in fortissimo and pianissimo, with cumulative impact that becomes overwhelming. And to the effect of this operation is added the effect of its orchestral context—the wonderful playing of the Concertgebouw Orchestra paced and shaped by Haitink—to which Perahia's playing is in part a response.

Richard Goode's playing in Mozart's concertos is made outstanding by its combination of sensitiveness with the strong enunciation—sustained to the ends of phrases—that one heard in Schnabel's playing of Mozart but usually doesn't hear today. Goode's performance of Schumann's Fantasia Op. 17 also reveals the technical powers and musical insight of an exceptional pianist and musician. And equal to these are his performances of Schubert's sonatas—the long-needed good performances of the ones Schnabel did not record, and the admirable ones of those he did. That is, inevitably Goode's performance of the Sonata in B flat differs in style and expressive effect from the Schnabel performance; and one must have both. Schnabel's occasional overexcited hurrying in the first movement makes one welcome the steadiness of Goode's performance; but in the slow movement Schnabel's individual expansive style—which, as it enlarges the music's shape, enhances its expressive force—produces a more tremendous utterance.

Malcolm Bilson's remarkably perceptive playing gives effect to every happening in the music of Haydn and Mozart that he plays, unfortunately, on reproductions of the unattractive-sounding fortepianos of that period.

Sensitivity, plasticity and grace are heard also in Krystian Zimerman's performances of Mozart sonatas and works of Chopin—notably in his exquisite performances of the two Chopin concertos with Giulini (his recording of Chopin's Waltzes, however, is flawed, for me, by innovative details of tempo and dynamics that I find unconvincing).

Emanuel Ax achieves his strongly enunciating playing in Mozart's Piano Concertos K.466 and 482 without hindrance or stimulation by the Dallas Symphony under Eduardo Mata; but his subsequent performances of K.453 and 456 have the coarse-sounding, stodgy, insensitive playing of the St. Paul Chamber Orchestra under Pinchas Zukerman, which is one possible reason for the playing by Ax that hasn't his characteristic sensitiveness, grace and tonal beauty. Those qualities are heard in his excellent performances of Beethoven's *Eroica* Variations and *Appassionata* Sonata, and in Chopin's solo pieces and concertos (the latter with beautiful-sounding contexts provided by the Philadelphia Orchestra under Ormandy). Ax's recording of Schumann's *Fanta-*

siestücke illustrates two occasional failings of his: the tempos that are too fast for clarity in *Aufschwung, In der Nacht* and *Traumeswirren;* and in *Des Abends,* marked *p* throughout, the agitatedly impassioned statement he makes out of what seems to me a quietly mediative piece.

Finally, Michael Rogers, an American whose career was gravely damaged at the outset by the nonsense written about him in the *New York Times,* amazed and delighted me then and later with a technical mastery that operated in the service of first-rate musical intelligence and taste to produce superb performances of the music of Beethoven, Schubert, Schumann and others [performances which so far have yet to be put on records].

String Players, Chamber Groups, and Instrumentalists Through the 1980s

Ax's playing with Yo-Yo Ma made their recordings of all of Beethoven's cello sonatas singular events. The sound that Ma produced from his cello, and the musical style of his use of that sound, resembled Feuermann's: one heard the same refinement, even the same timbre, in the sound; the same unfailing rightness and elegance—astonishing in one so young at the time—in the shaping of the sound in phrase after phrase. And what he did was complemented at every point by the sensitive playing of Ax— notably in Op. 102 No. 2, in the long dialogue of the slow movement's middle section that attains the sublimity one hears in much of Beethoven's late writing, then in the piano's restatements of, and the cello's comments on, the meditative statements of the movement's opening section, and then in the raptly meditative transition to the cello's announcement of the theme of the work's concluding and less interesting fugue.

And what Ma achieved overwhelmingly in these works he achieves as well in his recordings of Haydn's Cello Concerto in D and of Schubert's great Quintet Op. 163, with the Cleveland Quartet [but not in the performances of Mozart's Divertimento K.563 with violinist Gidon Kremer and violist Kim Kashkashian, nor in their recording of Schubert's Quartet Op. 161 (with cellist

Daniel Phillips), which are damaged beyond even Ma's power to redeem them by the grotesque playing of Kremer].

Mstislav Rostropovich has recorded impressive performances of Dvořák's Cello Concerto and Tchaikovsky's *Variations on a Rococo Theme*. And some years ago Natalia Gutman recorded Boccherini's delightful Cello Concerto in D (with the Moscow Conservatory Chamber Orchestra under Mikhail Terian) with not only distinguished musical taste, but extraordinary grace and elegance.

The Cleveland Quartet in the 1970s and '80s was an ensemble of the first rank—four players of virtuoso caliber who operated with perfection of ensemble execution, beauty of balanced tone, unusual freedom in the shaping of the music with nuances of tempo and dynamics, and an expressive intensity that was very exciting—for example in Schubert's *Death and the Maiden* Quartet. However, this intensity also resulted at times in the excessive vehemence heard in the group's recording of Haydn's Op. 76 No. 2. Moreover, from the start the players had a tendency toward fast tempos that in some instances were damaging to the effect of the music: their record-breaking tempo in the fugal concluding movement of Beethoven's Quartet Op. 59 No. 3, for example— faster even than the excessively fast tempo of the Guarneri performance—was one in which the detail of the progression could not be heard even by a listener who knew the music well.

But the quartet produced superb performances of Haydn's Op. 64 No. 5, Schubert's Quintet Op. 163 (with Yo-Yo Ma) and his Octet for strings and winds Op. 166 (with assisting artists), and Beethoven's Quartets Opp. 18, 59, 74 (*Harp*), 95, 127 and 135. [In 1988 the first violinist, Donald Weilerstein, left the group; and at this writing, the re-constituted quartet has not made any recordings.]

From the start the Guarneri Quartet, the Cleveland's peer in North America, has performed at the highest level of instrumental virtuosity, tonal beauty, ensemble precision and musical understanding, but has revealed something less than flawless musical judgment. It has revealed this in three ways: in questionable details of tempo (e.g. the finale of Op. 59 No. 3 that is too fast, the third movement of Beethoven's Op. 130 that is too sluggish, and the finale of Schubert's Op. 161, marked *allegro assai*, that merely ambles along ineffectively); in its general tendency to slow down second subjects excessively; and in its occasional lapses of taste (e.g. the italicizing swells at the return of the opening three-note cello figure, marked *decrescendo*, in the Minuet of Schubert's Op. 29, the cellist's mannered statement of the second subject in the opening movement of Mozart's K.589, his slide in the slow movement of K.590, and the first violin's arch anticipatory retardations in the second movement of Beethoven's Op. 59 No. 3, before bars 42 and 49).

The Guarneri's performances of Mozart's six quartets dedicated to Haydn, Beethoven's so-called middle quartets and Schubert's *Trout* Quintet Op. 114 (with Ax) exhibit the fewest such defects, though as against the intense expressiveness of the Guarneri's recording of the Mozart works, I prefer the more contained expressiveness and elegance of style of the Budapest Quartet's performances of the 1950s.

The Orlando Quartet's performances of Haydn's rarely played and recorded masterpieces, the Quartets Op. 54 Nos. 1 and 2, are the first in years to be recorded by a group capable of giving effect in these works to Haydn's moment-to-moment unexpected varying of volume, melodic and harmonic direction, phrase length, and rhythmic grouping and accent. And they do as well with Nos. 4 and 6 of Op. 76. The Tokyo Quartet also has made a superb recording of several of Haydn's quartets—his Op. 20 Nos. 4 and 5 and all of Op. 76. And equally fine playing has been done by the Alban Berg Quartet in its recordings of all ten of Mozart's mature quartets and of Schubert's Quintet Op. 163 (with the cellist Heinrich Schiff). Other recordings to date by these three ensembles have been, in different ways and to varying degrees, less satisfying.

The two violinists today of the stature of Ma, Pollini, Ax and Perahia in their fields are Itzhak Perlman and Anne-Sophie Mutter. Some of Perlman's most beautiful-sounding and sensitive playing can be heard in his recordings of the concertos of Beethoven (with Giulini) and Tchaikovsky (with Leinsdorf), Beethoven's sonatas for violin and piano (with Ashkenazy) and

Tchaikovsky's Trio (with Ashkenazy and the cellist Lynn Harrell). Mutter began her recording career in 1979 while still in her early teens with a notable recording in which she played Mozart's Concertos K.216 and 219 with flawless tone and phrasing (and admirable support by von Karajan). [And her performances since then have been on a level with those first ones.]

Two other instrumentalists who stand out above the rest are the oboist Heinz Holliger, and the trumpet player Wynton Marsalis, who plays in Haydn's Trumpet Concerto (under Raymond Leppard), and in lesser works, with the remarkable beauty of tone, fluidity and ease, and musical sensitiveness that one heard in Dennis Brain's playing of the horn.

Singers Through the 1980s

This period has also had its remarkable singers: Among the sopranos, Jessye Norman's singing, now lovely, now not, now expressive, now not, is nevertheless extraordinarily beautiful at its best, as it is in Gluck's *Alceste* with Gedda and in Mahler's *Des Knaben Wunderhorn* with John Shirley-Quirk, conducted by Haitink. Renata Scotto sang the role of Desdemona in Levine's recording of *Otello* (with Placido Domingo and Sherrill Milnes) more expressively than anyone else I have heard (and with beautiful high notes in the first and fourth acts that she did not produce in the same period at the Metropolitan). Margaret Price's lovely soprano had the timbre of youth a few years ago that made her own Desdemona in Solti's recording (with tenor Carlo Cossutta and baritone Gabriel Bacquier) not only ear-ravishing but touching; and though one hadn't thought Price's voice suitable for Wagner's *Tristan und Isolde*, at microphone range it has sufficient amplitude in Carlos Kleiber's superb recording of the work.

Judith Blegen has contributed her marvelously beautiful, crystalline singing to recordings of both opera and oratorio. Lovely singing has been done as well by Ruth Welting, Felicity Palmer, Margaret Marshall, Christiane Eda-Pierre, Agnes Baltsa, Ileana Cotrubas, Martina Arroyo, Kiri Te Kanawa, Lucia Popp, Lucia Valentini-Terrani, and Katia Ricciarelli. And Netania Davrath made a recording of Musorgsky's *Songs and Dances of Death* (with Erik Werba) in which every expressive point of the subtly inflected vocal declamation was admirably realized.

Frederica von Stade's intelligent, musical use of her beautiful mezzo-soprano—notably in her characterization of Cherubino in *Figaro*—left one unprepared for her inexpressive performance on records of Berlioz's *Les Nuits d'été* (with Ozawa) and for her poor singing of arias by Rossini—the successions of phrases which begin with an exaggerated pianissimo, erupt into an exaggerated fortissimo, and end with a return to the exaggerated pianissimo.

The outstandingly beautiful and powerfully expressive tenor singing of this period has been that of Placido Domingo—almost exclusively in nineteenth-century opera. Such sensitive use of another beautiful tenor voice was what one heard from José Carreras early in his career (e.g. in von Karajan's recording of *Don Carlo*), but his later performances have offered an unvaryingly powerful sound that becomes tiresome.

A recording of Verdi's *I Masnadieri* conducted by Richard Bonynge had excellent singing by a tenor new to me, Franco Bonisolli. And a number of recordings have offered outstandingly fine performances of eighteenth-century opera and oratorio by Anthony Rolfe Johnson, good ones by Francisco Araiza in both opera and Schubert's songs, and by Stuart Burrows in an even wider repertory. Peter Schreier's effective use of his beautiful tenor can be heard in oratorio, opera and *Lieder*, but his singing at its best was heard on a 1972 recording of Schumann's *Dichterliebe*, where it benefited by the contexts Norman Shetler provided with his realizations of Schumann's important writing for the piano.

As for Luciano Pavarotti, his powerful tenor lacks the sensuous warmth and ease of flow required by nineteenth-century operatic *cantilena*, and it becomes constricted and otherwise unattractive as it rises. His remarkable accuracy in dealing with sensational high notes doesn't make the brassy, rasping sound of the voice or his insensitive use of it any more agreeable to my ear. But incredibly Levine obtained musically admirable singing from him in the title role of Mozart's *Idomeneo* at the Metropolitan, and if that performance is ever issued, the recording will contain the one distinguished achievement of Pavarotti's career.

Among the operatic baritones are Piero Cappuccilli, Yevgeny Nesterenko, John Shirley-Quirk and the exceptional Leo Nucci. Sherrill Milnes was the sumptuous-voiced Iago in Levine's recording of *Otello* with Domingo, and his voice retained its steadiness and power later when it no longer had its earlier luster and warmth. Benjamin Luxon used another magnificent baritone voice to impressive effect in recordings of songs by Musorgsky, among other things. But one has to report both Håken Hagegard's expressive use of a fine baritone voice in a distinguished performance of Schumann's *Dichterliebe* cycle (with Thomas Schuback) and his unenlivening use of a less beautiful voice a year later in Schubert's *Winterreise* (with Emanuel Ax).

The outstanding basses in this period have included Ruggero Raimondi, Bonaldo Giaiotti, Samuel Ramey and Gwynne Howell. Robert Lloyd's performance as Osmin in Colin Davis's recording of Mozart's *The Abduction from the Seraglio* is the best, in voice and comic gift, I have ever heard, though also, no doubt, because of Davis's perceptive conducting of these passages. Outstandingly fine, too, is José Van Dam's singing as Sarastro in von Karajan's later recording of Mozart's *The Magic Flute*. And in a number of roles, notably those in Wagner's music-dramas, James Morris uses a voice that is outstanding not only in its beauty but its power.

Jazz 1920s–1940s

A word, finally, about jazz performance—the creative jazz of the period from the 1920s through the 1940s. The jazz performances I call creative were the freely improvisatory "hot" ones by small groups of players—as against the well-oiled performances of written-out arrangements by large bands. In an early Louis Armstrong cornet solo one heard something similar to what is so exciting in a formal piece by Haydn or Berlioz: the moment-to-moment working of a mind, observed this time in the very process of creation and operating with inventive exuberance that is controlled by a sense for coherent developing form. Armstrong's recordings—first with his Hot Five and Hot Seven (1925–28), with Earl Hines at the piano (1928), and the later ones with large commercial bands—documented his playing and singing from the time when these operated in the framework and context of the integrated performances of the Hot Five and Seven that were still close to their New Orleans origins of group improvisation, to the time when a big band merely provided a plushy background for the solo entertainer who began with a sensitively ornamented trumpet statement of a current song hit, continued with an extravagantly free vocal treatment of it, and carried this to its climax in a final spectacular trumpet solo. And listening to the groups of performances together one can perceive how much better the Hot Fives and Sevens were, as wholes, than the performances of the Earl Hines combination, brilliant and exciting though these were; and also how much better Armstrong's own work was in those early performances, superb and beautiful though it was in later ones—e.g. the 1928 *Muggles* and *West End Blues* with Hines, the 1929 *I Can't Give You Anything but Love.* Within the framework and context of the Hot Five and Seven performances Armstrong's solos, no matter how impassioned, how fantastic, how breathtaking in their virtuosity, remained under control and completed their developing structure; but already in the performances with Hines the spectacular got to be formless at times, as in those series of ever higher high notes; and this was carried to its occasionally incoherent extreme in the concluding exhibitions of trumpet virtuosity of the 1929 performances.

Armstrong did some of his finest creative playing with singers—with Ma Rainey, Bertha Hill and most notably with Bessie Smith. Smith's recordings document the change in the material she sang—from the authentic blues with which she began as a Black folk singer, to the popular songs and novelty numbers of her later years as a vaudeville entertainer. They also documented the succession of jazz musicians who recorded with her—from Clarence Williams, the pianist of her first recording of *Down Hearted Blues* in 1923, pianist James P. Johnson, Armstrong, cornetist Joe Smith, clarinetist Buster Bailey, trombonist Charlie Green, tenor saxophonist Coleman Hawkins and others of Fletcher Henderson's band, to the group including trombonist Jack Teagarden, tenor saxophonist Chu Berry and pianist Buck Washington that played at her last recording session ten years later. But they documented no change in the magnificent voice and style: the long phrases with their powerful momentums and tensions and wonderful inflections of rhythm and pitch that one heard at the beginning were heard all the way to the end, and exercised their effect in her every performance, no matter of what or with whom. Which didn't keep one from preferring the performances of the best music with the best players; and for me these were the *Cold in Hand Blues, You've Been a Good Ole Wagon, Reckless Blues* and *St. Louis Blues* that Smith recorded with Armstrong in 1925, and the *Baby Doll* and *Lost Your Head Blues* that she recorded with Joe Smith in 1926. Smith did some beautifully sensitive trumpet-playing around her singing; and Armstrong produced on muted cornet a progression of delicate, florid and derisive comment that got to be hilariously funny.

Another of the great cornet players of the time was Bix Beiderbecke. The one phrase of the late Otis Ferguson that has remained in my memory is his characterization of a Beiderbecke performance years ago: "as fresh and glistening as creation itself." It was more successful than my own attempts to describe what made the playing unique and, for some people, more exciting and moving than any other: "the unfailing continuity in the varied invention; the tensile strength of the continuous line of cornet sound, and at the same time its delicacy; the boldly soaring attack or rise to a high point, the sensitive fall away from this high point or at the end of a phrase." I find these terms inadequate; but I have no better ones now for what, in Beiderbecke's first phrase in *I'm Coming, Virginia* with Frankie Trumbauer's Orchestra, sends chills down my spine and brings tears to my eyes. This was one of many of his outstanding recorded performances—with Trumbauer's band in *Singin' the Blues, Clarinet Marmalade, Ostrich Walk,* and *Riverboat Shuffle,* and with his own group in *Jazz Me Blues, Sorry, Since My Best Gal Turned Me Down, Thou Swell* and *Ol' Man River*—the last two being examples of his wonderfully inventive "straight" playing of hit songs.

Beiderbecke played for a time in the brilliant band of Jean Goldkette (a small group of whose best players made up the Trumbauer band), and Beiderbecke can be heard in a chorus toward the end of their recording of *Clementine*. Later on he played in Paul Whiteman's band, in which one heard him at most for a full chorus, sometimes merely for a phrase, sometimes only in the background with the rest of the brass. But even the phrase detached itself from its dull surroundings as something exquisite and perfect; and even playing along with the others in the background he stood out from them, not through aggressiveness but solely through the distinctive quality of his style. I recommend *Lonely Melody, From Monday On* and *Sugar*.

Recording gives permanent life to these performances only as long as the records continue in print; and a number of outstanding performances have had their lives ended for long stretches of time by the discontinuance of, first, the original recording, and then of the reissues. There was a *Wild Man Blues* with Armstrong playing as part of clarinetist Johnny Dodds's Black Bottom Stompers that had an Armstrong cornet solo that was more controlled and less extravagant than the version he recorded the same year as leader of his own Hot Seven; but it is the latter that turns up in most Armstrong albums. And there were the superb performances by Armstrong and Teagarden at a 1947 concert in New York's Town Hall.

Extraordinarily beautiful invention by the trumpeter Buck Clayton and the clarinetist and tenor saxophonist Lester Young, both of the Basie Orchestra, were to be heard in the Kansas City Six's performances of *I Want a Little Girl* (Clayton and Young) and *Good Morning Blues* (Clayton). The trumpeter Charles Shavers did beautiful playing, with noteworthy contributions by Teddy Bunn on guitar, in *Wild Man Blues* with Johnny Dodds and His Chicago Boys and in the same group's *29th and Dearborn*. Another superb performance was trumpeter Bunny Berigan's *Tillie's Downtown Now* with Bud Freeman on tenor saxophone, Claude Thornhill at the piano, Grachan Moncur on bass, Eddie Condon on guitar and Cozy Cole on drums. [Enjoyable too were Red McKenzie's performances on kazoo with his Mound City Blue Blowers in *Hello Lola, One Hour* and *Fire House Blues*.]

Among the best performances of the pianist Fats Waller were *I Believe in Miracles, You're Not the Only Oyster in the Stew* and *Honeysuckle Rose*. There was the unique *Honky Tonk Train Blues* of pianist Meade "Lux" Lewis. Another fine pianist, Joe Sullivan, at his best in his solo recordings of *Gin Mill Blues* and *Honeysuckle*

Rose, played also with the cornetist Muggsy Spanier and the clarinetist Frank Teschemacher in several famous examples of the exciting Chicago ensemble style: the Chicago Rhythm Kings *There'll Be Some Changes Made* and *I've Found a New Baby,* the Miff Mole *Shim-Me-Sha-Wabble,* the McKenzie and Condon's Chicagoans *China Boy* and *Sugar,* and the Condon Footwarmers *Makin' Friends,* featuring the superb Teagarden. Later Spanier and his short-lived 1939 Ragtime Band recorded an outstanding series of performances that included *Dipper Mouth Blues, At the Jazz Band Ball, Riverboat Shuffle* and *At Sundown.*

Some of Jess Stacy's best solo piano playing could be heard in *Carnegie Jump, Carnegie Drag* and *I Can't Believe You're in Love with Me,* recorded with two groups of players brought together for the purpose. There was also his playing in Gene Krupa and his Chicagoans' *The World Is Waiting for the Sunrise,* with drums played by Krupa and string bass by Israel Crosby, after whom the same group's *Blues of Israel* was rightly named; *Blues of Israel,* in fact, was one of the finest improvised performances ever recorded, with outstanding contributions by Stacy and Crosby, Joe Harris, trombone, Nate Kazebier, trumpet, Dick Clark, saxophone and Allan Reuss, guitar.

Gene Krupa's Chicagoans was a small group drawn from Benny Goodman's first large band. Wonderful early performances by Goodman with his own small, especially assembled groups included the *Basin Street Blues* he recorded in 1931 with players who included Teagarden, *Texas Tea Party,* which he recorded in 1932 with Teagarden and Sullivan, *I Gotta Right to Sing the Blues,* and the masterpiece of the lot, *Moonglow,* recorded in 1933 with Teagarden again and the then great Teddy Wilson at the piano (this performance is not to be confused with the vastly inferior *Moonglow* recorded some years later by the Benny Goodman Quartet). Later in the 1930s Goodman, at the same time as he was recording performances of written arrangements with his large band, recorded improvised performances with Krupa and Wilson as the Benny Goodman Trio (Dave Tough sometimes replaced Krupa), of which *Someday,Sweetheart, Tiger Rag* and *Exactly Like You* were excellent. Later performances of what became the Benny Goodman Quartet suffered from the addition of Lionel Hampton's vibraphone and from the appalling deterioration in Wilson's playing, in which one heard him mechanically retracing the patterns of a style that originally had been created by living impulse.

As for Goodman's big bands, their performances were interesting only on the rare occasions when the noise was interrupted by improvised solos, for the most part by Goodman, as in *Stardust*, a second *Basin Street Blues* (Teagarden's trombone solo and the spirit of the entire performance made the earlier one superior), *St. Louis Blues, Alexander's Ragtime Band* and, best of all, *One O'Clock Jump* with Stacy.

A number of the best—i.e. the early (1927 to 1931)—Duke Ellington performances were those in which the band was still small (ten or twelve players), the arranged ensembles and backgrounds were still quite simple in harmony and style, leaving plenty of room for the soloists to play with freedom and at length, and the playing of the entire band had the relaxed freedom and vitality of jazz performance. Among these were the superb *Swanee Rhapsody, Swing Low* and *Ducky Wucky;* the outstanding *East St. Louis Toodle-oo, Wall Street Wail* and *Tiger Rag;* and the fine early *Black and Tan Fantasy* (the version originally on Victor) with Bubber Miley's trumpet-playing. Fine, too, were Jelly Roll Morton's *West End Blues* with his New Orleans Jazzmen, trumpeter Frankie Newton's *Blues My Baby Gave to Me* and the small Kirby Orchestra's *Undecided* and *It Feels Good* with Bailey, Shavers and the pianist Billy Kyle. The performances of Count Basie's Orchestra in *Good Morning Blues* and *Don't You Miss Your Baby* were worth hearing, too, for the distinctive style of Basie's piano-playing and for the extraordinary solos on muted trumpet of Clayton, who was heard also at the beginning of Teddy Wilson's *Can't Help Lovin' Dat Man* and immediately after Billie Holiday's affected singing of *He's Funny That Way*. And worth hearing as well were trumpeter Cootie Williams's *West End Blues;* the Henry Allen (trumpet) and Jay C. Higginbotham (trombone) *Indiana;* clarinetist Sidney Bechet's *Texas Moaner, Georgia Cabin* and *I'm Comin', Virginia;* and "Wild Bill" Davidson's *Ugly Chile, That Da-Da Strain, Panama* and *That's a Plenty*.

And the performances of Mildred Bailey—each made a delight by the exquisite inflection of the lovely small voice in phrasing whose subtle displacement of accents was controlled by a feeling for the shape of the phrase (as against the extravagant freedom with rhythm and notes in Billie Holiday's later singing that made what was sung no longer recognizable as the phrases of the song)—offered with Bailey's singing the exciting playing of small groups that at different times included Bailey's husband, Red Norvo, playing xylophone, Berigan and Shavers, trumpet, Buster Bailey, clarinet, Johnny Hodges and Russell Procope, alto saxophone, John Kirby, bass, and Mary Lou Williams, Kyle and Ellis Larkins, piano. And several performances recorded late in 1935—in particular *Someday, Sweetheart* and *Willow Tree*—were made especially notable by the fresh and richly inventive playing Teddy Wilson was doing at the time (1934–36). Wilson also contributed marvelous playing to Norvo's own *I Surrender, Dear, Blues in E flat, The Night Is Blue* and *With All My Heart,* and to the performances of *What a Little Moonlight Can Do, Miss Brown to You, I Wished on the Moon* and others that Wilson recorded at that early time with the young Billie Holiday.

If you wish to find out more about the jazz of this period, Wilder Hobson's *American Jazz Music* (Norton, 1939) offered the best introduction at the time to the jazz heard until the Second World War; [and if you want a formal, analytical and encyclopedic survey, two volumes by Gunther Schuller—*Early Jazz* (Oxford, 1968) and *The Swing Era* (Oxford, 1989)—will provide that].

29

Recorded Performances

INTRODUCTION

The subject of this chapter is some of the best, or best available, recorded performances of the music discussed in the earlier chapters of this book.

The first thing to mention about the choice of recordings is that it is selective: it doesn't evaluate all the performances of all the works of all the composers mentioned, which one person couldn't even hear; instead it limits itself for the most part to the best works discussed in Part One, although certain inferior compositions—by Wagner and Shostakovitch, for example—have been included for readers who want to judge their worth for themselves on the basis of a good recording. As well, certain eighteenth century and earlier pieces have been substituted for some of the ones mentioned in Part One that have been hard to find on records over the years.

This chapter limits itself further to mentioning only what seems to be the best performance or performances of each work. The recommendations of the best performances will reveal that in performance as in music a good critic does his own listening and evaluating and may reach conclusions which differ from those of other critics and from generally held opinion. Generally held opinion—whose effect was bad enough seventy years ago but has been enormously increased by present-day publicity media like record magazines and radio programs—regards all performances by well-known performers as valid, so that one can say that one pianist's performance of Chopin's G-minor Ballade is different from another's, but not that one is an effective realization of the piece of music and the other a monstrous distortion of it.

In the eyes of a record company any work it issues cannot be less than a masterpiece, and the musician who performs it is not only a great artist but exactly the right great artist for the work. Actually the company is out to sell records, and the records that sell are the ones made by the currently celebrated players, and of these a very small number indeed are what can be called great artists—that is, musicians who are endowed not only with fleet fingers but with musical understanding and taste and integrity. Moreover, even a great artist is not equally great in everything he or she does. A musician does better with the music of one composer than with another. For the music, if it amounts to anything, is not a mere spinning of notes, but in each case a product of human imagination and feeling; and musicians bring to these their own imagination and feeling, which may match better in one case than in another. But a record company that uses performers only because of the selling-power of their currently celebrated names is not concerned with what, if anything, they do well; and the result is instance after instance of poor matching of performer to music. It must be added that an artist who does well with a certain work in one recording may not do as well the next time, whether because of age or because of changes in temperament and taste.

The omission from this book of the names of many well-known artists does not, therefore, represent generally held opinion. It represents personal judgment, inevitably; but that does not mean that the recommendations will be arbitrary. We hear a piece of music as it comes to us through a player's mind; it sounds different as it comes through different minds; and we judge a performance by considering whether the character, the quality, the significance it imparts to the music is what our own understanding of the composer and the work leads us to believe correct.

However, your ears will be doing your listening for you. The recommendations in this book are given on the assumption that they have been asked for. Once you have read them, you are free to disregard them—to decide that you prefer someone else's records of certain pieces to the ones recommended here.

In the list below the best performance, reproduced adequately, is preferred to the poorer one that is reproduced with more beautiful sound, though in most instances if nothing is said about the recorded sound one may assume that it is satisfactory. In a few cases there wasn't space to list all of the outstanding performances of a piece; in others there weren't many to choose from, though more than in the days before it became so profitable to reissue old recordings. In general, the most recent outstanding performance is given, along with any from the past that are so remarkable as to belong in a basic library regardless of age (which is to say that only some, not all, of the recordings referred to in Chapter 28 are mentioned here). If a work has been recorded by a particular artist more than once, and if one of those performances is to be preferred, the names of collaborating artists or the date will serve to make it plain which one that is—e.g. "von Karajan, Berlin Philharmonic—*1962*" indicates that this particular Berlin Philharmonic recording of von Karajan's is preferable to his others with the same orchestra and to those with other orchestras. Monophonic recordings are set off in parentheses. One should not reject these out of hand: their sound, as reproduced on digital Compact Discs, is usually astonishingly more spacious, ample and warm than on earlier issues.

As for the omission of catalogue numbers, records today are so soon withdrawn and reissued under new numbers—in many cases by record companies other than the original ones—that the majority of these numbers soon cease to have any reference value. Consequently, the name of the record company is given here only for certain live performances in the public domain that have been issued in better sound by one company than another.

It has been pointed out, correctly, that lists such as this begin to be out of date the moment they go to the printer; it has been argued that they are therefore without value—which, however, is incorrect: the good performances mentioned below will remain good performances no matter what others are issued; a number have already become enduring classics of recorded performance. This doesn't mean that such a record will be the only one of a specific work to listen to years from now; but it does mean that it will be at least one of the ones to listen to—and perhaps the first. And although often recordings are deleted rapidly from the catalogues, many of them are re-issued frequently, also.

Thomas Hathaway / after B. H. Haggin

RECOMMENDED RECORDINGS (1991)

Composers are listed alphabetically by last name; a separate section at the end of this chapter lists some anthologies and collections of early music and English madrigals.

Key signatures are given only for works commonly identified that way; likewise with catalogue and opus numbers. In the case of composers whose works have been catalogued more than once, the catalogue number used in Part One of this book is given first, and the most commonly encountered alternatives after it.

Parentheses indicate an older, monophonic recording.

If two or more performances of the same piece are given, the listings are arranged in descending order of preference (the degree of difference may be slight). If there is no preference, the recordings are listed alphabetically by the name of the first artist named for each—e.g. Ashkenazy, Israel Philharmonic, Mehta; Pollini, Vienna Philharmonic, Böhm.

Albéniz

Ibéria for piano   Aldo Ciccolini; Alicia de Larrocha—*her later recorded performances are more mannered than her first one of the 1960s.*

Bach, C. P. E.

Keyboard Fantasia in C W.59 No. 6   Malcolm Bilson, fortepiano.
Magnificat   Ledger, Choir of King's College Cambridge, etc.

Songs—Canzone scordate (Gérard Souzay, baritone).

Symphonies Leppard, English Chamber Orchestra; Karl Richter, Munich Bach Orchestra; Geraint Jones, Little Orchestra of London; Pinnock, English Consort—*period instruments.*

Bach, J. S.

Arias, songs, and vocal excerpts Janet Baker.

(The) Art of the Fugue Ristenpart, Chamber Orchestra of the Saar; Helmut Walcha, organ; —*excerpts:* Glenn Gould, organ.

Brandenburg Concertos (6) Benjamin Britten, English Chamber Orchestra; Leppard, English Chamber Orchestra; Klemperer, Philharmonia Orchestra.

Cantatas Rilling, Gächinger Cantorei; Guest, St. John's College Choir; Willcocks, King's College Choir; Karl Richter, Munich Bach Choir.

Capriccio on the Departure of His Most Beloved Brother Igor Kipnis, harpsichord.

Chorales Rilling, Gächinger Cantorei.

Christmas Oratorio Rilling, Gächinger Cantorei.

Chromatic Fantasy and Fugue in D minor (Greta Kraus, harpsichord); (George Malcolm, harpsichord—*first recording, 1950s*); András Schiff, piano; (Wanda Landowska, harpsichord).

Concerto in D minor for violin or keyboard (Joseph Szigeti, violin, New Friends of Music, Stiedry); Glenn Gould, piano, Leningrad Academic Symphony, Slovak—*in preference to his recording with the Columbia Symphony and Bernstein;* (Wanda Landowska, harpsichord, with orchestra under Bigot); George Malcolm, harpsichord, with orchestras under Münchinger and, later, Menuhin.

Concerto in A minor for violin, or in G minor for keyboard Nathan Milstein, violin, with orchestra under Harry Blech; Glenn Gould, piano, Columbia Symphony, Golschmann; Arthur Grumiaux, violin, English Chamber Orchestra, Leppard.

Concerto in E for violin, or in D for keyboard Glenn Gould, piano, Columbia Symphony, Golschmann; Arthur Grumiaux, violin, English Chamber Orchestra, Leppard.

Concerto in D minor for two violins   Felix Ayo and Roberto Michelucci, with I Musici; Arthur Grumiaux, with Koji Toyoda and ensemble under Grumiaux, and, later, with Hermann Krebbers and members of the Orchestre de la Suisse Romande; Nathan Milstein and Erica Morini, with ensemble under Milstein.

Easter Oratorio   Münchinger, Stuttgart Chamber Orchestra, etc.; (Prohaska, Vienna Chamber Orchestra, etc.).

English Suites   András Schiff, piano.

Goldberg Variations   András Schiff, piano; Anthony Newman, harpsichord; (Wanda Landowska, harpsichord—*first recording, 1930s*); Glenn Gould, piano—*although his two recordings contain much that is musically unconvincing along with playing that is excitingly effective.*

Italian Concerto   (George Malcolm, harpsichord—*his first recording, 1950s*); Robert Wooley, harpsichord; Glenn Gould, piano.

Magnificat   Rilling, Gächinger Cantorei.

Mass in B minor   Rilling, Gächinger Cantorei, etc.; Klemperer, Philharmonia Orchestra, etc.; Karl Richter, Munich Bach Choir, etc.

Motets   Gardiner, English Baroque Soloists, etc.—*period instruments.*

Musical Offering—Ricercare   Münchinger, Stuttgart Chamber Orchestra; Marriner, Academy of St. Martin in the Fields.

Organ Music   Peter Hurford; (Anton Heiller); Lionel Rogg; Karl Richter; Helmut Walcha.

Partitas (6) for keyboard   András Schiff, piano—*with reservations about his mannered style in No. 1;* Trevor Pinnock, harpsichord—*with the same reservations; —No. 1:* (Dinu Lipatti, piano); Glenn Gould, piano; (Wanda Landowska, harpsichord—*her recording of the 1930s*).

Partitas and Sonatas for unaccompanied violin   (Joseph Szigeti); Nathan Milstein.

St. John Passion   Rilling, Gächinger Cantorei, etc.; Gardiner, Monteverdi Choir, etc.—*period instruments.*

St. Matthew Passion   Rilling, Gächinger Cantorei, etc.; Gardiner, Monteverdi Choir, etc.—*period instruments;* Karl Richter, Munich Bach Choir, etc.; Klemperer, Philharmonia Orchestra, etc.

Sonatas for flute and keyboard   Robert Aitken, with Greta Kraus, harpsichord.

Sonatas for violin and keyboard   James Buswell, with Fernando Valenti, harpsichord.

Suites for unaccompanied cello   (Pablo Casals—*his recordings of the 1930s*); Pierre Fournier; János Starker.

Suites, or Overtures, (4) for orchestra   Klemperer, Philharmonia Orchestra; Menuhin, Bath Festival Orchestra; Leppard, English Chamber Orchestra; Gardiner, English Baroque Soloists—*period instruments*.

Toccatas for keyboard   Fernando Valenti, harpsichord.

(The) Well-Tempered Clavier   Mieczyslaw Horszowski, piano; Glenn Gould, piano—*with reservations about his frequent perversities of tempo and touch*.

Bartók

Bluebeard's Castle   Ludwig, Berry, under Kertesz.

Concerto for Orchestra   Boulez, New York Philharmonic; Reiner, Chicago Symphony; Solti, Chicago Symphony.

Concertos (3) for piano   *Nos. 1 and 2*—Maurizio Pollini, Chicago Symphony, Abbado; *No. 3*—Vladimir Ashkenazy, Chicago Symphony, Solti.

Concerto for viola   (William Primrose, viola, New Symphony, Tibor Serly).

Music for Strings, Percussion and Celesta   Boulez, BBC Symphony; Reiner, Chicago Symphony.

Quartets (6)   Tokyo Quartet.

Rhapsodies (2) for violin and orchestra   (Emanuel Vardi, New Symphony, Tibor Serly).

Sonata No. 1 for violin and piano   David Oistrakh and Sviatoslav Richter; (Isaac Stern and Alexander Zakin).

Beethoven

Andante Favori for piano   (Artur Schnabel).

An die ferne Geliebte (song-cycle)   Dietrich Fischer-Dieskau.

Bagatelles Opp. 33, 119 and 126 for piano (Artur Schnabel);
Jacob Lateiner—*Op. 126.*

Choruses—Elegiac Song, Opferlied, Calm Sea and Prosperous Voyage
and *Bundeslied* Michael Tilson Thomas, London Symphony,
etc.

Concertos (5) for piano Murray Perahia, Concertgebouw Orchestra, Haitink; (Artur Schnabel, London Symphony Orchestra, Sargent); Maurizio Pollini, Vienna Philharmonic under Böhm and Jochum; Stephen Bishop-Kovacevich, BBC and London Symphony orchestras under Colin Davis; Vladimir Ashkenazy, Israel Philharmonic, Mehta.

Individual piano concertos No. 1—Glenn Gould, Columbia Symphony, Golschmann; *No. 2*—(William Kapell, NBC Symphony, Golschmann); Gould with Bernstein; *No. 3*—Van Cliburn, Philadelphia Orchestra, Ormandy; Gould with Bernstein; Radu Lupu, Israel Philharmonic, Mehta; *No. 4*—(Artur Schnabel, Chicago Symphony, Frederick Stock—*better orchestra and better recording than the older Sargent set*); Leon Fleisher, Cleveland Orchestra, Szell; *No. 5 (Emperor)*—(Schnabel with Stock—*same comment applies as for No. 4*); Cliburn with Reiner; (Gould, Toronto Symphony, Ancerl—*television broadcast, whose reproduction will vary with the company issuing the recording; the performance is enormously superior to the one Gould recorded with Stokowski*).

Concerto for violin Arthur Grumiaux with various orchestras and conductors, most notably the Concertgebouw Orchestra, Colin Davis; (Joseph Szigeti, with a studio orchestra—the so-called British Symphony—in his first recording, and the New York Philharmonic in his second, both under Walter); Nathan Milstein, Philharmonia Orchestra, Leinsdorf; Itzhak Perlman, Philharmonia Orchestra, Giulini; David Oistrakh, French National Orchestra, Cluytens.

Creatures of Prometheus—complete ballet Menuhin, Bath Festival Orchestra; Abravanel, Utah Symphony.

Fantasy in G minor Op. 77 for piano (Artur Schnabel).

Fidelio Behrens, Hofmann, under Solti; Dernesch, Vickers, under von Karajan; (Bampton, Peerce, under Toscanini); Ludwig, Vickers, under Klemperer.

Grosse fuge See: *Quartet Op. 133.*

Mass in C Guest, St. John's College Choir; Colin Davis, London Symphony Orchestra, etc.; Giulini, Philharmonia Orchestra, etc.; Beecham, Royal Philharmonic, etc.

Missa Solemnis (Toscanini, NBC Symphony, Milanov, Castagna, Bjoerling, Kipnis, etc.—*1940 concert performance, whose reproduction will vary with the company issuing the recording; the Music and Arts edition has acceptable sound*); (Toscanini, NBC Symphony, Lois Marshall, Merriman, Conley, Hines, etc.—*1953*); Jochum, Concertgebouw Orchestra, Giebel, Höffgen, Häfliger, Ridderbusch, etc.; Colin Davis, London Symphony, Tomowa-Sintow, Payne, Tear, Lloyd, etc.

Overtures (Toscanini); Colin Davis; Haitink; Maazel—*with the Israel Philharmonic.*

Quartets (16) for strings (Budapest Quartet—*1951–52*).

Individual string quartets
Op. 18 (6)—Cleveland Quartet; (Budapest Quartet—*Nos. 1–4, No. 6, and part of No. 5, all recorded in the 1930s and '40s*); *Op. 59 (3)*—Cleveland Quartet; Guarneri Quartet; Quartetto Italiano; (Budapest Quartet—*Nos. 2 and 3, recorded 1937, 1941*); *Op. 74 (Harp)*—(Budapest Quartet—1937); Cleveland Quartet; Guarneri Quartet; Quartetto Italiano; Weller Quartet; *Op. 95*—(Budapest Quartet—*1941*); Cleveland Quartet; Guarneri Quartet; Weller Quartet; *Op. 127*—(Budapest Quartet—*1942*); Quartetto Italiano; Yale Quartet; *Op. 130*—Quartetto Italiano; Fitzwilliam Quartet; *Op. 131*—(Budapest Quartet—*1940*); Quartetto Italiano; Yale Quartet; *Op. 132*—(Budapest Quartet—*1942*); Quartetto Italiano; Yale Quartet; Fitzwilliam Quartet; *Op. 133 (Grosse Fuge)*—Quartetto Italiano; Fitzwilliam Quartet; *Op. 135*—(Budapest Quartet—*1940*); Quartetto Italiano; (Toscanini, NBC Symphony strings—*Lento and Vivace*).

Quintet Op. 29 Guarneri Quartet with Zukerman; (Budapest Quartet with Katims—*1945*).

Serenade for string trio Op. 8 Grumiaux Trio; (Szymon Goldberg, Paul Hindemith, Emanuel Feuermann).

Sonatas (5) for cello Yo-Yo Ma and Emanuel Ax; János Starker and Rudolf Buchbinder; (Pablo Casals, with Mieczyslaw

Horszowski and Otto Schulhof—*1930s*); (Pierre Fournier and
Artur Schnabel); Mstislav Rostropovitch and Sviatoslav Richter.

Sonatas (32) for piano Claude Frank; (Artur Schnabel—*with
reservations about his occasional excessive distentions of phrase and
the occasional tempo that is too fast for clarity or accuracy*).
Individual piano sonatas
Op. 2 (3)—Vladimir Ashkenazy; *Op. 7*—Murray Perahia; Arturo
Benedetti Michelangeli; *Op. 10 (3)*—Vladimir Ashkenazy; *Op.
13 (Pathétique)*—Van Cliburn; *Op. 14 (2)*—Ashkenazy; *Op.
22*—Perahia; *Op. 26*—Ashkenazy; Sviatoslav Richter; *Op. 27
(2): No. 1*—Ashkenazy; *No. 2 (Moonlight)*—Cliburn; Radu
Lupu; *Op. 28 (Pastoral)*—Ashkenazy; (Edwin Fischer); *Op. 31
(3): No. 2*—Perahia; Maurizio Pollini; Stephen Bishop-
Kovacevich; Clara Haskil; *No. 3*—Perahia; Bishop-Kovacevich;
Haskil; *Op. 53 (Waldstein)*—Pollini; Emanuel Ax; Lupu; Ash-
kenazy; *Op. 57 (Appassionata)*—Cliburn; Ax; *Op. 78*—
Ashkenazy; *Op. 79*—Pollini; Ashkenazy; *Op. 81a (Les Adieux)*—
Cliburn; Perahia; Pollini; Ax; *Op. 90*—Ashkenazy; *Op. 101*—
Pollini; *Op. 106 (Hammerklavier)*—Ashkenazy; Pollini; (Glenn
Gould); *Op. 109*—Pollini; Alfred Brendel; *Op. 110*—Pollini;
(Edwin Fischer); Brendel; *Op. 111*—(Fischer); Jacob Lateiner;
Pollini.

Gould's 1967 broadcast performance of the Hammerklavier *Sonata—reproduced with acceptable sound in the Music and Arts
edition—is the only one of his Beethoven sonata performances that,
today, does not seem too wilfully distorted to be a valid statement of
the music. It has unusually slow tempos in the first movement that,
nevertheless, one can accept, some bizarreries in the trio of the
otherwise well-played second movement that one cannot accept,
uncommonly lyrical and involved playing—for Gould—in the great
third movement that is very moving to hear, and the most extraordinarily clarifying performance of any of the fugal finale.*

Sonatas (10) for violin (Fritz Kreisler and Franz Rupp); Itzhak
Perlman and Vladimir Ashkenazy; (Arthur Grumiaux and
Clara Haskil); David Oistrakh and Lev Oborin.
Individual violin sonatas (Fritz Kreisler and Sergei Rachmanioff

—*Op. 30 No. 3*); (Joseph Szigeti and Artur Schnabel—*Op. 24 (Spring) and Op. 96*); (Joseph Szigeti and Béla Bartók—*Op. 47, Kreutzer*).

Songs Fischer-Dieskau.

Symphonies (9) (Toscanini, NBC Symphony—*1949–1952*); Haitink, Concertgebouw Orchestra, and, earlier, with the London Philharmonic; Wand, North German Radio Orchestra; von Karajan, Berlin Philharmonic—*1960s*).

Individual symphonies *No. 1*—Michael Tilson Thomas, English Chamber Orchestra; *No. 2*—Solti, Chicago Symphony; *No. 3 (Eroica)*—(Toscanini, NBC Symphony—*1939 and 1953*); Colin Davis, BBC Symphony; *No. 4*—(Toscanini, BBC Symphony); Carlos Kleiber, Bavarian Radio Orchestra; Colin Davis, BBC Symphony; *No. 5*—Carlos Kleiber, Vienna Philharmonic; Michael Tilson Thomas, English Chamber Orchestra; Muti, Philadelphia Orchestra; *No. 6 (Pastoral)*—Michael Tilson Thomas, English Chamber Orchestra; Colin Davis, BBC Symphony; (Toscanini, NBC Symphony —*1941 concert performance, whose reproduction will vary with the company issuing the recording*); *No. 7*—(Toscanini, BBC Symphony—*1935*, New York Philharmonic—*1936*); Carlos Kleiber, Vienna Philharmonic; Guido Cantelli, Philharmonia Orchestra; Colin Davis, London Symphony; *No. 9 (Choral)*—Solti, Chicago Symphony, etc.; (Toscanini, NBC Symphony, etc.—*1938 concert performance, whose reproduction will vary with the company issuing the recording; the Music and Arts edition is excellent*).

Trios (11) for piano, violin and cello Stern, Rose, Istomin Trio.

Individual piano trios *Op. 1 No. 2*—(Alexander Schneider, Pablo Casals, Eugene Istomin); *Op. 70 No. 2*—(Schneider, Casals, Istomin); *Op. 97 (Archduke)*—Trio di Trieste—*1960s*.

Trios (3) for strings Op. 9 Arthur Grumiaux, etc.

Variations for piano *Thirty-two Variations in C minor*—(Artur Schnabel); Radu Lupu; Rudolf Buchbinder; *Eroica Variations Op. 35*—(Schnabel); Emanuel Ax; Buchbinder; Clifford Curzon, Louis Lortie; *Diabelli Variations Op. 120*—(Schnabel); Stephen Bishop-Kovacevich.

Bellini

Concerto for oboe   Heinz Holliger, Geneva Baroque Orchestra, Auberson.

Operas

(I) Capuleti ed i Montecchi   Gruberova, Baltsa, under Muti.

Norma   (Callas, Stignani, Filippeschi, under Serafin); Caballé, Domingo, under Cillario.

(Il) Pirata   Caballé, etc., under Gavazzeni.

(I) Puritani   (Callas, di Stefano, under Serafin).

(La) Sonnambula   (Callas, Cossotto, Monti, under Votto).

Arias and vocal excerpts by singers other than those mentioned above: Nicolai Gedda, (Lois Marshall), Zinka Milanov, (Lina Pagliughi), (Rosa Ponselle), (Tito Schipa), Beverly Sills, (Giulietta Simionato), Joan Sutherland, (Cesare Valletti).

Berg

Sonata Op. 1 for piano   Anton Kuerti.

Violin Concerto   Itzhak Perlman, Boston Symphony, Ozawa; Pinchas Zukerman, London Symphony, Boulez.

Wozzeck   Wächter, Silja, under Dohnányi; Fischer-Dieskau, Lear, under Böhm; (Farrell, Harrell, under Mitropoulos).

Berlioz

Béatrice et Bénédict   Eda-Pierre, Baker, Watts, Tear, under Colin Davis.

Benvenuto Cellini   Eda-Pierre, Gedda, under Colin Davis.

Choruses: Sara la baigneuse, Méditation religieuse, La Mort d'Ophélie   Colin Davis.

(La) Damnation de Faust   Colin Davis, London Symphony, Veasey, Gedda, Bastin, etc.; Prêtre, Orchestre de Paris, Baker, Gedda, Bacquier, etc.; Markevitch, Lamoureux Orchestra, Rubio, Verreau, Roux, etc.; Ozawa, Boston Symphony, Mathis, Burrows, McIntyre, etc.

(*L'*) *Enfance du Christ*   Colin Davis, London Symphony, Baker, Tappy, Allen, Bastin, etc.

Harold in Italy   (Toscanini, NBC Symphony, Carlton Cooley, viola—*1949 concert performance, whose reproduction will vary with the company issuing the recording*); Colin Davis, London Symphony, Nobuko Imai, viola; (Toscanini, NBC Symphony, Cooley—*1953*).

(*La*) *Mort de Cléopâtre*   Baker, London Symphony, Gibson; Pashley, English Chamber Orchestra, Colin Davis.

(*Les*) *Nuits d'été*   (Steber, orchestra under Mitropoulos); Baker, Philharmonia Orchestra, Barbirolli; Leontyne Price, Chicago Symphony, Reiner; de los Angeles, Boston Symphony, Münch; Norman, London Symphony, Colin Davis.

Overtures   Colin Davis; Münch; (Toscanini).

Requiem   Colin Davis, London Symphony, etc.; Münch, Boston Symphony Orchestra, etc.

Romeo and Juliet   (Toscanini, NBC Symphony, etc.); Colin Davis, London Symphony, etc.;   —*orchestral excerpts:*   (Toscanini, NBC Symphony).

Songs   Sheila Armstrong, (Eleanor Steber), (Maria Kurenko).

Symphonie fantastique   Colin Davis, Concertgebouw Orchestra; Boulez, London Symphony; von Karajan, Berlin Philharmonic; Haitink, Vienna Philharmonic.

Te Deum   Abbado, European Community Youth Orchestra and Chorus; Colin Davis, London Symphony, etc.

(*Les*) *Troyens*   Veasey, Vickers, etc., Royal Opera, Colin Davis; —*final scenes:*   Baker, London Symphony, Gibson.

Bernstein

Fancy Free—suite   Bernstein, New York Philharmonic.

Trouble in Tahiti   Williams, Patrick, under Bernstein; (Wolff, Atkinson, under Winograd).

Bizet

(*L'*) *Arlésienne—suites* (2)   Beecham, Royal Philharmonic; Gardiner, Lyons Opera Orchestra.

Carmen Bumbry, Vickers, under Frühbeck de Burgos—*with original spoken dialogue;* de los Angeles, Gedda, under Beecham—*with sung recitatives;* —*orchestral suite:* (Toscanini, NBC Symphony).

Jeux d'Enfants for piano duet Alfons and Aloys Kontarsky; Arthur Gold and Robert Fizdale.

Symphony in C Beecham, French National Radio Orchestra; Gardiner, Lyons Opera Orchestra.

Variations chromatiques for piano Glenn Gould.

Bloch

Quartet No. 2 (Musical Arts Quartet)

Quintet No. 1 for piano and strings (Johana Harris, Walden Quartet); Grant Johanessen, New World Quartet.

Schelomo János Starker, Israel Philharmonic, Mehta; (Emanuel Feuermann, Philadelphia Orchestra, Stokowski).

Voice in the Wilderness János Starker, Israel Philharmonic, Mehta.

Blow

Ode on the Death of Mr. Henry Purcell Deller Consort; (Russell Oberlin, Charles Bressler, New York Pro Musica).

Boccherini

Concerto in D for cello Natalia Gutmann, Moscow Chamber Orchestra, Terian; *the performance by Mstislav Rostropovich with the Zürich Collegium Musicum under Sacher may be good.*

Quartets—particularly Op. 6 Nos. 1 and 3, Op. 58 No. 2 (New Music Quartet); Quartetto Italiano; Carmirelli Quartet.

Quintets Carmirelli Ensemble; Academy of St. Martin in the Fields; Marlboro Festival ensemble under Carmirelli.

Trios Carmirelli Ensemble.

Symphonies Leppard, English Chamber Orchestra—*Op. 12;* Ephraikian, Filarmonici di Bologna—*Op. 35;* Caracciolo, Scarlatti Orchestra—*Op. 37.*

399

Borodin

In the Steppes of Central Asia   Markevitch, Lamoureux Orchestra.
Polovtsian Dances from Prince Igor   Ansermet, Orchestre de la
Suisse Romande; Mackerras, London Philharmonic; (Stokow-
ski, Philadelphia Orchestra).

Brahms

Academic Festival Overture   (Toscanini, NBC Symphony).
Concertos (2) for piano   No. 1 in D minor—Leon Fleisher, Cleveland Orchestra, Szell; Van Cliburn, Boston Symphony,
Leinsdorf; *No. 2 in B flat*—Rudolf Serkin, Cleveland Orches-
tra, Szell; Van Cliburn, Chicago Symphony, Reiner.
Concerto for violin   Arthur Grumiaux, Concertgebouw Orches-
tra, van Beinum; Nathan Milstein, Vienna Philharmonic, Jo-
chum; (Joseph Szigeti, Hallé Orchestra, Harty).
Concerto for violin and cello (Double Concerto)   (Mischa Mis-
chakoff, Frank Miller, NBC Symphony, Toscanini); Isaac
Stern, Yo-Yo Ma, Chicago Symphony, Abbado.
(Ein) Deutsches Requiem (German Requiem)   Klemperer, Philhar-
monia Orchestra, etc.
Handel Variations   ⎫
Haydn Variations   ⎬   *See: Variations*
Paganini Variations   ⎭
Serenade No. 1   Haitink, Concertgebouw Orchestra.
Songs (Marian Anderson), Janet Baker, Dietrich Fischer-
Dieskau, (Mattiwilda Dobbs), (Elena Gerhardt), (Hans Hotter),
(Alexander Kipnis), (Lotte Lehmann), Christa Ludwig, (Elis-
abeth Schumann), Elisabeth Schwarzkopf, Irmgard Seefried,
Benita Valente.
Symphonies (4)   Wand, North German Radio Orchestra; (Tos-
canini, NBC Symphony—*1951–52*); von Karajan, Berlin Phil-
harmonic—*1960s;* Klemperer, Philharmonia Orchestra.
Individual symphonies   No. 1—(Toscanini, NBC Symphony—
*1940 concert performance, whose reproduction will vary with the
company issuing the recording*); von Karajan, Vienna Philharmonic; (Cantelli, Philharmonia Orchestra); *No. 2*—Haitink,

Concertgebouw Orchestra; Kertesz, Vienna Philharmonic; *No. 3*—Cantelli, Philharmonia Orchestra; Abbado, Dresden State Orchestra; Kertesz, Vienna Philharmonic; *No. 4*—Carlos Kleiber, Vienna Philharmonic; Haitink, Concertgebouw Orchestra.

Variations on a Theme of Handel Van Cliburn; (Leon Fleisher).

Variations on a Theme of Haydn (Toscanini, New York Philharmonic—*1936*, NBC Symphony—*1952*); Abbado, Dresden State Orchestra; Haitink, Concertgebouw Orchestra; Giulini, Philharmonia Orchestra.

Variations on a Theme of Paganini John Lill; Victor Merzhanov.

Britten

Albert Herring Cantelo, Fisher, Pears, Evans, under Britten.

(A) Ceremony of Carols Guest, St. John's College Choir; Willcocks, King's College Choir.

Folk Song arrangements Benjamin Luxon.

(Les) Illuminations Eda-Pierre, Audoli Ensemble, Audoli; Pears, English Chamber Orchestra, Britten; Tear, Philharmonia Orchestra, Giulini.

(A) Midsummer Night's Dream Harwood, Harper, Brannigan, Pears, under Britten.

Peter Grimes Pears, Watson, under Britten; Vickers, Harper, under Colin Davis; —*Four Sea Interludes:* Giulini, Philharmonia Orchestra; —*Four Sea Interludes and Passacaglia:* Handley, Ulster Symphony.

St. Nicolas Willcocks, Academy of St. Martin in the Fields, Russell, Tear.

Serenade for Tenor, Horn and Strings Pears, Tuckwell, London Symphony, Britten; Tear, Clevinger, Chicago Symphony, Giulini.

(The) Young Person's Guide to the Orchestra Britten, London Symphony; Giulini, Philharmonia Orchestra.

Bruckner

Mass in E minor Mehta, Vienna Philharmonic, etc.; Wörmsbächer, Bergedorfer Chamber Choir, etc.

Symphonies (9) No. 4—von Karajan, Berlin Philharmonic; *No. 9*—Wand, North German Radio Symphony.

Te Deum (Forster, Berlin Philharmonic and St. Hedwig's Cathedral Choir, Giebel, Höffgen, Traxel, Frick); Mehta, Vienna Philharmonic and State Opera Chorus, Blegen, Lilowa, Ahnsjö, Meven; (Walter, New York Philharmonic and Westminster Choir, Yeend, Lipton, Lloyd, Harrell).

Bull

Harpsichord music   Thurston Dart; Trevor Pinnock.

Busoni

Concerto for piano   Garrick Ohlsson, Cleveland Orchestra and men's chorus, Dohnányi.

Byrd

Keyboard music   Thurston Dart, harpsichord; Davitt Moroney, harpsichord; Glenn Gould, piano.
Lute music   Paul O'Dette.
String music   Fretwork ensemble under Michael Chance.

Vocal music
(The) Great Service   Tallis Scholars; Cleobury, King's College Choir.
Madrigals   Deller and Wenzinger Consorts; Hilliard Ensemble; Ledger, Pro Cantione Antiqua.
Masses for Four and Five Voices   Tallis Scholars; Deller Consort; Guest, St. John's College Choir; Willcocks, King's College Choir.

Carter

Concerto for piano   Ursula Oppens, Cincinnati Orchestra, Gielen.
Sonata for piano   Charles Rosen; Paul Jacobs.

Quartets Composers String Quartet—*Nos. 1 and 2;* Juilliard Quartet—*No. 2.*

Cavalli

La Calisto (realized by Leppard) Baker, Cotrubas, Kubiak, under Leppard.
Giasone Dubosc, Banditelli, Chance, under Jacobs—*period instruments.*
Xerse Nelson, Feldman, Poulenard, under Jacobs—*period instruments.*

Chabrier

España Ansermet, Orchestre de la Suisse Romande.
Marche joyeuse Ansermet, Orchestre de la Suisse Romande; Jordan, ORTF Orchestra.
Suite pastorale Ansermet, Orchestre de la Suisse Romande; Jordan, ORTF Orchestra.
Dix Pièces pittoresques for piano Aldo Ciccolini.
(Le) Roi malgré lui Hendricks, Garcisanz, Gino Quilico, under Dutoit; —*Fête polonaise:* Ansermet, Orchestre de la Suisse Romande; Jordan, ORTF Orchestra.

Chant

See: Plainchant *in the* Music Before 1500 *section at the end of this chapter.*

Cherubini

Coronation Mass Muti, Philharmonia Orchestra, etc.
Medea Farrell, Turp, Flagello, under Gamson—*excerpts;* (Callas, Barbieri, Petri, under Gui—*1953 live performance, whose reproduction will vary with the company issuing it.*)
Quartets (6) Melos Quartet.

Requiem in C minor (Toscanini, NBC Symphony, etc.); Muti, Philharmonia Orchestra, etc.

Requiem in D minor Horst Stein, Orchestre de la Suisse Romande, etc.; Markevitch, Czech Philharmonic, etc.

Symphony in D minor (Toscanini, NBC Symphony); Boettcher, Philharmonia Orchestra.

Chopin

Andante Spianato and Grand Polonaise Op. 22 Krystian Zimerman; Emanuel Ax; Artur Rubinstein.

Ballades (4) Vladimir Ashkenazy; Emanuel Ax; Van Cliburn— *No. 3.*

Barcarolle (Dinu Lipatti); Murray Perahia; Van Cliburn; Vladimir Ashkenazy.

Berceuse Murray Perahia.

Concertos (2) for piano Emanuel Ax, Philadelphia Orchestra, Ormandy; Krystian Zimerman, Los Angeles Philharmonic, Giulini; Murray Perahia, Israel Philharmonic, Mehta.

Individual concertos No. 1—Van Cliburn, Philadelphia Orchestra, Ormandy; (Dinu Lipatti, Zürich Tonhalle Orchestra, Ackermann); Maurizio Pollini, Philharmonia Orchestra, Kletzki; Artur Rubinstein, New Symphony Orchestra of London, Skrowaczewski; *Concerto No. 2*—Vladimir Ashkenazy, London Symphony, Zinman.

Études Opp. 10 and 25 (12 each) Maurizio Pollini; Vladimir Ashkenazy—*his recording of the 1960s;* Louis Lortie—*with reservations about the metallic sound of the piano in the loudest passages.*

Trois nouvelles études Vladimir Ashkenazy—*his first recording, made in the 1960s.*

Fantaisie Op. 49 Van Cliburn; Murray Perahia; Youri Egorov.

Fantaisie-Impromptu Op. 66 Murray Perahia; Artur Rubinstein; Vladimir Ashkenazy—*with reservations about the fast tempos of the first sections.*

Impromptus (3) Murray Perahia; Artur Rubinstein; Mieczyslaw Horszowski.

Mazurkas Nikita Magaloff; Artur Rubinstein.

Nocturnes (21) Peter Katin; Vladimir Ashkenazy.

Polonaises (7)   Maurizio Pollini; Van Cliburn—*Polonaise Op. 53.*
Polonaise-Fantaisie Op. 61   Maurizio Pollini; Emanuel Ax; Vladimir Ashkenazy.
Preludes (24)   Nelson Freire; Garrick Ohlsson; Murray Perahia; Maurizio Pollini.
Scherzos   Vladimir Ashkenazy; Sviatoslav Richter; Van Cliburn—*Scherzo No. 3.*
Sonatas (3) *for piano*   *No. 1*—Vladimir Ashkenazy; *No. 2* (*Funeral March*)—Van Cliburn; Murray Perahia; Maurizio Pollini; Artur Rubinstein; *No. 3*—Cliburn; Perahia; Pollini; Rubinstein; (Dinu Lipatti); Emanuel Ax.
Sonata for cello   János Starker and Sigeo Neriki; Paul Tortelier and Aldo Ciccolini.
Songs   Teresa Zylis-Gara, with Halina Czerny-Stefanska; Elisabeth Søderstrøm, with Vladimir Ashkenazy.
Trois nouvelles études   *See after: Études.*
Waltzes   (Dinu Lipatti—*especially the Besançon Festival recital performance*); Artur Rubinstein; Peter Katin.

Copland

Appalachian Spring   Copland, Columbia Chamber Orchestra; Slatkin, St. Louis Symphony;   —*Suite:* Copland, London and Boston symphony orchestras.
Billy the Kid   Slatkin, St. Louis Symphony—*complete;*   Copland, London Symphony—*suite.*
Music for the Movies and *Music for the Theater*   Dennis Russell Davies, Orchestra of St. Luke's.
Rodeo—*complete:*   Slatkin, St. Louis Symphony;   —*suite:* Copland, London Symphony.
(*The*) *Tender Land:*   Clements, Cassilly, New York Philharmonic, under Copland—*abridged;*   Comeaux, Dressen, Orchestra of the Plymouth (Minnesota) Music Series, under Brunelle—*complete, but only adequately sung;*   —*orchestral suite:* Copland, Boston Symphony.

Corelli

Concerti Grossi (Società Corelli); Fasano, Virtuosi di Roma; I Musici; Marriner, Academy of St. Martin in the Fields; Gracis, Solisti dell' Orchestra Scarlatti; McGegan, Philharmonia Baroque—*period instruments*.

Cornelius

(The) Barber of Baghdad Czerwenka, Gedda, Schwarzkopf, under Leinsdorf.

Couperin, F.

Concerts Royaux for winds, etc. Heinz Holliger, with Aurèle Nicolet, Thomas Brandis, Christianne Jacottet, etc.

Harpsichord music George Malcolm; Rafael Puyana; Kenneth Gilbert.

Leçons de Ténèbres No. *1*—(Hugues Cuénod, with Daniel Pinkham); Nos. *1, 2* and *3*—(Hugues Cuénod, Gino Sinimberghi, etc.—*in which Cuénod's voice is more threadbare than in the earlier record of No. 1*); Judith Nelson, Emma Kirkby, etc.—*singing well but with less expressive force than Cuénod.*

Motets Isabelle Poulenard, Jill Feldman, Gregory Reinhart, under Davitt Moroney.

Pièces en concert for viola da gamba and figured bass Jordi Savall, Christophe Coin, Ton Koopman—*period instruments.*

Couperin, L.

Harpsichord music Albert Fuller; Davitt Moroney.

Dallapiccola

Tartiniana (Bernstein, Columbia Symphony).

Debussy

Orchestral music

Images for orchestra (*Gigues, Ibéria and Rondes de Printemps*) Boulez, Cleveland Orchestra; Michael Tilson Thomas, Boston Symphony; (Toscanini, NBC Symphony—*Ibéria*).

(*La*) *Mer* Michael Tilson Thomas, Philharmonia Orchestra; (Toscanini, Philadelphia Orchestra—*1941*); (Toscanini, NBC Symphony—*1950*); (Cantelli, Philharmonia Orchestra); Boulez, Philharmonia Orchestra; von Karajan, Berlin Philharmonic—*1960s;* Haitink, Concertgebouw Orchestra; (Koussevitzky, Boston Symphony—*with reservations about his disregard for the score in some instances*).

Nocturnes (*Nuages, Fêtes and Sirènes*) Michael Tilson Thomas, Philharmonia Orchestra; (Toscanini, NBC Symphony—*omits Sirènes*); (Cantelli, Philharmonia Orchestra—*omits Sirènes*).

Prélude à L'Après-midi d'un faune Boulez, Philharmonia Orchestra; (Cantelli, Philharmonia Orchestra); Haitink, Concertgebouw Orchestra; Michael Tilson Thomas, Boston Symphony.

Opera

Pelléas et Mélisande Spoorenberg, etc., under Ansermet; (Danco, Mollet, under Ansermet); Søderstrøm, Shirley, under Boulez; von Stade, Van Dam, under von Karajan; (Joachim, Jansen, under Désormière).

Piano music

Children's Corner Arturo Benedetti Michelangeli.

Études Garrick Ohlsson; Paul Jacobs.

Estampes Van Cliburn—*La Soirée dans Grenade* and *Jardins sous la pluie*.

(*L'*) *Isle joyeuse* Van Cliburn; Jane Coop.

Images for piano Arturo Benedetti Michelangeli; Van Cliburn—*Reflets dans l'eau*.

Preludes Arturo Benedetti Michelangeli; Jorge Bolet.

Suite bergamasque Garrick Ohlsson.

Quartet in G minor Guarneri Quartet; (Budapest Quartet—*1940*).

Delibes

Coppélia   Ansermet, Orchestre de la Suisse Romande; Bonynge, with the Orchestre de la Suisse Romande and the National Philharmonic.

Delius

Appalachia, Brigg Fair, Irmelin—prelude, Koanga—closing scene, North Country Sketches, Paris, Summer Night on the River, Walk to the Paradise Garden Beecham, Royal Philharmonic; (Beecham, London Philharmonic).
In a Summer Garden   Ormandy, Philadelphia Orchestra.

des Prés   *See:* Josquin

Donizetti

Anna Bolena   (Callas, Simionato, Rossi-Lemeni, under Gavazzeni); Sills, Verrett, Burrows, Plishka, under Rudel; Suliotis, Horne, Alexander, Ghiaurov, under Varviso.
Don Pasquale   Sciutti, Oncina, Krause, Corena, under Kertesz; Freni, Winbergh, Nucci, Bruscantini, under Muti.
(L') Elisir d'amore   Cotrubas, Domingo, Wixell, Evans, under Pritchard; Bonney, Winbergh, Weikl, Panerai, under Ferro.
Lucia di Lammermoor   (Callas, di Stefano, Gobbi, under Serafin); Caballé, Carreras, Ramey, under Lopéz Cobos.
Lucrezia Borgia   Caballé, Kraus, Verrett, Flagello, under Perlea.
Maria Stuarda   Sills, Farrell, Burrows, Louis Quilico, under Ceccato.

Arias and vocal excerpts by singers other than those mentioned above:
(Licia Albanese), (Jussi Bjoerling), (Fernando Corena), Nicolai Gedda, Marilyn Horne, Alfredo Kraus, (Tito Schipa), Cesare Siepi, Beverly Sills, Joan Sutherland.

Dowland

Lachrimae, or Seaven Teares   London Philomusica, Dart; Consort of Musicke, Rooley—*period instruments;* Dowland Consort, Lindberg—*period instruments;* Fretwork ensemble under Michael Chance—*period instruments.*

Lute Songs   Rogers Covey-Crump and Jacob Lindberg; Alfred Deller and Desmond Dupré; Russell Oberlin and Joseph Iodone; Nigel Rogers and Paul O'Dette.

Songs or Ayres   Hilliard Ensemble; Golden Age Singers, Bream; Consort of Musicke—*with reservations about the voices of the soprano and bass in their solos.*

Collections   Janet Baker; Hugues Cuénod; Peter Pears.

Dufay

Missa L'Homme armée   Hilliard Ensemble.
Missa Se la face ay pale   Early Music Consort, Munrow.
Chansons   Hilliard Ensemble.

Dukas

(The) Sorcerer's Apprentice   Ansermet, Orchestre de la Suisse Romande; (Cantelli, Philharmonia Orchestra); Levine, Berlin Philharmonic; (Toscanini, NBC Symphony).

Dunstable

Motets   Hilliard Ensemble.

Dvořák

American Suite   Michael Tilson Thomas, Berlin Radio Symphony.
Carnival Overture   Kertesz, London Symphony; Szell, Cleveland Orchestra.

Concerto for cello János Starker, London Symphony, Dorati; Mstislav Rostropovich, Berlin Philharmonic, von Karajan; Lynn Harrell, London Symphony, Levine; (Pablo Casals, Czech Philharmonic, Szell); (Feuermann, National Orchestral Association, Barzin—*this 1940 concert performance, issued on commercial records for the first time in 1990, was recorded later than the studio version with Taube that was on 78s*).

Czech Suite Jordan, Chamber Orchestra of Lausanne.

Gypsy Songs Op. 55 Peter Schreier.

Legends Kubelik, English Chamber Orchestra; Leppard, London Philharmonic.

Quartet Op. 51 (Budapest Quartet).

Quartet Op. 96 (American) Guarneri Quartet; (Budapest Quartet—*1940*).

Quintet Op. 81 Emanuel Ax with the Cleveland Quartet; Stephen Bishop-Kovacevich with Berlin Philharmonic Octet members; Clifford Curzon with the Vienna Philharmonic Quartet; (Clifford Curzon with the Budapest Quartet); Artur Rubinstein with the Guarneri Quartet.

Serenade for Strings Marriner, Academy of St. Martin in the Fields; Leppard, English Chamber Orchestra.

Serenade for Winds Schneider, Chamber Orchestra of Europe; Kertesz, London Symphony; Marriner, Academy of St. Martin in the Fields.

Slavonic Dances Opp. 46 and 72 Kubelik, Bavarian Radio Orchestra; Szell, Cleveland Orchestra.

Stabat Mater Kubelik, Bavarian Radio Orchestra, Mathis, Reynolds, Ochman, Shirley-Quirk, etc.

Symphonic Variations Kubelik, Bavarian Radio Orchestra; Colin Davis, London Symphony; Kertesz, London Symphony.

Symphonies No. 7—Colin Davis, Concertgebouw Orchestra; Levine, Chicago Symphony; Kubelik, Berlin Philharmonic; Andrew Davis, Philharmonia Orchestra; *No. 8*—Giulini, Chicago Symphony; von Karajan, Vienna Philharmonic—*1960s;* Kubelik, Berlin Philharmonic; Szell, Cleveland Orchestra; *No. 9 (From the New World)*—(Toscanini, NBC Symphony—*both the 1953 recording and the concert performance that preceded it; the last is excellently reproduced in the Nuova Era edition (a two-disc set with other less satisfactory material) and in the Virtuoso single-disc*

edition); Levine, Chicago Symphony; Colin Davis, Concertgebouw Orchestra.
Trio Op. 65 Raphael Trio; Kim-Ax-Ma Trio.

Egk

Quattro Canzoni Irmgard Seefried, Bavarian State Orchestra, Egk.

Von Einem

Concerto for piano Op. 20 (Gerty Herzog, Berlin Radio Symphony, Fricsay).

Elgar

Enigma Variations (Toscanini, NBC Symphony—*1951*); Solti, Chicago Symphony; (Toscanini, BBC Symphony—*1935*).

de Falla

(*El*) *Amor brujo* Marina de Gabarain, Orchestre de la Suisse Romande, Ansermet; Victoria de los Angeles, Philharmonia Orchestra, Giulini.
Nights in the Gardens of Spain Alicia De Larrocha, London Philharmonic, Frühbeck de Burgos.
Seven Popular Spanish Songs Marilyn Horne and Martin Katz.
(*The*) *Three-Cornered Hat—complete* Victoria de los Angeles, Philharmonia Orchestra, Frühbeck de Burgos; Jan De Gaetani, New York Philharmonic, Boulez; Teresa Berganza, Orchestre de la Suisse Romande, Ansermet; —*Suite:* (Cantelli, Philharmonia Orchestra).
(*La*) *Vida breve—Dance* Ansermet, Orchestre de la Suisse Romande; Lopéz Cobos, Cincinnati Symphony.

Farnaby

Harpsichord music Thurston Dart; Igor Kipnis; Trevor Pinnock.
Vocal music Deller Consort.

Fauré

Pelléas et Mélisande—incidental music Andrew Davis, Philharmonia Orchestra; Ansermet, Orchestre de la Suisse Romande; Marriner, Academy of St. Martin in the Fields; Irving, New York City Ballet Orchestra.
Pénélope Norman, Taillon, Van Dam, under Dutoit.
Requiem Cluytens, Paris Conservatory Orchestra, de los Angeles, Fischer-Dieskau, etc.; Ansermet, Orchestre de la Suisse Romande, Danco, Souzay, etc.; Andrew Davis, Philharmonia Orchestra, Popp, Nimsgern, etc.
Shylock—incidental music Irving, New York City Ballet Orchestra.

Franck

(Les) Éolides Cluytens, Belgian National Orchestra; Jordan, Basle Symphony.
Prelude, Chorale and Fugue Sviatoslav Richter; (Alfred Cortot).
Psyché—complete Fournet, Prague Symphony; (van Otterloo, Hague Philharmonic); —*Section 4 (Psyché and Eros)*: Giulini, Philharmonia Orchestra; (Toscanini, NBC Symphony).
Quartet Fitzwilliam Quartet.
Quintet (Clifford Curzon and the Vienna Philharmonic Quartet).
Rédemption—Morceau symphonique Cluytens, Belgian National Orchestra; Jordan, Basle Symphony.
Sonata for violin Itzhak Perlman and Vladimir Ashkenazy.
Symphony in D minor Cantelli, NBC Symphony; Andrew Davis, Philharmonia Orchestra; (Toscanini, NBC Symphony—*both the 1952 performance and the one from 1940, which is acceptably reproduced in the Music and Arts edition*); (Beecham, London Philharmonic).

Variations symphoniques (Walter Gieseking, Philharmonia Orchestra, von Karajan); Leon Fleisher, Cleveland Orchestra, Szell.

Gabrieli, A.

Motets for choirs, brass, strings and organ Gardiner, Monteverdi Choir, London Baroque Soloists and Philip Jones Brass Ensemble—*period instruments.*

Gabrieli, G.

Canzoni e sonate Philip Jones Brass Ensemble; London Cornet and Sackbutt Ensemble—*period instruments*; Canadian Brass with the Boston Symphony and New York Philharmonic Brass Societies.
Motets for choirs, brass, strings and organ Gardiner, Monteverdi Choir, London Baroque Soloists and Philip Jones Brass Ensemble—*period instruments.*
Symphoniae sacrae Taverner Choir; Ambrosian Singers, Denis Stevens.

Gershwin

Porgy and Bess Leontyne Price, Warfield, under Henderson—*abridged.*
An American in Paris Michael Tilson Thomas, New York Philharmonic; (Toscanini, NBC Symphony).
Rhapsody in Blue Michael Tilson Thomas, pianist and conductor, Los Angeles Philharmonic; Gershwin (*from a piano roll*), Columbia Jazz Band, Michael Tilson Thomas; (Gershwin, piano, Paul Whiteman Orchestra—*abridged*).
Second Rhapsody Michael Tilson Thomas, pianist and conductor, Los Angeles Philharmonic.
Overtures Michael Tilson Thomas, Buffalo Philharmonic.

413

Gesualdo

Madrigals Gardiner, Monteverdi Choir; Rooley, Consort of Musicke; Robert Craft conducting various vocal ensembles.
Motets Gardiner, Monteverdi Choir.
Responsories Tallis Scholars; Deller Consort.

Gibbons

Anthems Deller Consort; Wulstan, Clerkes of Oxenford.
Harpsichord music Thurston Dart; Trevor Pinnock; Glenn Gould, piano.
Madrigals Pro Cantione Antiqua of London; Rooley, Consort of Musicke; Deller Consort; Hugues Cuénod.

Glinka

Russlan and Ludmilla—Overture Mackerras, London Philharmonic.
Songs Jennie Tourel; Galina Vishnevskaya.

Gluck

Alceste Norman, Gedda, under Baudo.
Don Juan (ballet) Marriner, Academy of St. Martin in the Fields.
Iphigénie en Aulide Moffo, Augér, Fischer-Dieskau, under Eichhorn.
Iphigénie en Tauride Montague, Aler, under Gardiner; (Massard, Simoneau, etc., Aix Festival, Giulini—*with reservations about the shrill voice of Neway*).
Orfeo ed Euridice von Otter, Hendricks, under Gardiner—*1866 version based on Berlioz's revisions, sung in French;* Lorengar, Horne, under Solti—*"Berlioz" version, sung in Italian;* (Simoneau, Danco, under Rosbaud—*Gluck's own French version of 1774*); Janowitz, Fischer-Dieskau, under Karl Richter—*"Berlioz" version, sung in German;* Forrester, Stich-Randall,

under Mackerras—*Gluck's original version of 1762, sung in Italian;* —*Act 2:* (Merriman, Gibson, NBC Symphony, under Toscanini —*"Berlioz" version, sung in Italian*).

Arias and vocal excerpts by singers other than those mentioned above: Janet Baker, Eileen Farrell, (Kathleen Ferrier), Nicolai Gedda, Hilde Güden.

Gounod

Faust De los Angeles, Gedda, under Cluytens.

Griffes

(The) Pleasure-Dome of Kubla Khan Ozawa, Boston Symphony.
Poem Kathleen Rudolph, CBC Vancouver Orchestra, Bernardi; (William Kincaid, Philadelphia Orchestra, Ormandy).
Roman Sketches Leonid Hambro.
Sonata for piano Leonid Hambro.

Handel

Instrumental music
Alexander's Feast See: Concerto Grosso in C.
Concerto for oboe No. 3 Heinz Holliger, English Chamber Orchestra, Leppard; (Marcel Tabuteau, Philadelphia Orchestra, Ormandy).
Concertos for organ George Malcolm, Academy of St. Martin in the Fields, Marriner; Simon Preston, Bath Festival Orchestra, Menuhin.
Concertos for strings and winds Leppard, English Chamber Orchestra.
Concerti Grossi Op. 6 Menuhin, Bath Festival Orchestra—*with George Malcolm's imaginative continuo-playing;* Leppard, English Chamber Orchestra; Marriner, Academy of St. Martin in the Fields.
Concerto Grosso in C (Alexander's Feast) Leppard, English Chamber Orchestra.

Overtures, etc. Leppard, English Chamber Orchestra; Bonynge, English Chamber Orchestra.

Royal Fireworks Music Leppard, English Chamber Orchestra; Menuhin, Bath Festival Orchestra; Boulez, New York Philharmonic.

Sonatas (6) Op. 1 for violin and continuo Suzanne Lautenbacher, violin, Johannes Koch, viola da gamba, Hugo Ruf, harpsichord; Julian Olevsky, violin, Martin Ormandy, cello, Fernando Valente, harpsichord.

Suites for harpsichord Thurston Dart; Anton Heiller.

Water Music Menuhin, Bath Festival Orchestra; Dart, London Philomusica; Leppard, English Chamber Orchestra; (Hewitt Chamber Orchestra).

Vocal music

Acis and Galatea Gardiner, English Baroque Soloists, Burrowes, Rolfe Johnson, Hill, White, etc.—*period instruments;* Marriner, Academy of St. Martin in the Fields, Gomez, Tear, Langridge, Luxon, etc.

Alcina Bonynge, London Symphony, Sutherland, Berganza, etc.—*with reservations about Sutherland's mannered crooning much of the time; she sings the arias in fast tempo breathtakingly, however.*

Alexander's Feast Deller, Orianna Concert Choir, Sheppard, Worthley, Bevan, etc.; Gardiner, English Baroque Soloists, Brown, Watkinson, Stafford, Robson, Varcoe, etc.—*period instruments.*

(L') Allegro ed il Penseroso Willcocks, London Philomusica, Morison, Watts, Pears, Alan, etc.; Gardiner, English Baroque Soloists, etc. —*period instruments.*

Ariodante Leppard, English Chamber Orchestra, Mathis, Burrowes, Baker, Bowman, Ramey, etc.

Belshazzar Harnoncourt, Vienna Concentus Musicus, Palmer, Lehane, Esswood, Tear, etc.

Chandos Anthems Willcocks, King's College Choir; Mann, Rutgers University Collegium Musicum, Boatwright, Bressler, Held, Miller, etc.

Dettingen Te Deum Gönnenwein, South German Madrigal

Choir, etc.; (van der Horst, Netherlands Bach Choir, etc.); Preston, Westminster Abbey Choir, etc.

Dixit Dominus Willcocks, King's College Choir, Zylis-Gara, Baker, etc.; Preston, Westminster Abbey Choir, Augér, Dawson, etc.

Israel in Egypt Preston, English Chamber Orchestra, Gale, Watson, Bowman, Partridge, etc.; Gardiner, English Baroque Soloists, Robson, Dawson, von Otter, Chance, etc.—*period instruments.*

Jephtha Marriner, Academy of St. Martin in the Fields, Margaret Marshall, Kirkby, Hodgeson, Esswood, Rolfe Johnson, Keyte, etc.; Gardiner, English Baroque Soloists, vocal soloists, etc.—*period instruments.*

Judas Maccabaeus Mackerras, English Chamber Orchestra, Palmer, Baker, Davies, Shirley-Quirk, etc.

Julius Caesar (Giulio Cesare) Rudel, New York City Opera, Sills, Forrester, Wolff, Treigle, etc.

(The) Messiah Colin Davis, London Symphony Orchestra, Harper, Watts, Wakefield, Shirley-Quirk, etc.; Leppard, English Chamber Orchestra, Palmer, Watts, Davies, Shirley-Quirk, etc.; *(Mackerras's otherwise good performance is spoiled by Harwood's and Esswood's poor singing; however, Baker's great singing in it—notably in* He Was Despised—*can be heard on the album of excerpts.)*

Ode for St. Cecilia's Day Willcocks, King's College Choir, Cantelo, Partridge, etc.; Ledger, King's College Choir, Gomez, Tear, etc.

Roman Vespers Philadelphia Concerto Soloists Chamber Orchestra, Blegen, Valente, Forrester, Garrison, Cheek, Korn.

Samson Leppard, English Chamber Orchestra, Baker, Watts, Tear, Shirley-Quirk, Luxon, etc.; Karl Richter, Munich Bach Orchestra, Young, Arroyo, Stewart, Flagello, etc.

Saul Mackerras, English Chamber Orchestra, Margaret Price, Armstrong, Davies, McIntyre, Dean, etc.

Semele Somary, English Chamber Orchestra, Armstrong, Watts, Tear, Diaz, etc.; Anthony Lewis, New Symphony Orchestra, Vyvyan, Whitworth, Watts, Herbert, etc.

Solomon Gardiner, English Baroque Soloists, Watkinson, Argenta, Hendricks, Rolfe Johnson, etc.—*period instruments;* Somary, English Chamber Orchestra, Armstrong, Palmer, Tear, Rippon, Diaz, etc.

Tamerlano Moriarty, Copenhagen Chamber Orchestra, Bogard, Killebrew, Simon, Steffan, etc.; Gardiner, English Baroque Soloists, Argenta, Findlay, Ragin, Chance, etc.—*period instruments.*

Theodora Somary, English Chamber Orchestra, Harper, Forrester, Lehane, Young, Lawrenson, etc.

Arias and vocal excerpts by singers other than those mentioned above: (Isobel Baillie), Lisa Della Casa, (Kathleen Ferrier), Dietrich Fischer-Dieskau, Marilyn Horne, (Maria Kurenko), Richard Lewis, (Lois Marshall).

Haydn

Cantatas

Ariana a Naxos Janet Baker, Raymond Leppard, fortepiano.

Berenice che fai Janet Baker, English Chamber Orchestra, Leppard.

Chamber music

Quartets—variously (Budapest Quartet), Orlando Quartet, (Schneider Quartet), Tokyo Quartet, Quartetto Italiano, Berg Quartet, Guarneri Quartet, Griller Quartet, Allegri Quartet, Cleveland Quartet, Lindsay Quartet, Weller Quartet, Aeolian Quartet.

Trios (31) for violin, cello and piano Beaux Arts Trio.

Trios (3) Op. 53 for strings Arthur Grumiaux, etc.

Choral music

(The) Creation Jochum, Bavarian Radio Orchestra, Giebel, Kmentt, Frick, etc.; von Karajan, Berlin Philharmonic Orchestra, Janowitz, Fischer-Dieskau, Krenn, Wunderlich, Berry, etc.; Solti, Chicago Symphony, Burrowes, Wohlers, Morris, Greenberg, Nimsgern, etc.; Willcocks, King's College Choir, Harper, Tear, Shirley-Quirk, etc.

Mass No. 2 (Great Organ Mass) Preston, Christ Church Cathedral Choir, Nelson, Watkinson, Hill.

Mass No. 3 (St. Cecilia Mass) Preston, Christ Church Cathedral Choir, Nelson, Cable, Hill, Thomas.

Mass No. 4 (Missa in honorem Sancti Nicolai) Furthmoser, Vienna Boys' Choir, etc.

Mass No. 5 (Small Organ Mass) Grossmann, Vienna Boys' Choir, etc.

Mass No. 6 (Missa Cellensis, or Mariazellermesse) Guest, St. John's College Choir, etc.

Mass No. 7 (Mass in Time of War) Willcocks, King's College Choir, etc.; Kubelik, Bavarian Radio Orchestra, etc.; Guest, St. John's College Choir, etc.

Mass No. 8 (Heiligmesse) Guest, St. John's College Choir, etc.

Mass No. 9 (Nelson Mass) Colin Davis, Bavarian Radio Orchestra, Hendricks, Lipovšek, Araiza, Meven.

Mass No. 10 (Theresienmesse) Guest, St. John's College Choir, etc.

Mass No. 11 (Creation Mass) Guest, St. John's College Choir, etc.

Mass No. 12 (Harmoniemesse) Guest, St. John's College Choir, etc.

(The) Seasons von Karajan, Berlin Philharmonic, Janowitz, Hollweg, Berry, etc.; Colin Davis, BBC Symphony, Harper, Davies, Shirley-Quirk.

Te Deum Gillesberger, Vienna Boys' Choir.

Concertos

Concerto in D for cello Yo-Yo Ma, English Chamber Orchestra, Garcia; János Starker, Philharmonia Orchestra, Giulini.

Concerto in D for keyboard George Malcolm, harpsichord, Academy of St. Martin in the Fields, Marriner; Vasso Devetzi, piano, Moscow Chamber Orchestra, Barshai; Igor Kipnis, harpsichord, London Strings, Marriner.

Concerto in E flat for trumpet Wynton Marsalis, National Philharmonic, Leppard.

Opera

(La) Vera Costanza Norman, Donath, Ahnsjö, under Dorati.
(Dorati made good recordings of a number of the other operas, as well.)

Piano music
Sonatas (62) for piano Malcolm Bilson, fortepiano; John McCabe, piano; Gilbert Kalish, piano.

Individual piano sonatas
Sonatas in C Hob.48/L.58, C minor Hob.20/L.33, C major Hob.50/ L.60, and F Hob.23/L.38 Emanuel Ax.
Sonata in E flat Hob.49/L.59 Glenn Gould—*his first recording, of the 1950s.*
Sonatas in C minor Hob.20/L.33 and G minor, Hob. 44/L.32 Charles Rosen.
Variations, etc., for piano Malcolm Bilson, fortepiano; John McCabe; Gilbert Kalish.

Symphonies—in sets
Nos. 44–49 Janigro, Radio Zagreb Orchestra.
"Middle" symphonies Leppard, English Chamber Orchestra; Marriner, Academy of St. Martin in the Fields; Dorati, Philharmonia Hungarica.
Late symphonies Nos. 82–87—Bernstein, New York Philharmonic; Marriner, Academy of St. Martin in the Fields; *Nos. 93–104*—Colin Davis, Concertgebouw Orchestra; Jochum, London Philharmonic.
Individual symphonies
No. 77—Leppard, English Chamber Orchestra; *No. 82*—Colin Davis, Concertgebouw Orchestra; *No. 83*—Glover, London Mozart Players; *No. 84*—Glover, London Mozart Players; Colin Davis, English Chamber Orchestra; *No. 86*—Colin Davis, Concertgebouw Orchestra; *No. 87*—Colin Davis, Concertgebouw Orchestra; *No. 88*—(Toscanini, NBC Symphony); Glover, London Mozart Players; Colin Davis, Concertgebouw Orchestra; Jochum, Berlin Philharmonic; *No. 91*—Colin Davis, Concertgebouw Orchestra; *No. 92 (Oxford)*—Colin Davis, Concertgebouw Orchestra; Marriner, Academy of St. Martin in the Fields; *No. 93*—(Cantelli, NBC Symphony); Solti, London Philharmonic; *No. 94 (Surprise)*—de Almeida, Orchestra Sinfonico di Roma; Leppard, Scottish Chamber Orchestra; Casals, Marlboro Festival Orchestra; Marriner, Academy of St. Martin in the Fields; *No. 95*—Casals, Marlboro Festival Orches-

tra; Britten, English Chamber Orchestra—*concert performance, whose reproduction will vary with the company issuing the recording; No. 96 (Miracle)*—de Almeida, Orchestra Sinfonico di Roma; Solti, Chicago Symphony; Haitink, Concertgebouw Orchestra; Marriner, Academy of St. Martin in the Fields; *No. 98*—(Toscanini, NBC Symphony); Jochum, Berlin Philharmonic; Leppard, Scottish Chamber Orchestra; *No. 99*— (Toscanini, NBC Symphony); Solti, London Philharmonic; Haitink, Concertgebouw Orchestra; *No. 100 (Military)*—Solti, London Philharmonic; Marriner, Academy of St. Martin in the Fields; *No. 101 (Clock)*—(Toscanini, New York Philharmonic); Marriner, Academy of St. Martin in the Fields; *No. 102*—Solti, London Philharmonic; *No. 103 (Drum Roll)*—Solti, London Philharmonic; Marriner, Academy of St. Martin in the Fields; *No. 104 (London)*—von Karajan, Vienna Philharmonic—*1960s;* Kempe, Philharmonia Orchestra; Klemperer, Philharmonia Orchestra; Marriner, Academy of St. Martin in the Fields; (Beecham, London Philharmonic); (Edwin Fischer and his chamber orchestra).

(Glover and Solti are recording other Haydn symphonies, as well.)

Hindemith

(The) Four Temperaments   (Leon Fleisher, Netherlands Chamber Orchestra, Goldberg); Gordon Boelzner, New York City Ballet Orchestra, Irving; (Hans Otte, Berlin Philharmonic, Hindemith).

Mathis der Maler—symphony   (Cantelli, NBC Symphony); Steinberg, Boston Symphony; (Hindemith, Berlin Philharmonic).

Quartet No. 3 Op. 22   (Coolidge Quartet).

Sonata Op. 11 No. 4 for viola and piano   Kim Kashkashian and Robert Levin.

Symphonic Metamorphoses on Themes of Weber   Abbado, London Symphony; Ormandy, Philadelphia Orchestra; (Hindemith, Berlin Philharmonic).

Humperdinck

Hänsel und Gretel Cotrubas, Søderstrøm, von Stade, under Pritchard.

Ingegneri

Miserere Ensemble "A Sei Voce."
Officium Hebdomadae Sanctae (Responsories for Holy Week) Ensemble "A Sei Voce."

Ippolitov-Ivanov

Caucasian Sketches (Kletzki, Philharmonia Orchestra); Rozhdestvensky, Moscow Philharmonic; Abravanel, Utah Symphony.

Isaac

Motets, etc. Pro Cantione Antiqua of London; Hilliard Ensemble with the Kees Bocke Consort.

Ives

Symphonies Nos. 2 and 3 Michael Tilson Thomas, Concertgebouw Orchestra.
(The) Unanswered Question Michael Tilson Thomas, Chicago Symphony; Bernardi, CBC Vancouver Orchestra.

Janáček

(The) Cunning Little Vixen Popp, Jedlička, Randová, under Mackerras; *—orchestral suite:* Mackerras, Vienna Philharmonic; Andrew Davis, Toronto Symphony.
Jenůfa Søderstrøm, Randová, Ochman, under Mackerras.
Idyll Gerard Schwarz, Los Angeles Chamber Orchestra.
Katya Kabanová Søderstrøm, Kniplová, Dvorsky, under Mackerras.

Lachian Dances Zinman, Rochester Philharmonic.

Piano music Ivan Moravec.

Quartets Nos. 1 and 2 Gabrieli Quartet.

Sinfonietta Kubelik, Bavarian Radio Orchestra; Abbado, London Symphony; Ozawa, Chicago Symphony.

Slavonic (Glagolitic) Mass Kubelik, Bavarian Radio Orchestra, Lear, Rössl-Majden, Häfliger, Crass, etc.; Kempe, Royal Philharmonic, Kubiak, Collins, Tear, Schöne, etc.

Josquin des Prés

Déploration sur la mort de Johannes Ockeghem Hilliard Ensemble; Pro Cantione Antiqua of London.

Missa La-Sol-Fa-Re-Mi Tallis Scholars.

Mass and Plainchant Pange Lingua Tallis Scholars.

Missa L'Homme armée Tallis Scholars.

Motets and Chansons (incl. the Ave Maria à 4) Hilliard Ensemble.

Lalo

Symphonie espagnole Isaac Stern, Philadelphia Orchestra, Ormandy.

di Lasso (Lassus)

Masses Preston, Choir of Christ Church Cathedral; Venhoda, Prague Madrigal Singers; Turner, Pro Cantione Antiqua of London.

Penitential Psalms I–VII Preston, Choir of Christ Church Cathedral; Turner, Pro Cantione Antiqua of London; Hilliard Ensemble.

Leclair

Sonata Op. 9 No. 3 for violin Arthur Grumiaux, with István Hajdu, harpsichord.

Loeffler

(*The*) *Death of Tintagiles* Indianapolis Symphony, Nelson.
Pagan Poem Stokowski, studio orchestra; (Hanson, Eastman-Rochester Symphony).
Poem (Hanson, Eastman-Rochester Symphony).

Lully

Alceste—selections Curtin, Cuénod, under Straight.
Dies Irae Paillard Chamber Orchestra and chorus.
Grand Motet (*Miserere*) (Anthony Lewis, chorus, Ritchie, Morison, Deller, Richard Lewis, Herbert, Boyce); Paillard Chamber Orchestra and chorus.
Marches and Fanfares Maurice André, trumpet, Pierre Cochereau, organ, with a wind ensemble under Birbaum.
Te Deum Paillard Chamber Orchestra and chorus.

Lutoslawski

Concerto for Orchestra Ozawa, Chicago Symphony; Rowicki, Warsaw Philharmonic.

Machaut

La Messe de Nostre Dame Parrott, Taverner Consort and Choir.
Songs Page, Gothic Voices.

Mahler

Kindertotenlieder (Dietrich Fischer-Dieskau, Berlin Philharmonic, Kempe), and, later, with Böhm; (Heinrich Rehkemper, Berlin State Opera Orchestra, Horenstein); (Kathleen Ferrier, Vienna Philharmonic, Walter); Janet Baker, Hallé Orchestra, Barbirolli, and, later, Israel Philharmonic, Bernstein.
(*Das*) *Klagende Lied* Elisabeth Søderstrøm, Evelyn Lear, Ernst Häfliger, etc., London Symphony, Boulez—*original version;*

Heather Harper, Norma Procter, Ilse Hollweg, etc., Concertgebouw Orchestra, Haitink—*Mahler's revised version.*

(Des) Knaben Wunderhorn Jessye Norman, John Shirley-Quirk, Concertgebouw Orchestra, Haitink; Elisabeth Schwarzkopf, Dietrich Fischer-Dieskau, London Symphony Orchestra, Szell.

(Das) Lied von der Erde Dietrich Fischer-Dieskau, Murray Dickie, Philharmonia Orchestra, Kletzki; Janet Baker, James King, Concertgebouw Orchestra, Haitink; (Kathleen Ferrier, Julius Patzak, Vienna Philharmonic, Walter); Christa Ludwig, Fritz Wunderlich, Philharmonia Orchestra, Klemperer.

Lieder aus der Jugendzeit (Anny Felbermayer, Alfred Poell, with Victor Graef, piano); Janet Baker, with Geoffrey Parsons, piano.

Lieder eines fahrenden Gesellen (Dietrich Fischer-Dieskau, Philharmonia Orchestra, Furtwängler); Fischer-Dieskau, Bavarian Radio Orchestra, Kubelik.

Rückertlieder Dietrich Fischer-Dieskau, Berlin Philharmonic, Böhm; Janet Baker, Philharmonia Orchestra, Barbirolli, and, later, London Symphony, Michael Tilson Thomas.

Songs (miscellaneous) (Marian Anderson); Janet Baker; (Anny Felbermayer); (Kathleen Ferrier); Dietrich Fischer-Dieskau; Marilyn Horne; Christa Ludwig; (Alfred Poell); Irmgard Seefried.

Symphony No. 1 Tennstedt, London Philharmonic; Abbado, Chicago Symphony; Solti, Chicago Symphony; Kubelik, Bavarian Radio Orchestra; (Walter, New York Philharmonic); Walter, Columbia Symphony.

Symphony No. 2 (Resurrection) Kubelik, Bavarian Radio Orchestra, Mathis, Procter, etc.; Abbado, Chicago Symphony, Neblett, Horne, etc.; Klemperer, Philharmonia Orchestra, Schwarzkopf, Rössl-Majden, etc.; Walter, New York Philharmonic, Cundari, Forrester, etc.

Symphony No. 3 Michael Tilson Thomas, London Symphony, Baker, etc.; Levine, Chicago Symphony, Horne, etc.; Tennstedt, London Philharmonic, Wenkel, etc.; Kubelik, Bavarian Radio Orchestra, Marjorie Thomas, etc.

Symphony No. 4 Levine, Chicago Symphony, Blegen; Solti, Chicago Symphony, Te Kanawa; Kletzki, Philharmonia Orchestra, Loose; (Van Otterloo, Hague Philharmonic, Stich-Randall).

Symphony No. 5 Tennstedt, London Philharmonic; Levine, Philadelphia Orchestra.

Symphony No. 6 Abbado, Chicago Symphony; Haitink, Concertgebouw Orchestra.

Symphony No. 7 Abbado, Chicago Symphony; Haitink, Concertgebouw Orchestra.

Symphony No. 8 (Symphony of a Thousand) Haitink, Concertgebouw Orchestra, etc.; Kubelik, Bavarian Radio Orchestra, etc.

Symphony No. 9 Levine, Philadelphia Orchestra; (Horenstein, Vienna Symphony); Walter, Columbia Symphony.

Symphony No. 10 Levine, Philadelphia Orchestra; Ormandy, Philadelphia Orchestra—*both recordings are of the entire work— which is to say, of the Adagio that Mahler orchestrated himself and the rest that was completed by Deryck Cooke from Mahler's short score and his notations for the orchestration; Levine's recording of the Adagio, however, can be obtained separately.*

Marenzio

Madrigals Concerto Vocale, Jacobs.

Martinů

Symphonies Nos. 3 and 6 Järvi, Bamberg Symphony; Neumann, Czech Philharmonic.

Méhul

Symphonies (4) Gulbenkian Foundation Orchestra, Swierczewski. (*Étienne-Nicolas Méhul's (1763-1817) rarely played works remind one of Cherubini's by their unpredictability, and of Berlioz's by certain arresting turns of phrase and, on a smaller scale, by their instrumental colors.*)

Mendelssohn

Concerto for Violin in E minor Arthur Grumiaux, with various orchestras; (Joseph Szigeti, London Philharmonic, Beecham);

(Fritz Kreisler, Berlin State Opera Orchestra, Leo Blech); Isaac
Stern, Philadelphia Orchestra, Ormandy—*his second recording,
of 1960;* Nathan Milstein, Philharmonia Orchestra, Barzin.
(A) Midsummer Night's Dream—complete Kubelik, Bavarian Ra-
dio Orchestra; Marriner, Academy of St. Martin in the Fields;
—*excerpts:* Colin Davis, Boston Symphony.
Octet Laredo, Schneider, Steinhardt, etc.; I Musici.
Overtures Dohnányi; Abbado.
Songs Peter Schreier, with Walter Olbertz, piano.
Symphony No. 3 (Scotch) Abbado, London Symphony; (Tos-
canini, NBC Symphony—*1941 concert performance, whose re-
production will vary with the company issuing the recording; the
Music and Arts edition has acceptable sound*); Solti, Chicago
Symphony; Marriner, Academy of St. Martin in the Fields.
Symphony No. 4 (Italian) (Koussevitzky, Boston Symphony);
Leppard, English Chamber Orchestra; (Cantelli, Philharmonia
Orchestra); (Toscanini, NBC Symphony); Marriner, Academy
of St. Martin in the Fields.
Symphony No. 5 (Reformation) Bernstein, New York Philhar-
monic; (Toscanini, NBC Symphony).

Meyerbeer

(Les) Huguenots Sutherland, Tourangeau, Arroyo, Vrenios, under Bonynge—*with reservations about Sutherland's unattractive
voice and phrasing in* O beau pays *and* Tourangeau's *in* Nobles
seigneurs.
(Le) Prophète Horne, Scotto, McCracken, under Henry Lewis—
*with reservations about the constriction of Scotto's and McCracken's
voices in their high ranges.*

Milhaud

(La) Création du monde Bernstein, Orchestre National de
France; Milhaud, Champs-Elysée Theater Orchestra.

Monteverdi

(L') Orfeo Michael, Watkinson, Tappy, etc., Lyons Opera, Cor-
boz; Rogers, Bowman, Dean, Partridge, Reynolds, Hamburg

Monteverdi Ensemble, Jürgens—*period instruments;* Rolfe Johnson, Baird, von Otter, etc., English Baroque Soloists, Gardiner—*period instruments.*

Madrigals of Books III, IV, VII, VIII, IX, X Various singers and ensembles under Leppard.

Miscellaneous madrigals Monteverdi Choir, Gardiner—*period instruments;* Harper, English, Cuénod, Bath Festival, Leppard; Rogers, Partridge, Keyte, Hamburg Monteverdi Ensemble, Jürgens—*period instruments;* Consort of Musicke, Rooley—*period instruments;* Concerto Vocale, Jacobs—*period instruments.*

Vespers of 1610 Scheidt, Regensburg Cathedral Choir, soloists; Munrow, London Early Music Consort, Ameling, Burrowes, Tear, Rolfe Johnson, etc.—*period instruments;* Gardiner, Monteverdi Choir, soloists—*period instruments;* Jürgens, Monteverdi Choir of Hamburg, soloists—*period instruments.*

Morley

Madrigals Hugues Cuénod; Deller Consort; Hilliard Ensemble; Morley Consort; Peter Pears, Pro Cantione Antiqua of London; Nigel Rogers.

Mozart

Chamber music

Divertimento in E flat K.563 for violin, viola and cello Arthur Grumiaux, etc.; Trio Italiano d'Archi; (Pasquier Trio).

Quartets (4) K.285 for flute and strings Paula Robison and the Tokyo Quartet.

Quartet K.407 for horn and strings Jacky Magnardi, with the Danish Quartet; (Dennis Brain, with the Carter String Trio and Eileen Grainger).

Quartet K.370 for oboe and strings Heinz Holliger and the Orlando Quartet; (Marcel Tabuteau, with Isaac Stern, William Primrose and Paul Tortelier); (Harold Gomberg, with Felix Galimir, Gabriel Banat and Alexander Kouguell).

Quartets (2) for piano and strings   K.478 in G minor—(New York Quartet: Mieczyslaw Horszowski, Alexander Schneider, Milton Katims and Frank Miller); Artur Rubinstein, with the Guarneri Quartet; (Artur Schnabel, with the Pro Arte Quartet); *K.493 in E flat*—(Eugene Istomin, Isaac Stern, Katims and Mischa Schneider); (George Szell, piano, with the Budapest Quartet); Artur Rubinstein, with the Guarneri Quartet.

Quartets (10) for strings K.387–590   (Budapest Quartet—*1953–55*); Quartetto Italiano; Berg Quartet; Chilingirian Quartet.

Individual string quartets   K.387, 421, 458, 465, 499 and 590—(Budapest Quartet—*1933–49*); *K.421*—Yale Quartet; *K.499 and 575*—Guarneri Quartet; *K.575 and 590*—Weller Quartet.

Quintet in A K.581 for clarinet   Gervase de Peyer and the Melos Ensemble; George Pieterson, with Arthur Grumiaux and others; Eduard Brunner, with the Hagen Quartet.

Quintet K.452 for piano and winds   Murray Perahia, piano, with the English Chamber Orchestra Winds; Vladimir Ashkenazy, with the London Wind Soloists; James Levine, with the Vienna-Berlin Wind Ensemble; (Walter Gieseking, with the Philharmonia Wind Quartet—*in which Dennis Brain played the horn part; another recording with Brain two years earlier had his own good playing and that of his oboist brother Leonard, the clarinetist Stephen Waters, and the same bassoonist, Cecil James, but only adequate playing by the pianist, Colin Horsley*).

Quintets (6) for strings K.174–614   (Budapest Quartet with Milton Katims—*K.406–614, recorded 1945–51;* and with Walter Trampler—*K.174, recorded in 1957); Arthur Grumiaux, etc.;* Danish Quartet.

Sonatas (16) K.296–547 for violin and piano   Arthur Grumiaux and Walter Klien; Szymon Goldberg and Radu Lupu; *K.301, 305, 377, 380, 526*—(Joseph Szigeti and Andor Foldes); *K.481*—(Szigeti and Artur Schnabel). *Szigeti's recordings with Foldes and Schnabel are of concert performances; the reproduction will vary with the company issuing the recordings; the Music and Arts editions have acceptable sound.*

Trio in E flat K.498 for clarinet, viola and piano   Gervase de Peyer, Melos Ensemble.

Choral music

Ave, verum corpus K.618   Colin Davis, London Symphony, Te Kanawa, etc.

Exsultate, jubilate K.165   Kiri Te Kanawa, London Symphony, Colin Davis; Judith Blegen, Mostly Mozart Orchestra, Schwarz.

Kyrie in D minor K.341   Colin Davis, London Symphony, etc.

Masonic Cantatas   de Waart, Philharmonia Orchestra, Hollweg, Partridge, Dean, etc.

Mass No. 5 in C minor and C major K.139   Abbado, Vienna Philharmonic, Janowitz, von Stade, Ochman, Moll, etc.

Mass No. 8 in F K.192 (Missa Brevis)   Kegel, Leipzig Radio Orchestra, etc.

Mass No. 16 in C K.317 (Coronation)   Colin Davis, London Symphony, Donath, Knight, Davies, Dean, etc.

Mass No. 18 in C minor K.427 (the Great)   Gönnenwein, Southwest German Chamber Orchestra, Mathis, Erwin, etc.; Colin Davis, London Symphony, Donath, Harper, Davies, Dean, etc.

Requiem in D minor K.626   Colin Davis, BBC Symphony, Donath, Minton, Davies, Nienstedt, etc.; Guest, St. John's College Choir, Kenney, Walker, Kendall, Wilson-Johnson, etc.; Giulini, Philharmonia Orchestra, Donath, Ludwig, Tear, Lloyd, etc.; Marriner, Academy of St. Martin in the Fields, Cotrubas, Watts, Tear, Shirley-Quirk, etc.; Kertesz, Vienna Philharmonic, Ameling, Horne, Benelli, Franc, etc.; Schreier, conducting the Dresden State Orchestra, Margaret Price, Schmidt, Araiza, Adam, etc.; (Walter, New York Philharmonic, Seefried, Tourel, Simoneau, Warfield, etc.).

Vesperae solennes de confessore K.339   Colin Davis, London Symphony, etc.

Concertos for brass and winds

Concerto in B flat K.191 for bassoon   (Leonard Sharrow, NBC Symphony, Toscanini); Gwydion Brooke, Royal Philharmonic, Beecham.

Concerto in A K.622 for clarinet   Gervase de Peyer, London Symphony, Maag; Alfred Prinz, Vienna Philharmonic, Böhm; (de Peyer, London Symphony, Collins).

Concerto No. 1 in G K.313 for flute   Jean-Pierre Rampal, Vienna Symphony, Guschlbauer.

Concertos (4) for horn   (Dennis Brain, Philharmonia Orchestra, von Karajan).

Concertos for piano
No. 9 in E flat K.271   Vladimir Ashkenazy, London Symphony, Kertesz; (Walter Gieseking, Berlin State Opera Orchestra, Rosbaud); Murray Perahia, playing and conducting the English Chamber Orchestra; Maria João Pires, Gulbenkian Foundation Orchestra, Guschlbauer.
No. 12 in A K.414   Benjamin Britten, playing and conducting the English Chamber Orchestra; Murray Perahia, English Chamber Orchestra; Vasso Devetzi, Moscow Chamber Orchestra, Barshai; András Schiff, Salzburg Camerata Academica Orchestra, Vegh.
No. 13 in C K.415 (387b)   Murray Perahia, English Chamber Orchestra; Maria João Pires, Gulbenkian Foundation Orchestra, Guschlbauer; Malcolm Bilson, fortepiano, English Baroque Soloists, Gardiner—*period instruments.*
No. 14 in E flat K.449   Murray Perahia, English Chamber Orchestra; Maria João Pires, Gulbenkian Foundation Orchestra, Guschlbauer; (Rudolf Serkin, Busch Chamber Players); András Schiff, Salzburg Camerata Academica Orchestra, Vegh.
No. 15 in B flat K.450   Murray Perahia, English Chamber Orchestra; Malcolm Bilson, fortepiano, English Baroque Soloists, Gardiner—*period instruments.*
No. 17 in G K.453   Richard Goode, Orpheus Chamber Orchestra; Murray Perahia, English Chamber Orchestra; Maria João Pires, Gulbenkian Foundation Orchestra, Guschlbauer.
No. 18 in B flat K.456   Murray Perahia, English Chamber Orchestra.
No. 19 in F K.459   (Artur Schnabel, London Symphony, Sargent); Richard Goode, Vienna Symphony Chamber Orchestra, Klopfenstein; Maurizio Pollini, Vienna Philharmonic, Böhm; Maria João Pires, Lausanne Chamber Orchestra, Jordan.
No. 20 in D minor K.466   Clara Haskil, Lamoureux Orchestra, Markevitch; Richard Goode, Vienna Symphony Chamber Orchestra, Klopfenstein; Maria João Pires, Lausanne Chamber Orchestra, Jordan; Emanuel Ax, Dallas Symphony, Mata.
No. 21 in C K.467   (Walter Gieseking, New York Philharmonic,

Cantelli—*concert performance, whose reproduction will vary with the company issuing the recording; an AS Discs edition can be expected to have good sound*); (Artur Schnabel, London Symphony, Sargent); (Dinu Lipatti, Lucerne Festival Orchestra, von Karajan); Maria João Pires, Gulbenkian Foundation Orchestra, Guschlbauer.

No. 22 in E flat K.482 Christian Zacharias, Dresden State Orchestra, Zinman; (Artur Schnabel, New York Philharmonic, Walter—*concert performance, whose reproduction will vary with the company issuing the recording*); (Edwin Fischer, ensemble under Barbirolli); Emanuel Ax, Dallas Symphony, Mata.

No. 23 in A K.488 Richard Goode, Orpheus Chamber Orchestra; Maurizio Pollini, Vienna Philharmonic, Böhm; (Walter Gieseking, Philharmonia Orchestra, von Karajan); (Artur Schnabel, New York Philharmonic, Rodzinski—*concert performance, whose reproduction will vary with the company issuing the recording*); Maria João Pires, Gulbenkian Foundation Orchestra, Guschlbauer.

No. 24 in C minor K.491 Glenn Gould, CBC Symphony, Susskind; Clara Haskil, Lamoureux Orchestra, Markevitch; (Walter Gieseking, Philharmonia Orchestra, von Karajan); (Edwin Fischer, London Philharmonic, Collingwood).

No. 25 in C K.503 Leon Fleisher, Cleveland Orchestra, Szell; Friedrich Gulda, Vienna Philharmonic, Abbado; Christian Zacharias, Bavarian Radio Orchestra, Zinman.

No. 27 in B flat K.595 Friedrich Gulda, Vienna Philharmonic, Abbado; (Mieczyslaw Horszowski, Perpignan Festival Orchestra, Casals); (Artur Schnabel, London Symphony, Barbirolli); (Rudolf Serkin, New York Philharmonic, Toscanini—*1936 concert performance, whose reproduction will vary with the company issuing the recording*).

(*At this writing, Pires is re-recording the concertos; her recent concert performances lead one to expect the new recordings to be superb, provided the as yet un-named conductor is a good one. And Bilson is recording all the concertos on fortepiano with Gardiner.*)

Concertos (5) K.207, 211, 216, 218, 219 for violin Arthur Grumiaux, London Symphony, Colin Davis; Jean-Jacques Kantorow, Netherlands Chamber Orchestra, Hager.

Individual violin concertos K.211, 216 and 218—Isaac Stern, with orchestras under Szell and Alexander Schneider; K.216 and 218—(Gerard Poulet, Austrian Symphony, Gaston Poulet); (Szymon Goldberg, Philharmonia Orchestra, Susskind); K.216 and 219—Anne-Sophie Mutter, Berlin Philharmonic, von Karajan; K.218—(Joseph Szigeti, London Philharmonic, Beecham); K.219—(Nathan Milstein, Festival Orchestra, Harry Blech); Roberto Michelucci, I Musici.

Divertimentos   See: *Chamber Music and Orchestral Music.*

Operas

(The) Abduction from the Seraglio (Die Entführung aus dem Serail)   Eda-Pierre, Burrowes, Burrows, under Colin Davis.

(La) Clemenza di Tito   Baker, Minton, Burrows, under Colin Davis.

Così fan tutte   Caballé, Baker, Gedda, Ganzarolli, under Colin Davis; (Souez, Helletsgruber, Nash, Domgraf-Fassbänder, under Fritz Busch); (Schwarzkopf, Merriman, Simoneau, Panerai, under von Karajan).

Don Giovanni   Sutherland, Schwarzkopf, Wächter, Taddei, under Giulini; (Souez, Helletsgruber, Brownlee, Baccaloni, under Fritz Busch); Margaret Price, Sass, Burrows, Weikl, under Solti; (Jurinac, Stader, Fischer-Dieskau, under Fricsay).

Idomeneo, Rè di Creta   Rinaldi, Tinsley, Shirley, under Colin Davis; Jurinac, Simoneau, Richard Lewis, under Pritchard— *with minor cuts.*

(The) Impresario (Der Schauspieldirektor)   Cotrubas, Welting, under Colin Davis.

(The) Magic Flute (Die Zauberflöte)   Cotrubas, Donat, Tappy, Boesch, Talvela, under Levine; Lorengar, Burrows, Prey, Deutekom, Talvela, under Solti; (Stader, Häfliger, Fischer-Dieskau, Streich, Greindl, under Fricsay); (Lemnitz, Roswänge, Hüsch, Berger, Streinz, under Beecham).

(The) Marriage of Figaro (Le Nozze di Figaro)   (Mildmay, Rautavaara, Domgraf-Fassbänder, under Fritz Busch—*the recitatives are omitted*); Te Kanawa, Popp, von Stade, Ramey, Allen, under Solti; Tomowa-Sintow, Cotrubas, von Stade, Van Dam, Krause, under von Karajan; Moffo, Schwarzkopf, Wächter,

Taddei, Cossotto, under Giulini; (Jurinac, Schöffler, Streich, under Böhm).

Mitridate, Rè di Ponto   Augér, Cotrubas, Hollweg, under Hager.

Overtures   Colin Davis; Haitink; Marriner.

(For individual arias and excerpts, see below, under Vocal music)

Orchestral music

Dances (Contredances and German Dances)   Boskovsky, Vienna Mozart Ensemble; (Litschauer, Vienna State Opera Orchestra).

Divertimenti K.136, 137 and 138 for strings   Glover, London Mozart Players.

Divertimento in D K.251 for oboe, horns and strings   Heinz Holliger, Hermann Baumann, with the Orlando Quartet; (Marcel Tabuteau, Perpignan Festival Orchestra, Casals).

Divertimento in B flat K.287 for strings and horns   (Toscanini, NBC Symphony Orchestra); (von Karajan, Philharmonia Orchestra); Marriner, Academy of St. Martin in the Fields; (Cantelli, NBC Symphony or New York Philharmonic—*concert performances, whose reproduction will vary with the company issuing them; an AS Discs edition can be expected to have excellent sound).*

Divertimento in D K.334 for strings and horns   Marriner, Academy of St. Martin in the Fields.

Masonic Funeral Music K.477 (See also under Choral Music)   Jochum, Bamberg Symphony; de Waart, Philharmonia Orchestra.

(Les) Petits Riens K.299b (ballet)   Entremont, conducting the Vienna Chamber Orchestra.

Serenade in D K.203 (189b) for winds, horns, trumpets and strings   Marriner, Academy of St. Martin in the Fields.

Serenade in D K.239 (Serenata notturna) for strings   Britten, English Chamber Orchestra; Marriner, Academy of St. Martin in the Fields.

Serenade in D K.250 (Haffner) for winds, horns, trumpets and strings   de Waart, Dresden State Orchestra; Colin Davis, Bavarian Radio Orchestra.

Serenade in D K.320 (Posthorn) for winds, horns, trumpets and strings   Levine, Vienna Philharmonic; Boskovsky, Vienna Mozart Ensemble; de Waart, Dresden State Orchestra.

Serenade in B flat K.361 (Gran Partita) for winds Klemperer, London Wind Quintet and Ensemble; de Waart, Netherlands Wind Ensemble; Collegium Aureum—*period instruments.*

Serenade in E flat K.375 for winds Klemperer, New Philharmonia Wind Ensemble; Schneider, Chamber Orchestra of Europe.

Serenade K.388 in C minor for winds (variant of String Quintet K.406) Klemperer, New Philharmonia Wind Ensemble; Schneider, Chamber Orchestra of Europe.

Serenade K.525 (Eine kleine Nachtmusik) for strings Glover, London Mozart Players.

Sinfonia Concertante in E flat K.364 for violin and viola Iona Brown, Josef Suk, Academy of St. Martin in the Fields; Arthur Grumiaux, Arrigo Pelliccia, London Symphony Orchestra, Colin Davis; (Isaac Stern, William Primrose, Perpignan Festival, Casals).

Symphony No. 25 in G minor K.183 Britten, English Chamber Orchestra; Kertesz, Vienna Philharmonic; Marriner, Academy of St. Martin in the Fields.

Symphony No. 28 in C K.200 Colin Davis, Dresden Radio Orchestra; Marriner, Academy of St. Martin in the Fields; Entremont, conducting the Vienna Chamber Orchestra.

Symphony No. 29 in A K.201 Britten, English Chamber Orchestra; (Cantelli, Philharmonia Orchestra); Entremont, conducting the Vienna Chamber Orchestra; Kertesz, Vienna Philharmonic; Marriner, Academy of St. Martin in the Fields; (Toscanini, NBC Symphony—*concert performance, whose reproduction will vary with the company issuing the recording*).

Symphony No. 31 in D K.297 (Paris) Glover, London Mozart Players; (Beecham, London Philharmonic); Marriner, Academy of St. Martin in the Fields.

Symphony No. 34 in C K.338 Glover, London Mozart Players; Kempe, Philharmonia Orchestra; (Beecham, London Philharmonic); Marriner, Academy of St. Martin in the Fields.

Symphony No. 35 in D K.385 (Haffner) (Toscanini, New York Philharmonic—*1929*); Glover, London Mozart Players; Kertesz, Vienna Philharmonic, Casals, Marlboro Festival Orchestra; Marriner, Academy of St. Martin in the Fields; (Beecham, London and Royal Philharmonic orchestras).

Symphony No. 36 in C K.425 (Linz) Glover, London Mozart Players; Kertesz, Vienna Philharmonic; (Beecham, London Philharmonic); (Van Otterloo, Hague Philharmonic); Marriner, Academy of St. Martin in the Fields.

Symphony No. 38 in D K.504 (Prague) Britten, English Chamber Orchestra; Glover, London Mozart Players; Colin Davis, BBC Symphony; Casals, Marlboro Festival Orchestra; Marriner, Academy of St. Martin in the Fields.

Symphony No. 39 in E flat K.543 Glover, London Mozart Players; (von Karajan, Philharmonia Orchestra); (Beecham, London Philharmonic); Casals, Puerto Rico Festival Orchestra; Colin Davis, London Symphony and Dresden State orchestras; Solti, Chicago Symphony; Marriner, Academy of St. Martin in the Fields.

Symphony No. 40 in G minor K.550 von Karajan, Vienna Philharmonic—*1960s;* Giulini, Philharmonia Orchestra; Britten, English Chamber Orchestra; (Toscanini, NBC Symphony—*1938–39*); (Toscanini, NBC Symphony—*1950*); (Toscanini, New York Philharmonic—*1936 concert performance, whose reproduction will vary with the company issuing the recording*); (Casals, Marlboro Festival Orchestra—*version without clarinets*); Kertesz, Vienna Philharmonic; Mehta, Israel Philharmonic—*version without clarinets.*

Symphony No. 41 in C K.551 (Jupiter) Colin Davis, BBC Symphony or Dresden State Orchestra; Casals, Marlboro Festival Orchestra; Giulini, Philharmonia Orchestra; Jochum, Boston Symphony; (Klemperer, Philharmonia Orchestra); (Beecham, London Philharmonic); Marriner, Academy of St. Martin in the Fields.

(At this writing, Glover is recording all of the major symphonies.)

Piano music

Fantasia in C minor K.475 Malcolm Bilson, fortepiano; Youri Egorov.

Rondos K.485, 494, 511—Malcolm Bilson, fortepiano; *K.494 and 511*—(Artur Schnabel).

Sonatas (17) for piano Malcolm Bilson, fortepiano.

Individual piano sonatas K.280, 281, 311, 330—Krystian Zimerman; *K.310*—(Dinu Lipatti); Maria João Pires; *K.330*—Van

Cliburn; (Glenn Gould—*his first recording, made in the 1950s*);
K.332, 333, 570—(Artur Schnabel).
Sonata in D K.448 for two pianos Vladimir Ashkenazy and
Malcolm Frager.
Variations (Walter Gieseking).

Vocal music
Concert arias and operatic excerpts Janet Baker, Judith Blegen,
Stuart Burrows, Lisa Della Casa, Anton Dermota, Nicolai
Gedda, Hilde Güden, (Maria Kurenko), (Frida Leider), (Tiana
Lemnitz), (Lois Marshall), Edith Mathis, Anna Moffo, (Ezio
Pinza), (Elisabeth Rethberg), (Anneliese Rothenberger), Paul
Schöffler, (Elisabeth Schumann), Graziella Sciutti, Irm-
gard Seefried, Cesare Siepi, Léopold Simoneau, Maria Stader,
(Eleanor Steber), Teresa Stich-Randall, Joan Sutherland.
Songs Peter Schreier; (Elisabeth Schumann); Elisabeth Schwarz-
kopf; Benita Valente.

Musorgsky

Boris Godunov Raimondi, Polozov, etc., under Rostropovich—
1872 version, with the St. Basil's scene of 1869; Talvela, Gedda,
etc., under Semkow—*same;* Shtokolov, etc., under Eltsin—
Act 2, only, in the 1869 version (except for Shuisky's 1872 descrip-
tion of the murdered Tsarevich), and with Shostakovitch's innocuous
revision of the orchestration. Rostropovich takes better tempos than
Semkow, but he rarely rises to dramatic climaxes, and his cast is
weaker. One wishes that Eltsin, who paces the music well, and
Shtokolov, who is a superior Boris, had recorded the entire opera.
(The complete 1872 version in the performance led by Fedoseyev is
feverishly conducted, stridently sung, and does not include the St.
Basil's scene.)
(The) Fair at Sorochinsk (completed by Shebalin) Matorin, Mish-
chevsky, Voinarovsky, Klenov, and others of the Stanislavsky
Theater, under Esipov.
Khovanshchina—entire opera, as completed by Rimsky-Kor-
sakov (Mark Reizen, etc., Bolshoi Opera, under Nebolsin);
—*excerpts from Musorgsky's own version:* (Dolukhanova, Pon-
triagin, Shevtzov, etc., Moscow Radio Orchestra, Kovalev);

—*choral excerpts, as completed by Rimsky-Korsakov:* Abbado, London Symphony Orchestra, etc.; —*Prelude to Act 1:* Solti, London Symphony; (Koussevitzky, Boston Symphony).

Night on Bare Mountain (Musorgsky's own version) Abbado, London Symphony Orchestra.

(The) Nursery (song-cycle) Elisabeth Søderstrøm, with Vladimir Ashkenazy; (Irmgard Seefried, with Erik Werba).

Pictures at an Exhibition—original piano version Viktor Yeresko; Sviatoslav Richter—*good except for his rushing of the Promenades;* Vladimir Ashkenazy—*the 1960s recording, which is good except for his distortion of the Goldenberg and Schmuyle episode; avoid Ashkenazy's later performance.*

Pictures at an Exhibition—orchestrated by Ravel (Toscanini, NBC Symphony Orchestra); Abbado, London Symphony Orchestra; (Cantelli, NBC Symphony); Giulini, Chicago Symphony.

Scherzo in B flat Abbado, London Symphony.

Songs and Dances of Death Benjamin Luxon, with David Willison, piano; Galina Vishnevskaya, with Mstislav Rostropovich, piano.

Songs—miscellaneous Benjamin Luxon; Jennie Tourel; Galina Vishnevskaya.

Sorochinsky Fair See: (The) Fair at Sorochinsk.

Sunless song-cycle Benjamin Luxon, with David Willison, piano; (Maria Kurenko, with V. Pastukhoff, piano).

Triumphal March (The Capture of Kars) Abbado, London Symphony.

Nicolai

The Merry Wives of Windsor (Die lustigen Weiber von Windsor) Mathis, Donath, Weikl, under Klee.

Nielsen

Symphony No. 4 (The Inextinguishable) von Karajan, Berlin Philharmonic.

Nin

Songs   Marilyn Horne, with Martin Katz.

Obrecht

Chansons and Motets   Early Music Consort of London, Munrow; Pro Cantione Antiqua of London, Turner.

Ockeghem

Intemerata dei Mater   Early Music Consort, Munrow.
Maria motets   Prague Madrigalists, Venhoda; Hilliard Ensemble.

Offenbach

(*La*) *Belle Hélène* (Linda, Dran, Giraud, Linsolas, under Leibowitz); Norman, Aler, Burles, Bacquier, under Plasson—*which may be better than the same conductor's* La Périchole *for the presence of Norman and Aler.*

(*La*) *Périchole* Linval, Monteil, Noguéra, under Markevitch. *Avoid Plasson's recording, which is spoiled by Berganza's straining voice and Carreras's dry tone, and by their stiff articulation, which is made more apparent by the expressiveness with which the un-named actors read the dialogue between numbers.*

Pachelbel

Organ music   (Luther Noss); Werner Jacob; Jean-Pierre Leguay.

Palestrina

Masses, Motets, Stabat Mater   Tallis Scholars; Pro Cantione Antiqua of London; Guest, St. John's College Choir; Hilliard Ensemble; Willcocks, King's College Choir.

THE LISTENER'S MUSICAL COMPANION

Parsons

Song—Pandolpho   Fretwork ensemble, Michael Chance.

Pergolesi

Stabat Mater   Jacobs, Concerto Vocale—*period instruments;* Abbado, London Symphony, etc.

Peri

Euridice   Coro Polifonico di Milano and Solisti di Milano, Ephraikian.

Piston

The Incredible Flutist   Kitayenko, Moscow Philharmonic; Mester, Louisville Orchestra.

Plainchant:

See Music Before 1500 *section at the end of this chapter.*

Poulenc

Concerto for Organ, Strings and Timpani   George Malcolm, Academy of St. Martin in the Fields, Iona Brown.

Praetorius

Dances from Terpsichore   Early Music Consort of London, Munrow—*period instruments.*
Motets from Musae Sionae   St. Alban's Cathedral Boys' Choir, Munrow.

Prés: *See:* Josquin des Prés.

Prokofiev

Alexander Nevsky Finnie, Scottish National Orchestra, Järvi; Obraztsova, London Symphony, Abbado.

Chout (The Buffoon, or, The Tale of the Buffoon)—complete ballet Susskind, London Symphony; —*suite:* Järvi, Scottish National Orchestra; Abbado, London Symphony.

Cinderella—complete ballet Previn, London Symphony; —*excerpts:* Järvi, Scottish National Orchestra; Slatkin, St. Louis Symphony.

Concertos (5) for piano No. 1—Sviatoslav Richter, Moscow Symphony, Kondrashin; Vladimir Ashkenazy, London Symphony, Previn; Gary Graffman, Cleveland Orchestra, Szell; *No. 2*— Ashkenazy and Previn; *No. 3*—Van Cliburn, Chicago Symphony, Hendl; Ashkenazy and Previn; Graffman and Szell; (Sergei Prokofiev, London Symphony, Coppola); *Nos. 4 and 5*—Ashkenazy and Previn.

Concerto No. 1 (of 2) for violin (Joseph Szigeti, London Philharmonic, Beecham); Isaac Stern, Philadelphia Orchestra, Ormandy; (David Oistrakh, London Symphony, von Matacic); Anne-Sophie Mutter, National Symphony, Rostropovich.

(The) Gambler soloists, chorus and orchestra of the All Union Radio, Rozhdestvensky—*good male solo voices but to varying degrees unpleasant female solo ones.*

Lieutenant Kije—suite Michael Tilson Thomas, Los Angeles Philharmonic; (Koussevitzky, Boston Symphony); Abbado, Chicago Symphony.

(The) Love for Three Oranges (L'Amour des trois oranges) Bacquier, Bastin, Lyons Opera, Nagano; —*orchestral suite:* Michael Tilson Thomas, Los Angeles Philharmonic; Järvi, Scottish National Orchestra; Ormandy, Philadelphia Orchestra.

(Le) Pas d'acier (The Steel Dance)—suite Järvi, Scottish National Orchestra.

(The) Prodigal Son Järvi, Scottish National Orchestra; Rozhdestvensky, USSR State Orchestra.

Romeo and Juliet—Suites Nos. 1, 2 and 3 Järvi, Scottish National Orchestra.

Scythian Suite (Ala and Lolly) Järvi, Scottish National Orchestra;

Abbado, Chicago Symphony; Markevitch, French National Radio Orchestra.

Sonatas (10) for piano No. 2—Tedd Joselson; No. 3—Gary Graffman; No. 6—Van Cliburn; No. 7—Marizio Pollini.

Symphonies (7) No. 1 *(Classical)*—(Toscanini, NBC Symphony); Giulini, Chicago Symphony; (Koussevitzky, Boston Symphony); No. 5—Järvi, Scottish National Orchestra; Schippers, Philharmonia Orchestra.

(The) Ugly Duckling Elisabeth Søderstrøm, with Vladimir Ashkenazy.

Visions fugitives for piano Tedd Joselson.

Puccini

(La) Bohème (Albanese, Peerce, under Toscanini); (de los Angeles, Bjoerling, under Beecham).

Madama Butterfly de los Angeles, Bjoerling, under Santini.

Tosca (Callas, di Stefano, Gobbi, under de Sabata).

Arias and vocal excerpts by singers other than those mentioned above: Carlo Bergonzi, Montserrat Caballé, José Carreras, Placido Domingo, (Eileen Farrell), Mirella Freni, Nicolai Gedda, (Frida Leider), (Lois Marshall), Sherrill Milnes, Anna Moffo, Leontyne Price, Katia Ricciarelli, Renata Tebaldi.

Purcell

Chacony and Pavane in G minor Camerata Bern.

Dido and Aeneas Baker, Clark, Sinclair, under Anthony Lewis —*avoid Baker's later recording, conducted by Bedford;* Mary Thomas, Sheppard, Bevan, under Deller—*period instruments;* (Flagstad, Schwarzkopf, Helmsley, under Jones); Veasey, Donath, Shirley-Quirk, under Colin Davis.

(The) Fairy Queen (Morison, Vyvyan, under Anthony Lewis —*avoid Vyvyan's later recording, conducted by Britten*).

Fantasias for strings (including the Fantasia in Five Parts on One Note) Marriner, Academy of St. Martin in the Fields; Menuhin, Bath Festival Orchestra.

Harpsichord music George Malcolm; Thurston Dart.

In Guilty Night (*Saul and the Witch of Endor*) Concerto Vocale, Jacobs—*period instruments;* Deller Consort—*period instruments.*

Jubilate Deo Deller Consort—*period instruments.*

King Arthur (Sheppard, Knibbs, etc., with the Deller Consort—*period instruments*).

Masque of Timon of Athens Dawson, Fisher, Covey-Crump, under Gardiner—*period instruments.*

Music for the Funeral of Queen Mary Gardiner, English Baroque Soloists—*period instruments;* (Geraint Jones, with chorus and orchestra); Guest, St. John's College Choir; Deller Consort—*period instruments.*

Ode for St. Cecilia's Day Cantelo, Deller, Ambrosian Singers, Tippett; Taverner Choir, Parrott—*period instruments;* Deller Consort—*period instruments.*

Remember Not, Lord, our Offenses Guest, St. John's College Choir.

Te Deum Willcocks, King's College Choir; Deller Consort—*period instruments.*

Tell Me Some Pitying Angel Concerto Vocale, Jacobs.

Thou Knowest, Lord, the Secrets of our Hearts (*Funeral Sentences*) Guest, St. John's College Choir; Gardiner, Monteverdi Choir —*period instruments.*

Arias and vocal excerpts by singers other than those mentioned above: (Isobel Baillie); (Kathleen Ferrier); Maureen Forrester; (Lois Marshall).

A collection including the Fantasia in Five Parts on One Note, *the* Golden Sonata, *and the songs* O Let Me Ever, Ever Weep!, I Attempt from Love's Sickness to Fly, Fairest Isle, Close thine Eyes, I Love and I Must *and* Tell Me Some Pitying Angel *was issued in an album of performances by April Cantelo, Della Jones, Maurice Bevan, John Gibbs, the harpsichordist George Malcolm, and the Academy of St. Martin in the Fields under Marriner. In another collection the soprano Edita Gruberova, trumpeter Wynton Marsalis, and the English Chamber Orchestra under Leppard perform various instrumental and vocal pieces.*

Rachmaninoff

Concerto No. 3 for piano   Van Cliburn, Symphony of the Air, Kondrashin; (Sergei Rachmaninoff, Philadelphia Orchestra, Ormandy).
Rhapsody on a Theme of Paganini   Van Cliburn, Philadelphia Orchestra, Ormandy; (Sergei Rachmaninoff, Philadelphia Orchestra, Stokowski).

Rameau

Dardanus   Eda-Pierre, von Stade, Van Dam, under Leppard.
Harpsichord music   George Malcolm; Kenneth Gilbert.
(Les) Indes galantes   Paillard Chamber Orchestra; Chapelle Royale, Herreweghe.

Ravel

Concertos for piano—Concerto in G, and Concerto in D for left hand   Louis Lortie, London Symphony, Frühbeck de Burgos.
Daphnis et Chloé—complete ballet   Boulez, New York Philharmonic; —*Suite No. 2:* (Koussevitzky, Boston Symphony); Boulez, Cleveland Orchestra; Haitink, Concertgebouw Orchestra; Abbado, Boston Symphony; (Cantelli, Philharmonia Orchestra); (Toscanini, NBC Symphony).
Piano music: Gaspard de la nuit, Miroirs, Sonatine, Le Tombeau de Couperin, La Valse—Louis Lortie; *Alborada del Gracioso*—(Dinu Lipatti).
(La) Valse, for orchestra   Abbado, London Symphony; Boulez, New York Philharmonic; Haitink, Concertgebouw Orchestra.

Respighi

Ancient Airs and Dances   Bernardi, CBC Vancouver Orchestra; Marriner, Academy of St. Martin in the Fields.
(La) Boutique fantasque   Andrew Davis, Toronto Symphony; Solti, Israel Philharmonic.

Fountains of Rome (Toscanini, NBC Symphony); Michael Tilson Thomas, Los Angeles Philharmonic.

Pines of Rome (Toscanini, NBC Symphony).

Rossiniana (Ansermet, Orchestre de la Suisse Romande).

Rimsky-Korsakov

Capriccio espagnol Argenta, London Symphony.

(Le) Coq d'or—suite Järvi, Scottish National Orchestra; (Ansermet, Orchestre de la Suisse Romande).

May Night Sapagena, Lisovsky, Pastushenko, under Fedoseyev.

Russian Easter Overture Markevitch, London Symphony; Rozhdestvensky, Orchestre de Paris; (Stokowski, Philadelphia Orchestra).

(The) Snow Maiden Arkhipova, Mosyakov, under Fedoseyev.

Arias, songs and vocal excerpts Nicolai Gedda.

Rossini

Operas

(The) Barber of Seville Baltsa, Araiza, Allen, Lloyd, under Marriner; Berganza, Alva, Prey, under Abbado; (de los Angeles, Alva, Bruscantini, under Gui).

(La) Cenerentola Baltsa, Araiza, under Marriner; Berganza, Alva, under Abbado; (de Gabarain, Oncina, under Gui).

(Le) Comte Ory Montague, Aler, under Gardiner; (Oncina, Roux, under Gui).

(La) Donna del lago Ricciarelli, Ramey, under Pollini.

Elisabetta, Regina d'Inghilterra Caballé, Carreras, under Masini.

(L') Italiana in Algeri Baltsa, Lopardo, under Abbado; (Simionato, Valletti, under Giulini); Valentini-Terrani, Araiza, under Ferro.

Mosè in Egitto Anderson, Raimondi, under Scimone.

Otello Carreras, von Stade, under Lopéz-Cobos.

Semiramide Sutherland, Horne, under Bonynge.

Tancredi Cuberli, Horne, Palacio, under Weikert.

(*Il*) *Turco in Italia* (Callas, Rossi-Lemeni, Gedda, under Gavazzeni); Caballé, Ramey, under Chailly.

(*Il*) *Viaggio a Reims* Ricciarelli, Gasdia, Ramey, under Abbado.

William Tell Studer, Merritt, under Muti; Caballé, Gedda, under Gardelli.

Arias and vocal excerpts by singers other than those mentioned above: (Fernando Corena), (Tito Schipa), Beverly Sills, (Conchita Supervia), (Renata Tebaldi), (Jennie Tourel).

Overtures (Toscanini); Gamba; Abbado; Giulini.

Other music

Missa di Gloria Handt, BBC Singers, etc.

Petite messe solennelle Sawallisch, Munich Vocal Ensemble, Lövaas, Fassbänder, Schreier, Fischer-Dieskau, etc.—*version with pianos;* Scimone, Ambrosian Singers, Ricciarelli, Zimmermann, Carreras, Ramey, etc.—*with pianos.*

Stabat Mater Giulini, Philharmonia Orchestra, Ricciarelli, Valentini-Terrani, Gonzales, Raimondi, etc.

Sonatas for two violins, cello and bass Scimone, I Solisti Veneti; I Musici; (Janigro, I Solisti di Zagreb).

de la Rue

Motets Pro Cantione Antiqua, London.

Ruggles

Complete works Michael Tilson Thomas, Buffalo Philharmonic.

Satie

Parade Abravanel, Utah Symphony.
Relâche Abravanel, Utah Symphony.
Piano music Aldo Ciccolini.

Scarlatti, A.

Madrigals Jürgens, Monteverdi Choir of Hamburg.
O magnum mysterium Poole, BBC Singers.

Su le sponde del Tebro Blegen, Columbia Chamber Ensemble, Schwarz.

Scarlatti, D.

Harpsichord sonatas (George Malcolm); András Schiff, piano; Luciano Sgrizzi; Scott Ross; (Greta Kraus); (Wanda Landowska—*the recordings of the 1930s*); (Dinu Lipatti, piano); (Robert Casadesus, piano).

Scheidt

Organ music Mireille Lagacé; Kurt Eichhorn.

Schönberg

Erwartung Silja, Vienna Philharmonic, Dohnányi.
Five Pieces for Orchestra Op. 16 Boulez, BBC Symphony.
Transfigured Night (Verklärte Nacht) von Karajan, Berlin Philharmonic; Boulez, Ensemble Intercontemporain—*version for sextet.*

Schubert

Chamber music
Arpeggione sonata Lynn Harrell, with James Levine, piano.
Octet Op. 166/D.803 Brymer, Tuckwell, Gatt and the Cleveland Quartet; Gervase de Peyer with the Melos Ensemble; Scott, Heller, Jolley and the Marlboro Festival ensemble.
Quartets
Nos. 1–11 Melos Quartet.
No. 12 in C minor (Quartettsatz) Quartetto Italiano; (Budapest Quartet—*1933*).
No. 13 in A minor Op. 29/D.804 (Budapest Quartet—*the 1933 recording especially*).
No. 14 (Death and the Maiden) Cleveland Quartet; (Budapest Quartet—*1953*); Quartetto Italiano.

No. 15 in G Op. 161/D.887 (Budapest Quartet); (Kolisch Quartet); Gabrieli Quartet.

Quintet for piano and strings (Trout) Emanuel Ax, with the Guarneri Quartet; Ingrid Haebler, with Grumiaux, etc.; Lamar Crowson, with the Melos Ensemble; (Mieczyslaw Horszowski, with the Budapest Quartet and bassist Moleux—*1950*); Christoph Eschenbach with the Koeckert Quartet; Jörg Demus, with the Schubert Quartet; (Artur Schnabel, with the Pro Arte Quartet).

Quintet in C Op. 163/D.956 for strings Arthur Grumiaux, etc.; Yo-Yo Ma, with the Cleveland Quartet; (Budapest Quartet—*1941*); (Isaac Stern, Alexander Schneider, Milton Katims, Pablo Casals, Paul Tortelier); Weller Quartet; Berg Quartet, with Heinrich Schiff.

Sonatas for violin Op. 137 Nos. 1 and 2/D.384 and D.385— Arthur Grumiaux and Paul Crossley; (Joseph Szigeti and Andor Foldes); *Op. 162/D.574*—Grumiaux and Crossley; (Fritz Kreisler and Sergei Rachmaninoff).

Trio No. 1 in B flat Op. 99/D.898 Trio di Trieste—*1960s;* (Jascha Heifetz, Emanuel Feuermann, Artur Rubinstein); Suk Trio; (Jacques Thibaud, Pablo Casals, Alfred Cortot).

Trio No. 2 in E flat Op. 100/D.929 Trio di Trieste—*1960s;* (Rudolf Serkin, with the Busch Quartet—*1930s*).

Choral Music

Mass No. 2 in G D.167 Sawallisch, Bavarian Radio Orchestra, Popp, Dallapozza, Fischer-Dieskau; Shaw, Atlanta Symphony, Upshaw, Gordon, Stone; Vienna Boys' Choir.

Mass No. 4 in C D.452 Sawallisch, Bavarian Radio Orchestra, Popp, Fassbänder, Dallapozza, Fischer-Dieskau.

Mass No. 5 in A flat D.678 Dennis Russell Davies, Carleton College Choir, Sabo, de Gaetani, Sperry, Guinn; Sawallisch, Bavarian Radio Orchestra, Donath, Fassbänder, Araiza, Fischer-Dieskau—*with reservations about Donath's tremulous voice.*

Mass No. 6 in E flat D.950 Guest, St. John's College Choir, Palmer, Watts, Bowen, Evans, Keyte; Shaw, Atlanta Symphony, Valente, Simpson, Siebert, Myers; Sawallisch, Bavarian Radio Orchestra, Donath, Fassbänder, Araiza, Fischer-Dieskau—*with reservations about Donath.*

Piano music

Allegretto in C minor D.915   Richard Goode; Maurizio Pollini; (Artur Schnabel).

Andantino varié Op. 84 No. 1/D.823 for piano four-hands   (Artur and Karl-Ulrich Schnabel).

Fantasie Op. 103/D.940 for piano four hands   András Schiff and Imre Rohmann—*in spite of the poor piano.*

Grand Duo   See: Sonatas.

Impromptus (8) *Op. 90/D.899 and Op. 142/D.935* (Artur Schnabel); Murray Perahia; (Dinu Lipatti—*Op. 90/D.899 Nos. 2 and 3*).

Klavierstücke (3) *D.946*   Maurizio Pollini; Gilbert Kalish.

Marches caractéristiques for piano four-hands   András Schiff and Imre Rohmann—*in spite of the poor piano;* (Paul Badura-Skoda and Jörg Demus).

Moments musicaux   Clifford Curzon; (Artur Schnabel).

Rondo for piano four-hands Op. 107/D.951   András Schiff and Imre Rohmann—*in spite of the poor piano;* (Paul Badura-Skoda and Jörg Demus).

Sonata in A minor Op. 42/D.784   Maurizio Pollini.

Sonata in D Op. 53/D.850   (Artur Schnabel); Vladimir Ashkenazy.

Sonata in G Op. 78/D.894   Vladimir Ashkenazy; Anton Kuerti.

Sonata in A Op. 120/D.664   Vladimir Ashkenazy; Leon Fleisher.

Sonata in A minor Op. 143/D.784   Vladimir Ashkenazy; Radu Lupu.

Sonata in C (incomplete) Op. Posth./D.840   Gilbert Kalish.

Sonata in C minor Op. Posth./D.958   Richard Goode; (Artur Schnabel); Maurizio Pollini; (Webster Aitken).

Sonata in A Op. Posth./D.959   Richard Goode; (Artur Schnabel); Maurizio Pollini; Radu Lupu; Christoph Eschenbach; (Webster Aitken—*for the sake of his performance of the second movement*).

Sonata in B flat Op. Posth./D.960   Richard Goode; (Artur Schnabel); Maurizio Pollini.

Sonata (Grand Duo) for piano four-hands   (Arthur Gold and Robert Fizdale); Abbado, Chamber Orchestra of Europe—*playing Joachim's orchestration.*

Wanderer Fantasy   Murray Perahia; Maurizio Pollini.

Orchestral music
Rosamunde—complete   Boskovsky, Dresden State Orchestra.
Symphonies Nos. 1–6   Marriner, Academy of St. Martin in the
Fields; Abbado, Chamber Orchestra of Europe.
Symphony No. 5   Haitink, Concertgebouw Orchestra;
(Toscanini, NBC Symphony).
Symphony No. 8 (Unfinished)   (Toscanini, NBC Symphony—
*uninterrupted run-through at the dress rehearsal of March 3rd,
1949; reproduction will vary with the company issuing the recording)*; (Toscanini, NBC Symphony—*1950*); Cantelli, Philharmonia Orchestra; Britten, English Chamber Orchestra; Abbado, Chamber Orchestra of Europe; Carlos Kleiber, Vienna
Philharmonic; Mannino, National Arts Center Orchestra; Giulini, Philharmonia Orchestra; Kertesz, Vienna Philharmonic;
Haitink, Concertgebouw Orchestra; (Beecham, London Philharmonic).
Symphony No. 9 (the Great C major)   (Cantelli, NBC Symphony—
*concert performance, whose reproduction will vary with the company
issuing the recording; the AS Discs edition has excellent sound)*;
(Toscanini, Phildelphia Orchestra—*1941*); (Toscanini, NBC
Symphony—*1953*); Haitink, Concertgebouw Orchestra; Kertesz, Vienna Philharmonic.

Songs
(Die) Schöne Müllerin   Dietrich Fischer-Dieskau, with Gerald
Moore; Lois Marshall, with Greta Kraus; Peter Pears, with
Benjamin Britten; Gérard Souzay, with Dalton Baldwin; Fran-
cisco Araiza, with Irwin Gage.
Schwanengesang   Dietrich Fischer-Dieskau, with Gerald Moore,
and later with Alfred Brendel; Hans Hotter, with Moore.
Winterreise   Dietrich Fischer-Dieskau, with Jörg Demus; Peter
Pears, with Benjamin Britten; (Hans Hotter, with Erik Werba
*—an even finer performance than Hotter's earlier one with Gerald
Moore*); Lois Marshall, with Anton Kuerti; Christa Ludwig,
with James Levine.
Single songs   Elly Ameling, (Marian Anderson), Janet Baker,
(Hugues Cuénod), Lisa Della Casa, (Mattiwilda Dobbs), (Kath-
leen Ferrier), Dietrich Fischer-Dieskau, (Kirsten Flagstad),

(Elena Gerhardt), (Hans Hotter), (Margarete Klose), Werner Krenn, (Lotte Lehmann), Christa Ludwig, (Margaret Ritchie), (Elisabeth Schumann), Elisabeth Schwarzkopf, Irmgard Seefried, Elisabeth Søderstrøm, (Richard Tauber).

Schumann

Carnaval Robert Casadesus; Guiomar Novaes; (Sergei Rachmaninoff—*with reservations*).

Concerto in A minor for piano (Dinu Lipatti, Philharmonia Orchestra, von Karajan); Artur Rubinstein, Chicago Symphony, Giulini; Van Cliburn, Chicago Symphony, Reiner; Stephen Bishop-Kovacevich, BBC Symphony, Colin Davis; Murray Perahia, Bavarian Radio Orchestra, Colin Davis—*with reservations about the distant and hollow recorded sound of the orchestra and the metallic sound of the piano.*

Davidsbündlertänze Murray Perahia; Stephen Hough.

Études symphoniques Murray Perahia; Maurizio Pollini; Robert Casadesus.

Fantasia Op. 17 Maurizio Pollini; Richard Goode; Clifford Curzon; Vladimir Ashkenazy; Stephen Hough.

Fantasiestücke Op. 12 Murray Perahia; Richard Goode.

Kinderszenen Clifford Curzon; Clara Haskil.

Kreisleriana Artur Rubinstein; Vladimir Ashkenazy; Anton Kuerti.

Manfred Overture Haitink, Concertgebouw Orchestra.

Papillons Murray Perahia; Robert Casadesus.

Quintet in E flat Op. 44 for piano and strings Artur Rubinstein and the Guarneri Quartet; (Clifford Curzon and the Budapest Quartet); (Rudolf Serkin and the Busch Quartet—*1930s*).

Sonatas for piano Op. 11—Maurizio Pollini; *Op. 22*—Murray Perahia.

Songs

Dichterliebe Dietrich Fischer-Dieskau, with Jörg Demus—*1950s recording especially;* Peter Pears, with Benjamin Britten; Thomas Allen, with Roger Vignoles; Håkan Hagegård, with Thomas Schuback; (Gérard Souzay, with Alfred Cortot); (Hans Hotter, with Hans Altmann).

Liederkreis Op. 24—Dietrich Fischer-Dieskau, with Christoph Eschenbach; Thomas Allen, with Roger Vignoles. *Op. 39*— Dietrich Fischer-Dieskau, with Christoph Eschenbach. *Myrthen* Dietrich Fischer-Dieskau, with Christoph Eschenbach.

Single songs by artists other than those mentioned above (Marian Anderson), Janet Baker, (Kirsten Flagstad), (Elena Gerhardt), (Mack Harrell), Werner Krenn, (Lotte Lehmann), Edith Mathis, (Lois Marshall), Elisabeth Schwarzkopf, Irmgard Seefried, (Richard Tauber).

Symphonies (4) Haitink, Concertgebouw Orchestra; (Toscanini, NBC Symphony—*No. 3 (Rhenish)*).

Waldszenen Robert Casadesus; (Clara Haskil); Artur Rubinstein—*excerpt: Vogel als Prophet*.

Schütz

Motets and Psalms Scheidt, Regensburg Cathedral Choir; Willcocks, King's College Choir.

St. Matthew Passion Rilling, Gächinger Cantorei; Fischer-Dieskau, Distler Chorale.

Symphoniae Sacrae Rilling, Gächinger Cantorei.

Weinachts-Historie (Christmas Story) Zöbeley, Munich Residenz Orchestra and Motet Choir.

Scriabin

Piano Sonata No. 3 Vladimir Ashkenazy.

Shapero

Symphony for Classical Orchestra Bernstein, Columbia Symphony Orchestra.

Shostakovitch

Concerto for Piano, Trumpet and Strings André Previn, New York Philharmonic, Bernstein.

Lady Macbeth of Mtsensk Vishnevskaya, Gedda, under Rostropovich.

Symphonies No. 1—Barshai, Vancouver Symphony; *No. 5*—Haitink, Concertgebouw Orchestra; *No. 9*—Barshai, Vancouver Symphony.

Sibelius

Concerto for violin   David Oistrakh, Philadelphia Orchestra, Ormandy; (Heifetz, London Philharmonic, Beecham).
Symphonies Nos. 2, 5 and 7   von Karajan, Berlin Philharmonic; Colin Davis, Boston Symphony; (Koussevitzky, Boston and BBC Symphony orchestras).
(The) Swan of Tuonela   Ormandy, Philadelphia Orchestra.

Smetana

(The) Bartered Bride   Lorengar, Wunderlich, under Kempe.
From Bohemia's Meadows and Fields   Kubelik, Boston Symphony.
(Die) Moldau   (Toscanini, NBC Symphony); Kubelik, Boston Symphony.
Trio in G minor Op. 15   Yuval Trio.

Strauss, Johann II

(Die) Fledermaus (Lipp, Güden, Wagner, Dermota, Patzak, Poell, under Krauss); Rothenberger, Holm, Fassbänder, Gedda, Fischer-Dieskau, Berry, under Boskovsky; (Streich, Schwarzkopf, Krebs, Gedda, under von Karajan).
(The) Gypsy Baron (Der zigeuner Baron) (Poell, Patzak, Loose, Anday, under Krauss); (Schwarzkopf, Gedda, Kunz, under Ackermann).
One Night in Venice (Eine Nacht in Venedig) (Schwarzkopf, Gedda, under Ackermann).
Wiener Blut (Spirit of Vienna) (Schwarzkopf, Loose, Gedda, under Ackermann); Rothenberger, Holm, Gedda, under Boskovsky.

Strauss, R.

Also sprach Zarathustra (*Thus Spake Zarathustra*) von Karajan, Vienna Philharmonic; Kempe, Dresden State Orchestra; (Reiner, Chicago Symphony—*his early recording, of 1954*).

Capriccio (Schwarzkopf, Gedda, Fischer-Dieskau, Wächter, under Sawallisch); —*final scene:* (Schwarzkopf, Philharmonia Orchestra, Ackermann).

Death and Transfiguration See: *Tod und Verklärung*.

Don Juan (Toscanini, NBC Symphony); von Karajan, Vienna Philharmonic; Kempe, Dresden State Orchestra.

Don Quixote (Toscanini, NBC Symphony, with Frank Miller— *1948 concert performance, whose reproduction will vary with the company issuing the recording*); (Toscanini, NBC Symphony, with Miller—*1953*); Szell, Cleveland Orchestra, with Pierre Fournier; Kempe, Dresden State Orchestra, with Paul Tortelier; (Ormandy, Philadelphia Orchestra, with Emanuel Feuermann); (Toscanini, NBC Symphony, with Feuermann— *1938 concert performance, whose closet-like sound, even in the good Music and Arts edition, gives little impression of anything but Feuermann's marvelous playing; both of Toscanini's later performances with Miller, which were well-recorded, and Feuermann's recording with Ormandy, are preferable*).

Elektra Nilsson, Resnik, under Solti; —*scenes:* Inge Borkh, Paul Schöffler, Chicago Symphony, Reiner.

Four Last Songs (Kirsten Flagstad, Philharmonia Orchestra, Furtwängler); (Elisabeth Schwarzkopf, Philharmonia Orchestra, Ackermann).

(Ein) Heldenleben (*A Hero's Life*) Michael Tilson Thomas, London Symphony; Kempe, Dresden State Orchestra; Reiner, Chicago Symphony.

Metamorphosen Franco Mannino, National Arts Center Orchestra; von Karajan, Berlin Philharmonic—*1960s*.

(Der) Rosenkavalier Schwarzkopf, Ludwig, Edelmann, under von Karajan; —*scenes:* (Lehmann, Schumann, Mayr, under Heger).

Salome Caballé, Richard Lewis, under Leinsdorf; —*final scene:* Inge Borkh, Chicago Symphony, Reiner; (Ljuba

Welitsch, Metropolitan Opera Orchestra, Reiner); (Welitsch, Austrian Radio Orchestra, von Matacic—*recording made a few years before the one with Reiner*).

Songs Dietrich Fischer-Dieskau, Lisa Della Casa, (Anny Felber-mayer), Nicolai Gedda, (Elena Gerhardt), (Lotte Lehmann), (Tiana Lemnitz), Christa Ludwig, (Alfred Poell), (Elisabeth Schumann), Elisabeth Schwarzkopf, Benita Valente.

Thus Spake Zarathustra See: *Also sprach Zarathustra.*

Till Eulenspiegel's Merry Pranks Michael Tilson Thomas, London Symphony; (Toscanini, NBC Symphony); von Karajan, Vienna Philharmonic.

Tod und Verklärung (*Death and Transfiguration*) (Toscanini, Philadelphia Orchestra—*1942*); (Toscanini, NBC Symphony—*1952*); von Karajan, Vienna Philharmonic; Kempe, Dresden State Orchestra.

Stravinsky

Agon (Stravinsky, Los Angeles Festival Orchestra); Irving, New York City Ballet Orchestra.

Apollon Musagètes (*Apollo*) (Stravinsky, RCA Victor Symphony); Stravinsky, Columbia Symphony; Ansermet, Orchestre de la Suisse Romande.

(Le) Baiser de la fée (*The Fairy's Kiss*) (Stravinsky, Cleveland Orchestra); Stravinsky, Columbia Symphony; Järvi, Scottish National Orchestra.

Canticum Sacrum (Stravinsky, Los Angeles Festival Orchestra).

Concerto for two pianos Paul Jacobs and Ursula Oppens.

Concerto for violin Isaac Stern, Columbia Symphony, Stravinsky; Anne-Sophie Mutter, Philharmonia Orchestra, Sacher.

Concerto in D for string orchestra (Stravinsky, RCA Victor Symphony); von Karajan, Berlin Philharmonic.

Danses concertantes (Stravinsky, RCA Victor Symphony); Colin Davis, English Chamber Orchestra.

Dumbarton Oaks concerto (Stravinsky, Dumbarton Oaks Orchestra); Stravinsky, Columbia Symphony.

(The) Firebird (*L'Oiseau de feu*) Stravinsky, Columbia Sym-

phony; Boulez, New York Philharmonic; Colin Davis, Concertgebouw Orchestra; Haitink, London Philharmonic.

(*L'*) *Histoire du soldat*   Stravinsky, with an ensemble headed by violinist Israel Baker.

In Memoriam Dylan Thomas   Stravinsky, with a choral ensemble.

Jeu de cartes (*The Card Game*)   Stravinsky, Cleveland Orchestra; Münch, Boston Symphony; Colin Davis, London Symphony; (Cantelli, Boston Symphony—*concert performance, whose reproduction will vary with the company issuing the recording; an AS Discs edition can be expected to have good sound*).

Mass   Stravinsky, Columbia Symphony woodwinds and chorus.

Movements for piano and orchestra   Stravinsky, Columbia Symphony, with Charles Rosen, piano; Salonen, London Sinfonietta, with Paul Crossley, piano.

(*Les*) *Noces* (*The Wedding*)   Stravinsky, American Concert Chorus, etc.; Craft, Orpheus Chamber Orchestra, etc.; Boulez, Théâtre Nationale.

Oedipus Rex   (Stravinsky, Cologne Radio Symphony, Pears, Mödl, Rehfuss, etc.); Stravinsky, Washington Opera Society, Shirley, Verrett, Gramm, etc.

Orpheus   Stravinsky, Chicago Symphony.

Petrushka   Michael Tilson Thomas, Philharmonia Orchestra; Stravinsky, Columbia Symphony; Levine, Chicago Symphony; Boulez, New York Philharmonic.

Pulcinella   (Stravinsky, Cleveland Orchestra); Stravinsky, Columbia Symphony.

(*The*) *Rake's Progress*   (Harrell and others of the Metropolitan Opera, Stravinsky); Reardon and others, Royal Philharmonic, Stravinsky.

Requiem Canticles   Craft, Columbia Symphony, etc.

(*Le*) *Sacre du printemps* (*The Rite of Spring*)   (Stravinsky, New York Philharmonic); Stravinsky, Columbia Symphony; Boulez, Cleveland Orchestra; Michael Tilson Thomas, Boston Symphony; Colin Davis, Concertgebouw Orchestra.

Scherzo fantastique   Boulez, New York Philharmonic; Stravinsky, Columbia Symphony.

Scènes de ballet   Stravinsky, CBC Symphony.

Symphonies of Wind Instruments   Boulez, New York Philharmonic; Stravinsky, Northwest German Radio Orchestra; Salonen, London Sinfonietta.

Symphony in C (Stravinsky, Cleveland Orchestra); Stravinsky, CBC Symphony.

Symphony in Three Movements (Stravinsky, New York Philharmonic); Stravinsky, Columbia Symphony.

Symphony of Psalms (Stravinsky, Columbia Symphony and chorus); Stravinsky, CBC Symphony and Festival Singers of Toronto.

Threni, for voices and instruments Stravinsky, Columbia Symphony, etc.

Tallis

Motet Spem in alium Tallis Scholars; Willcocks, King's College Choir.

Other motets, anthems, etc. Willcocks, King's College Choir; Tallis Scholars; Wulstan, Clerkes of Oxenford.

Harpsichord music Trevor Pinnock.

Instrumental music Michael Chance, Fretwork ensemble.

Tartini

Cello Concerto in A Enrico Mainardi, Lucerne Festival Strings, Baumgartner.

Tchaikovsky

Concertos for piano No. *1*—Van Cliburn, RCA Victor Symphony, Kondrashin; (Vladimir Horowitz, NBC Symphony, Toscanini—*1943 especially*); Vladimir Ashkenazy, London Symphony, Maazel; *No. 2*—Igor Zhukov, Moscow Radio Symphony, Rozhdestvensky; Peter Donahoe, Bournemouth Symphony, Barshai; (Shura Cherkassky, Cincinnati Symphony, Susskind—*Siloti edition, which makes cuts in the first and second movements*); *No. 3*—Peter Donahoe, Bournemouth Symphony, Barshai.

Concerto for violin   Arthur Grumiaux, various conductors and orchestras; Itzhak Perlman, Boston Symphony, Leinsdorf; Isaac Stern, Philadelphia Orchestra, Ormandy; Stern, National Philharmonic, Rostropovich; Vladimir Spivakov, Slovak Philharmonic, Košler; Boris Belkin, Philharmonia Orchestra, Ashkenazy; (Bronislaw Huberman, Philadelphia Orchestra, Ormandy—*1946 concert performance, whose reproduction will vary with the company issuing the recording; the Music and Arts edition has good sound*); (Huberman, Berlin State Opera Orchestra, Steinberg—*1930s*).

(The) Enchantress   Glushkova, Kuznetzov, Moscow Radio Symphony, Provatorov.

Eugene Onegin   Kubiak, Weikl, Burrows, under Solti; Freni, Allen, Shicoff, under Levine; —*Letter scene:* (Ljuba Welitsch, Philharmonia Orchestra, Susskind); —*Lensky's aria:* (Leonid Sobinov, with orchestra); (Jussi Bjoerling, orchestra under Grevillius); Nicolai Gedda, Philharmonia Orchestra, Galliera.

Francesca da Rimini   Giulini, Philharmonia Orchestra; Dorati, National Philharmonic.

Iolanta   Vishnevskaya, Gedda, under Rostropovich; Sorokina, Atlantov, others of the Bolshoi Theater, Ermler—*both with reservations about the lead soprano.*

(The) Maid of Orleans (Jeanne d'Arc)   Arkhipova, others of the Moscow Radio Orchestra, Rozhdestvensky—*with some reservations about the women's voices.*

Manfred Symphony   Michael Tilson Thomas, London Symphony; (Toscanini, NBC Symphony—*Toscanini made a cut in the last movement*).

Méditation Op. 42 No. 1 for violin   Isaac Stern, National Symphony, Rostropovich; Itzhak Perlman, Israel Philharmonic, Mehta.

(The) Nutcracker—complete   Michael Tilson Thomas, Philharmonia Orchestra; Ansermet, Orchestre de la Suisse Romande; Previn, London Symphony and Royal Philharmonic orchestras; Andrew Davis, Toronto Symphony; —*suite:* von Karajan, Berlin Philharmonic; (Toscanini, NBC Symphony—*1940 concert performance, whose reproduction will vary with the company issuing the recording*).

Overture 1812 von Karajan, Berlin Philharmonic, chorus.

(The) Queen of Spades (Pique-Dame) Vishnevskaya, Gugaloff, under Rostropovich.

Romeo and Juliet (Toscanini, NBC Symphony); (Cantelli, Philharmonia Orchestra); Giulini, Philharmonia Orchestra; (Koussevitzky, Boston Symphony).

(The) Seasons for piano Antonin Kubalek.

Serenade for Strings Op. 48 von Karajan, Berlin Philharmonic—1960s; Marriner, Academy of St. Martin in the Fields; Leppard, English Chamber Orchestra.

Sleeping Beauty Previn, London Symphony; Ansermet, Orchestre de la Suisse Romande.

Sonata in G Op. 37 for piano (Grand Sonata) Sviatoslav Richter.

Songs Dietrich Fischer-Dieskau, Robert Tear, Jennie Tourel, Galina Vishnevskaya.

Suites for orchestra Nos. 2, 3 and 4—Michael Tilson Thomas, Los Angeles Philharmonic and Philharmonia Orchestra—*and Thomas's superb performance of No. 1 if he records it; his performance with the Chicago Symphony was broadcast.*

Symphonies
No. 1 *(Winter Dreams)*—Michael Tilson Thomas, Boston Symphony; Haitink, Concertgebouw Orchestra; *No. 2 (Little Russian)*—Abbado, Chicago Symphony; Maazel, Vienna Philharmonic; *No. 3*—Haitink, Concertgebouw Orchestra; Maazel, Vienna Philharmonic; *No. 4*—(Cantelli, NBC Symphony—*concert performance, whose reproduction will vary with the company issuing the recording; the Music and Arts edition has good sound*); Maazel, Berlin and Vienna Philharmonic orchestras; von Karajan, Berlin Philharmonic; Argenta, Orchestre de la Suisse Romande; *No. 5*—Maazel, Vienna Philharmonic; (Cantelli, Boston Symphony—*concert performance, whose reproduction will vary with the company issuing the recording; an AS Discs edition can be expected to have good sound*); Abbado, Chicago Symphony—*in spite of occasional distortions;* Klemperer, Philharmonia Orchestra; (Beecham, London Philharmonic); *No. 6 (Pathétique)*—(Toscanini, Phildelphia Orchestra); Abbado, Vienna Philharmonic; (Cantelli, Philharmonia Orchestra).

Swan Lake Bonynge, National Philharmonic; Ansermet, Orchestre de la Suisse Romande—*with cuts.*

The Tempest Abbado, Chicago Symphony.
Trio Jascha Heifetz, Gregor Piatigorsky, Artur Rubinstein.
Variations on a Rococo Theme for cello Mstislav Rostropovich, Berlin Philharmonic, von Karajan.
Voyevode Abbado, Chicago Symphony.

Telemann

Hamburger Ebb und Fluht (Water Music) Wenzinger, Schola Cantorum Basiliensis; Cologne Musica Antiqua.
Concertos for recorder Michala Petri, etc.
Concertos for trumpet(s) in various combinations Maurice André, etc.

Thomas

Mignon Horne, Welting, von Stade, under Almeida; *—Overture:* (Toscanini, NBC Symphony).

Thomson

Acadian Songs and Dances (from Louisiana Story) (Ormandy, Philadelphia Orchestra); Landau, Westphalian Symphony.
Filling Station (Barzin, New York City Ballet Orchestra).
Four Saints in Three Acts (Thomson, conducting an ensemble and various good soloists—*abridged*); Allen, Matthews, etc., Orchestra of Our Time, Thome.
(The) Mother of Us All Godfrey, Dunn, Vanni, under Leppard—*with reservations about Dunn.*
Synthetic Waltzes for two pianos (Arthur Gold and Robert Fizdale).

Tippett

(The) Midsummer Marriage Royal Opera, Colin Davis.
Symphony No. 2 Colin Davis, London Symphony.

Tomkins

Madrigals   Pears, Wilbye Consort; Ambrosian Singers.
Harpsichord music   Thurston Dart; Trevor Pinnock.
Sacred music   Rose, Magdalen College Choir.

Vaughan Williams

Blake Songs   Robert Tear, with Neil Black, oboe.
English Folksong Suite   Boult, London Philharmonic and London Symphony orchestras.
Fantasia on a Theme by Thomas Tallis   Boult, London Philharmonic; Marriner, Academy of St. Martin in the Fields.
Fantasia on Greensleeves   Boult, London Philharmonic; Marriner, Academy of St. Martin in the Fields.
(The) Lark Ascending   Boult, Philharmonia Orchestra, with Hugh Bean, violin.
Mass in G minor   Willcocks, King's College Choir.
Symphonies   Boult, London Philharmonic and Philharmonia orchestras; Previn, London Symphony.

Verdi

Chamber music
Quartet   Guarneri Quartet.

Choral music
Four Sacred Pieces   Giulini, Philharmonia Orchestra, etc.; Solti, Chicago Symphony, etc.; (Toscanini, NBC Symphony—*Te Deum*).
Requiem   (Toscanini, NBC Symphony, Nelli, Barbieri, di Stefano, Siepi, etc.—*1951*); (Toscanini, NBC Symphony, Milanov, Castagna, Bjoerling, Moscona, etc.—*1940 live performance, whose reproduction will vary with the company issuing the recording; the Music and Arts edition has acceptable sound*); Solti, Vienna Philharmonic, Sutherland, Horne, Pavarotti, Talvela, etc.—*avoid Solti's Chicago set with Baker and Lucchetti;* (Cantelli,

Boston Symphony, Nelli, Turner, Conley, Moscona, etc.—
*concert performance, whose reproduction will vary with the company
issuing the recording; this Boston performance has better singing by
the chorus than Cantelli's New York Philharmonic performance
does*).

Operas

Aida (Nelli, Tucker, under Toscanini); Ricciarelli, Domingo,
under Abbado; Leontyne Price, Vickers, under Solti; Simionato, Bergonzi, under von Karajan; (Callas, Tucker, under
Serafin).

Aroldo Caballé, Cecchele, Manno, under Queler.

Attila Deutekom, Bergonzi, Milnes, under Gardelli.

(Un) Ballo in maschera (Nelli, Peerce, Moscona, under
Toscanini); Caballé, Carreras, Wixell, under Colin Davis; Margaret Price, Pavarotti, Bruson, under Solti.

(Il) Corsaro Norman, Caballé, Carreras, under Gardelli.

Don Carlo (five-act version) Caballé, Domingo, Milnes, Raimondi, under Giulini; Tebaldi, Fischer-Dieskau, Bergonzi,
Ghiaurov, under Solti.

(I) Due Foscari Ricciarelli, Carreras, Ramey, under Gardelli.

Ernani Freni, Domingo, under Muti—*reported to be good.*

Falstaff (Valdengo, Nelli, under Toscanini); Gobbi, Schwarzkopf, under von Karajan; Bruson, Ricciarelli, under Giulini;
Evans, Simionato, under Solti.

(La) Forza del destino Leontyne Price, Domingo, under Levine;
Arroyo, Bergonzi, under Gardelli.

(Un) Giorno di regno Norman, Carreras, under Gardelli.

(I) Lombardi Deutekom, Domingo, under Gardelli.

Luisa Miller Caballé, Pavarotti, under Maag—*Pavarotti's voice is
agreeable-sounding in its lower range but constricted and unattractive as it rises.*

Macbeth Verrett, Domingo, under Abbado; Cossotto, Carreras,
under Muti.

(I) Masnadieri Caballé, Bergonzi, under Gardelli; Sutherland,
Bonisolli, under Bonynge.

Nabucco Dimitrova, Domingo, Cappuccilli, under Sinopoli; Suliotis, Gobbi, Prevedi, under Gardelli—*can be expected to be good.*

Otello (Vinay, Nelli, under Toscanini); Domingo, Scotto, under

Levine; Vickers, Rysanek, under Serafin—*avoid Vickers's later recording with von Karajan;* Cossutta, Margaret Price, under Solti

Rigoletto Ghiaurov, Cotrubas, Domingo, under Giulini; (Gobbi, Callas, di Stefano, under Serafin); (Warren, Berger, Peerce, under Cellini); —*Act 4:* (Warren, Milanov, Peerce, NBC Symphony, Toscanini).

Simon Boccanegra Freni, Carreras, under Abbado.

Stiffelio Sass, Carreras, under Gardelli—*Sass is not in good voice.*

(La) Traviata Cotrubas, Domingo, under Carlos Kleiber; (Callas, Kraus, under Ghione); (Albanese, Peerce, under Toscanini).

(Il) Trovatore Plowright, Domingo, under Giulini; Leontyne Price, Domingo, under Mehta; (Callas, di Stefano, under von Karajan); Ricciarelli, Carreras, under Colin Davis; (Milanov, Bjoerling, under Cellini).

(I) Vespri Siciliani Arroyo, Domingo, under Levine.

Arias and vocal excerpts by singers other than those mentioned above: Grace Bumbry, (Maria Cebotari), Suzanne Danco, (Eileen Farrell), (Benvenuto Franci), (Nicola Fusati), Nicolai Gedda, (Julius Patzak), (Alexander Kipnis), (Frida Leider), (Tiana Lemnitz), Anna Moffo, (Claudia Muzio), Leo Nucci, (Lina Pagliughi), (Ezio Pinza), (Rosa Ponselle), (Elisabeth Rethberg), (Helge Roswänge), (Bidú Sayão), (Tito Schipa), Graziella Sciutti, Cesare Siepi, (Eleanor Steber).

Overtures (Toscanini); Giulini; Abbado; Chailly.

Victoria (Vittoria)

El Siglo de oro Pro Cantione Antiqua of London.

Masses O magnum mysterium and *O quam gloriosum* Hill, Choir of Westminster Cathedral.

Motets Ascendens Christus and *O quam gloriosum* Hill, Choir of Westminster Cathedral.

Officium Defunctorum (Requiem) Tallis Scholars.

Responsories O vos omnes and *Tenebrae factae sunt* Hill, Choir of Westminster Cathedral.

Other works Tallis Scholars; Guest, St. John's College Choir.

Vivaldi

Vocal works

Beatus vir   Coro Polifonico di Roma, Virtuosi di Roma, Fasano.

Credo   Coro Polifonico di Roma, Virtuosi di Roma, Fasano; I Solisti Veneti, etc., Scimone.

Gloria in D   Willcocks, King's College Choir, Baker, Vaughan, Partridge, Keyte, etc.

Stabat Mater   Shirley Verrett, Virtuosi di Roma; Aafje Heynis, Solisti di Milano, Ephraikian.

Instrumental music

Il Cimento dell' armonia e dell' invenzione—complete (the first four concertos make up The Four Seasons; *see below*)   I Musici, with Felix Ayo.

(L') Estro armonico   I Musici; Vienna State Opera Orchestra, Rossi.

(The) Four Seasons (first four concertos of Il Cimento dell' armonia, etc.)   Paul Peabody, Philharmonia Virtuosi, Kapp; I Musici, with either Felix Ayo or Roberto Michelucci; Jan Tomasow, with I Solisti di Zagreb, Janigro.

(La) Stravaganza Op. 4   Alan Loveday, Academy of St. Martin in the Fields, Marriner.

Concertos for flute or recorder   Michala Petri, Academy of St. Martin in the Fields, Iona Brown.

Concertos for two horns   Timothy Hill and Douglas Brown, Academy of St. Martin in the Fields, Marriner.

Concertos for oboe   Pierre Pierlot, I Solisti Veneti, Scimone; David Reichenberg, English Concert, Pinnock—*period instruments.*

Concerto in D minor for viola d'amore   Renzo Sabatini, Virtuosi di Roma, Fasano; Günther Lemmen, Collegium Aureum, Reinhardt—*period instruments.*

Concertos for violin (miscellaneous)   Nathan Milstein and ensemble.

Concerto in C major for violin and two cellos   Arrigo Pelliccia, Massimo Amfitheatrof, B. Mazzacurati, Virtuosi di Roma, Fasano.

Concertos and Sinfonias for string orchestra and harpsichord   Capella Savaria, Nicholas McGegan, harpsichord and conductor—*period instruments.*

Sonatas for cello Nos. 1, 2, 3 and 5—Antonio Janigro, with Robert Veyron-Lacroix, harpsichord.
Sonatas for violin Op. 2 No. 2—Arthur Grumiaux, with István Hajdu, harpsichord.

Wagner

Lohengrin Silja, Thomas, Vinay under Sawallisch; Grümmer, Ludwig, Thomas, Fischer-Dieskau, Frick, under Kempe.
(Die) Meistersinger (Grümmer, Schock, Ferdinand Frantz, under Kempe); Bailey, Bode, Kollo, under Solti.
Parsifal Waltraud Meier, Peter Hofmann, Estes, Sotin, under Levine; —*Act 3, and scenes from Acts 1 and 2:* (Pistor, Brongeest, Ludwig Hofmann, under Muck—*1927–28*).
(Der) Ring des Nibelungen—complete (Das Rheingold, Die Walküre, Siegfried, Götterdämmerung) Behrens, Morris, Metropolitan Opera, Levine; (Flagstad, Svanholm, Frantz, Weber, etc., La Scala, Furtwängler—*1950 live performances, whose reproduction will vary with the company issuing the recording*). —*Die Walküre:* (Rysanek, Suthaus, Mödl, Klose, Ferdinand Frantz, Vienna Philharmonic, Furtwängler); —*Die Walküre, Acts 1 and 2:* (Lehmann, Melchior, Fuchs, Hotter, with the Vienna Philharmonic and Berlin State Opera orchestras under Walter and Seidler-Winkler—*even more notable for the great singing of Hotter and Fuchs as Wotan and Brünnhilde in Act 2, and for the extraordinarily beautiful sounding and well integrated playing of the orchestra(s), than for the contributions of Lehmann and Melchior in Act 1; the sound is astonishing for the 1930s and faithfully reproduced on the Danacord reissue*). See also below: *Excerpts.*
Tannhäuser Silja, Bumbry, Windgassen, Wächter, Greindl, under Sawallisch.
Tristan und Isolde Margaret Price, Kollo, under Carlos Kleiber; (Flagstad, Suthaus, etc., Philharmonia Orchestra, Furtwängler); Gray, Mitchinson, under Goodall; Dernesch, Vickers, under von Karajan; (Flagstad, Melchior, under Beecham—*live recording, whose reproduction will vary with the company issuing the recording; the Music and Arts edition has acceptable sound*).
Wesendonck Lieder Marilyn Horne, Royal Philharmonic, Anthony Lewis; (Flagstad, Vienna Philharmonic, Knapperts-

busch); (Eileen Farrell, with Stokowski and, later, with Bernstein).

Excerpts and concert pieces Boulez; (Cantelli—*including concert performances, whose reproduction will vary with the company issuing the recording; the AS Discs edition has good sound*); (Furtwängler); Haitink; Klemperer; (Muck); Stein; (Toscanini—*including the superb concert performances of 1953, whose excellent sound is well reproduced by the Music and Arts and Fonit-Cetra editions*).

Vocal excerpts by singers other than those mentioned above (Peter Anders), (Fernand Ansseau), Otto Edelmann, (Paul Franz), Hilde Güden, Hans Hopf, (Frida Leider), (Emmy Leisner), Kurt Moll, Maria Müller, Birgit Nilsson, Karl Ridderbusch, Paul Schöffler, Friedrich Schorr.

Walther

Organ music Kenneth Gilbert.

Walton

Belshazzar's Feast Luxon, London Philharmonic, Solti; Shirley-Quirk, Royal Philharmonic, Previn.

Façade Scales, West, London Mozart Players, Glover; Ashcroft, Scofield, London Sinfonietta, Walton; (Sitwell, Horner, ensemble under Prausnitz); (Sitwell, Pears, London Opera Group, Collins).

Partita for orchestra Szell, Cleveland Orchestra.

Troilus and Cressida Baker, Cassilly, English, Lloyd, Luxon, under Foster; —*excerpts:* Schwarzkopf, Richard Lewis, Monica Sinclair, under Walton.

Weber

Arias and vocal excerpts Eileen Farrell; (Kirsten Flagstad).

Concertos (2) for clarinet Gervase de Peyer, with orchestras under Frühbeck de Burgos and Colin Davis.

Concertos (2) for piano Malcolm Frager, North German Radio Orchestra, Andreae.

Euryanthe Norman, Hunter, Gedda, under Janowski.

(Der) Freischütz Janowitz, Mathis, Schreier, under Carlos Kleiber.

Grand Duo Concertante Op. 48 for clarinet and piano David Shifrin and William Doppman.

Invitation to the Dance (orchestrated by Berlioz) (Toscanini, BBC Symphony); (Leopold Stokowski, Philadelphia and studio orchestras); *See also: Piano Music.*

Konzertstück for piano and orchestra Alfred Brendel, London Symphony, Abbado.

Oberon Nilsson, Hamari, Domingo, Prey, under Kubelik.

Overtures Kubelik; (Toscanini).

Piano music *Invitation to the Dance, Momento capriccioso, Rondo brillante, Sonatas (4)* Garrick Ohlsson; Dino Ciani—*Sonatas Nos. 2 and 3.*

Quintet Op. 34 for clarinet and strings Gervase de Peyer, with the Melos Ensemble; Eduard Brunner, with the Hagen Quartet; David Shifrin, with the Sequoia Quartet.

Symphonies (2) Schönzeler, London Symphony; Sawallisch, Bavarian Radio Orchestra; Boettcher, Philharmonia Orchestra—*No. 1.*

Variations Op. 33 for clarinet and piano on a theme from Silvana David Shifrin and William Doppman.

Webern

Five Movements (Fünf Sätze) Op. 5 for string quartet Quartetto Italiano; Boulez, London Symphony—*orchestral version.*

Five Pieces (Fünf Stücke) Op. 10 for orchestra Boulez, London Symphony; von Karajan, Berlin Philharmonic.

Passacaglia Op. 1 for orchestra Boulez, London Symphony; von Karajan, Berlin Philharmonic.

Quartets 1905 and Op. 28 (1938) Quartetto Italiano.

Six Pieces (Sechs Stücke) Op. 6 for orchestra Boulez, London Symphony; von Karajan, Berlin Philharmonic.

Songs *Opp. 3 and 4*—Heather Harper, with Charles Rosen; *Opp.*

8, 12, 13 and 14—Heather Harper, with an ensemble under Boulez.

Symphony for Small Orchestra (i.e. winds, harp and string quartet) Op. 21: Boulez, London Symphony; von Karajan, Berlin Philharmonic.

Transcriptions —*of the Ricercare from Bach's Musical Offering:* Boulez, London Symphony; —*of German Dances by Schubert:* (Webern, Frankfurt Radio Orchestra).

Variations Op. 30 for orchestra Boulez, London Symphony.

(*The complete works of Webern were recorded in the 1970s by various artists under the supervision of Pierre Boulez.*)

Weelkes

Madrigals and Motets Pears, Wilbye Consort; Pro Cantione Antiqua of London; Hilliard Ensemble.

Willaert

Motets Rifkin, Boston Camerata Motet Chorus.

Wilbye

Madrigals Pears, Wilbye Consort; April Cantelo, Maurice Bevan, Deller Consort; Pro Cantione Antiqua of London; Hilliard Ensemble.

Wolf

(*Der*) *Corregidor* (Fuchs, Teschemacher, Erb, under Elmendorff).

Italian Serenade (Budapest Quartet—*1933*); (New Music Quartet); Guarneri Quartet; I Musici; Hagen Quartet.

Penthesilea Gerdes, Vienna Symphony.

Quartet in D minor (New Music Quartet); Lasalle Quartet.

Songs

Italian Songbook Dietrich Fischer-Dieskau and Irmgard Seefried, with Jörg Demus and Erik Werba, pianists; Elly Ameling and Tom Krause, with Irwin Gage, piano; Fischer-Dieskau and Christa Ludwig, with Daniel Barenboim—*whose lifeless quiet playing and banging loud playing are equally damaging to the music;* —*selections:* Dietrich Fischer-Dieskau, with Hertha Klust.

Spanish Songbook Dietrich Fischer-Dieskau and Elisabeth Schwarzkopf, with Gerald Moore—*Schwarzkopf's singing is good in the religious songs, but mannered and affected in the secular ones.*

Mörike Lieder (Gérard Souzay, with Dalton Baldwin, piano); Dietrich Fischer-Dieskau, with Gerald Moore—*studio recording and a Salzburg recital, 1961; avoid Fischer-Dieskau's less satisfactory recordings with Barenboim and Richter.*

Individual songs Janet Baker, Lisa Della Casa, Mattiwilda Dobbs, (Kathleen Ferrier), Dietrich Fischer-Dieskau, (Elena Gerhardt), (Mack Harrell), (Hans Hotter), (Alexander Kipnis), (Lotte Lehmann), (Tiana Lemnitz), Christa Ludwig, Benjamin Luxon, Lois Marshall, (Alfred Poell), (Elisabeth Schumann), Elisabeth Schwarzkopf, Irmgard Seefried, (Leo Slezak), Gérard Souzay, (Blanche Thebom), Benita Valente.

MUSIC BEFORE 1500

Plainchant

Gregorian Chant
Chants de l'église de Rome (Roman chants of the 7th and 8th centuries) Ensemble Organum, Pérès.
Music for Holy Week Schola Antiqua, Blackley.
Chant for Eastertide Capella Antiqua, Ruhland.

Ambrosian Chant
Chants for the Church of Milan Ensemble Organum, Pérès.

9th-13th Centuries—Monophonic

Anon: The Play of Daniel Ensemble directed by David Wulstan.
Hildegard of Bingen: A Feather on the Breath of God Gothic
Voices, Page.

12th-15th Centuries—Polyphonic

Anon.: Le Chansonnier Cordiforme (15th Century Songbook)
Consort of Musicke, Rooley.
Anon.: Mass for Christmas Day, and *1210 Aquitaine Polyphony*
Ensemble Organum, Pérès.
Medieval English Music Early Music Consort of London,
Munrow.
Various Early Music Consort of London, Munrow.

English Madrigalists

English Lute songs Julianne Baird, with Ronn MacFarlane, lute.
(The) Triumph of Oriana (madrigals assembled in 1601 in honor of
Queen Elizabeth I) Pro Cantione Antiqua of London, Par-
tridge.
Various The Deller Consort; (Russell Oberlin, countertenor).
See also, above: Blow, Bull, Byrd, Dowland, Dunstable, Farnaby,
Gibbons, Johnson, Morley, Purcell, Tallis, Tomkins, Weelkes and
Wilbye.

Inquiries about recordings issued after this chapter
went to press (1991) may be directed to:
Recommended Recordings, Post Box 5428, Station A
Toronto, Ontario, Canada, M5W 1N6.

Bibliography

1. BOOKS ABOUT COMPOSERS

Bach, J. S.
Forkel, Johann Nikolaus, *Johann Sebastian Bach: His Life, Art and Work,*
Charles Sanford Terry, translator (London, 1920)

Beethoven
The Letters of Beethoven, Emily Anderson, translator and editor (New
York, 1961)
Sullivan, J. W. N., *Beethoven—His Spiritual Development* (London, 1927)
Thayer, Alexander W., *Beethoven,* Elliot Forbes, editor (New York, 1921,
'67)
Turner, W. J., *Beethoven* (London, 1924, '33)
(*See below:* 5. Further reading)

Berlioz
Berlioz, Hector, *Memoirs* (Paris, 1870); translated into English by Elea-
nor and Rachel Holmes (London, 1884); Holmes translation
revised by Sir Ernest Newman (London, 1932, '35); translated by
David Cairns (New York, 1969, '75, '77)
Berlioz: A Selection from His Letters, Humphrey Searle, translator and
editor (New York, 1966)
New Letters of Berlioz, 1830–1868, Jacques Barzun, translator and editor
(New York, 1954)
Cairns, David, *Berlioz* Vol. I (London, 1989)
Turner, W. J., *Berlioz—the Man and His Work* (London, 1934)
Wotton, Tom, *Hector Berlioz* (London, 1935)
(*See below:* 3. Berlioz; 4. Strunk)

BIBLIOGRAPHY

Brahms
Gal, Hans, *Johannes Brahms* (London, 1961, '75)

Copland
Berger, Arthur, *Aaron Copland* (New York, 1950)
(*See below:* 5. Further reading)

Griffes
Maisel, Edward M., *Charles Tomlinson Griffes* (New York, 1943)

Haydn
Geiringer, Karl, *Haydn* (New York, 1946, '61, '68, '82)

Mozart
Die Briefe W. A. Mozarts und seiner Familie, Ludwig Schiedermair, editor
    (Munich, 1914)
Mozart. Briefe und Aufzeichnungen—Gesamtausgabe, W. A. Bauer and
    O. E. Deutsch, editors (Kassel, 1962)
The Letters of Mozart and His Family, Emily Anderson, translator and
    editor (London, 1938); revised by Anderson, A. Hyatt King and
    Monica Carolan (New York, 1966)
Dent, Edward J., *Mozart's Operas* (London, 1913, '47)
Girdlestone, Cuthbert, *Mozart and His Piano Concertos* (New York, 1948,
    '58)
Turner, W. J., *Mozart—The Man and His Works* (London, 1938); revised
    and edited by Christopher Raeburn (London, 1965)

Musorgsky
The Musorgsky Reader, J. Leyda and S. Bertensson, editors (New York,
    1947, '70)
(*See below:* 1. Rimsky-Korsakov; 3. Porter; Marnold; Sackville-West; 5.
    Further reading)

Rimsky-Korsakov
Rimsky-Korsakov, Nicolai, *My Musical Life*, Judah A. Joffe, translator
    (London and New York, 1923, '42, '74)

Rossini
Toye, Francis, *Rossini—A Study in Tragi-Comedy* (New York, 1947)

Scarlatti
Kirkpatrick, Ralph, *Domenico Scarlatti* (New York, 1953)

Schubert
Schubert: Memoirs by His Friends, Otto Erich Deutsch, editor (London,
    1958)
Gal, Hans, *Schubert and the Essence of Melody* (London, 1974)

BIBLIOGRAPHY

Strauss, Richard
*A Working Friendship: The Correspondence between Richard Strauss and
Hugo von Hofmannsthal,* Hans Hammelmann and Oswald Osers,
translators (New York, 1962)

Stravinsky
Igor Stravinsky: Selected Correspondence, Robert Craft, editor (New York,
1982, 1984)
Stravinsky, Igor, and Robert Craft:
Conversations with Stravinsky (New York, 1958)
Memories and Commentaries (New York, 1959)
Expositions and Developments (New York, 1962)
Dialogues and a Diary (New York, 1963)
Themes and Episodes (New York, 1966)
Retrospectives and Conclusions (New York, 1969)
Craft, Robert, *Stravinsky: Chronicle of a Friendship, 1948/71* (New York,
1972)
Craft, Robert, and Vera Stravinsky, *Stravinsky in Pictures and Documents*
(New York, 1978)

Tchaikovsky
The Life and Letters of Tchaikovsky, Rosa Newmarch, translator and editor
(London, 1906, New York, 1973)
Piotr Il'ych Tchaikovsky: Letters to His Family: An Autobiography, Galina
von Meck, translator and editor (New York, 1973, '81)

Verdi
Budden, Julian, *The Operas of Verdi* (New York, 1973, '78, '81)
Toye, Francis, *Verdi—His Life and Work* (New York, 1946)
Walker, Frank, *The Man Verdi* (New York, 1962)
(See also: 5. Further reading)

Wagner
Gal, Hans, *Richard Wagner* (London, 1963, '76)
Robert W. Gutman, *Richard Wagner: The Man, His Mind, and His Music*
(New York, 1968)
(See below: 4. Capell)

Wolf
Walker, Frank, *Hugo Wolf* (New York, 1952)

2. BOOKS ABOUT PERFORMERS AND JAZZ

Beecham
Beecham, Sir Thomas, *A Mingled Chime—Leaves from an Autobiography* (London, 1944)
Jefferson, Alan, *Sir Thomas Beecham* (New York, 1979)
Reid, Charles, *Thomas Beecham—An Independent Biography* (New York, 1962)

Caruso
Caruso, Dorothy, *Enrico Caruso: His Life and Death* (New York, 1945)

Flagstad
Flagstad, Kirsten, *The Flagstad Manuscript,* Louis Biancolli, editor (New York, 1952)

Jazz
Hobson, Wilder, *American Jazz Music* (New York, 1939)
Schuller, Gunther, *Early Jazz* (New York, 1968)
Schuller, *The Swing Era* (New York, 1989)

Koussevitzky
Smith, Moses, *Koussevitzky* (New York, 1947)

Toscanini
Antek, Samuel, *This Was Toscanini* (New York, 1963)
Haggin, B. H., *Arturo Toscanini: Contemporary Recollections of the Maestro,* Thomas Hathaway, editor (New York, 1989)
Sachs, Harvey, *Toscanini* (New York, 1978)

3. MUSICAL REVIEWS, ESSAYS, ETC.

Berlioz, Hector
  Les Grotesques de la musique (Paris, 1859)
  Les Soirées de l'orchestre (Paris, 1853); published in English as *Evenings in the Orchestra,* Charles E. Roche, translator (London, 1929); Roche translation revised by Jacques Barzun (New York, 1956); translated by C. R. Fortescue, with notes by David Cairns (London, 1963)
  À Travers chants (Paris, 1862)
  (*See also:* 4. Strunk)

Cairns, David, *Responses* (New York, 1973)

BIBLIOGRAPHY

Craft, Robert
  Current Convictions (New York, 1977)
  Prejudices in Disguise (New York, 1974)
  Present Perspectives (New York, 1984)
Hale, Philip, *Philip Hale's Boston Symphony Program Notes,* John N. Burk,
  editor (New York, 1935)
Hanslick, Eduard, *Vienna's Golden Years of Music—1850–1900,* Henry
  Pleasants III, translator and editor (New York, 1950); re-issued as
  Eduard Hanslick, Music Criticisms 1846–99 (New York, 1950, '63)
Marnold, Jean, *Musique d'autrefois et d'aujourd'hui* (Paris, 1911)
Porter, Andrew, *Music of Three Seasons* (New York, 1978)
Sackville-West, Edward, and Desmond Shawe-Taylor, *The Record Guide*
  (London, 1951)

Shaw, George Bernard
  London Music in 1888–89, as heard by Cornetto di Bassetto (London,
  1937)
  Music in London, 1890–94 (London, 1932)
  How To Become a Musical Critic—Previously Uncollected Writings, Dan
  Lawrence, editor (New York, 1961)
  All of the above, plus *The Perfect Wagnerite* (London, 1898; revised
  1930) and further uncollected musical writings, issued in *Shaw's
  Music,* Dan Lawrence, editor (New York, 1981)

Thomson, Virgil
  The Musical Scene (New York, 1945)
  The Art of Judging Music (New York, 1948)
  Music Right and Left (New York, 1951)
  Music Reviewed 1940–1954 (New York, 1967)
  The Virgil Thomson Reader, Rockwell, editor (New York, 1981)
  (*See below:* 5. Further reading)

Turner, W. J.
  Music and Life (London, 1921)
  Variations on the Theme of Music (London, 1924)
  Musical Meanderings (London, 1928)
  Facing the Music—Reflections of a Music Critic (London, 1933)
  Music—An Introduction to Its Nature and Appreciation (London, 1936)

4. GENERAL

Abraham, Gerald
  A Hundred Years of Music (London, 1938, '49)

BIBLIOGRAPHY

This Modern Music (New York, 1933) (published in England as *This Modern Stuff*)

Capell, Richard, *Opera* (London, 1930, 1948)

Copland, Aaron
  Music and Imagination (New York, 1952)
  Our New Music (New York, 1941)
  (*See below:* 5. Further reading)

Dent, Edward J., *Opera* (London, 1940, '49)
Huxley, Aldous, *Music at Night and Other Essays* (London, 1931)
Lambert, Constant, *Music Ho!* (London, 1934)
Nabokov, Nicholas, *Old Friends and New Music* (New York, 1951)
Phillips, Lois, *Lieder Line by Line (and Word by Word)* (New York, 1979)
Straeten, Edmund van der, *The History of the Violoncello, the Viol de Gamba, Their Precursors and Collateral Instruments* (London, 1915, '71)
Strunk, Oliver, editor, *Source Readings in Music History* (New York, 1950)

Tovey, Donald F.
  Essays in Musical Analysis (London, 1935)
  The Main Stream of Music and Other Essays (London, 1949)
  (*See also:* 5. Further reading)

5. FURTHER READING
(NOT MENTIONED IN THE TEXT)

Berger, Arthur, *The Music of Aaron Copland* (New York, 1945)
Calvocoressi, M. D., and Gerald Abraham, *Musorgsky* (New York, 1946)
Copland, Aaron, *Copland on Music* (New York, 1960)
Copland, Aaron, with Vivian Perlis, *Copland* (2 vols.) (New York, 1984, '90)
Selected Letters of Virgil Thomson, Tim Page, editor (New York, 1988)

Tovey, Donald F.
  Beethoven (London, 1944, '64)
  Articles from the Encyclopaedia Britannica (London, 1944)

Selected Letters of Giuseppe Verdi, Charles Osborne, translator and editor (New York, 1971)

Index of Musical Terms

Reference is made to pages on which a term is defined or illustrated, not to every place the term occurs. Where there is more than one page reference, boldface numbers indicate primary definitions.

INDEX OF MUSICAL TERMS

Index of Performers
and Musical Organizations
(Chapters 1–28)

Boldface page numbers in longer entries differentiate between commentary and passing mention.

Names beginning with "de" and its variants are listed by prefix: *de*lla Casa, Lisa. Names prefixed by "von," "I," "Le" and their variants are listed by surname: *K*arajan, Herbert von; *M*usici, I; l'*O*rchestre de la Suisse Romande (exception: *L*os Angeles Philharmonic).

479

INDEX OF PERFORMERS AND ORGANIZATIONS

INDEX OF PERFORMERS AND ORGANIZATIONS

INDEX OF PERFORMERS AND ORGANIZATIONS

INDEX OF PERFORMERS AND ORGANIZATIONS

Index of Jazz Musicians

Separately listed bands named after band leaders are listed by the leader's surname, not by his first name—e.g. Dodds, Johnny: and His Chicago Boys.

General Index

Boldface page numbers in the composer entries differentiate between commentary and passing mention.

Composers' first names and dates, as a rule, are given in the index only for those composers not discussed in Part One; full names and dates for the others are given at the ends of chapters.

Not indexed here are: performers, jazz musicians and musical terms (these are indexed separately); composers or works mentioned in passing in Chapter 28, *Great Performers*, except those not discussed at all in Part One; composers and works listed alphabetically in Chapter 29 (recommended recordings).